STRUGGLING WITH HISTORY

SOCIETY AND HISTORY IN THE INDIAN OCEAN

For many centuries the lands around the Indian Ocean have exchanged people, goods, and ideas. This series provides a platform for anthropological and historical research on social life in the region with a view to the consequences of these exchanges. The editors of the series solicit manuscripts based on original and sensitive approaches to the region through archives, ethnography, languages, texts, and visual and material culture.

Editors:
Anne K. Bang (University of Bergen)
Kai Kresse (University of St Andrews)
Scott S. Reese (Northern Arizona University)
Edward Simpson (Goldsmiths College)

are grateful to the organisers and audiences of these events for their valuable comments and questions. Liese Hoffmann worked especially hard with us to prepare the text for publication, and we benefited from technical advice by Svenja Becherer and Michael Schulz.

Joy Adapon, Isabella Lepri, Scott Reese and Mark Harris have graciously read and commented on various drafts of pieces of this book, and especially the Introduction. Apart from our contributors, we would like to thank David Parkin for supporting this project from the outset. Finally, a special note of thanks goes to both Michael Lambek and Michael Pearson for agreeing to open and close the book with kind words and prose that wears only lightly their own significant contributions to scholarship.

Notes on Language and Text

Words from a number of languages other than English appear in this book. This reflects the range of languages spoken in the region. We have attempted to keep the method of transliteration (particularly of Arabic) as simple as possible, prioritising readability and the appearance of the text. The chapters retain a regional linguistic flavour, and at times regional sub-variants are used rather than the common standardised terms (e.g. 'shehe' in southern Swahili instead of 'sheikh' or the Arabic 'shaykh'). Words common to Indological literature and works on Hinduism and Islam, and the names of people, places and communities appear in non-italicised anglicised form. Other technical terms appear in italics and are explained, often in parenthesis, on their first occurrence. There are a number of other notable quirks in the text: some contributors have preferred to use 'West Asia' over 'the Middle East'; Bombay was renamed as Mumbai in 1995, but the old name appears often in references and in the text where it is convenient for it to do so. Primary sources have been cited as footnotes; secondary sources appear as bibliographic entries.

PREFACE AND ACKNOWLEDGEMENTS

This book owes its existence to a workshop at the University of St Andrews in April 2004, hosted by CASKE, the Centre for the Study of Anthropological Knowledge and Ethics, based in the Department of Social Anthropology. It was greatly helped by funding from the School of Philosophy and Anthropological Studies, for which we would like to thank Peter Clark. The workshop itself became one of those memorable events in which scholarship, academic discussion, and an open social atmosphere merge into a fruitful whole. For this, we thank all the participants for their respective contributions.

The workshop took methodological naivety as a starting-point. Quite simply, our aim was to attempt getting inside the language and idioms of the work of other scholars working in other sectors of the western Indian Ocean. This was successful to a degree – as much as one could hope for in two days – as we discuss below in the Introduction. It is hoped that the workshop and this resulting volume will pave the way for longer-term collaborations, which, in time, may allow us to visit one another's field-sites and perceive the shores of the Indian Ocean through the eyes and languages of our colleagues and friends. Some of those who participated in the workshop have, for various reasons, not been able to contribute their work to this collection. They are Mohamed Bakari, Jim Brennan, Jan-Georg Deutsch, Zulfikar Hirji and Beatrice Nicolini. We are grateful to them for contributing to the ongoing discussion that has made this book what it is and for entering into the spirit of the occasion. Tom Widger made excellent transcripts of our discussions.

Some of the ideas discussed in the Introduction have been aired in papers presented during 2006, at a conference on Cosmopolitanism in Keele (hosted by the Association of Social Anthropologists), an Indian Ocean workshop in London (organised by Shihan De Silva and Clifford Pereira at the Commonwealth Institute), and at a round-table discussion hosted by the Centre of Modern Oriental Studies (ZMO) in Berlin. We

CONTENTS

Columbia University Press
Publishers Since 1893
New York
Copyright © 2008 Columbia University Press
All rights reserved

Library of Congress Cataloging-in-Publication Data
Struggling with history : islam and cosmopolitanism in the western indian ocean
/ Edward Simpson & Kai Kresse, editors.
    p. cm.
Includes bibliographical references and index.
ISBN 978-0-231-70023-8 (cloth : alk. paper)—
ISBN 978-0-231-70024-5 (pbk. : alk. paper)
I. Simpson, Edward, 1971- II. Kresse, Kai. III. Title.

DS339.S77 2007
303.48'21824—dc22

                                        2007020790
∞
Columbia University Press books are printed on permanent and durable acid-free
paper.
This book is printed on paper with recycled content.
Printed in India

c 10 9 8 7 6 5 4 3 2 1
p 10 9 8 7 6 5 4 3 2 1

References to Internet Web sites (URLs) were accurate at the time of writing.
Neither the author nor Columbia University Press is responsible for URLs that
may have expired or changed since the manuscript was prepared.

EDWARD SIMPSON & KAI KRESSE
editors

STRUGGLING WITH HISTORY
Islam and Cosmopolitanism in the
Western Indian Ocean

Columbia University Press
New York

challenged to take seriously the Being and Act of God himself in his revelation.

There are two basic issues here. On the one hand, it is the very substance of the Christian faith that is at stake, and on the other hand, it is the fundamental nature of scientific method, in its critical and methodological renunciation of prior understanding, that is at stake. This is the great water-shed of modern theology: either we take the one way or the other—there is no third alternative. That does not mean to say that one must wholly follow Barth on the one hand or wholly follow Bultmann on the other, but that one must go either in the direction taken by Barth or in the direction taken by Bultmann. The way of Barth leads to the establishment of Christianity on its own solid God-given foundations and to the pursuit of theology as a free science in its own right; the way of Bultmann leads to the dissolution of Christianity in secular culture and to the pursuit of theology as an expression of a reactionary, existentialist way of life.

A recent statement of Barth, published in the *Christian Century* sums up well his own reaction to the challenge of Bultmann.[1]

'Among the undertakings which I have seen my theological contemporaries pursue and complete, Rudolf Bultmann's "demythologisation" of the New Testament has occupied me most of all—less because of its concrete problematic propositions than because it seemed to me a highly impressive resumption of the theme and method of the type of theology fostered by Schleiermacher; Bultmann's work thus gave me occasion to submit to a new consideration, examination and sharpening my own point of departure acquired 40 years ago in a deviation from the Schleiermacherian tradition. I could not in conclusion follow Bultmann in respect to his particular thesis and much less still in respect to his fundamental method, in which I saw theology in spite of all safeguards being led anew into Egyptian or Babylonian captivity to a particular philosophy. From association with the young theological generation studying in Basel it seemed to me as if the interest in a decidedly existentialist interpretation, for a while devouring everything else, as in former days the interest in an historical-critical interpretation did likewise, would soon diminish. Yet from another perspective the situation can appear different, and I would not be surprised if existentialist interpretation should still have a noteworthy future in the diverse forms given it by Bultmann's disciples. What is certain is that one must be grateful to Bultmann for the warning that the not yet completed emanci-

[1] *The Christian Century*, 20 Jan., 1960, p. 74 f.

pation of theology will not be so easy as some (including very likely, some of my readers and friends) would have it. To me it is significant that present-day Old Testament scholars, especially in regard to the old, yet always new, theme of "faith and history", are on the whole on much better ground than the authoritative New Testament men, who to my amazement have armed themselves with swords and staves and once again undertaken the search for the "historical Jesus"—a search in which I now as before prefer not to participate.'

That does not of course mean that Barth has no concern for the real historical Jesus Christ or is sceptical about successful research into what the New Testament has to say of him, but that the attempt to find a 'Jesus' apart from his Gospel, a Jesus apart from the concrete act of God in him, a 'Jesus' that can be constructed out of the historical records by means of criteria derived from secular sources alone, is a failure to understand the New Testament. The real, objective, historical Jesus is the Jesus Christ who cannot be separated from his self-revelation or from his Gospel, for that Revelation and Gospel are part of the one historical Jesus Christ who is to be understood out of himself, and in accordance with his own being and nature. To use the language of John Calvin, it is not a 'bare Christ' or 'naked Christ' that is the object of our faith, but 'Christ clothed with his Gospel', 'Christ clothed with his acts and promises', the 'whole Christ', for that is the only Jesus Christ there ever was, and is and ever will be. Any other 'Christ' would only be a construct of our imagination or an objectification of our own creative spirituality.

If this whole Jesus Christ is the proper object of our faith, then scientific exegesis and interpretation of the New Testament must be accompanied by and tested by the critical and constructive inquiry of dogmatics, through which we allow Jesus Christ in his objective, historical and divine reality to disclose himself to us and to speak to us the very Word of God which he is himself.[1]

3. Jesus Christ and Culture

If Jesus Christ is only man and not God himself in human existence, if the Incarnation is only an objectified construct of our religious self-consciousness, then Christianity is only a transient expression of human

[1] Cf. John McIntyre, *Anselm and his Critics*, p. 55: 'Theological interpretation is an essential part of the determination of the facts which constitute the Christian faith, and so-called impartial historical criticism is by itself unqualified to achieve that end.'

culture that emerged out of the stream of time and will be submerged again as the course of civilisation advances on in its great achievements, and theology becomes only an ideological interpretation of the structures of man's historical existence and self-understanding. But if Jesus Christ is the one Word of God become flesh, the very Son of God come into our human existence in space and time, for us and for our salvation, then as the one Truth of God he is the centre of all truth and the creative source of all that is good and beautiful and true, and of all true culture. A dogmatic theology that takes its inquiry seriously cannot stop short of inquiring into the relevance of the concrete act of God in Jesus Christ for our redemption, but must go on to inquire into its relevance for all creation. It cannot stop short of the significance of Jesus Christ for the life of the Church but must go on to inquire into his universal and cosmic significance, and therefore into the relation of the Church to the world, and of its mission to universal human activity. If in Jesus Christ God himself became man and has entered into our historical and creaturely existence, within its continuities and rhythms and operations, and has forever bound it up with his own eternal Being as Creator and Saviour, then all things in heaven and earth, and all knowledge and truth and art, are made to pivot upon this axis: Jesus Christ as the one Truth of God and the Light of life. But the obverse of that fact is also inescapable, that the one Truth of God, in its creative and saving work, has taken the way of the historical Jesus Christ in the midst of all historical reality. Therefore it is here, in the historical reality of Jesus Christ, and indeed in his *humanity*, that we are to discern the one Truth of God at work in and behind all truth.[1]

It is for this reason that Barth finds the word *scientia* too narrow to convey the full significance of the knowledge of Jesus Christ as the Truth of God. It requires to be enlarged through what the Old Testament called 'wisdom', the *sophia* of the Greeks or the *sapientia* of the Latins. This gives us a concept of knowledge and wisdom that embraces the entire existence of man. The Truth which we know in Jesus Christ is the Light of life; it is Truth by which we can live and which throws its light upon the whole of our being, upon all its moments and activities and aspirations. To live by this Truth is the meaning of Christian knowledge—it is to live in the light of the knowledge of God, to live with an enlightened reason, and therefore to be sure of our own existence and of the ground and goal of all that happens.

---

[1] Cf. Barth's essay 'Philosophie und Theologie' in *Philosophie und Christliche Existenz*, pp. 94f, 101f, and *CD* IV.3 § 69.2 'The Light of Life'.

'A quite tremendous extension of the field of vision is indicated by this', Barth says. 'To know this object in its truth means in truth to know no more and no less than all things, even man, even oneself, the cosmos and the world. The Truth of Jesus Christ is not one Truth among others; it is *the* Truth, the universal Truth that creates all truth as surely as it is the Truth of God, the *prima veritas* which is also the *summa veritas*. For in Jesus Christ God has created all things, He has created all of us. We do not exist apart from Him, but in Him, whether we are aware of it or not; and the whole cosmos exists not apart from Him but in Him, borne by Him, the Almighty Word. To know Him is to know all. To be touched and gripped by the Spirit in this realm means being led into all truth.'[1]

We will not attempt to follow out in detail the way in which Barth relates the voice of Christ to the cosmos, or the Truth of Christ to the universe of truths which concerns us in the cultural life of man. It will be sufficient to indicate how, on the ground of the Incarnation, Barth refuses to develop any abstract doctrine of the Logos of God apart from his unity with the humanity of Jesus Christ, or any abstract doctrine of man, that is, an independent anthropology, but only a doctrine of man in his essential reality and wholeness in relation to God, and to his fellow-man, and so to the world at large.

Just as in his doctrine of creation, Barth expounds the Covenant of Grace as the internal presupposition and ground of creation, and expounds the creation as the external presupposition and ground of the Covenant, so he thinks of Jesus Christ, the concrete fulfilment of the Covenant, in a constitutive relation both to the eternal election of God and to the whole of creation, for in him all things are gathered up and reconciled and made good in the divine good-pleasure. It is therefore only in Jesus Christ that we can understand the essential nature of the creaturely world and only in him that we can see properly and discern the ultimate meaning of all creaturely being and continuity and activity. It is in his great reconciling work that God has finally made good his work of creation, and therefore it is in the faithfulness of God incarnate in Jesus Christ that we can understand the independent distinctiveness of creation, its terrestrial truth, and its constant meaning, which persist in spite of all sin and corruption for the sake of the divine glory which in Jesus Christ overflows for all that God has made. Jesus Christ is the final establishment of the creation of God, and therefore it is only in and through him that the meaning of creaturely being and the rhythm of its

[1] *Dogmatics in Outline*, p. 26.

NOTES ON CONTRIBUTORS

Anne Bang is Research Fellow at the University of Bergen. She has studied, and published widely on, cultural and religious relations between South Arabia (Yemen and Oman) and East Africa (Zanzibar in particular) in the nineteenth and twentieth centuries. Her book *Sufis and Scholars of the Sea. Family Networks in East Africa, c. 1860-1925* was published in 2003 by RoutledgeCurzon in the *Indian Ocean Series*. She is working on a monograph on Norwegian trading activities in East Africa in the early twentieth century, and has recently extended her research to South Africa (Durban and Cape Town).

Helene Basu was recently appointed Professor of Anthropology at the University of Muenster, Germany, after a long period with the Department of Anthropology at the Free University, Berlin. She has conducted extensive fieldwork in Gujarat, western India, and published widely in both German and English on black African communities in India and more recently on the Charan, a caste of sacred bards. Her book publications include *Von Barden und Königen. Ethnologische Studien zur Göttin und zum Gedächtnis in Kacch* (Peter Lang, 2004); *Embodying Charisma* (co-edited with Pnina Werbner, Routledge 1998); *Habshi-Sklaven, Sidi-Fakire: Muslimische Heiligenverehrung im westlichen Indien* (Berlin, 1995).

Felicitas Becker recently joined Simon Fraser University, Vancouver, as Assistant Professor in African History. Her study of rural Muslims in twentieth-century Tanzania, *Becoming Muslim: The Spread of Islam in Southeast Tanzania, ca. 1880-2000*, was made possible by a British Academy Post-doctoral Fellowship and will be published as a British Academy monograph. Her articles focus on colonial and post-colonial Tanzania, especially Tanzanian Muslims. Her current research is on responses to the AIDS pandemic among East African Muslims.

Gwyn Campbell is Canada Research Chair in Indian Ocean World History at McGill University. His most recent publications include *An Economic History of Imperial Madagascar, 1750-1895: The Rise and Fall of an Island Empire* (Cambridge UP, 2005); and, as (co)editor, *Abolition and Its Aftermath in Indian Ocean Africa and Asia* (Routledge, 2005); *Slavery and Resistance in Africa and Asia* (Routledge, 2005); *Resisting Bondage in Indian Ocean Africa and Asia* (Routledge, 2005); *The Structure of Slavery in Indian Ocean Africa and Asia* (Frank Cass, 2004). His monograph *Africa and the Indian Ocean World from early times to 1900* is to appear in the *Cambridge Economic History of Africa Series*.

Nile Green is Lecturer in South Asian Studies at Manchester University. He has written more than twenty-five articles on Islam in South Asia and Iran. His monograph *Indian Sufism since the Seventeenth Century: Saints, Books and Empires in the Muslim Deccan* is published with Routledge. At present he is preparing a book on Sufism and Islamic reform in the princely state of Hyderabad and 'A Brief History of Sufism' for Blackwell.

Kai Kresse is Lecturer in Anthropology at the University of St Andrews and Research Fellow at the Zentrum Moderner Orient in Berlin (2006–2008). He was Evans-Pritchard Lecturer at All Souls College, Oxford, in 2005. His monograph *Philosophising in Mombasa: Knowledge, Islam, and Intellectual Practice on the Swahili Coast* is published with Edinburgh UP. He has published articles on the Swahili coast and African philosophy and edited collections on the African philosophers H. Odera Oruka (Peter Lang, 1997) and V.Y. Mudimbe (*Journal of African Cultural Studies*, 2005), and on Cultural Philosophy (Wehrhahn, 2001).

Michael Lambek is Professor of Anthropology at the University of Toronto and at the LSE, University of London. He has carried out fieldwork in the western Indian Ocean since 1975, among Malagasy speakers of Mayotte and in northwest Madagascar, leading to three monographs: *Human Spirits: A Cultural Account of Trance in Mayotte* (Cambridge UP, 1981), *Knowledge and Practice in Mayotte: Local Discourses of Islam, Sorcery, and Spirit Possession* (University of Toronto Press, 1993), *The Weight of the Past: Living with History in Mahajanga, Madagascar* (Palgrave-Macmillan, 2002). Among his numerous other publications is *A Reader in the Anthropology of Religion* (Blackwell, 2002).

Filippo Osella is Senior Lecturer in Anthropology at the University of Sussex. Initial research on rural Kerala, South India, examining issues of stratification, identity and social mobility among an ex-'untouchable' community, as reflected in a monograph he co-authored with Caroline Osella, *Social Mobility in Kerala: Modernity and Identity in Conflict* (Pluto, 2000). Further fieldwork in Kerala led to publications on consumption, on micro-politics and on masculinity. From 2002-2005, he pursued an ESRC research project, with Caroline Osella, on consumption practices, popular culture and social reproduction in an urban area in South India.

Caroline Osella is Lecturer in Anthropology with reference to South Asia at SOAS, University of London. Her research focuses on the ways in which projects of identity crafting are brought back to the body, while socially constructed bodies are differentiated to reflect class, ethnic and gender differences and forge social hierarchies. This has led to the books, co-authored with Filippo Osella, *Social Mobility in Kerala: Modernity and Identity in Conflict* (Pluto, 2000), and *Masculinities in South Asia* (Kali for Women, Delhi, 2003; Zed Press, 2003). From 2002-2005, she pursued an ESRC research project, with Filippo Osella, on consumption practices, popular culture and social reproduction in an urban area in South India.

Michael Pearson is Adjunct Professor at the University of Technology in Sydney. He has written, co-authored or edited fifteen books and about sixty articles and book chapters. Among his books are *Port Cities and Intruders: The Swahili Coast, India and Portugal in the Early Modern Era* (Johns Hopkins UP, 1998), *Pilgrimage to Mecca: The Indian Experience,*

1500-1800 (Markus Wiener, 1996), *Pious Passengers: The Hajj in Earlier Times* (Hurst, 1994), *The Indian Ocean* (Routledge, 2003), and, co-edited with Ashin Dasgupta, *India and the Indian Ocean, 1500-1800* (Oxford UP, 1999).

Scott Reese is Associate Professor in History at the University of Northern Arizona. He is currently completing a book manuscript on Sufi sheikhs and Islamic discourses on the Somali coast in the nineteenth and twentieth centuries, and engaged in further research on colonial Aden. He has published widely on Islam in Africa and the Western Indian Ocean, and edited the volume *The Transmission of Learning in Islamic Africa*, published by Brill in 2004.

Edward Simpson is Lecturer in Anthropology at Goldsmiths College, London. He is the author of a series of journal articles and book chapters on Muslims, migration and politics in Gujarat and the Indian Ocean. More recently, he has written on the political economy of natural disasters in South Asia. He published a monograph *Muslim Society and the Western Indian Ocean: The Seafarers of Kachchh* with Routledge in 2006.

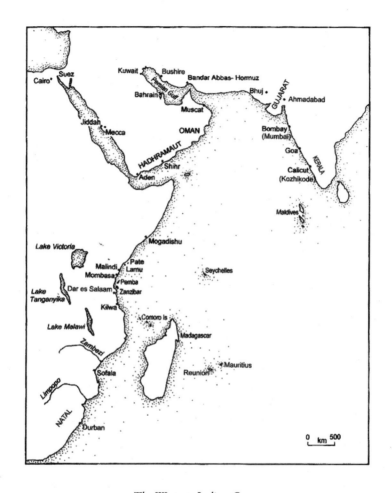

The Western Indian Ocean

FOREWORD

Michael Lambek

Over the last decade or so an increasing number of scholars working along the Indian Ocean, and especially in its western half, i.e., from the west coast of South Asia across to the east coast of Africa, have been shifting from primarily continental perspectives, as specialists in South Asia, Middle East, or East Africa, to examine the connections between their diverse localities and hence to considering in what sense these localities and connections constitute a common 'region' or even a 'system.' Several histories have been written and a series of conferences and workshops have been held, at times in little communication with one another, and mostly in the global north. Perhaps most importantly, a cohort of younger scholars have been trained who are fluent in one or more of the languages of the Indian Ocean littoral and who can thus begin to do justice to the cosmopolitanism of the region's inhabitants. By 'cosmopolitanism' I mean only, for the moment, their fluency in multiple languages, familiarity with and acknowledgment of alternate modes of religiosity and social practices, and their easy mobility between sites where one or another of these languages, modes, and practices are dominant.

This volume reflects admirably the fruits of this scholarship and represents the latest phase of the effort of thinking through what constitutes the Indian Ocean as a region and how to characterise the fluency of its inhabitants. This trajectory could be described as a kind of hermeneutic circle or spiral—we can only recognise the region through understanding the specific localities and movements between them, and we understand the localities and movements better as components of a regional system. The editors leaven their excitement at this intellectual project with some scepticism as to how far the systematisation of a totality can go, a scepticism I share. For one thing, at different times and in different places, micro-regional interactions have been much more significant than macro-regional ones. The Mascarenes (Mauritius and

Réunion), for example, share connections with the societies and processes discussed in this volume, yet they are also different enough that their absence from it does not constitute a huge gap. One might speak of localised but overlapping repertoires of practices rather than of uniformity at any of the relevant levels of inclusion (for instance, locality, region and Indian Ocean world).

The hermeneutic spiral entailed in understanding the practices, processes, relations, ideas and trajectories operating at any one level in relation to those operating at levels of greater or lesser encompassment is, of course, paralleled in the activities of the inhabitants of the region themselves—as they are engaged in making sense of their lives, setting ethical and practical goals and standards at multiple levels of inclusion, drawing on trans-oceanic ties to establish local identities, and drawing on local ties to establish trans-oceanic relations and identities. The chapters in this volume focus on this multi-levelled and recursive process mainly in the domain of religion and with respect to what one could call social or political imaginaries, but they could equally examine a range of other domains, such as kinship or culinary practices (topics tantalisingly introduced here in the chapter by the Osellas).

At each location along the Indian Ocean littoral there is a kind of a tension or pull between the maritime world and the continental, land-based one. This plays out quite differently at each site. How much the sea constitutes a centre around which the ports lie and how much the water forms the boundaries between discrete land masses is always going to be a matter of balance, both in the practical and political activities of the region's inhabitants and in scholarly judgment, and it will surely vary from place to place and over time, depending on the particular historical circumstances, themselves the conjunction of many factors. The point is, perhaps, that their littoral locations have allowed the inhabitants of the ports to escape some predations of land-based states, while also enabling them to expand trade in both directions (that is, both maritime and terrestrial).[1]

---

1   Certainly, in northwest Madagascar the Sakalava state remained upstream and maintained very careful relations with the Islamic ports of trade (Lambek 2002a; Vérin 1986).

In attempting to conceptualise a maritime region the contributors to this volume follow previous scholarship on the Mediterranean and the Atlantic, but it is clear that, despite evident historical connections between the Indian Ocean and each of these other regional systems, the nature of the Indian Ocean *qua* region or system is quite specific. The Atlantic system, so well depicted by Mintz (1985), was constituted through European domination and especially the triangulation between West African sources of slaves and markets, New World plantations, and emergent industrialism in the UK and Western Europe. With European passage around the Cape of Good Hope, the western Indian Ocean became a part of the Atlantic system (the Mascarenes developing along a trajectory remarkably similar, in some respects, to that of the Caribbean). But Indian Ocean mobility is much older and broader than this and, as many of these chapters admirably elucidate, the older traditions of trade, movement, and localisation were continuous alongside – and in articulation with – European mercantilism, piracy, and eventually colonialism and post-colonialism. A difference from the Mediterranean system (itself connected to the Indian Ocean by means of both Egypt and Middle Eastern routes, as some chapters show) is that Indian Ocean distances are much larger and, for the most part, the Indian Ocean littorals have not been under the full control of extensive or competing empires like those of the Romans or the Ottomans. As a result, one could suggest, Indian Ocean ports have had more autonomy than their Atlantic or Mediterranean counterparts.

Despite the ambiguity concerning the Indian Ocean as an integrated region there is a remarkable unity in the volume. The large majority of chapters are case studies from towns, strung like pearls around the coastal perimeter – moving from west to east, north from Natal (Green) along the East African coast through southern Tanzania (Becker), Zanzibar (Bang), Kenya (Kresse), across to Aden (Reese) and over to Iran (Green), Gujarat (Simpson, Basu), Bombay (Green, again), and down the west coast of India to Kerala (Osella and Osella). Indeed, perhaps the most striking pattern to emerge from this book is the comparability of Indian Ocean trading ports as primary socio-political units. What the contributions (aside from Campbell's superb historical overview) share is that the units of study are specific kinds of localities in which the urban community has been more important than the state and in which ties are primarily to people in other cities rather than hinterlands and, more broadly, across the Islamic ecumene. Thus, locality and trans-locality take on a particular hue and so too do politics, which often centre on forms of Islamic practice or, in the South Asian cases, the tension between Muslim and Hindu political and historical imaginaries, but also enable the flourishing of minority ethno-religious groups such as Parsis, Jews, Christians, Ismailis or Bohras.

Going out on a limb, I suggest that the chapters show implicitly but cumulatively a kind of elective affinity between Islam and relatively autonomous cities, polities where the state is either absent, irrelevant, or at some degree of arm's length.[2] If, as is often asserted, Islam does not afford the relatively sharp distinction between church and state, or religion and politics, characteristic of European thought and practice, this may be because the polities most congenial or proper to Islam (at least, Sunni Islam) are not states (extensive, agrarian, bounded, nested, hierarchical and bureaucratic), but rather political entities that resemble more the Greek *polis* – face-to-face communities of citizens. Much as the ancient *polis* at its best offered a democratic citizenship, while also (unfortunately) maintaining a hierarchy between citizens and slaves, so too the Muslim communities of the Indian Ocean littoral maintained a more-or-less democratic civic culture combined with social stratification. As in ancient Greece, economic enterprise was relatively private in contrast to the public sphere of the market place and the mosque, and the former was often underpinned by slave labour. Slaves or former slaves, in turn, had their semi-public arenas, like those furnished by spirit possession and religious devotionalism.

The chapters illuminate certain vehicles and processes for articulating ethical and political concerns afforded by Islam, and thus recurrent in these largely Muslim urban enclaves. They offer a fascinating repertoire of Muslim politics and history in their purest sense, that is, centred not

---

2　One might expand the comparison from maritime cities to the urban enclaves found in the desert regions of the Middle East and North Africa.

around conquest, warfare, kingship, or rule, but on the conduct of communal life, a politics that occurs in and through Islam. Such a politics must balance the 'certain knowledge' manifest in the Qur'an with the 'contestable authority' of its expositors, an authority that is gained or lost through ethical comportment (Lambek 1993: 162–92; Messick 1989). Concomitantly, the chapters demonstrate the historical vitality of Islam, a religious tradition that is far from static or homogenous but continuously generating its own internal lines of debate and contestation. There is a sense in this volume both of the specificity of history, as citizens face particular challenges of colonialism, nationalism, modernism and so forth, but also of something more generally characteristic of the Islamic milieu and of the dynamics intrinsic to Islam itself as a particular kind of social order of knowledge.

This book thus advances our understanding of the nature of Islamic political life, a life made possible in and through the ongoing conversation of Muslims by means of their discursive tradition. This includes – centrally, but not uniformly – the uses of the past and the kinds of historicity, historical legitimation and historically inflected social and political imaginaries shaped by particular forms of the social reproduction of knowledge. We see this both where Muslims are the large majority or engaged mainly in debating with each other and where they constitute some kind of minority and are engaged in debating, articulating with, or defending themselves from, some form of colonialism or nationalism. Indeed, we see the awkwardness of fit between Islam and the nation state, awkward because Islam and the Islamic socio-political imaginary are at once both larger and more encompassing and smaller and more intimate than the nation. The politics of Islam and the reproduction of Islamic tradition are better suited to civic milieux and inter-city or inter-regional networks of scholars than to the powers, orders, bureaucracies and ideologies of the nation state.

What the contributors describe as cosmopolitanism might be defined as the conduct of public life in such urban milieux, a style of comportment characterised by urbanity, learning and debate, by virtues of mutual respect and tolerance. This is a kind of gracious civility that comes from a combination of Muslim (and other religious) traditions of learning and cultivation of virtuous dispositions and of living in well-knit and at least partially autonomous yet internally diversified communities, communities with relatively clear spatial boundaries yet seeing themselves also as part of a world of relatively similar places.[3] These are (or were) towns in which ships are met, unloaded and boarded, and strangers welcomed through the universality of Muslim hospitality and the communities of prayer, mosque and Sufi brotherhoods, but also communities based historically on the slave trade, constituted by social hierarchies of various kinds, and engaged in hard-played tournaments of prestige.[4] This is, as Marc Swartz (1991) wrote of the Swahili, 'the way the world is' (*Dunia, Bwana*). But as the contributors to this exciting book show, even as the horizons of 'cosmopolitan' knowledge and sophistication expand from local and regional to national, trans-national and global levels, this civility comes under increasing challenge.

This book is crammed with far more ideas and much richer scholarship than I have been able to indicate here; it is an honour and pleasure to be able to invite you to its feast.

---

3   On virtuous disposition within Islam, see Mahmood (2004) and Hirschkind (2006); on virtuous practice as it articulates between Islam and alternate traditions, see Lambek (2002a, 2002b).

4   See, for example, el Zein (1974) on Lamu and Meneley (1996) on Zabid.

Bibliography

Hirschkind, C. 2006. *The Ethical Soundscape: Cassette Sermons and Islamic Counterpublics*. New York: Columbia University Press.

Lambek, M. 1993. *Knowledge and Practice in Mayotte: Local Discourses of Islam, Sorcery, and Spirit Possession*. Toronto: University of Toronto Press.

—— 2002a. *The Weight of the Past: Living with History in Mahajanga, Madagascar*. New York: Palgrave-Macmillan.

—— 2002b. 'Nuriaty, the Saint and the Sultan: Virtuous Subject and Subjective Virtuoso of the Post-Modern Colony', in R. Werbner (ed.), *Post-Colonial Subjectivities*. London: Zed.

Mahmood, S. 2004. *Politics of Piety: The Islamic Revival and the Feminist Subject*. Princeton: Princeton University Press.

Meneley, A. 1996. *Tournaments of Value: Sociability and Hierarchy in a Yemeni Town*. Toronto: University of Toronto Press.

Messick, B. 1989. 'Just Writing: Paradox and Political Economy in Yemeni Legal Documents', *Cultural Anthropology*, 4.1.

Mintz, S. 1985. *Sweetness and Power: The Place of Sugar in Modern History*. New York: Viking Penguin.

Swartz, M. 1991. *The Way the World Is: Cultural Processes and Social Relations Among the Mombasa Swahili*. Berkeley: University of California Press.

Vérin, P. 1986. *The History of Civilization in Northern Madagascar*. Rotterdam: A. A. Balkema.

El Zein, A.H. 1974. *The Sacred Meadows: A Structural Analysis of Religious Symbolism in an East African Town*. Evanston: Northwestern University Press.

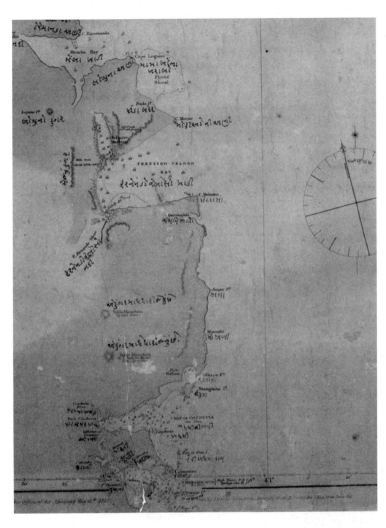

Memba Bay to Mozambique

Riyadha Mosque, Lamu (Kenya)

INTRODUCTION

COSMOPOLITANISM CONTESTED: ANTHROPOLOGY AND HISTORY IN THE WESTERN INDIAN OCEAN

Edward Simpson and Kai Kresse

This book investigates the relationship between history and anthropology in the western Indian Ocean with reference to both Islam and cosmopolitanism. It explores how social groups have been formed in the past and are explained today by selective recourse to that past or to the pasts of others. The chapters take the form of case studies which focus either on particular ports and seaboards or on the social exchange between ports and seaboards. Each is inspired by different yet overlapping heuristic interests, describing the contours and dynamics of social life past and present, along the shores of East Africa, the Arab Peninsula and western India. Taken as a whole, the chapters bring anthropology and history together to scrutinise the tangle of narratives, practices and visions that have shaped social imagination of those living along the ocean's shores.[1] In this introduction, we sketch out the structure of the book and the contribution it makes to the study of the

---

1   There have been a number of other important attempts at drawing connections between the Middle East, South Asia and Africa. Notable among contemporary historians and anthropologists to have worked on these themes are Edward Alpers, Charles Lindholm, David Parkin, Ulrike Freitag and Sanjay Subrahmanyam. We have also benefited from the proceedings of a workshop held in Heidelberg in 1999, the 'Middle East/South Asia Project' at University of California Santa Barbara, the 'Indian Ocean Project' at University of California Los Angeles and publications by the former 'Indian Ocean Group' at the Zentrum Moderner Orient in Berlin, the Routledge Indian Ocean Series, and the journal *Comparative Studies of South Asia, Africa and the Middle East*. Recent work on the Mediterranean has again approached similar themes (Bayly and Fawaz 2002) as has well-known work on other oceans.

Indian Ocean and to social theory. Some of our conclusions remain in
the form of questions rather than as definitive statements; these indicate
pathways for future research, following and pushing further the
perspective outlined here.

Struggles with history, it appears to us, underlie much of the sociality
and patterns of connectedness in the western Indian Ocean; thus, it
seems suitable that studies of the region should also struggle with history.
The roles of history we have in mind are many and varied, both for the
people we study and for us as researchers. Here we explore several of the
roles history plays as a way of approaching the study of the region. Our
initiative is also in response to the fact that the adjective 'cosmopolitan' is
frequently used as an epithet in relation to the Indian Ocean, often in a
somewhat lazy sense to suggest population movement and the sharing
and inter-mingling of cultural values. This, clearly, needs to be
scrutinised and qualified. Any conception of 'cosmopolitan society', we
think, ought to reflect the historical struggles on which it builds. Our
approach, which seeks to be empirically based and conceptually sensitive,
investigates the effects of a dynamic history of population movement and
trade on society in particular places at particular times. The picture we
draw is of shifting patterns of social division and of ethnic and religious
rivalries; these things, we suggest, are what different societies of the
western Indian Ocean have, fundamentally, in common. In the broadest
sense, this book examines how, why and under what circumstances
people attempt to change or re-affirm the social and moral orders in
which they find themselves.

We see little point in attempting to provide yet another new
definition of 'cosmopolitanism', but we will briefly characterise our
understanding of its significance here.[2] Whatever else it may signify, the
term clearly, and etymologically, refers to the idea of being part of a

---

2 Vertovec and Cohen provide six useful perspectives on cosmopolitanism (2002: 1–22).
   Other stimulating and empirically-based reflections on cosmopolitanism can be found
   in Breckenridge et al. (2002) and Beck (2004). Appiah (2006) illustrates why, despite
   the considerable hype about it these days, cosmopolitanism is still a good word to think
   with.

broad social project that exists outside the confines of kinship, ethnicity or nationality. Importantly, for us, 'cosmopolitanism' envelops a consciousness of human diversity. It refers to a sense of living beyond the mundane collective boundaries of everyday life and is suggestive of a trans-communal society. In this society, people are conscious of the differences between themselves and cognisant of other patterns of obligation from which they may well be excluded. Thus, in one sense, cosmopolitanism can be seen as normative 'goal': to live in peace with one another and willingly subscribe to the same basic principles. In another sense, cosmopolitanism can also be seen as a factual 'challenge': how to create or envisage wider unity when faced with social diversity. It is cosmopolitanism in this latter form that we wish to take up, for it seems of greater relevance for the kind of social and historical investigation that we are interested in. That is not to deny the possibility (and indeed, the reality) of encountering normative ideas about cosmopolitanism at work in the societies we study, but these are not our main concern here. If the 'challenge' of cosmopolitanism lies in how the present is negotiated to shape a more agreeable future for such a diverse society, then reference to the past is particularly salient as a way of underpinning this process – a kind of conglomeration of pasts held in common.

As anthropologists, we have separately conducted ethnographic fieldwork on the littorals of the Indian Ocean: Simpson in western India and Kresse on the Swahili coast of East Africa. During this research we have had to struggle with history and people's sense of the past in different ways. Narratives about the past inevitably take on different densities and emphasises depending on the context. In this sense, history sometimes appears to explain how the social world has become what it is; at other times, history has little or nothing to say about contemporary social orders. We then have to ask: why is this so? Any attempt to answer such a research-led question inevitably produces another new narrative about the past – one which, from an anthropologist's perspective, emerges ideally from the confluence of our scholarship and the judgements and narratives of our friends and informants. As most people who have conducted ethnographic research will be aware, not everyone in the field knows the same array of things in equal depth or detail – why, indeed, might they be expected to? One often encounters experts on the past, as well as those who have little or selective interest in what went before. This is an interesting fact in its own right and clearly has profound implications for understanding how societies work as well as making it very difficult to speak in general terms about the past on the behalf of others; however, this uneven distribution of knowledge is not only seen among individuals in the same place because it is also true that different societies have different degrees of interest in the past as well as different methods of recording, recounting and erasing what has gone before. Thus, the struggles with history that concern us here are at once personal, theoretical, methodological and ethnographic, and at all levels are placed, we think, in stark relief by the comparative approach of this book.

Dealing with the past, the present and the revealing tensions of social change is a notoriously perilous task for some very well-known practical, disciplinary and methodological reasons. There is, as J.D.Y. Peel has recently suggested, 'an expository problem' in creating a linear narrative for accounts of human action: 'put history before sociology, and the narrative may not be fully intelligible; put society or culture first, and it may well appear as too given and reified, too independent of historical agency at all' (2000: 47). In the Indian Ocean, the past weighs heavily on littoral society and the effects of centuries of trade and population exchange are evident to even the most innocent of travellers. The sense of who was an insider and who was an outsider has changed over time and versions and visions of past and present and the ways in which their relationships were conceptualised have been many and fluctuating. Merchants, warriors and slaves have moved in and out of the fields that anthropologists and historians study, sometimes leaving sociological legacies and at other times not. Mombasa, for instance, in the course of its social history known to us, has integrated a variety of people of 'African', 'Arab' and 'South Asian' descent in a wider sense into its urban sphere. Not infrequently these people came from intermediary ports of residence (such as Lamu, Zanzibar, Barava, Kismayu, Abu-Dhabi and Bahrain) rather than their places of ethnic origin. A range of languages, other than Swahili, Arabic and English, can be heard in the city; among them are Gujarati, Kachchhi, Urdu, Somali, Mijikenda, Luo and other upcountry African languages. Islamic traditions characterise many, but far from all, of the local communities in religious terms (for example, Sunni-Shafi'i, Ibadhi, or the Shi'a-Ithna'ashari, -Bohora and -Isma'ili), in each case signifying different trans-local networks spanning across the Indian Ocean, while Hinduism and Christianity are also publicly visible.

In the Old Town of Mombasa, the ethnic origins of friends and neighbours reflect the wide spectrum of places mentioned above. Over generations, marriages have affirmed existent family and group structures or shaped them anew, with and against the lines of custom and convention. These ties provide illustrations of a local social fabric that reflects Indian Ocean links. Belief in Islam is what unites the Old Town community, yet also what sets groups apart, as sub-factions compete with each other. The social networks of neighbouring people overlap, inter-sect, but clearly also differ. Before venturing further into the dynamics and tensions seen in Mombasa and the other settings explored in this book, we will cast more light on our own disciplinary perspective and on the inter-disciplinary relationships we are cultivating here.

Anthropology and History
Over two decades ago, Bernard Cohn, an anthropologist who spent much time among historians, provocatively suggested that: 'as chronology is to the historian so authenticity is to the anthropologist' (1981: 240). In another essay written at about the same time (1980), he invented the two fictitious anthropologists Phillias Fillagap and Lucy Lacuna who were to toil endlessly to plug holes in the ethnographic record, domesticating data and turning it into knowledge. Historians may have often blushed at the ways in which their anthropological colleagues clumsily treat the past, at their quest for evidence to support what they see in the present, and at their all-too-often naive use of archival materials which on occasion leads to an ahistorical view of society. Anthropologists on the other hand, have often been no less derisory about the historians' gloss on social diversity and complexity. The archive, it is suggested, obscures as much as it reveals and, on the

whole, elevates events, charters and treaties over and above the contingencies of social life. For Cohn, a fruitful relationship between the disciplines was to be found in a categorical shift in the research practices of his fictional anthropological pals, who were to exchange the collection of objective social facts for the study of the construction of cultural categories and the process of that construction. This is essentially the approach taken in this book, with the caveat that we lay more emphasis on society than on culture.

The debate about the relationship between anthropology and history of course takes for granted that we know what the disciplines are and that they could or should be brought together (see Comaroff 1982). Both before and after Cohn debates about the relationship between the disciplines have been repeated often, and a cursory study of this genealogy reflects significant changes within disciplines themselves. For the British anthropological tradition, there is some dispute about whether it has always taken history seriously, and how successful it was in doing so. A general debate on this topic took on a particular vigour in the 1950s, after E.E. Evans-Pritchard (1950: 123) picked up Maitlands' (1936: 249) phrase '[...] by and by anthropology will have the choice of becoming history or nothing'.[3] In subsequent decades, the continuing spat spawned other creative insights: there were no societies as isolated, or indeed as 'primitive', as it had been claimed and change was something that people did to themselves as well as had done to them.[4]

---

3 Although Evans-Pritchard is well-known for his concern that anthropology needs more history, elsewhere he also suggested that history should become more anthropological (1962: 64), which suggests he saw an inter-dependent relationship between disciplines of equal worth.

4 The wrangling was given vigour by the contrasting views of Radcliffe-Brown, who carefully distinguished between social anthropology and history on both practical and methodological grounds. He drew this distinction however, not out of a dislike of history as has often been claimed, but to clarify the difference between the historical explanation of institutions and their theoretical understanding (1952: 3; also see Smith 1962). The contrasting positions of these respected intellects provoked some wonderful debates that now seem dated and frightfully self-referential about the correct nature of the relationship between structure, function and social change (see Lewis 1968; Gellner 1964 for example).

Meanwhile, other historians tried to work out their relationship to anthropology and ethnography. One of the most fruitful series of ideas to emerge from these debates, in which Cohn also played a key role, was about the way in which colonial history was itself an ethnographic product of a particular set of concerns, classificatory exercises and relations of power.

By taking this path of entry into the debate we can see a continuity of concerns and inter-disciplinary questions, across schools, periods and approaches, at least within anthropology. We think here of Johannes Fabian's (1983) post-colonial critique of anthropology which questioned the basic parameters of the discipline itself. His thesis was that anthropology fundamentally misrepresented people from elsewhere because its practices were based on the Euro-centrism inherent to prevailing knowledge and power structures. According to him, the 'anthropological Other' thus remained part of another world, set apart from that of the anthropologist. Fabian's solution to this problem was to be found in a particular way of including history: anthropologist and ethnography were to be bound together, coevally, within the same narrative and temporal framework. Only then could anthropology claim to be a true documentation of social life, rendering it understandable in its own terms.[5]

Obviously, Fabian and Evans-Pritchard are from different eras and influenced by different scholarly trends. Yet, they seem to share a similar basic message: anthropology must be historical or be nothing. Evans-Pritchard (1962), writing from a colonial vantage, had already placed an explicit emphasis on the need to study 'our own' societies and 'others' in the same terms and following the same basic principles. In Fabian's case, this call is prompted by the heightened post-colonial sensitivity to the influence and effects of knowledge and power. Both authors are exemplary in their treatment of the past and their work illustrates ways in which anthropology can avoid manufacturing what Fred Cooper recently

---

5 Fabian's later work shows how history complements the ethnographic project of anthropology and keeps it alive as a just endeavour. This he has pursued in different ways (1997, 1990, 1986).

called 'ahistorical history' (2005: 17); namely, writing which purports to address the relationship of past to present but does so without interrogating the way processes unfold over time. Here, Cooper is concerned with the conceptual framework for the study of colonialism and its aftermath. Seeing colonialism as a cluster of tensions between external appropriations and impositions, and internal responses and agencies, he suggests research along the following lines:

We can examine the constraint imposed by the insinuation of Western social categories into daily life and political ideology in conquered spaces without assuming that the logic immanent in those categories determined future politics. We can recognize the instability and contested nature of colonizing ideologies and ask how political leaders in the colonies sought to reintegrate, appropriate, deflect, and resist the political ideas they gleaned from colonial rulers, their own experience, and their connections across colonial boundaries (2005: 32).

That said, the colonial encounter in South Asia and East Africa clearly did produce some ethnographic and indeed historical knowledge in particular ways that perhaps altered the shape of pre-colonial society forever.[6] This knowledge was often Orientalist, intelligence led or evolutionist. This is perhaps the most fearsome of the histories we have had to struggle with as researchers working in the Indian Ocean. It is difficult to see around and through, and despite more recent work of the Subaltern Studies Group and others, it was still often the monumental tomes of the colonial gazetteers to which we were referred for regional histories when we started our post-graduate careers. If there was irony in being directed to such sources, then it was veiled too heavily to be appreciated at the time.

The influence of the techniques and methods of colonial history have spilled out into the world to interact with other local forms of knowledge. The ethnographies we read as background material to our own work tend to build on colonial sources, the first being written as part of the colonial project (see Simpson 2006: 33–39). The claims

---

6　There has also been considerable work on the ways in which colonialism and its practices influenced ideas about caste (Dirks 2001; Peabody 2001) and language (Blackburn 2003; Fabian 1986; Robinson 2003: 66–104; Zaman 1999).

contained within these works may have left the page and taken on meanings of their own. What our friends and informants know and say is clearly influenced to some degree by a legacy of the colonial encounter as well as by the thoughts of other powerful interest groups. Of course, these processes have not simply influenced the ways in which events are interpreted and the methods of establishing a relationship between different events; they have also deeply affected the categorisation of space and place, as administrative and linguistic boundaries congealed with ethnic and religious boundaries during the period of colonialism.

We mention this here to draw attention to the fact that the very stuff of anthropology – social organisation, conceptions of the individual and the collective body and so forth – have very real histories that have unfolded over time, been influenced by colonialism and its aftermath in various ways, and have changed both in and of themselves but also in their relationship to other things. Knowing something of a history is one thing, knowing what do with it in relation to other kinds of social activity that may not have such known histories is quite another.

Space and History
When we cast our eyes from land to sea we have to struggle again with history because anthropologists and historians usually write very different kinds of books about the Indian Ocean and only rarely have they written books together (see Horton and Middleton 2000 for an example). We will return to this matter shortly, but first we wish to introduce the discussion with a more prosaic observation on the written history of the Indian Ocean. Given our preceding discussion on the unfolding of time and colonialism, what can a contemporary ethnographer expect to gain from reading a historian's text such as K.N. Chaudhuri's (1985) seminal and sophisticated *Trade and Civilisation in the Indian Ocean: An Economic History from the Rise of Islam to 1750* and its sequel (1992), *Asia Before Europe*? There can be no certainty that any of the phenomena or trade routes Chaudhuri describes survive today. If there is such a resemblance then there is nothing to say that that particular phenomenon has not vanished and reappeared in response to some other need rendering it unrelated to that described by Chaudhuri. Does this

mean Chaudhuri's work is simply well-written background material for what came next? Could the lacking sense of temporal continuity be restored by reading *Trade and Civilisation* in tandem with other books written about the period from 1750 to today?

We dress these profound issues in a somewhat caricatured garb to make them stand out clearly. There is of course no simple answer to either question and we raise them because in this book we have taken care not to reproduce the problems they suggest: namely, we have exercised caution when faced with scenarios that invite comparison and that may alluringly suggest continuity over time or space.

One of the most striking things about the history of the Indian Ocean, as it exists in scholarly accounts, is the centrality many leading historians give to spatial metaphors and spatial theories, and here Chaudhuri also excels.[7] This is strange however because the resources of history ('records' for simplicity's sake, although we realise this will not please everyone) and the conventional research methods employed by the discipline do not strike us as naturally offering a way into theorising about the experience of space through travel, or indeed about the often diverse nature of the connections between people and places.

The French historian Fernand Braudel (1972) pointed to the fact that the unity of a culture or territorial unit can also be defined by the movements of people across the mass of water at its centre rather than by

---

7   This is not the place to present a comprehensive bibliography of scholarly work on the western Indian Ocean. However, although we focus primarily on Chaudhuri's work, we have also read and been influenced by the following: Arasaratnam (1990), Bang (2003), Boxer (1969), Curtin (1984), Das Gupta and Pearson (1987), Fair (2001), Freitag (2003), Freitag and Clarence-Smith (1997), Gilbert (2004), Pearson (1976), Pouwels (1987), Prins (1965), Reda Bhacker (1992), Risso (1995), Sheriff (1987), Subramanian (1997) and Toussaint (1966). Throughout this work, spatial metaphors are far more elaborate and numerous than their temporal cousins. While there can be no doubt that such discussions have been useful for illustrating the changing boundaries of the region and of patterns of trade within it, the question remains: just whose view of space and travel are we presented with in such accounts? While this question may seem irrelevant for those focusing on patterns of regional trade or the operation of inter-regional economies, the question should be far from irrelevant for those interested in the perspectives of people who live and work in the region. We have found it illuminating to read the literature with this question firmly in mind.

the lands around its periphery. In his view, the Mediterranean region was a place of human activity defined by the journeys, exchanges, and the cultures of those that traversed its waters and lands. Similarly, Chaudhuri (1985) has illustrated how the Indian Ocean unites people and places through recognised systems of exchange, yet it also divides by distance, changing environmental conditions and cultural difference. In his view, travel, movements of population, climate, waves of colonisation, mastery of sea travel and, at times, Islam, give unity to the Indian Ocean. Diversity is to be seen in social systems and cultural traditions such as food, clothing, housing and, at times, in Islam – when its expansion created distinct zones of political tension. To both the features of unity and diversity we might, for example, add language, where unity is given in some areas by a specialised business tongue, a recognised common language such as Hindi or English in modern India, Swahili in East Africa or, on a grander scale, the predominance of Arabic among Muslims for prayer, ritual action and legal and philosophical concepts (see Parkin 2000). Language obviously also suggests diversity because of the range of local languages and dialects which can be used to afford privacy and discretion.

Other historians have cast their spatial metaphors differently. Kenneth McPherson (1993), for example, defines the Indian Ocean 'world' by the shifting boundaries of long-distance maritime trade. He is however careful to stress that this world does not form a homogenous area and that commonalities between regions, such as those we have just mentioned, were carried by trade. Similarly, Michael Pearson (2000, 2003) has argued the Indian Ocean is not bound together by a nebulous notion of commonality or structure. He suggests that the people of the littorals identify strongly with their own countries but are also bound up in more general patterns of loyalty, such as belonging to the Muslim world.

David Parkin has suggested that spatial tropes, perhaps like those we have just described, are 'useful fictions' (2000: 1). Recently, the claim has been heard that the division and naming of continents, culture areas, civilizations, world regions and so on is arbitrary and discursive rather than scientific. For example, Martin Lewis and Kären Wigen (1997), a geographer and an historian, examine the origins of the ways in which the continents have been classified from antiquity to the present. They show the influence of imperialism, environmental determinism and nation state-ism on the ways in which we think about global spaces. Other recent writing on the Indian Ocean has set out to re-imagine it as the 'cradle of globalisation' or as a zone of 'space on the move' (Deutsch and Reinwald 2002). Some of this work, drawing on James Clifford (1997) and others, focuses on migration, new communication technologies, changing modes of production and consumption, and political identities within a framework of globalisation.

This literature exaggerates the potential for deconstructing the fictions of space and the fluidity of social and political boundaries. If we are precise rather than general in our thinking, we can then see that to properly understand spatial relationships then the role of ideas, knowledge, human practices and social institutions also needs to be considered, as Pearson implies by pointing to the importance of national loyalties in the Indian Ocean. To historicise boundaries and idioms of classification to show how these things have changed over time, as Lewis and Wigen do, is well and good. Political boundaries, modes of administration, nation state-ism and imperialism are however extremely potent categories in the present. Who for example would think of the heavily militarised border shared between India and Pakistan simply as an 'arbitrary and discursive' phenomenon? To show that boundaries and spaces have histories in which they have changed shape is one thing, dealing with the significance of the contemporary form seems quite another.

In some ways, it is impossible to refute the various unity and diversity theses we have outlined above and the importance of the multiple loyalties in an individual's experiences. The terms of the model are a broad church by any standard and it is possible to see evidence of both diversity and unity in practically any social setting if that is what one is looking for. Following Chaudhuri however, and this is what a contemporary ethnographer can take from his work, the principal argument made through the chapters of this book is simply that distinct patterns of social diversity create the impression of unity. In the following pages, we will explain what we mean by this and how this influences our understanding of western Indian Ocean societies. First, however, we wish to show how movement tends to divide rather than unify the spaces of the western Indian Ocean.

Movement and Space

It is well documented that the movement of people in the Indian Ocean intensified with European colonial expansion during the nineteenth and early twentieth centuries, and perhaps changed character as it did so. However, there is compelling evidence to suggest that western India and parts of the coast of East Africa have in various ways been exchanging populations, ideas and goods for millennia. Ethnographic research suggests that such exchanges are reflected in the contemporary social, architectural and religious fabric of the regions. Yet, it is worth dwelling for a moment on what this means because it seems to us that contrary to some prevailing notions of Indian Ocean historicity, human connectivity in the region (that is to say connections across the Indian Ocean) tends actually to be rather limited. Some scholars have taken the movement of goods through the ports of the region as an axiomatic sign of cosmopolitanism. Here, there seems to be a general confusion of people and things because while some goods have wonderful migration histories, the individuals who traded such items tended to act merely as nodal brokers between different legs of the goods' journey and only travelled occasionally, perhaps seasonally, themselves. There is however more at stake here than the idea that goods moved a great deal and people moved much less.

In our view, what movement and migration there was (and is) tended to create new or modified divisions in the population both at home and away rather than creating a unified oceanic society. This is especially clear when the research focus is placed upon social practices such as endogamy, community taxation and community-specific leadership structures, and in some cases community-specific religious practices and languages. In many cases (but obviously not all), the experience of migration and trade solidified and modified the boundaries suggested by caste and religion. Here we have in mind elite Muslim groups such as

Aga Khani Khojas (Isma'ilis) for whom patterns of community growth and decline in the Indian Ocean context are well known, but also Indian Hindu castes such as Lohanas and Bhatiyas for whom these things are equally true but much less familiar in academic writing.

We have also noted that much of the writing about movement in the Indian Ocean tends to treat different places as if they were all equal in their worth. However, it seems the values accorded to places, spaces and destinations vary quite dramatically from any particular viewpoint on the Indian Ocean. Thus, the role of the Hijaz in the mind of Muslim travellers is obviously quite different to the position it occupies in the imagination of Hindu travellers; Mumbai has a special significance for Khojas, and so forth. Similar patterns of salience are also found in visa and immigration practices of various countries, such that from the perspective of Gujarat it is generally felt that Muslims are more readily granted visas for the Emirates and Hindus for Oman (this has a history). Muslims in post-colonial Kenya are often given permission only to travel to the Arab Gulf countries, if fortunate enough to obtain visas (or even passports). Importantly, then, the different values given to space, place and, indeed, history, are important resources in the politics of home, and migrants may attempt to use the financial or moral gains of their own journeys to enhance their standing locally. Thus our argument: without social diversity, the unity of the Indian Ocean is a hollow idea – and so is cosmopolitanism and its theoretical corollaries.

Highly significant social differences define the characters of port towns, despite centuries of inter-mingling populations. Therefore, the impression of unity in the Indian Ocean, we suggest, is derived from particular kinds of social diversity which are recognisable to people within the region as they move through space and time.

In a sense, cosmopolitanism may well, on occasion, be an economic strategy, a vehicle for trade, rather than a meaningful cultural or social identity or a political project. As one of our informants put this: 'the more bits of languages I speak, the more saris I can sell to South Asians in the bazaars of Dubai.' And, albeit on a different scale, as a Muslim cloth merchant in Gujarat said: 'the more I know about Hindu religious ceremonies, when they take place and why, the more cloth it allows me to sell them. They laugh that I know the gifts they make to their deities when a child is born. I change my stock depending on their religious calendar.' Fitting as these functional characterisations of cosmopolitan behaviour are, economic strategy signifies just one of several levels on which cosmopolitanism is played out socially.

By contesting the primacy of a simple notion of 'cosmopolitanism' (or the lazy view of it, as we said at the beginning) as a way of looking at the Indian Ocean, we are able to explore local views and experiences of travel and the daily grind of life that do not necessarily bear directly on notions of elitism or tolerance, that much of the social theory literature suggests. Rather than viewing patterns of movement and trade as forces which inevitably reduce social diversity, we suggest this history has created societies in which differences are recognised and individuals are, to a greater or lesser extent, equipped with the skill to navigate through such differences. If it makes sense to speak generally of 'Indian Ocean cosmopolitanism', it is in this sense of social contestation based on a struggle with history that is not so much shared as held in common. Struggling with history, we suggest, for both researchers and researched, is an ethnographic project as well as a cause of methodological anxiety and an existential fact.

In some senses, other disciplines at work within the region, geography and archaeology for instance, are well aware of these kinds of issues. We now turn to a somewhat unlikely source to illustrate what we mean. In 1946, James Hornell, published the monograph *Water Transport: Origins and Early Evolution*. This volume was the culmination of decades of study and in it he classified the vessels he knew around the coast of India (and elsewhere). He used criteria more-or-less of his own making, for classifying certain vessels as sub-types of other types and so on.[8] Everyone who has subsequently written on the coastal and estuarine sailing traffic of India has to refer to this work, and, inevitably, gets bogged down in discussing the merits of Hornell's classificatory schema in order to produce their own, one which is typically based primarily on

---

8 There are interesting parallels between Hornell's project and the British colonial practices of census and cultural documentation referred to earlier.

what they perceive to be Hornell's errors. But there is a serious problem with this kind of classificatory exercise and that is that the people who use and build such vessels often have alternative methods of classification, which rely more on location, function, size, quality of materials and what kind of person the boat's owner is than on the particular shape of a boat or the method of its assembly. Consequently, two boats that look the same may have different names just as two boats that do not look the same may have the same name if they are owned or crewed by the same kind of people.

The worldly-sounding problem of ship classification also raises two further significant methodological problems for the study of the Indian Ocean. The first, to which we have alluded, is the persistence of regional traditions in an area with a long history of population exchange. The design of many ships visible in the Indian Ocean today has clearly been influenced by European, Arabian and Persian techniques and technologies. However, the particular combination of techniques deployed in a particular place continues to produce identifiable regional traditions, such that ships built in Yemen are distinguishable from ships built in western India or from those built on Lamu Island.[9] Ships, as artefacts of historical inter-change, cannot empirically reveal the diversity from which they are formed, a problem also well known to marine archaeologists, including, incidentally, Hornell. Furthermore, and more importantly, the persistence of regional traditions in ship construction has not been eroded by centuries of exchange and trade, nor completely extinguished by modern technology. Today, in the port of Mumbai or in a Dubai creek, aside from national ensigns, it is possible to tell more-or-less accurately where a vessel is from by its design and decoration despite the fact such vessels operate under similar environmental and economic conditions – a few decades ago, this was similarly possible in Mombasa (see Jewell 1976), before the frequency of visiting sailing-boats rapidly decreased. To discern such differences obviously requires knowledge and

---

9   As documented, for instance, in a fascinating piece of ethnography, where the Swahili poet Ahmed Sheikh Nabhany describes all the stages of building a large sailing-boat (*jahazi*) in an epic poem which has been translated (Miehe and Schadeberg 1979); see also Prins (1965).

skill, but as we discuss later in relation to social forms, this also tends to mean that the eye is drawn to the familiar at the expense of the unfamiliar: not all things are equally seen. The second related issue of which ships are both an example and a provocative metaphor relates to names and naming. In comparative projects there is always the problem of ensuring that units of analysis are in fact comparable. Throughout this project we have been plagued by many of the assumptions we set out to deconstruct. We have taken the time to converse about the construction and assumptions of ethnographic and historical work from other regions: the intellectual genealogy, conventions, fashions and weaknesses. At a very simple level, we have seen how contemporary scholarship on East Africa is of quite a different character to that written on South Asia. There are of course good ethnographic and historical reasons for this aside from the particular history of intellectual endeavour. This problem notwithstanding, it became quite clear that many assumptions we brought to the table about religious and ethnic categories and names proved quite misleading in comparative discussion. What we have in mind here is primarily categories such as 'Sunni', 'Salafi' and 'Bohra'. On another level, however, we could probably extend the discussion terms to include others such as 'merchant', 'hinterland', 'port' and 'nationalism'. Or, to put this problem in terms of a question: does the term 'Sunni' have exactly the same connotations in the social life of South Asia as it does in East Africa, including the actual meaning of denomination? Probably not, but how does one go about determining how not and why not when one's own knowledge of what the term means is derived from field research in a particular region? This has proved to be a challenging question and one that quite rapidly begins to point to the ontological limitations of ethnography. However, we would like to share two particularly illustrative examples that also reflect our concern with movement and the fragmentation of space.

The Daudi Bohras (commonly also spelled as 'Vohra' in India, known as 'Bohoras' in East Africa and Bohri in Kerala, an incidental observation that reinforces the general point we are about to make) are a well-known group within the Indian Ocean. They are Shi'as, mostly originating from Gujarat, who for at least the last two hundred years have been a regular presence in most of the commercial centres of the Indian Ocean. It is also well known that they have a strong religious leader who is supported by tiers of lesser-leaders and well-defined institutions and customary law. More than most other groups, they invest considerable time and effort in maintaining the cohesion of their community, they have community-specific taxation and loan schemes, and they quite literally attempt to ostracise their bad apples. For them, social and financial security lie within the community to which they submit, and fundamental personal decisions – about succession in family business, for instance – are made (if possible) following the advice of their primary leader, who in turn visits his communities all around the world, strengthening their local footing while reaffirming global ties. Despite this however, disputes over legitimacy and succession among the Daudi Bohra leadership are well documented. It is also clear that as other communities of migrant Daudi Bohras formed in East Africa during the late nineteenth century they gradually, and sometimes consciously, changed character, both in relation to the new society in which they found themselves but also in terms of their own religious practices and ideas about leadership (see Blank 2001). Even this group, one that has invested so much in imposing homogeneity upon themselves, has however found that migration within the western Indian Ocean brought about change and social fragmentation. On one level, it makes sense to talk of a Daudi Bohra community in a trans-oceanic sense because there is a clear rhetoric of community cohesiveness and patterns of leadership that allows for this assertion to stand. But at another level, differences in actual practices between the migrant settlements, however inter-linked they are, suggest an alternative picture of community fragmentation such that Daudi Bohras visiting India from Africa will notice that in India things are done slightly differently and that the politics of gossip or prestige operate through other channels. However, many East African Bohras may never travel to India, while Gujarati is their first language, their Swahili rudimentary, and they are consistently identified by fellow citizens (of whatever origin) as a distinct 'Indian' community.

The second example we have in mind tells a similar tale but also creates a concrete link between migration within the western Indian Ocean and other patterns of global migration. While Simpson was conducting fieldwork in Gujarat a few years ago, he was visited by an Isma'ili (an Aga Khani Khoja) from London who was interested in exploring her roots, or at least what she imagined her roots to be. Her grandparents had left western India by ship for East Africa in the early part of the twentieth century. Her family remained in Africa for many decades until they were forced to leave for Britain in the 1970s. In Gujarat, we spent our time visiting Khoja cemeteries, shrines and rest houses, all in various states of abandonment and decay. Often, she refused to accept that some of the sites we visited belonged to her community and she suggested that she had been brought to the wrong place in error; sometimes she was quite vehement about this. She complained that the decorations were wrong, the worship of images and so forth that we saw in these places made her feel uneasy because they were not the same as she remembered from her childhood in East Africa, let alone from when her family had moved to Leicester, a city in the East of England. She left feeling disappointed at not recognising her past in the lives of Khojas still living in Gujarat. Despite her embarrassment about what she had seen in the community's religious buildings, she was however able to arrange access to these usually difficult to access places by simply making a phone call to representatives of local Khoja community organisation. 'Being' Khoja worked for her in terms of contacts and networks – even if 'being' Khoja in terms of religious practice and memory did not. At the heart of her disappointment was a 'slippage' where, gradually over the decades, debates about orthodoxy and practice amongst migrants in Africa and later in Britain had slowly and imperceptibly transformed popular practices within her family to the point that she no longer recognised them in India and was made to feel uncomfortable by what she saw. This is not of course to say that religious practice in India had maintained the same form since her ancestors had departed, as perhaps she had assumed to be the case.

As researchers we have become acutely aware of such differences being revealed as our informants confront social difference while moving back and forth across the Ocean. Often our friends and informants and the writers of records however do not worry about, or perhaps are not always aware of, these kinds of distinctions. This again returns us to the problem of seeing.

Seeing and Equivalence

We now turn to develop the idea of 'equivalence' and the implications of this idea for social relationships and the ways in which littoral society operates. Chaudhuri (n.d.) uses the term in a paper that remains unpublished (as far as we know) in which he also seemingly struggles to explain obvious differences in a region the disparate parts of which clearly have so much in common.[10] He turns to consider the politics of vision and theories of resemblance. In the way we understand his use of a theory of equivalence it means that sailors grow up on one littoral and when they travel somewhere else the new coast they encounter reminds them of their home; this creates visual and therefore emotional and psychological bonds that people share, or, in the language we have been using, have in common. In our view, it might not only be the coastline however that creates the sense of an imagined community through the experience of equivalence.

Equivalence might also be found in the striking similarities in patterns of vernacular architecture and its usage in the Indian Ocean. Here we have in mind features such as street-side verandas which serve as meeting-points for men of the neighbourhood, hosting friendships and political debate.[11] Indeed, equivalence might also be something as simple

---

10 Chaudhuri presumably derives the term from mathematics, like his earlier use of set theory in *Trade and Civilisation* (and more explicitly in 1992). However, the term has a history in both anthropology and sociology in relation to comparative methods. See Smith (1969) for an early but thorough discussion of the key issues surrounding the notion of 'equivalence' in cross-cultural research; also see Didier and Simpson (2005).

11 Called *barazas* and *otlas* in Swahili and Gujarati respectively, they operate according to variable criteria (such as age, status, or ethnic, religious and political background), granting almost open or only highly restricted access to others. On *barazas* in Zanzibar see Loimeier (2005) and in Kenya see Kresse (2005). We are unaware of comparable literature on the phenomena in Gujarat. Also note here Filippo and Caroline Osella's

as the familiar design and motifs of wooden doors at the Swahili coast and in Gujarat that shield private courtyards from busy bazaars (see Barton 1924). These examples take us from the general and non-specific down to the specifics at street level. It is at street level that we have also seen a strong use for the idea of equivalence as a way of looking at comparative ethnography. Our contention here is that just as travellers or merchants may see something of home in the street architecture of distant places they may also recognise the shape and characteristics of their home society in the societies of the places they visit.

As a way into this idea we start at the level of popular demographic stereotypes which reflect a loose division of labour in many seaboard towns of the Indian Ocean. In such commercial towns there are often Parsis, Banians, Hadhramis and, more particularly, Daudi Bohras with their distinctive beards and embroidered skull caps pedalling ironmongery; there may also be vaguely discernable groups of Baluchis and Pathans in Africa who came as mercenaries in the past; and there are South Indians now working as airport cleaners (for instance) in the modern Emirates. Beyond the stereotype however each figure in this list is suggestive of a broader community, perhaps endogamous, and of a particular form of social organisation structured by a hierarchy and formal institutions. In short, there are clearly defined social groups scattered around the Indian Ocean, whose practices and customs (such as beards, drumming or rituals) have migrated with them albeit, as we have discussed, changing as they do so. The traveller, sailor or migrant recognises these people as the equivalents of people and communities from home and is thus able to use suitable terms of address with confidence and, perhaps, even imagine an appropriate social position in relation to the new but superficially familiar stranger. Behind the simplifying mask of such demographic equivalence, which may exist more in the illusions of imagination than in reality, we suggest there are some more fundamental social equivalences.

---

discussion in this volume (Chapter 9) of equivalent street-side men's clubs in Kerala and how they are recreated after a fashion by migrants from Kerala in the Emirates.

Looking to the past again for a moment, a number of recent publications on the history of South Asian merchants in the Indian Ocean have questioned the idea of unity and power provided by caste, kinship and natal affiliations. The impetus for this work has been to counter the legacy of colonial ethnological scholarship to which caste was central. Claude Markovits (2000), for example, suggests that the role of caste has been over-played in analysis of the organisation of mercantile networks.[12] From our vantage, caste retains more significance than Markovits allows. Today, caste, as it is practiced and understood in western India, serves as an important medium for both migration and trade. Caste does not of course determine everything but its presence is strongly felt and for the purposes of our argument, caste is a prime example of the ways in which equivalences operate.[13] Today, Muslim saints (*pir* and *bawa*) from western India organise their visits to Tanzania through the caste networks of their followers in India. Not always, but commonly, jobs in the Emirates are secured through networks of caste. Caste clearly overlaps with patterns of friendship, and, in the case of the saints, with patterns of patronage, but voyages organised through these kinds of networks tend to allow the traveller to remain within these networks overseas. We exaggerate the point to make it of course, but many migrants (we do not claim all migrants), whether they are merchants, saints or labourers, do not venture overseas with the wide eyes of a tourist keen on sampling new foods and meeting the locals, let alone to understand local principles of social organisation. Saints from

---

12 In this instance the assertion is odd given that it is based on evidence from Sind where caste is well-known not to exist in the same form as elsewhere in South Asia.

13 In the anthropological literature on South Asia there is a long-running and somewhat tendentious debate on the question of whether Muslims have caste of an equivalent form to that found among Hindus. Most contributions to this debate ignore the fact that there is considerable regional variation in the structure and function of caste among Hindus and tend to draw on abstract models of what caste is and does (such as Dumont 1980). Here we assume that Muslims do have caste (known variously as *biraderi, jati* and *jamat* in local languages). These groups tend to be endogamous, have a collective sense of identity based on a generally shared past and perhaps a legal code and elected or hereditary patterns of leadership. Such collective forms of organisation do not encompass all Muslims but are particularly pronounced among mercantile classes.

Gujarat tend to regard black Tanzanians as not worthy of their interest; similarly, one *pir* who had tried his hand at white-collar labour migration to Dubai a few years earlier (before deciding being a saint was more lucrative) had found, despite his pious reputation at home, that he was treated very badly and most 'natives' of the Emirates did not think him worthy of their interest for reasons he did not entirely understand. In both cases, he found solace in familiar networks. As is often rightly claimed, such networks facilitate movement and travel; however, they also seem to serve another, perhaps more conservative and less obvious but no less important purpose, and that is as a form of equivalence, which we think makes travel possible, eases discomfort, and essentially allows people to be blind (to not see) to the differences between home and the place they have travelled to.

As the example of the wandering *pir* also suggests, religion, and particularly Islam, underpins many of the social networks that span the Indian Ocean. These networks often encompass lesser networks of kinship, community and trade. Muslims of the Swahili coast, for instance, have commonly belonged to the Sunni-Shafiʿi *madhhab* (legal school of Islam); yet, upon closer inspection this coast also harbours communities defined by adherence to other Islamic doctrines, which often is almost equivalent to membership in an ethnic group (the Shiʿa-Ithnaʿashari and -Ismaʿilis for example). We previously noted that both Pearson and Chaudhuri cautiously suggested that at times Islam gave unity to the Indian Ocean. Indeed, at times Islam undeniably provides a unifying point of reference; however, at other times, the generality of this statement is questionable because of various linguistic, ethnic, legal and doctrinal differences that are also emphasised among Muslims in the region. We do not wish to discount the importance of an imagined Muslim community (although this may also take many forms), but it will have to be conceded by insiders and outsider observers alike that especially among Muslims who share apparently similar beliefs factionalism and creative rivalries often exist.

Such factionalism is so frequently described in the academic literature (as well as in many of the chapters of this book) that it leads us to suggest that the most fundamental of social equivalences, at least for Muslims, is a general tendency in society to exist between reformists and those they seek to oppose; significantly, this division also appears similar from the perspective of those opposed by the reformists. This type of division has typically, yet somewhat unsatisfactorily, been described as a contrast between 'universalist' and 'particularist', 'Great' and 'Little' traditions, 'sharia-minded Islam' and 'mysticism' (Eickelman 1981: 202–203; also Geertz 1968), or the 'High Islam of the scholars' and 'Low Islam of the people' (Gellner 1992: 9). In a recent reformulation of this dichotomy Parkin (2000: 12) has argued for a softer distinction, between what he calls ontological dualists and monists. The dualists see an unbridgeable gap between themselves and Allah; the monists see themselves as being at one with Allah or other forms of divine power such as cults of saints. Despite the differences in terminology in the models just described, the former class of people is generally associated with mosques, scripture, literacy, monotheism, egalitarianism, ritual sobriety and the absence of mediators and graven images; the latter is associated with provincial life, personalised relationships with the divine, social and religious hierarchy, elaborate ritual practices and a general proliferation of sacred objects and places.

But how useful is this dichotomy, however formulated, for understanding specific people and practices in everyday life? We would like to go a step further and point out that many Muslims – that is as thinking, doubting and believing individuals with particular life histories, be they vassals or scholars – tend to oscillate between these extremes, or even inhabit both conceptual spaces simultaneously. The two parts of this model are then best seen as general tendencies rather than as clear-cut groups, a point also made by Parkin (2000). Along the Swahili coast, for instance, people remember examples of reformist sheikhs who pushed for social egalitarianism and sobriety in ritual practice while they also participated in certain kinds of *maulidi* celebrations (on the Prophet's birthday and other occasions) or *ziyara* (ritual visits to graves). There are also examples of scholars who have renounced some of the reformist ideologies for which they were once famed and feared, and, through a renewed framework of Islamic interpretation, returned to some of the practices they had previously rejected. As Zaman has put it recently: 'the very effort to preserve Islam "unchanged" in a rapidly changing world involves considerable redefinition of what Islam means, where to locate it in society, and how best to serve its interests' (2002: 86). This reminds us of the intellectual and rhetorical effort that so-called 'traditional scholars' invest when responding to the challenges of social and political change and ideological confrontation. When we investigate Islamic discourse within the public sphere (as in Eickelman and Anderson 1999) we gain a sense of the specific contours and dimensions of rivalries between some Muslims. These are again shaped by a whole variety of factors: the doctrinal frameworks of *madhhab*, trans-local networks of Islamic ideologies (and the type of funding they may or may not attract), the use of particular languages and rhetoric in sermons and lectures, and the presentation and contestation of 'Islamic history' (see also Zaman 2002: 6, 113). But what matters also, and perhaps more than can often be unveiled in short-term or through archival research, are personal rivalries between individual leading figures within the Muslim community, which may again be traced to doctrinal, ideological and ethnic differences, but also, significantly, to personal animosities and competition for status and social prestige.

These examples of the complexity of Islamic debates remind us that the social life of Muslims is not adequately explained through recourse to stark dichotomies, such as those we outlined above.[14] Yet, stark dichotomies are not without their uses and are indeed often used by Muslims themselves as a method of describing and seeing differences in religious and social practice. It also seems that many of those travelling the littorals make generalisations about what they see as they move from one place to another, as the new coast they encounter reminds them of their home. Thus we suggest the tension between reformists and their

---

14 This general point runs through the work of Eickelman (1981, 1985), also in collaboration with Piscatori (1990, 1996). It is also well developed in Asad's work on Islam as 'discursive tradition' (1986), recently revisited by Zaman (2002: 6). In work on Indian Ocean societies we have found Bowen (1993) on the eastern Indian Ocean region and Lambek on the Comoros (1993) to be useful in the way they discuss internal conflicts over knowledge in Muslim societies. Lambek (2002) also gives a particularly sensitive account of social experience and history in Madagascar.

Others is a strong form of equivalence and offers a way into society for the visitor. Consequently, we ask ourselves: how do internal debates in Muslim societies, and the ways in which strangers can make themselves feel at home within these debates, relate to our earlier discussion of cosmopolitanism?

In our view, competing interpretations of orthodoxy and legitimacy can be seen as rival forms of cosmopolitanism: all share the goal of uniting Muslims by insisting on universal standards and practices; yet, propagating a sectarian agenda also inevitably gives rise to the disunity of factionalism. Individuals may well be aware of differences in the politics of practice between rival groups but can ignore such differences at convenient times and when a new shore reminds them of their home. The ways in which Islam is worked out and socially negotiated may be thought of as akin to a conception of 'cosmopolitanism' as a regulative idea (in a Kantian sense), a practical goal that humans have accepted and internalised in order to make headway towards it. In other words, Islamic ideologies can be described as cosmopolitanisms at work in society, structured within the general theological structure imparted by the history of Islam. Thereby, visions of the *umma*, the global Muslim community of believers, are pronounced, advocated and rehearsed in specific circumstances around the world.

Of course, the networks of kin, caste and religion we have invoked are constantly compromised by the individual's desire for profit or perhaps by a desire for a relationship with a more-personal God. All such categories however, even as fleetingly imagined forms of unity, are enduring signs of a unity through equivalence because they are shared and acted upon by other travellers. Society in the Indian Ocean is not simply characterised by an unshakable sense of unity, or by the inextricable erosion of difference as time passes and 'progress' takes place; rather, the social history of the Indian Ocean has created what we may call an ever-changing community of strangers. Placing ethnography above history for a moment, we could say that the Indian Ocean hosts a society based on the fact that it knows enough about itself to know that it does not, really, exist. Or, in other words, the historical experience of commonality at the street level that shapes the region has led to a consciousness of social diversity and a largely-assumed knowledge of social differences. This view of things dissolves the idea of simple unity and along with it the view of a trans-oceanic 'community' with a 'shared' history.

Approach, Method and Chapters
The contributors to this book are both historians and anthropologists and have long-term engagements with the Indian Ocean region and its peoples. The strength of their work and the depth of their knowledge hopefully provide a good basis for our comparative perspective. Each chapter emerges from a wider research project to which the contributor was already committed prior to the idea of this book. All authors have made use of their 'working experience of both the field and the archive' (Cohn 1981: 221). They have also invested in long-term fieldwork and broadly support Cohn's vision of an 'anthropological history' (1981: 216).[15] To a significant degree, the research presented in the following chapters explores internal perspectives on social life, based upon primary sources (oral and written, historical and contemporary) from a wide spectrum of languages used within the littoral societies in focus: Arabic, Hindi, Malayalam, Gujarati, Urdu, Farsi and Swahili. We take this fact, of research following the paths of regional discourses held in these languages – rather than being confined to the colonial archive and its language – as a promising and liberating sign for the future.[16] This can be seen as taking regional traditions of ethnographic (and also historiographic) writing a step further (after Fardon 1990), from within, so to speak. The nine chapters of this book address the following themes.

In Chapter One, Gwyn Campbell makes a case for the re-imagination of the role of Africa in the history of the Indian Ocean. He suggests that many scholars have sidelined the role of the continent in pursuit of their own regional biases and that in fact Africa had played a

---

15 On the importance of fieldwork for historians and the relevance of local historiographies from an anthropological perspective also see Keyes Adenaike and Vansina (1996) and Harneit-Sievers (2002).
16 On wider related issues argued with regard to intellectual decolonisation in Africa, see also Wiredu (1996) and Ngugi (1986).

central role in trade in the Indian Ocean up until the nineteenth century. Campbell makes two other strong claims to support his case. First, Africa has been conventionally regarded as an Islamic periphery in relation to the dominant centre formed by today's Middle East. This, he suggests, is fundamentally wrong because Islam in its many forms allowed vast swathes of Africa (not simply the coastal regions) to become part of a broader Indian Ocean trading society. His second related claim is that the conventional division of Africa into northern and sub-Saharan regions is based primarily on colonial categories that obscure important pre-existing networks that linked the regions. The chapter counters many of the conventional wisdoms about the ways in which the littorals of the Indian Ocean are inter-related historically.

In Chapter Two, Edward Simpson explores a similar problem of how territory is given a particular form, namely the history and shape of human relationships within the Indian Ocean from the perspective of modern South Asia. He explores two common narratives about the past and the foundation of the town of Bhuj in western India. The first narrative assimilates the origins of the town to the religious and cultural traditions of the Hindu nation. In this view, the western coast of India is the boundary of a self-contained and clearly-defined cultural unit, India, the integrity of which is at constant risk from foreign invaders from the ocean. The second narrative assimilates the town historically to Sind, the Indian Ocean, to Islam and to patterns of knowledge, language and material culture that migrated with people from the lands to the west. Both versions of the foundation myth seek to establish a claim in the historical development of Bhuj, the former for Hinduism and the latter for Islam. Both narratives also draw on an impenetrable tangle of colonial and post-colonial scholarship and concerns. While these narratives are clearly political expedient, they also suggest radically different ways of imagining the historical relationship between the land and the ocean. The former narrative is largely self-referential and suggestive of stasis; the latter is driven by movement, conquest and social transformation, and a drift of people, things and Islam with the monsoon winds from west to east.

In Chapter Three, Nile Green describes the movement of Sufis in the western Indian Ocean, notably, but not exclusively, between Iran, Bombay, Bushire and Natal. He describes a series of networks that wax and wane in response to colonial policies and economics in the Indian Ocean, but he also suggests how the experience of travel has left a cultural imprint on land. Travel in the Sufi tradition of South Asia has been given a discursive role that has shaped the ways in which the experience of travel has been recorded in Persian and Urdu sources. The Sufis remembered their journeys and these memories became part hagiography; often, the hagiography reflects the vulnerability of those at sea. Green suggests that the experience of the anxieties of the sea voyage and the relief at sighting and setting foot on land has become a master trope of storytelling. Arguably, this is an equivalence accessible to all oceanic travellers, with strong parallels with the experience of hajj and the transformative effects of the experience, which perhaps also goes someway to explaining the apparent elective affinity between Sufism and littoral manifestations of Islam throughout the Indian Ocean.

In Chapter Four, Anne Bang examines the effects of colonialism on the cosmopolitan nature of urban Zanzibar. She asks to what extent the colonial presence represents an end to distinctive patterns of cosmopolitanism of the nineteenth century. By examining conflict in and around the mosques over the nature of authentic religious practice, the transformation of the court system and the politics of an early beach resort ('Zanzibar's Brighton'), Bang shows first how imperialist conceptions of race and power eventually re-ordered relationships between different groups of 'natives' (of the Indian Ocean), reminding us that over time the demographic equivalents are not simply static categories in fixed relationships to one another. Secondly, she shows how some of those colonised appropriated colonial values as society was re-ordered afresh.

In Chapter Five, Scott Reese focuses on religious discourse in colonial Aden in the 1930s. In common with most ports of the region but more emphatically so because of its strategic significance for the British Empire, the Muslims of Aden were ethnically heterogeneous, thrown together largely by colonial happenstance. Reese explores how particular individuals constructed new forms of Muslim community that downplayed differences in class, ethnicity and economic status in favour of adherence to particular doctrine, in this case pro-Salafi and anti-Salafi. During the 1930s, trans-local discourses of religious reform were adapted to the needs of particular individuals in Aden. He tells us, for instance, about a Salafi-oriented reformist Sayyid of Hadhrami origin (a butcher by profession), who actively campaigned against Sufi activities. The scenario Reese describes is an important one because it demands the use of a vocabulary that lends itself to the idea of demographic equivalence (a Salafi or a Hadhrami Sayyid) but then removes some of the certainty the terms may convey by conjoining them and forcing us to rethink the meaning of the new category. Reese's chapter also draws to our attention how competing groups of Muslims sought to use the newly imposed colonial structures of political administration to advance their own factional and doctrinal interests, particularly against their ideological adversaries – who in some ways seem to be personal rivals for social status more than anything else.

In Chapter Six, Kai Kresse analyses the use of historical narratives by Islamic scholars in Mombasa. Here again the opposition between reformists and their Others takes varied forms, often questioning common assumptions. For example, conversion from Sunni-Shafi'i *madhhab* to Shiism (of the Ithna'ashari variety) has become a significant phenomenon within the coastal Muslim community. This process was initiated by proselytising groups such as the Bilal Muslim Mission in the 1960s, pushed forward by the success of the Islamic revolution in Iran in 1979, and has continued under the influence of particular charismatic individuals who struggled to make their version of the past publicly acceptable. Clearly, debates about Muslim practice impinge on all levels of personal conduct. Simple defamation of the ideas or personalities of others is seldom a successful strategy, and there is a constant struggle between competing factions to gain a following also through argument and persuasion. Kresse shows how the presentation of historical knowledge is used as a persuasive form of rhetoric to highlight some of the shifting contours of the debates about Islam in East Africa and its changing relationship to ideas from other shores. In this example, both

Sunni-Shafiʿi and Shiʿa-Ithnaʿashari communities traditionally defined themselves largely along ethnic lines. Now they have to come to terms with the task of integrating 'strangers' (new converts of different ethnic origins) to their fold, they also run the risk of insiders becoming strangers. This can perhaps be seen as a shift from one kind of cosmopolitanism to another; or, at least, as a shift in the construction and negotiation of collective Islamic identities. Despite the changes in the ways collective identities are imagined the fundamental equivalence of reformists and their Others survives largely unscathed.

In Chapter Seven, Felicitas Becker reassesses some of the conventional wisdoms about coastal-hinterland relationships in southern Tanzania during the twentieth century. Based on a wealth of oral sources, she suggests that neither the coastal towns nor the regional Islamic networks have become as redundant as has been claimed. By focusing on the idea of networks to critically examine the relation between the nodes of particular networks, their competitors, and their surroundings, Becker shows how networks allow for the possibility of parallel, yet hardly connected social groupings in the same social setting. She makes the point that a research focus on just one group can tell a story that simply does not reflect the fortunes or networks of another group resident in the same place. If we step away from the intricate details of the historical ethnography of southern Tanzania, then there are clear lessons to be drawn from this analysis for the study of the relationship between network, place and narrative for the Indian Ocean as a whole.

In Chapter Eight, Helene Basu considers the related patterns of exchange between South Asia and East Africa of people and practices. She describes how Islam along the Swahili coast has often incorporated an inter-mingling of practices related to Sufism, healing and spirit possession, the so-called *ngoma* performances that John Janzen (1992) previously investigated in a wide-ranging comparative study of central and south-eastern Africa. Looking across the ocean to Gujarat in India one encounters a similar constellation in rituals performed by Sidis, a Muslim community of former African slaves and seamen. Basu situates the Sidis in the broader context of the migration of East African spirit possession cults, recognising what she is investigating on both shores of the Indian Ocean. She analyses the practices of Sidis in a comparative and historical framework in order to suggest that drumming and spirit possession are things which resemble a deep structure of grammar capable of generating comparable but distinct practices across time and space.

In Chapter Nine, Filippo and Caroline Osella describe the patterns and consequences of migration of the Koyas (a Muslim community from Calicut) from South India to the Middle East. They explore empirical connections between local phenomena and broader trends to show how the experiences of travel and labour provide a narrative trope that allows people to make sense of their position in the world. They suggest that these international migration practices both reinforce and undermine historical notions of urban cosmopolitanism through which Koyas define their own and their city's identity. Koyas tend to cluster in particular areas of Calicut in matrilineal joint families; yet, they are also engaged with trade and connections to the Arab world that have a long and significant history. Together, these discursive resources allow Koyas to both assimilate themselves to and distinguish themselves from other Muslim and non-Muslim communities and play into broader patterns of identity politics. Here again, in a cosmopolitan society, the division between reformers and their Others plays a part in defining the meaningful sections of society, and thus a mechanism through which strangers may integrate themselves.

Beyond the Indian Ocean, a similar characterisation of cosmopolitanism to that described above is also found in the recent work of the philosopher Kwame Anthony Appiah (2006) who sees the challenge of cosmopolitanism as living in a 'world of strangers'. The worlds of familiar strangers described in the chapters of this book also call to mind a metaphor for human history from the work of J.D.Y. Peel. He suggests that history may best be imagined as 'a multi-coloured woollen cord, with component fibers of different lengths [...] that give it structure by pulling both together and against one another' (2000: 9). If this image is appropriate, then it takes a common effort of historical and anthropological research to identify, disentangle and interpret the multiple fibers (of narrative and experience, of knowledge and practice, belief and vision) that have shaped the social imagination, in this case, of the people living along the shores of the western Indian Ocean.

We have stated that struggling with history is an ethnographic project as well as a methodological concern. This suggests that there is no one simple or ideal relationship between anthropology and history, either as disciplines or as forces at work in the world, as the societies we study make use of the past in very different ways to engage with the present.

The images placed in front of this introduction are intended to evoke the kinds of scenarios we have in mind. The cartographic image (also on the front cover of this book) is the southern section of sheet five of a survey of the coast of East Africa conducted by the Hydrographic Office of the London Admiralty. The base print originates from the 1824 survey conducted by Captain Owen from the decks of the HMS Leven. The full cartographic sheet shows two degrees of latitude from Pemba in the north to the town of Mozambique in the south (the southern-most part of this coast appears on the cover from Memba Bay to Mozambique). In the middle of the nineteenth century, with the decline of the Portuguese influence, the map was amended many times as the British grew increasingly interested in the region. They sounded inlets to detect risky shoals and safe anchorages, and made elaborate notes on the ocular demonstrations of geographical features and flora. Sometime later, the map was heavily annotated in the Gujarati script by at least two scribes. While many of their annotations are straight-forward transliterations of English names, others deviate in spelling; perhaps suggesting that the Gujaratis knew how to pronounce the names of these places from personal experience. The suspicion that they had knowledge of the coast is further strengthened by the fact that they also often disagreed with the British map. For instance, the location of some geographical features such as Table Mountain (translated, rather than merely transliterated, into Gujarati on the map as 'Mejnu Dungar'), are different to those marked by previous British surveyors.

The map was unearthed in Gujarat by a local antiques dealer from urban rubble following an earthquake in 2001. The image (as well as the biography of travel we can perhaps imagine for the map as it changed hands) evokes an ever-shifting coastline, often intriguingly inconsistent, as the world-views suggested by the geography of Portuguese place names, the results of British intelligence-led surveys, and the annotations of Gujarati merchants converge.

The second image depicts the Riyadha Mosque in Lamu. Built in 1901 as a mosque and college by Sayyid Habib Saleh (d.1935), it became the central religious and educational institution of the Sufi Alawiyya networks in East Africa, and retains this status even today. It was modelled and named after a mosque in Say'un, Hadhramaut, which was initiated and run by Sayyid Ali Muhammad al-Hibshy (d. 1914). From him, Habib Saleh also adopted the distinctive *maulidi* poems and their performances (involving rhythmic bodily movements and the use of hand-held drums) which came to be known as al-Hibshy. Like other forms of *maulidi* they became an important vehicle for Islamisation in East Africa. Despite several decades of opposition from local reformists, they continue to be performed today.

Habib Saleh, who was a Hadhrami Sayyid born in the Comoros, is credited with opening up Islam to the underprivileged in Lamu and initiating social reform within the hierarchical urban community, dominated by local patricians (*waungwana*). He is remembered and venerated to this day, and his grave is visited by a sizable faction of the many thousands of Muslims who come to Lamu for the annual *maulidi* celebrations. His descendents remain in charge of the Riyadha Mosque and College, and their networks (as part of the Alawiyya) reach far south and west into the upcountry region, to Tanzania, Kenya and Uganda. Links are also maintained sea-wards with the Comoros and the Hadhramaut, and also with Oman where one of his great-grandsons lives and works as a university teacher.[17] Often cast as 'traditionalist', this kind of Islam, linked to the privileged position of sayyids, has been opposed

---

17 For background on the Riyadha Mosque see Bang (2003: 144–47), Farsy (1989), Freitag (2003: ch.6), Khitamy (1995), Lienhardt (1959) and el-Zein (1974).

by various strands of reformism (linked to global debates within the *umma*), and again defended and re-affirmed from within. Such dynamics, explored in similar forms in various chapters of this book, are indicative of a global, living and contested heritage of Islam. In this way, the picture of a building, a material artefact used as religious and educational institution, represents many of the layers of meaning associated with these particular social networks and their histories that span the western Indian Ocean.

The photograph also depicts three women strolling by the Riyadha Mosque (to the right and front). They are dressed in the way that is considered proper for coastal Muslim women. The combination of the long black robe and the cloth covering the head is called *buibui* (also meaning 'spider' in Swahili). It is worth noting that this term has been applied to various changing fashions of black over-gowns and veils over the last few decades.

An unfinished building is visible on the left of the picture. A satellite dish on its roof is a reminder of other kinds of connections to the wider world. In Lamu and elsewhere, satellite television is used as much for Mecca-TV and *al-Jazira* as it is for the Bollywood Movie Channel and CNN.

In the spirit of these images, the chapters of this book together examine what cosmopolitanism means in the context of the western Indian Ocean. They describe cosmopolitanism at work (and as a contested idea) in struggles over social identity and conceptions of legitimacy. Our thoughts on travel and equivalence have emerged from reading and discussing these chapters with one another. While the terms of reference might vary from place to place, the social mechanisms we have described allow travellers to see the politics of home in distant ports, and by thus recognising home in what they see, they are able to participate meaningfully and contribute to the reproduction and transformation of the social order.

Bibliography

Appiah, K.A. 2006. *Cosmopolitanism: Ethics in a World of Strangers.* Princeton: Princeton University Press.

Arasaratnam, S. 1990. 'Recent Trends in the Historiography of the Indian Ocean, 1500 to 1800', *Journal of World History.*

Asad, T. 1986. *The Idea of an Anthropology of Islam.* Occasional Paper Series, Center for Contemporary Arab Studies. Washington D.C.: Georgetown University.

Bang, A.K. 2003. *Sufis and Scholars of the Sea. Family Networks in East Africa, 1860–1925.* London: RoutledgeCurzon.

Barton, F.R. 1924. 'Zanzibar Doors', *Man,* 24.

Bayly, C.A., and L. Fawaz 2002. 'Introduction: The Connected World of Empires', in L. Fawaz and C.A. Bayly (eds), *Modernity and Culture: From the Mediterranean to the Indian Ocean.* New York: Colombia University Press.

Beck, U. 2004. *Der kosmopolitische Blick oder: Krieg ist Frieden.* Frankfurt: Suhrkamp.

Blackburn, S. 2003. *Print Folklore, and Nationalism in Colonial South India.* New Delhi: Permanent Black.

Blank, J. 2001. *Mullahs on the Mainframe. Islam and Modernity among the Daudi Bohras.* Chicago & London: The University of Chicago Press.

Bowen, J. 1993. *Muslims Through Discourse: Religion and Ritual in Gayo Society.* Princeton: Princeton University Press.

Boxer, C.R. 1969. *The Portuguese Seaborne Empire, 1415–1825,* London: Hutchinson.

Braudel, F. 1972 [originally pub. 1948]. *The Mediterranean and the Mediterranean World in the Age of Philip II* (Vols I and II) (trans. S. Reynolds), London: Collins.

Breckenridge, C.A., S. Pollock, H.K. Bhabha and D. Chakrabarty (eds) 2002. *Cosmopolitanism.* Durham: Duke University Press.

Chaudhuri, K.N. 1985. *Trade and Civilisation in the Indian Ocean: An Economic History from the Rise of Islam to 1750.* Cambridge: Cambridge University Press.

—— 1992. *Asia Before Europe: Economy and Civilisation from the Rise of Islam to 1750.* Cambridge: Cambridge University Press.

—— n.d. 'The Middle East & South Asia Through the Eyes of the Beholder: An Outline of a Theory of Equivalence', Keynote Lecture to the Conference on Comparative Studies of South Asia and the Middle East, University of California Santa Barbara, 2000.

Clifford, J. 1997. *Routes: Travel and Translation in the Late Twentieth Century.* Cambridge: Harvard University Press.

Cohn, B.S. 1980. 'History and Anthropology: The State of Play', *Comparative Studies in Society and History*, 22.2.

—— 1981. 'Anthropology and History in the 1980s: Towards a Rapprochement', *Journal of Interdisciplinary History*, 12.2.

Comaroff, J.L. 1982. 'Dialectical Systems, History and Anthropology: Units of Study and Questions of Theory', *Journal of Southern African Studies*, 8.2.

Cooper, F. 2005. *Colonialism in Question: Theory, Knowledge, History.* Berkeley: University of California Press.

Curtin, P. 1984. *Cross-cultural Trade in World History.* Cambridge: Cambridge University Press.

Das Gupta, A., and M.N. Pearson (eds) 1987. *India and the Indian Ocean, 1500–1800.* New Delhi: Oxford University Press.

Deutsch, J-G., and B. Reinwald (eds) 2002. *Space on the Move. Transformations of the Indian Ocean Seascape in the Nineteenth and Twentieth Century.* Berlin: Klaus Schwarz Verlag.

Didier, B.J., and E. Simpson 2005. 'Islam along the South Asian Littoral'. *ISIM Review*, 16.

Dirks, N. 2001. *Caste of Mind: Colonialism and the Making of Modern India.* Princeton: Princeton University Press.

Dumont, L. 1980 [revised edition, originally pub. 1966]. *Homo Hierarchicus. The Caste System and its Implications.* Chicago: The University of Chicago Press.

Eickelman, D.F. 1981. *The Middle East. An Anthropological Approach.* New Jersey: Prentice-Hall.

—— 1985. *Knowledge and Power in Morocco: The Education of a 20th Century Notable.* Princeton: Princeton University Press.

Eickelman, D.F., and J.W. Anderson (eds) 1999. *New Media and the Muslim World: The Emerging Public Sphere.* Bloomington: Indiana University Press.

Eickelman, D.F., and J. Piscatori (eds) 1990. *Muslim Travellers: Pilgrimage, Migration and the Religious Imagination.* London: Routledge.

—— 1996. *Muslim Politics.* Princeton: Princeton University Press.

Evans-Pritchard, E.E. 1950. 'Social Anthropology: Past and Present (the Marett Lecture)', *Man*, 50.

—— 1962. *Essays in Social Anthropology.* London: Faber and Faber.

Fabian, J. 1983. *Time and the Other: How Anthropology Makes its Object.* New York: Colombia University Press.

—— 1986. *Language and Colonial Power: The Appropriation of Swahili in the Former Belgian Congo 1880–1938.* Cambridge: Cambridge University Press.

—— 1990. *History from Below: The 'Vocabulary of Elisabethville' by André Yav. Texts, Translation and Interpretive Essay.* Amsterdam: John Benjamins Publishers.

—— 1997. *Remembering the Present: Painting and Popular History in Zaire.* Berkeley: University of California Press.

Fair, L. 2001. *Pastimes and Politics: Culture, Community and Identity in Post-Abolition Urban Zanzibar, 1890–1945.* Oxford: James Currey.

Fardon, R. (ed.) 1990. *Localising Strategies: Regional Traditions of Ethnographic Writing.* Edinburgh: Scottish Academic Press.

Freitag, U. 2003. *Indian Ocean Migrants and State Formation in the Hadhramaut: Reforming the Homeland.* Leiden: Brill.

Freitag, U., and W.G. Clarence-Smith 1997. *Hadhrami Traders, Scholars, and Statesmen in the Indian Ocean, 1750s–1960s.* Leiden: Brill.

Geertz, C. 1968. *Islam Observed: Religious Development in Morocco and Indonesia.* New Haven: Yale University Press.

Gellner, E. 1964. *Thought and Change.* London: Weidenfeld and Nicolson.

—— 1992. *Muslim Society.* Cambridge: Cambridge University Press.

Gilbert, E. 2004. *Dhows and the Colonial Economy of Zanzibar, 1860–1970.* Oxford: James Currey.

Harneit-Sievers, A. 2002. *A Place in the World: New Local Historiographies from Africa and South Asia.* Leiden: Brill.

Hornell, J. 1946. *Water Transport: Origins and Early Evolution.* Cambridge: Cambridge University Press.

Horton, M., and J. Middleton 2000. *The Swahili: The Social Landscape of a Mercantile Society.* Oxford: Blackwell.

Janzen, J. 1992. *Ngoma: Discourses of Healing and Spirit Possession in Central Africa.* Berkeley: University of California Press.

Jewell, J.H. 1976. *Dhows in Mombasa.* Nairobi: East African Publishing House.

Keyes Adenaike, C., and J. Vansina (eds) 1996. *In Pursuit of History: Fieldwork in Africa.* Oxford: James Currey.

Khitamy, A. b.S. 1995. 'The Role of the Riyadha Mosque-College in Enhancing the Islamic Identity in Kenya', in M. Bakari and S.S. Yahya (eds), *Islam in Kenya.* Nairobi: MEWA.

Kresse, K. 2005. 'At the *Baraza*: Socializing and Intellectual Practice at the Swahili Coast', in T. Falola (ed.), *Christianity and Social Change in Africa: Essays in Honor of J.D.Y. Peel.* Durham: Carolina Academic Press.

Lambek, M. 1993. *Knowledge and Practice in Mayotte: Local Discourses of Islam, Sorcery, and Spirit Possession.* Toronto: University of Toronto Press.

—— 2002. *The Weight of the Past: Living with History in Mahajanga, Madagascar.* London: Palgrave.

Lewis, M.W., and K.E. Wigen 1997. *The Myth of Continents: A Critical Metageography.* Berkeley: University of California Press.

Lewis, I.M (ed.) 1968. *History and Social Anthropology.* London: Tavistock Publications.

Lienhardt, P. 1959. 'The Mosque College of Lamu and its Social Background', *Tanzania Notes and Records.*

Loimeier, R. 2005. 'The Baraza: A Grassroots Institution', *ISIM Review* 16.

Maitland, F.W. 1936. *Selected Essays.* Cambridge: Cambridge University Press.

Markovits, C. 2000. *The Global World of Indian Merchants, 1750–1947.* Cambridge: Cambridge University Press.

McPherson, K. 1993. *The Indian Ocean: A History of People and the Sea.* Delhi: Oxford University Press.

Miehe, G., and T. Schadeberg (eds) 1979. *Sambo ya Kiwandeo. The Ship of Lamu Island, by Ahmed Sheikh Nabhany.* Leiden: Afrika-Studiecentrum.

Ngugi wa Thiong'o 1986. *Decolonising the Mind: The Politics of Language in African Literature.* Oxford: James Currey.

Parkin, D. 2000. 'Inside and Outside the Mosque: A Master Trope', in D. Parkin and S.C. Headley (eds), *Islamic Prayer Across the Indian Ocean. Inside and Outside the Mosque*. Richmond, Surrey: Curzon.

Peabody, N. 2001. 'Cents, Sense, Census: Human Inventories in Late Precolonial and Early Colonial India', *Comparative Studies of Society and History*, 43.4.

Pearson, M.N. 1976. *Merchants and Rulers in Gujarat: The Response to the Portuguese in the Sixteenth Century.* Berkeley: University of California Press.

—— 2000. 'Consolidating the Faith: Muslim Travellers in the Indian Ocean World', *UTS Quarterly: Cultural Studies and New Writing*. 6.2.

—— 2003. *The Indian Ocean*. London: Routledge.

Peel, J.D.Y. 2000. *Religious Encounter and the Making of the Yoruba.* Bloomington: Indiana University Press.

Pouwels, R.L. 1987. *Horn and Crescent: Cultural Change and Traditional Islam on the East African Coast, 800–1900.* Cambridge: Cambridge University Press.

Prins, H.J. 1965. *Sailing from Lamu: A Study of Maritime Culture in Islamic East Africa.* Assen: van Gorcum and Comp. N.V.

Radcliffe-Brown, A.R. 1952. *Structure and Function in Primitive Society.* Glencoe: The Free Press.

Reda Bhacker, M. 1992. *Trade and Empire in Muscat and Zanzibar. The Roots of British Domination.* London: Routledge.

Risso, P. 1995. *Merchants and Faith: Muslim Commerce and Culture in the Indian Ocean.* Boulder: Westview Press.

Robinson, F. 2003. *Islam and Muslim Society in South Asia.* New Delhi: Oxford University Press.

Sheriff, A. 1987. *Slaves, Spices and Ivory in Zanzibar: Integration of an East African Commercial Empire into the World Economy, 1770–1873.* London: James Currey.

Simpson, E. 2006. *Muslim Society and the Western Indian Ocean: The Seafarers of Kachchh.* London: Routledge.

Smith, M.G. 1962. 'History and Social Anthropology', *The Journal of the Royal Anthropological Institute of Great Britain and Ireland,* 92.1.

Smith, R.J. 1969. 'The Concept of Equivalence: A Polemical Analysis', *The Journal of American Folklore*, 82.326.

Subramanian, L. 1987. 'Banias and the British: The Role of Indigenous Credit in the Process of Imperial Expansion in Western India in the Second Half of the Eighteenth Century', *Modern Asian Studies*, 21.3.

Toussaint, A. 1966. *History of the Indian Ocean*. London: Routledge and Kegan Paul.

Vertovec, S., and R. Cohen 2002. 'Introduction: Conceiving Cosmopolitanism', in S. Vertovec and R. Cohen (eds), *Conceiving Cosmopolitanism: Theory, Context, and Practice*. Oxford: Oxford University Press.

Wiredu, K. 1996. *Cultural Universals and Particulars: An African Perspective*. Bloomington: Indiana University Press.

Zaman, M.Q. 1999. 'Commentaries, Print and Patronage: "Hadith" and the Madrasas in Modern South Asia', *Bulletin of the School of Oriental and African Studies* 62.1.

―――― 2002. *The Ulama in Contemporary Islam: Custodians of Change*. Princeton: Princeton University Press.

1

ISLAM IN INDIAN OCEAN AFRICA
PRIOR TO THE SCRAMBLE:
A NEW HISTORICAL PARADIGM

Gwyn Campbell

The history of Islam in East Africa has received relatively little historical attention. This chapter discusses the historiographical context for the study of Islam in this region, and argues for a reassessment of what constituted East Africa and the economic role there of Islam in the context of the rise of the first global economy. Traditional Euro-centric histories have tended to portray Islam as a monolithic politico-religious institution, with a Middle-Eastern core and a wide-flung periphery that included much of Muslim Africa, with a political empire that was eroded by the technologically superior and more adaptable modernising forces of Europe. In East Africa the chief economic impact of Muslim intervention was the creation of a slave export trade.

This chapter argues that the economic role of Islam in the Indian Ocean regions and in East Africa needs to be reconsidered. Islam created a *Pax Islamica* over vast regions that stimulated economic and cultural development over the entire Indian Ocean World. Moreover, in overall terms, Europeans who entered the Indian Ocean region from the end of the fifteenth century failed to establish durable monopolies or critically weaken Muslim economic networks. The central focus of this chapter is on Muslim economic influence in Indian Ocean Africa – a concept critical to understanding to the historical role of Islam in East Africa. It is argued that Indian Ocean Africa, here defined as eastern Africa from the Cape to Cairo and the islands of the western Indian Ocean, formed an integral part of the wider Muslim trading world and that in Indian

Ocean Africa, as elsewhere, Muslims maintained vibrant commercial relations with non-Muslim communities, and that western capitalist and imperialist expansion did not totally undermine Muslim influence, as traditionally thought.

Background: bibliographical approaches to Islam in Indian Ocean Africa. The Euro-centric tradition
Traditional Euro-centric histories generally analyse Islam in a negative light. They consider that non-Western societies possessed insuperable institutional and ideological obstacles to modernisation. In Asia, the centralised civilisations of China, India and Mesopotamia, while impressive in size, stifled the individual enterprise and freedom of thought that in Europe expanded during the Renaissance and Reformation, gave rise to early capitalism, flourished during the Enlightenment and ultimately underpinned the emergence of modern industrial society. In particular, although between the eighth and eleventh centuries polities governed by Islamic law developed a unified body of beliefs, those polities subsequently failed to evolve: Islamic precepts obstructed the development of individualism, the entrepreneurial spirit and the democratic impulse, failed to develop primogeniture or lift the ban on usury, and in general constrained the drive to maximise economic returns – key elements in the emergence of capitalism in Europe. Rather, Muslim investment was channelled into essentially unproductive activities such as school and mosque construction, and poor relief (Segal 2001: 6). As Richard Eaton notes of the Euro-centric approach to Islam:

Since the eleventh century, it was the fate of Islamic civilization to serve in the European imagination as a wholly alien 'other,' a historic and cosmic foil against which Europeans defined their own collective identity as a world civilization (1993: 2).

In the Euro-centric view, the foundations for individual liberty and modernisation in Asia were laid with the imposition of external, specifically European and Christian forces in the nineteenth and twentieth centuries (Eaton 1993: 1–36; Frank 1998).

Africa receives shorter thrift than Asia in Euro-centric histories. Characterised by small decentralised tribal polities focused on the rule of elders, and a multiplicity of animist and ancestral beliefs, Africa was trapped in a primitive inertia that Islam accentuated rather than challenged: In East Africa, Muslims developed a slaving network that inflicted war, famine and servitude on hapless Africans. However, Islamic religious influence was limited to the littoral until the nineteenth century when, propelled by a combination of European commercial expansion and rising external demand for slaves and ivory, Muslim traders forged trade links with the interior. The limited scholarly attention to Islam in Eastern Africa also reflects demographic factors: while Africa's share of the world Muslim population was considerable (Eaton 1993: 23), East Africa today possesses only about three percent of the world's Muslim population, less than any other region except China and the Balkans (one percent each). In consequence, eastern Africa is considered largely peripheral to the Muslim world.

The Asia-centric Traditions
Since the 1980s an Asia-centric School has emerged to challenge the Euro-centric historical approach. Kirti Nayaran Chaudhuri (1992) and others, adapting Ferdinand Braudel's concept of a Mediterranean 'maritime' economy, argue for the early emergence of an Asian economy based on a maritime trade network that ran from the Near to Far East (A. Reid 1988, 1993). Emphasising the rise of a cluster of great production centres (Mesopotamia, India and China) linked by the monsoons, these scholars argue that Asia developed the first 'global economy', a durable and sophisticated complex of long-distance production and exchange. Some scholars, such as Chaudhuri (1992) and André Wink (1996) associate the rise of this global economy with the development of Islam from the seventh century (see also A. Reid 1988, 1993). Indeed, Wink argues that Islam underpinned the creation of a 1000-year Indian Ocean civilisation:

Already long before the arrival of the Portuguese, the region from East Africa and Ethiopia to Arabia, the Yemen, Persia, India and the Indonesian Archipelago, increasingly acquired a unitary Islamic identity, a distinctive historical personality, which made it the largest cultural continuum of the world. (1996: 4)

Others associate the first global economy with economic developments in Sung China between 960 and 1279 (Abu-Lughod 1989; Moldelski and Thompson 1996). Most consider that the European economy achieved dominance over the Asian economy from the mid-eighteenth. century, although Andre Gunder Frank (1998) argued that Western economic superiority was achieved only in the nineteenth century and that Asia is currently fast eroding Western dominance (Abu-Lughod 1989, Chaudhuri 1992, 1985; Modelski and Thompson 1996: 142–5, 156; Wink 1996; see also Cain and Hopkins 1992: 150–81). At the same time, scholars of the Muslim world have moved away from the traditional idea of Islam as a monolithic institution, and begun to explore its plurality of communities, over time and space (Eaton 1993: 4).

However, Asia-centric scholars share the Euro-centric view that Africa was of peripheral economic importance. It furnished Asia with raw materials, tropical exotica and slaves but Africans played a passive role in this exchange which was dominated by foreign (Arab, Persian and Indian), chiefly Muslim, traders operating from enclaves on the east coast of Africa that, isolated from the African interior, were orientated exclusively to maritime trade. Chaudhuri attempts to explain the marginal, largely submissive role of Africans by reference to a unique 'African' mode of development:

The exclusion of East Africa from our civilisational identities needs a special word of explanation. In spite of its close connection with the Islamic world, the indigenous African communities appear to have been structured by a historical logic separate and independent from the rest of the Indian Ocean. (Chaudhuri 1992: 36)

Asia-centrists have similarly paid scant attention to the expansion of Islam in East Africa. In part, this stems from their focus on state-building – a preoccupation they share with Eurocentrists: Islamic polities in eastern Africa were small and exercised limited power.

The Afro-centric Tradition .

The first serious scholarly attempts to revise the traditional image of a historically inert Africa arose in the 1960s, when a post-colonial Liberal School of historical thought demonstrated the vitality of indigenous African forces (see Hopkins 1977; Oliver and Fage 1988). However, the Liberal School largely subscribes to the conventional wisdom that the first decisive phases in global economic development were the European 'discoveries' and subsequent domination of the New and Indian Ocean worlds – a view reinforced by Marxist and 'Underdevelopment' scholars, who consider that Western capitalist forces decisively shaped subsequent non-European history (see Coquery-Vidrovitch 1989; Fanon 1968;).

Over recent decades, an Afro-centric School has emerged that, like the Asia-centric School, has reacted strongly against the presuppositions of the Euro-centric tradition. In particular, Afro-centric scholars have assertively sought to place Africans at the centre of pre-nineteenth-century historical developments in Africa. The debate over East African history has focused on what Christopher Ehret (1998) has termed the 'Classical Age' starting in c.1500 B.C.E. following which entrepreneurial Bantu-speaking peoples discovered iron smelting and introduced sedentary agriculture to the region.

This debate has impacted on the study of Islam in eastern Africa. Arguing on the basis of the Bantu structure of Kiswahili, Afro-centrists deny non-African Muslims a significant role in the formation of the Swahili civilisation. Rather, they argue that Bantu-speakers, on reaching the east coast of Africa, adopted a maritime lifestyle, and from the eight century forged city ports and a maritime commercial network that underpinned a Swahili civilisation which thrived until the arrival of Europeans in the fifteenth century. Indeed, the Afro-centric interpretation of the historical impact of Islam in eastern Africa largely converges with the Euro-centric view: Islam is associated overwhelmingly with the slave export trade, the subordination of indigenous African economic activity to external 'Arab' interests and the displacement of women from economically important and independent roles. Asia- and Afro-centric scholars have succeeded in modifying the conventional picture only marginally by stressing that some African male slaves

achieved military and/or political positions of considerable importance in
Muslim countries (see Ali 1996; Catlin and Alpers 2004; Jayasurya and
Pankhurst 2001; Harris 1993; Rashidi 1993).

A Reassessment: The Indian Ocean World and Indian Ocean Africa

It is here argued that the historical role of Islam in eastern Africa can
only be fully understood by discarding traditional geographical (North
versus sub-Saharan Africa; West, Central, East and Southern Africa) and
political divisions (stemming essentially from colonial boundaries).
Rather, Islam in eastern Africa should be considered in terms of the
Indian Ocean World and Indian Ocean Africa.

The Indian Ocean World

The Indian Ocean World is here taken to comprise all regions directly
involved in the long-distance maritime trade network of the first global
economy, an economy which was regulated by the monsoon system of
the Indian Ocean and South China Sea. The Indian Ocean World
economy thus comprises the entire area from the Cape to Cairo to
Calcutta to Canton. The main maritime trade network complimented
the older overland trans-Asian 'silk road.' In the western Indian Ocean
World, both converged on two main trading hubs: the Persian Gulf and
Red Sea. This formed the economic context for the rise of Islam. The
first Muslim conquests, in the Fertile Crescent and Red Sea regions,
captured the two main routes from the Indian Ocean to Egypt and the
Mediterranean. The next targets were the overland 'Silk Route' and the
Persian Gulf region: In the seventh century, Islam captured the Persian
Sassanid Empire, brought Persia and Iraq under common rule, and
dominated the chief overland route to Syria (Abu-Lughod 1989: 209;
Pearson 2000: 37; S. Reid 1993: 14–15; Strathern 1993: 13). Although
Medina and Mecca remained the spiritual foci of Islam, its centre of
power shifted from Arabia to Damascus under the Umayyad dynasty
(661–750) and to Baghdad under the Abbasids between 750 and 1258
(Eaton 1993: 12–13).

The traditional interpretation is that Islam declined as an economic
and political force from the tenth to thirteenth centuries as Turkish

military slaves asserted control over key Islamic institutions, the Mongols conquered the Abbasids in 1258 and the caliphate passed to the Mamluks of Egypt (Eaton 1993: 19–20; Martin 1976: 3). Also, Chinese merchants under the patronage of the southern Sung dynasty (969– 1279) wrested from their Muslim competitors control over freight and passenger shipping between China and South-East Asia and India (Lo 1955: 499). However, the Chinese failed to dominate the western Indian Ocean and the collapse of Chola and Chinese naval power from the mid-thirteenth and mid-fifteenth centuries respectively permitted Muslim traders to extend their domination of Indian Ocean World maritime trade to the degree that some scholars have termed the Indian Ocean from the mid-thirteenth to early sixteenth century an 'Islamic Lake'(Lo 1955: 499; Modelski and Thompson 1996: 142, 144; Mollat 1971: 303, 306; Panikkar 1945: 7–8; Varthema 1863: 151). Islam played an instrumental and, over a millennium, a durable role in the creation of the Indian Ocean World global economy, creating what André Wink refers to as an Indo-Islamic civilisation:

Already long before the arrival of the Portuguese, the region from East Africa and Ethiopia to Arabia, the Yemen, Persia, India and the Indonesian Archipelago, increasingly acquired a unitary Islamic identity, a distinctive historical personality, which made it the largest cultural continuum of the world. (Wink 1996: 4)

Indian Ocean Africa

Euro-centric, Asia-centric and Afro-centric scholars have tended to assume that the only region of Africa upon which the Indian Ocean World trade network had a direct bearing was East Africa – with the latter having played a marginal role in it.[1] It is here argued that, by contrast, the Indian Ocean World global economy had a significant impact on all parts of Africa washed by the Indian Ocean or its Red Sea extension (South Africa, Mozambique, Tanzania, Kenya, Somalia, Djibouti, Ethiopia and Eritrea, Sudan, Egypt, Madagascar, and the Comoro, Mascarene and Seychelle Islands), as well as on landlocked

---

1 See, for example, Chaudhuri (1985) who almost completely omits Africa.

regions in the interior including Lesotho, Swaziland, Botswana, Malawi, Zimbabwe, Zambia, Rwanda, Burundi and Uganda, which possessed important trade outlets to those waters. This embraced a vast eastern portion of the African continent covering most of the area, from Cairo to the Cape, which is here termed Indian Ocean Africa.

This new geographical structure permits a reappraisal of the role of Africa in the Indian Ocean World, and of Islam in Indian Ocean Africa, that breaks the association of both in traditional histories with the African slave export trade. A new historical paradigm emerges in which important links become apparent, not only between Indian Ocean Africa regions, but also between Indian Ocean Africa and the Indian Ocean World. These ensured important exchanges of capital, people, commodities, technology and ideas, albeit ones that fluctuated over time, and demonstrate that Indian Ocean Africa played an integral part in the creation and development of the Indian Ocean World global economy.

Islam and the Indian Ocean World Global Economy
Non-Euro-centric scholarship argues that Islam helped mold the administrative, legal, educational and spiritual structures that underpinned the expansion of the Indian Ocean World global economy from the seventh century. While such structures were forged in the Islamic heartland *(Dar al-Islam)*, their influence spread further, carried by Muslim traders and missionaries to regions throughout the Indian Ocean World, from Indonesia to Africa, where a number of local authorities adopted and adapted those aspects of Islam that most promoted the integration of their region into the Indian Ocean World economy (see Leur 1967: 114; Meilink-Roelofsz 1962: 6). Islamic rulers in Damascus and Baghdad adopted from previous Persian and Roman imperial regimes an efficient administrative structure, mints and coinage, a standing army, a postal service and a tax system based on land revenue. From the start, these greatly enhanced production and trade in the Islamic heartland, and to newly conquered territories (Donini 1991: 26–30; Eaton 1993: 13).

Also, by the ninth century, Islam had developed a comprehensive legal framework.[2] It comprised a body of law (the *shari'a*) shaped by 'consensus' (prevailing learned interpretation of the Quran and hadith), 'analogy' (permitting scholars to incorporate elements from other, notably Christian, Jewish, Zoroastrian, Roman and Sasanian legal traditions), and 'precedent' (whereby in the *Dar al-Kufr* – lit. 'house of unbelievers' – or non-Islamic societies, pre-Islamic customary law could be recognised). The result was a unified yet flexible legal framework for economic activity across much of the Indian Ocean World. The political decentralisation characteristic of the region favoured the spread of Islamic legal practice, especially in the largely autonomous mercantile communities that dominated port cities, while local authorities in the *Dar al-Kufr* frequently summoned Muslim holy men and scholars for legal advice or adjudication.[3]

In addition, Islam expounded tolerance and universalism. The Quran expressly condemned racism, tribalism and nationalism, while Muslim powers generally proved relatively tolerant of Jews, Christians and Zoroastrians who as 'people of the book' (that is to say they possessed scriptural traditions similar to the Quran) could be granted the status of *dhimmi*, or protected communities (Robinson 2004: 18; Segal 2001: 6).[4] For instance, the Umayyads (661–750) tolerated and made little effort to convert conquered Jews, Christians and Zoroastrians (Robinson 2004: 9). Even under the Abbasids (750–1258) when Islamisation and Arabisation accelerated, non-Muslims continued to prosper, some being appointed to official positions (Adler 1907: 39, 42, 51, 63; Robinson 2004: 9). In addition, in order to increase revenue from international commerce, Muslim authorities generally assured security of person and

---

2 The *hadith*, which developed by the ninth century, are a collection of traditions about the life of the Prophet *(Sira)* or what he approved – as opposed to the *sunna*, which denotes the way he lived his life and constitutes the second source of Islamic jurisprudence; see Robinson (2004: 12–14); see also – *http://www.usc.edu/dept/MSA/ fundamentals/hadithsunnah/* (accessed on 16th June 2006).

3 See e.g. Spooner, B. 'Indian Ocean: Cradle of Globalization' – *http://www.accd.edu/ sac/history/keller/IndianO/Spooner.html* (accessed on 16th June 2006).

4 See footnote 3.

property to all merchants visiting or residing in the main entrepôts, irrespective of ethnicity, religion or culture, in return for a tax on their trade. Thus, in 1442 Abd al-Razzak al-Samarqandī commented of Hormuz, then the premier Persian Gulf port:

> Travellers come here from all countries, and, in turn, bring merchandise and can get everything they wish with no trouble at all. There are many people of all religions in this city and no one is allowed to insult their religion. That is why this city is called the citadel of security. (Samarqandī quoted in Ricks 1970: 354, n. 78)

While Islam and Arabisation did not always overlap, the expansion of the Muslim trading network led to the increasing use of Arabic as a *lingua franca* over much of the Indian Ocean World (Duyvendak 1949: 19–20; Eaton 1993: 8, 16–19; Hornell 1946: 231; S. Reid 1993: 13, 15; Robinson 2004: 9; Strathern 1993: 33; Tibbetts 1971: 2). The use of written Arabic, facilitated by the teaching of the Quran, as a canonical scripture, and the adoption of paper making from the end of the eighth century, greatly promoted accuracy in commercial transactions, as well as legal security.[5]

The advantages of conversion to Islam were thus considerable. Membership of any distinct club based on religion, ethnicity or other social communality could be economically advantageous in terms of building bonds of mutual trust and confidence that were critical to the establishment of trade networks, access to credit and promotion of commercial frontiers over a wide geographical area. Members of the political and mercantile classes were particularly attracted to a religion that embraced much of the Indian Ocean World and beyond, and in which commerce and Islam increasingly overlapped, due to the often close involvement of merchants in the *tariqa* (Sufi brotherhoods) – which greatly promoted Muslim trade as well as Islam in the *Dar al-Kufr*.

---

5   See Becker (1999), Duyvendak (1949: 19–20), Eaton (1993: 8, 16–19), Marvazī (1942: 18, 67–8), S. Reid (1993: 13, 15), Robinson (2004: 11–12), Strathern (1993: 33) and Tibbetts (1971: 2). The Arab adoption of Chinese paper-making followed the defeat of a Chinese army and capture of Chinese paper-makers in Samarqand by Islamic forces in 751.

Due to the *tariqa*-merchant alliance, Islam by the late thirteenth century dominated the main Indian Ocean World maritime trade routes between the Red Sea and Indonesia (Gray 1890: 470–71; Martin 1976: 1), while converts along those routes took advantage of the *hajj* and other Islamic pilgrimages to advance their commercial interests and create or consolidate long distance trading contacts. Pilgrimages also served to encourage debate and the spread of new ideas (Ahmad 1947: 8–9; see also Robinson 2004: 16, 18–19; Segal 2001: 18).

However, mass conversion to Islam, in both the Middle-Eastern heartland and beyond, occurred only when core aspects of pre-existing belief systems were accommodated. This again reflected the flexibility and pragmatism of Islam that enabled it to move beyond being the religion of the conqueror to becoming the religion of the conquered. In sum, the Euro-centric image of Islam as a monolithic and uniform structure needs to be thoroughly revised. Although it held certain core tenets, it was a complex and flexible system, forms of which varied regionally and over time (Eaton 1993: 14–16).

Islam in Indian Ocean Africa: A New Paradigm
The traditional division between North and sub-Saharan Africa closely corresponds with the medieval Arab division between the African *Dar al-Islam* (incorporating the southern Mediterranean basin from Morocco to Egypt) and the African *Dar al-Kufr* which was subdivided into four great ethno-geographical communities: the Nubia of the Nile valley above the first cataract; the Habasha of Ethiopia; the Zanj of the east coast, from variously Zeila or Mogadishu to Mozambique; and the Sudan in sub-Saharan West and Central Africa (Donini 1986: 54; Ismail 1968: 7–13). Within Indian Ocean Africa, Trimingham (1964: xi–xii) ascribes to Egypt a 'Basic Near-Eastern Islamic culture' which contrasts with the 'Hamitic-Negro' culture of Eastern or Nilotic Sudan, the 'North-Eastern Hamitic' culture of the eastern Horn plains of Eritrea, Ethiopia and Somalia, and the Swahili culture of coastal East Africa. While from the thirteenth century, the expansion of Islam occurred predominantly in India and Africa (Eaton 1993: 24–25), most historians have assigned to

sub-Saharan Indian Ocean Africa a peripheral role in Islamic history.[6] However, the new paradigm that discards traditional geographical and political divisions and recognises the Indian Ocean Africa as a historically significant region allows for a radical, more holistic, assessment of the historical role of Islam both within Indian Ocean Africa and in terms of vibrant linkages between Indian Ocean Africa and the wider Muslim community of the Indian Ocean World.

(i) Egypt: the Dar al-Islam in Indian Ocean Africa
Egypt, indisputably part of the *Dar al-Islam*, has traditionally been discussed less in relation to Africa than to the Middle East. It nevertheless formed an integral part of both the Indian Ocean World and of Indian Ocean Africa. First, Egypt was of critical importance to the Indian Ocean World global economy. One of the world's major commercial crossroads, it linked the Indian Ocean to the Mediterranean basin, the Middle East to northern Africa, and both, via its Sudanese hinterland, to West and East Africa: Gold and pilgrims regularly flowed from West Africa to the Sudan and on to Egypt or across the Red Sea to Jeddah and Mecca;[7] and trade links were forged via the Nile to other regions of Indian Ocean Africa, Islamic merchants from Cairo venturing far south into the wetter lands of the Upper Nile (Kapteijns and Spaulding 1982: 29; O'Fahey and Spaulding 1974: 16; Trimingham 1964: 2).[8] The fertile Nile valley also constituted a major grain granary for surrounding regions (Fahny 1950: 23–7).

Egypt thus formed a primary target for the early Islamic powers. The Arab invasion of 639 was led by 'Amr b. al-'As, a former trader to Egypt, who was fully aware of its commercial and strategic importance (Christides 1999; Hunwick 1996). The traditional interpretation is that Egypt prospered under the Arab conquerors, the Shiite Fatimids (973–1171), Ayyubids from 1171 to 1250 (Dols 1977: 144), and 'Turkish'

---

6 Notable exceptions are Robinson (2004) and Levtzion and Pouwels (2000).
7 Many stopped en route to work, and some settled; see Robinson (2004: 171–72) and Donini (1991: 60–1).
8 Anon. 'The Advent of Islam in East Africa': *http://baobab.harvard.edu/narratives/islam/EastTrade.html.* (accessed on 5th March 2005).

Mamluks (1250 to 1382) before entering a long period of decline from the 'Circassian' Mamluk period (1382 –1517).

The initial period of prosperity is reflected in demographic expansion: Egypt's population grew from about 2.4 million at the end of the twelfth century to around 4 million by the mid-fourteenth century. This was accompanied by urbanisation, notably the growth of Alexandria and of Cairo which, alongside Baghdad, Cordova and Delhi, became one of the Islam's major administrative capitals (Dols 1977: 149, 151–3). Cairo also developed into a principal manufacturing and commercial centre through which passed the major commodities, including spices, flowing between the Indian Ocean World and Mediterranean basin (Bryson and Padoch 1981: 10–12; Eaton 1993: 14; Lo 1955: 496–7; Martin 1975: 368, n. 4). Indeed, Cairo dominated Mediterranean trade between the tenth and thirteenth centuries (Eaton 1993: 14; Gran 1980: 523; Pires 1990: 4). Alexandria also boomed, Benjamin of Tudela (*c.*1170) noting that it was 'a commercial market for all nations' visited by merchants from west and east, including some from 'India, Zawilah, Abyssinia, Lybia, El-Yemen, Shinar and Esh-Sham, or Syria (Adler 1993: 76; Donini 1991: 22). To further maritime trade, the Egyptian regime embarked on a major shipbuilding and canal construction programme. Consequently, the Egyptian fleet dominated much of the Mediterranean to the west and the Red and Arabian Seas to the east (Becker 1999: 152; Fahny 1950: 23, 28, 36–9, 47, 80–3, 95–6).

Simultaneously, Egypt promoted trade with its southern hinterland (Kapteijns and Spaulding: 29; O'Fahey and Spaulding 1974: 16; Trimingham 1964: 2).[9] Indeed, so important were the Red Sea and Nile, the resources of North-East Africa, and the Sudan and areas beyond, that the Egyptian state adopted an imperial policy to bring those regions under its control, through military subjugation, commercial dominance and colonial settlement (Eaton 1993: 13; O'Fahey and Spaulding 1974: 16–17).

The economic decline of Egypt from the late fourteenth century has traditionally been ascribed to Circassian Mamluk policy, notably state

---

9   See footnote 8.

monopolies, refusal to invest in new techniques, and high taxes. Agricultural and industrial production fell sharply, trade stagnated and the population declined sharply until the early sixteenth century when the regime fell to the Ottomans (Dols 1977: 47–8, see esp. 47, n. 4).[10]

However, a marked decrease in state-controlled production and trade occurred only in the fifteenth century, well after the economy in general had sharply declined. This points to other causal agents, especially the Black Death which repeatedly hit Egypt from 1347 provoking a drastic and sustained fall in urban and rural populations, the impoverishment of surviving peasants and, in combination with climatic factors, notably droughts and excessive rains, a decline in agricultural production, the irrigation infrastructure, transport and communications (Dols 1977: 57, 60, 150–1, 154–5, 159–62, 164–7, 183).[11] Nevertheless, when plague epidemics relented, there were periods of economic recovery, as during the reign of Sultan Barquq (1382–99), and neither trade nor the fiscal system collapsed. Indeed, the Portuguese in the early sixteenth century discovered that the vital Red Sea spice trade was firmly controlled by the Mamluks,[12] while Pires (1512) emphasised the importance of Alexandria in east–west trade:

The merchandise which these people take to India comes from Venice in Italy. It comes to Alexandria, and from the Alexandria warehouses it comes by river to the factors in Cairo, and from Cairo it comes in caravans with many armed people. It comes to Tor, but this is not often, because on account of the nomad robbers they need many armed people to guard the merchandise. But at the time of the Jubilee (Jubileu), which is held every year in Mecca on the first day of February, when many people come, [the merchandise] is sent to Mecca with them. And from there it comes to Jidda and from Jidda it comes to the warehouses they have in Aden and from Aden it is distributed to Cambay, Goa, Malabar, Bengal, Pegu and Siam. (Pires (1512) quoted in Francis 2002: 171)

---

10 Mujani, W.K. 'The Economic Decline of Circassian Mamluks in Egypt, 1468–1517'.– *http://www.ehs.org.uk/ehs/conference2004/assets/mujani.doc.* (accessed on 16th June 2006).
11 See footnote 10.
12 See footnote 10.

The chief aim of Egypt's Muslim rulers was to maximise state revenue. In consequence, as was the case with governments in many other parts of the *Dar al-Islam*, they adopted a pragmatic and tolerant attitude to other religions. They initially refrained from proselytisation and Arabisation. Indeed, the first Arab governor followed his Byzantine predecessors in ratifying the appointment of Coptic Church patriarchs (Hunwick 1995), while the Coptic language persisted until the eleventh or twelfth century (Eaton 1993: 13). The eventual decline of the Coptic religion occurred primarily as a result of the 1347–1349 plague which caused high mortality among monks and, due to peasant abandonment of much of the irrigation system, undermined the economy of Coptic monasteries (Dols 1977: 167–68).

Some non-Muslims were appointed to important positions: In the early Caliphate, the naval centres of Alexandria, Dumyat (Damietta) and Rosetta were administered by Christian officials (Fahny 1950: 30). Again, merchants of other faiths (notably 'of the book') received state protection in return for political allegiance and taxation. Alexandria and Cairo in particular attracted traders of many origins, including some from Ethiopia. As in other Indian Ocean World entrepôts, each merchant community had its own quarters (Eaton 1993: 14). One of the most important was that of the Jewish Karimi whose wealth was built on spices (Adler 1993: 72; see also Donini 1991: 22; Marsot 1990: 2). In the 1160s, 7,000 'very rich' Jews serviced by two major synagogues, inhabited Fustat, or Old Cairo (Adler 1993: 69–71). Moreover, this tolerance was extended to the indigenous population: By the late Middle Ages there had occurred in Egypt extensive intermarriage and a breakdown of local ethnic prejudice (Dols 1977: 153).

Islamisation increased as the Muslim trade network flourished and imperial frontiers expanded. Proselytisation in Lower Egypt was significant from 716, but was slower further south. Nubia, from the seventh century a tribute state of Egypt, was visited by Arab merchants, miners, pilgrims and nomads, some of whom settled. As a result, the northernmost Nubian kingdom of Maris became Muslim and was assimilated into Egypt.[13] Following the sack of 'Aydhab in 1272 by Christian forces from Makuria, Egyptian rule was imposed and Arab 'Urban soldiers from Upper Egypt settled there. The 'Urbān subsequently expanded south into lands with higher rainfall, and in the mid-fourteenth century Egypt imposed an Islamic puppet dynasty on Makuria (Eaton 1993: 13; O'Fahey and Spaulding 1974: 16–17). Despite this, Islam, like Christianity before it, remained nominal. In a pattern duplicated in other Indian Ocean World regions, the converted, rulers and the ruled, maintained traditional indigenous beliefs and practices, such as, in the case of the Sudan, the veneration and exclusion of the monarch (Eaton 1993: 24–5; O'Fahey and Spaulding 1974: 18).

However, Egypt also became the focal point of Islamic learning and thus influenced the faithful throughout the Muslim world. Alexandria, which had a long-established reputation as a cultural centre, developed twenty academies by the 1160s (Adler 1993: 75) and a vibrant community of scholars, some of whose works, translated into Arabic, had a considerable influence on Islamic science (Donini 1991: 21–2). Yakut (1179–1229) noted of the scholars and alchemists of Alexandria Museum:

The place of their sessions is like stairs, where they sit divided into classes. On the lowest level sat the alchemists, making gold from silver by chemical means. Next to these stairs there was a spring of water able to cure leprosy. (Yaqut quoted in Donini 1991: 22).

Of more enduring importance were Cairo's scholarly institutions, including the observatory, established in 996 (Ahmad 1947: 79) and al-Azhar University (988), 'the oldest university in the world' and most famous centre of scientific learning alongside Baghdad (Donini 1991: 23). Following the restoration in Egypt of the orthodox Sunni regime under Saladin (1169), the Mongol destruction of Baghdad (1258), and the establishment of the caliphate in Egypt (1261), Cairo became and remained the world centre of Sunni scholarship (Dols 1977: 149; Donini 1991: 20; Robinson 2004: 19–20). Islamisation was facilitated by

---

13 Anon. 'The Role of Islam in African Slavery' – *http://africanhistory.about.com/library/weekly/ aa040201a.htm* (accessed on 16th June 2006).

Egypt's role as a major producer of papyrus parchments, used by all
Caliphs until the tenth century, and subsequently of paper (Eaton 1993:
16; Fahny 1950: 2; Marvazi 1942: 18, 67–8).

From the thirteenth century Al-Azhar wielded enormous influence
over developments in Islam in both the *Dar al-Islam* and *Dar al-Kufr*,
including the rest of Indian Ocean Africa. Its scholars constantly re-
evaluated the realities of the religious frontier in Africa, notably the need
to accommodate other cultures and religions (Donini 1991: 20). Al-
Azhar was also connected to other Indian Ocean Africa centres of Islamic
learning, including Kutranj, on the Blue Nile in Sudan and at Lamu on
the Swahili coast (Hunwick 1995), and attracted other Indian Ocean
Africa students: Those from Ethiopia were housed in a special hostel
(riwaq al-jabartiyya) maintained by the Islamic community in Ethiopia
(Robinson 2004: 113).

The Rest of Indian Ocean Africa

As noted, the rest of Indian Ocean Africa was of major economic interest
to Muslim Egypt. However, this needs to be placed in its proper context,
notably the historical role of maritime and overland routes to and within
Indian Ocean Africa. The Nile, the world's longest river (6,695km) and
the Great Rift Valley (arching from the Red Sea coast to the Zambesi
Delta) had from the earliest times formed major routes for the movement
of people, commodities, technology and ideas. Moreover, via the various
tributaries of the Nile they interconnected. At the same time, their
northern termini converged on western hubs of trans-Indian Ocean
World trade: Egypt and the Straits of Bab el Mandeb and Gulf of Aden.
By at least the B.C.E./C.E. changeover, important maritime trade routes
linked Egypt, Ethiopia and Southern Arabia to the East African coast at
least as far south as the 'metropolis' of Rhapta, probably situated in the
Rufiji Delta, opposite Mafia (Casson 1989; Chami 1999: 238–41).

Following the first Arab Muslim conquest, Egypt became an integral
part of the *Dar al-Islam*, but maintained vital connections with the rest
of Indian Ocean Africa. With the important exceptions of the Shia
Fatimid dynasty in Egypt (969–1171) and Zanzibari kharijites of Omani
extraction, Muslim Africans were orthodox Sunni. Moreover, Indian

Ocean Africa Muslim communities maintained regular contact with one another and with Muslim communities elsewhere (Robinson 2004: 7–8, 18, 37). There was thus considerable economic and other exchange between Indian Ocean Africa and the wider Muslim world. For instance, from the Islamic conquest of Sind (711), Arab merchants spread Indian agricultural techniques including the cultivation of hard wheat, rice, sugar cane, new varieties of sorghum, spinach, artichoke and eggplant, and cotton – a key industrial crop – throughout the Islamic world and beyond. Indeed, cotton diffusion in Africa paralleled that of Islam (Eaton 1993: 17). African products also proved of considerable significance to the Indian Ocean World economy in which African merchants were engaged. For example, in 1442 traders from Egypt, Ethiopia and Zanzibar were noted in the Persian Gulf entrepôt of Hormuz (Samarqandī (1442) quoted in Ricks 1970: 354, n. 78), while seventy years later, passengers travelling to and from Malacca on Gujarati ships included merchants from Cairo, Ethiopia, Kilwa, Malindi, Mogadishu and Mombasa (Pires 1944: 46).

(i) The Dar al-Hiyad (Ethiopia) and
Bilad as-Sudan (Sudan, lit. 'Land of the Blacks')
The history of Islam in North-East Africa has often been portrayed as a battle between the expanding forces of militant Islam and Christian Ethiopia. However, commercial and other economic relations indicate a more complex story. North-East Africa, located opposite Arabia, the birthplace and spiritual heartland of Islam, straddled the northern (Red Sea) *termini* of the Great Rift Valley and the Atbara and Abbaj (Blue Nile) tributaries of the Nile (leading to Sudan and Egypt). It was thus, like Egypt, an important crossroads between Indian Ocean Africa and the rest of the Indian Ocean World.

Prior to the rise of Islam, Aksum (based in Tigray province of Ethiopia) and its Red Sea port of Adulis largely dominated regional trade. However, the 541–542 plague, which first manifested itself on the overland caravan route from Ethiopia to Egypt (Dols 1977: 16–17), and the expansion of the Sasanian Empire, notably its occupation of Yemen in 570, undermined Aksum's influence and Persian merchants came to dominate Red Sea trade until the rise of Islam (Robinson 2004: 5, 111).

North-East Africa quickly drew the attention of Muslim traders in Arabia, Persia (following the Arab conquest of 640) and Egypt, notably from the Fatimid era, 969–1171 (Pires 1990: 14; Robinson 2004: 92). Ethiopia was a source of gold, ivory, civet musk and slaves, and Somalia of frankincense, animal skins, rhinoceros horn, tortoiseshell, ambergris, gold, beeswax, sandalwood and ivory.[14] These commodities, in high demand in Indian Ocean World markets, were exchanged for Chinese coins and porcelain (Duyvendak 1949: 16–17), Persian pearls, piece goods, dates and dried fish (Ricks 1970: 353, 355), coarse Cambay cloth, some silks, white cloths and spices (Hasan 1928: 137–8), Egyptian opium and (probably Egyptian) glass and other beads, as well as crystal, rosewater and dried roses (Pires 1990: 8–9, 13). Siraf merchants dominated this exchange until Siraf was devastated by an earthquake in 977, following which Yemeni merchants competed fiercely for the trade of North-East Africa – to the extent that naval battles erupted between Aden and Kish, the Persian port that succeeded Siraf (Ricks 1970: 352–54).

Thereafter, North-East African exports were stimulated by rising demand in India and China (Barendse 2002: 13; Ricks 1970: 355) where African ivory, frankincense, rhinoceros horns (used to neutralise poison) and tortoiseshell (for the manufacture of girdles) were particularly valued. Chinese imports from the Africa-Arabia-Persian Gulf area increased by 943 percent between 1049–53 and 1175 (Duyvendak 1949: 16), and Chinese ships (under Cheng Ho) visited Mogadishu and Brava in 1417–1419 and 1421–1422 (Duyvendak 1949: 16–17; Mills 1970: 13–14; Wallenstein 1998: 177; see also Lo 1955: 493). Although the Chinese fleet thereafter disappeared from the Indian Ocean, Egyptian, Arab, Persian and Indian ships continued to visit North-East Africa (Barbosa 1918: 129; Pires 1990: 14). Pires (1944: 8) noted that in 1512 Arabs from Aden and the Hadhramaut dominated Ethiopian exports,

---

14 For Ethiopia see Donald (1986: 21) and Roland and Fage (1988: 558). For Somalia see Duyvendak (1949: 16) and Ricks (1970: 353, 355).

comprising chiefly gold, ivory, horses, slaves and provisions. Ethiopians also travelled along the main Indian Ocean World maritime trade routes: For instance, in *c.*1518, Barbosa noted the presence of 'Abyssinian' merchants in Bengala at the mouth of the Brahmaputra River in North-East India (Hasan 1928: 145).

At the same time, North-East Africa attracted Arab settlers fleeing the harsh geography and arid climate of the Arabian Peninsula. Yemenites established a sultanate in Zeila in the seventh century and from the ninth century a number of Muslim polities emerged in Ethiopia (Zewde 1991: 9).

The advance of the Muslim trading and settler frontiers ensured that Islam had become dominant in Eritrea by the eleventh century and in the East Ethiopian highlands by the mid-thirteenth century by which time many Somalis had also converted. By the fourteenth century, a line of Muslim settlements dominated the main caravan routes from Zeila to the Sudan, and from the Red Sea coast to the Rift Valley (southeast of the Ethiopian highlands) and the plateau (to the south and west) resulting in the conversion to Islam of the elites of the Cushitic Sidama kingdoms to the south (Donham 1986: 21; Oliver 1988: 558). Wilfred Schoff (2001: 75) considers that regular trade and pilgrim routes also connected the Red Sea coasts of Ethiopia and the Sudan to Upper Senegal (see also Robinson 2004: 171–2).

By the thirteenth century, the same processes had resulted in the conversion to Islam of many coastal Somalis, and Saylac, an *entrepôt* on the Somali north coast, developed into an important centre of Muslim culture and learning. Arab immigration between the thirteenth and twentieth centuries in turn promoted Somali migration south, ultimately to the Tana River and the fertile Harer plains, in Ethiopia. From the fifteenth century centralized Islamic states emerged, notably Adal which at its zenith in the sixteenth century extended from Saylac, the capital, through the fertile valleys of the Jijiga, and the Harer, to the Abyssinian highlands. Islamic influence also spread south along the Somali east coast. Barbosa (*c.*1518) commented that Mogadishu 'belonged' to the 'Moors' and that 'All the people speak Arabic; they are dusky and black and some of them white' (Barbosa quoted in Hādī 1928: 137–8), while from the fifteenth century Sufi mystics settled in the Benadir hinterland. By the eighteenth century, the majority of Somalis had converted to Islam.[15] Although the expanding Muslim frontier sometimes created tensions, it did not assume the uniformly military or antagonistic form conventionally ascribed to it. Muslims accorded Ethiopia special status. Not only were Christians 'people of the book' but from 615 to 628 Aksum had granted refuge to 100 of Muhammad's followers fleeing persecution by the Prophet's Meccan opponents: in consequence Christian Ethiopia was deemed to be *Dar al-Hiyad* (or *Dar al-Sulh*), a region with a non-Muslim government, but distinct from the *Dar al-Kufr* in that it was considered to be at peace with Muslims and exempt from *jihad* (Robinson 2004: 5, 111–2). Moreover, despite rivalry, Ethiopian, 'pagan' and Muslim traders interacted commercially. For example, 'pagans' to the south of the Ethiopian highlands traded with the small Muslim states of Somalia that possessed important links to the Indian Ocean World (Levine 1974: 44; Robinson 2004: 113–14). Moreover, general Islamic commercial dominance did not prevent 'Christian' commercial influence from expanding along a north-south axis between the Dahlak Islands and the river Awash in the fourteenth century (Donham 1986: 21). As significantly, sufficient numbers of Oromo, a pastoral people who expanded into much of southern Ethiopia from the early sixteenth century, had converted to Christianity and become settled agriculturalists by the late seventeenth century for Emperor Iyasu I (1682–1706) to force them to settle along the northern edge of the River Abbay (Blue Nile) as a buffer against further Oromo incursions.[16]

The relatively cordial relations between the different religious communities in North-East Africa stemmed from a commercial rationale, from religious tolerance, and from shared linguistic and cultural traits (Levine 1974: 44). Moreover, whereas the merchant and

---

15 Anon. *http://www.mudulood.com/PageMudbefore1960.html* (accessed on 21st April 2005).

16 Anon. *http://www.unu.edu/unupress/unupbooks/uu08ie/uu08ie0n.htm* (accessed on 10th March 2005).

political elites often learned Arabic, in a pattern repeated elsewhere in Indian Ocean Africa and the wider Indian Ocean World, Arabicisation did not necessarily follow conversion. Consequently, in North-East Africa the mass of converts to Islam retained indigenous languages and cultures common to their non-Muslim neighbours (Ismail 1968: 11; Robinson 2004: 43, 113). In addition, the Christian hierarchy in Ethiopia maintained good relations with the Islamic regime in Egypt in order to retain its close links with the Coptic Church whose patriarch in Alexandria continued to appoint the bishop in Ethiopia until the 1950s (Robinson 2004: 113–14).

Relations between the different groups worsened as a result of a combination of human and natural forces. First, by the start of the sixteenth century a lively demand had developed in Indian sultanates, chiefly Bengal, for Ethiopian slaves. In response, some Islamic groups on the Red Sea coasts of Ethiopia and Somalia raided the highlands on horseback, capturing and exporting large numbers of Ethiopians (Pires 1990: 8, 14). This created tensions that were exacerbated by natural blights, notably drought and disease. Droughts often hit Yemen and could cause some impoverished Arabs to migrate, just as aridification in Central Asia from *c.* 1150–1200 led some Tashkent weavers and cap-makers to migrate to Egypt and Mogadishu (Bryson and Padoch 1981: 10–12; Lo 1955: 496–7; Martin 1975: 368, n. 4). Again, an exceptionally cool northern hemisphere summer associated with sulphur rich volcanic eruptions in 1414 probably provoked the 1415 Ethiopian invasion of the Muslim kingdom of Ifat in Somalia. Outbreaks of disease also increased emigration. Thus the 1438–1439 plague epidemic in the Yemen (Dols 1977: 311) led to a significant Arab migration to East Africa and to Somalia (promoting the Islamic Audel expansion into Galla territory).[17] However, the greatest tension occurred during a period of recurrent droughts between the early sixteenth and late eighteenth centuries when poor Arab immigration increased and the different groups competed fiercely for resources, notably fertile soil and water

---

17 Anon. *http://www.collectornetwork.com/article_postal_br* (accessed on 10th March 2005).

sources (Oliver 1988: 588–89; Robinson 2004: 114–15). This was probably the origin of the bitter 1527–1543 *jihad* in Ethiopia led by Imam Ahmad ibn Ibrahim (Gragn) and of the late sixteenth-century capture of Muslim regions, such as Inarya and Bosha, by Ethiopian Christian forces. It also underpinned the Galla offensive in Somalia that caused the Audel Empire to fragment into a number of small emirates and sultanates (Boxer 1968: 36; Levine 1974: 77).[18]

Nevertheless, harsh conditions in Arabia also enhanced trading opportunities in North-East Africa. Egypt had long been a major source of grain for Arabia, but the onset of major drought in the early sixteenth century also resulted in the export via Zeila, Berbera and the Suakin islands of 'much meat, fish, wheat, rice, barley and millet' to Jidda, in 1512 'a great trading city' of about 5,000 inhabitants and Mecca, of 1,000 (Pires 1944: 8, 1990: 11). Subsequent Egyptian (Ottoman) control of the Red Sea ensured the continuation of this trade, while the flow to the Red Sea of Indian Ocean World commodities, notably spices, halted by the Portuguese in the first decade of the sixteenth century had by mid-century recovered (Godinho 1996: 11). Moreover, merchants from North-East Africa continued to participate in Indian Ocean World trade. Saylac (until its decline in the mid-seventeenth century), Berbera, Mogadishu, Merca and Barawa were all important ports, exporting coffee, gold, ivory, frankincense, ostrich feathers, civet and Ethiopian slaves to markets in the Middle East, China and India (Barbosa 1918: 129; Donham 1986: 21; Levine 1974: 44; Oliver 1988: 558; Pires 1944: 8; Robinson 2004: 113–14) Further, even in European dominated centres such as Goa following the Portuguese takeover, the foreign merchant community included Ethiopians (Mathew 1990: 141).

(ii) Dar al-Harb/Kufr (Zanj or East Africa)
'Zanj', the term used by medieval commentators from the Middle East for the East African ('Swahili') coast from the Benadir coast of Somalia to

---

18 See footnote 17.

Sofala[19] constituted a region as vital to Islamic commerce as other Indian
Ocean World regions from the eighth to fifteenth centuries (Ricks 1970:
339–57).

As occurred in the Red Sea and Horn regions, Arabs became the
dominant mercantile group on the Zanj coast following the Islamic
invasion of Persia in 640 (Ricks 1970: 342–3), although during the
Baghdad-based Abbasid dynasty (750–1258), Persian traders regained
ascendancy. Persian merchants expanded their trading frontier south to a
lengthy littoral area they called *Bilad as-Sufala*, *i.e.* 'low-lying land', with
a capital 'Sofala' near Beira in Mozambique, adjoining Hwfl/ Waq-waq
(possibly Madagascar, the Comores or part of the African mainland then
inhabited by Khoisan-speakers), which was reputedly the richest in goods
(Elkiss 1981: 3 incl. n. 1–2; Hodges and Whitehouse 1983: ch. 6).[20]
From the eleventh century they probably traded as far as Pondoland
(Hasan 1928: 134) and were aware from second-hand reports of a
treacherous sea-route around the Cape into the Atlantic (Ahmad 1947:
12; Elkiss 1981: 3). Moreover, while most foreign merchants dealt with
coastal entrepôts, at least one enterprising Sirafi visited the interior
(Hodges and Whitehouse 1983: ch. 6).

Al-Mas'ūdī (d. 956) who visited East Africa at least twice, the last
occasion being in 916/17, provides the earliest detailed written account
of Zanj. He noted that ships sailed regularly from the Persian Gulf
(Oman and Siraf) directly to the main Zanj port of Qanbalu, probably
Unguja, Zanzibar Island (Ricks 1970: 349).[21] The round-trip from Sohar
in Oman to Sofala was nearly 12,000km. To China it was 16,000km
(Hodges and Whitehouse 1983: ch.6). East African commerce was as
important to Siraf, a 'large town [...] merchants' haunt [...] the

---

19 'Zanj' probably derived from the Indian 'Zanzibar' meaning 'country of the black man'
   or possibly from the Persian term *'zangi'* (meaning 'Egyptian, Ethiopian, Moor or
   Negro; a savage') see Devic (1883: 9–10, 15–16) and Fisher (1967: 967). Some
   commentators considered that there were communities of Zanj as far north as the
   Somali and Ethiopian border (Devic 1883: 24–6).

20 Horton, M. 'East Africa, Persian Economic, Political, and Cultural Relations Through
   1900' – *http://www.iranica.com/articles/v7/v7f6/v7f655.html* (accessed on 16th June
   2006).

21 See footnote 20.

emporium of Fars'[22] and a principal hub of Indian Ocean World commerce at its commercial zenith in the tenth century, as trade with the Far East (Ricks 1970: 343–45, 349). For instance, the lack of wood along the Red Sea and Persian Gulf littorals obliged local shipbuilders to import East African as well as Indian timber (Boxer 1968: 15), while the elite of Siraf, possessed magnificent houses 'built of teakwood brought from Zanj country' that 'were several stories high, built to overlook the sea' (quoted in Hasan 1928: 115; see also Ricks 1970: 346). Other East African exports to Aden, Sohar and Siraf included ivory, ambergris, gold, wild animal skins and pearls – in exchange for glass, from the Middle East, and pottery from the Middle East and from China[23] to which Zanj (Sofala) commodities were shipped via India, notably the port of Somnath on the river Sarsati [Saraswati] until its destruction in 1038 by Sultan Mahmud (Ahmad 1947: 146, 149).

After the 977 earthquake that devastated Siraf, the centre of Muslim trade with East Africa passed to Arabia (Ricks 1970: 352–3). However, following Idrisi (mid-twelfth century), Arab commentaries on East Africa appear to be recitations of previous texts (Devic 1883: 31–2), indicating a possible loss of first hand contact – until the early fourteenth century (Elkiss 1981: 8). This may well reflect a stronger Indian involvement in Zanj trade from *c*.1200–1300 when there was an increase in exports of ivory, gold and iron to India where the ivory and gold was used chiefly to manufacture jewellery and the iron to fashion a variety of products including steel swords that were subsequently exported to the Persian Gulf and other Indian Ocean World markets (Barbosa 1918: 15; Elkiss 1981: 4; Ricks 1970: 355). In Zanj, the local production of glass beads, pottery, textiles and iron declined sharply, replaced by imported goods, probably of mostly Indian origin (Nurse and Spear 1985: 17–19). Moreover, despite the emphasis in conventional histories on the slave trade, slave exports from East Africa remained limited until the ninth or tenth century C.E. and did not dramatically expand until the mid to

---

22 Minorsky, V. (trans. and ed.) 1937. *Hudūd al-ʿAlam* [The Regions of the World]. London: Luzac. – quoted in Ricks (1970: 346).

23 Sung dynasty coins have been uncovered at Zanzibar; see Ahmad (1947: 146) and Duyvendak (1949: 16–17).

late-eighteenth century. Even then, there is considerable debate as to
whether slaves or ivory were the most import export commodities (Alpers
1967, 1975; Campbell 1988a: 165–192, 1988b: 1–27, 2005: ch. 9;
Sheriff 1986, 1987).

Early Portuguese accounts confirm both the Indian connection and
that any loss in Arabian and Persian involvement had been temporary.
Barbosa (*c.*1518) observed that the Bazaruto Islands, between Sofala (to
the north) and Inhambane (to the south) were reputed for their pearls
which together with ambergris, which at Bazaroto was of good quality,
were collected and exported in quantity by local Muslims. He also noted
a significant gold trade down the Zambezi to Mangalo, at the mouth of
the Cuama (a Zambezi river delta). Mangalo was linked commercially to
'Angoya' (probably Angoche). Other exports included ivory, millet, rice
and meat, while cottons, silks and beads dominated imports (Barbosa
1918: 4–5, 15).

Export commodities from South-East Africa were shipped north by
'Muslim' agents to the ports of Mombasa, Malindi and Kilwa (Barbosa
1918: 15) from where most were re-exported. Thus Pires (*c.*1512) noted
that Cambay and Arabian merchants (mostly from Aden) purchased
commodities at Kilwa (the main collection point for goods from further
south)[24], Malindi and Mombasa, that were shipped to Zeila and Berbera
where they were exchanged for horses owned by local Muslims (Pires
1944: 14). These probably formed part of the extensive trade in Arabian
and Persian horses to India that may have started in the first century
C.E. (Hasan 1928: 142–3), while Barbosa (*c.*1518) comments that
Malindi and Mombasa were visited by merchant ships from Dio [Diu]
near Hormuz, from where ships also sailed to the Persian Gulf, Malacca
and China (1918: 129).

---

24 By the fourteenth century, immediately prior to the coming of the Portuguese, Kilwa
possessed political and economic hegemony over neighbouring ports along the Swahili
coast, including Chole, Sanje ya Kati, Zanzibar and Sofala, with looser influence over
Angoche, Quilemane, the Kerimbas, the Comoros and northwestern Madagascar; see
Barbosa (1918: 18).

Archeological evidence (a mosque) demonstrates that Islam became established on the Zanj coast from the late eighth century (Horton 1996: 123, 126, 155). The Muslim community in Zanj initially comprised mainly foreign merchants: Istakhri (mid-tenth century) commented that the Zanj were not Muslim and Moqaddicci (eleventh century) excluded Zanj from his geography of Islamic countries (Devic 1883: 24–27). This stemmed from the logistics of trade: as the monsoon regime petered out south of Zanzibar, foreign merchants were obliged to establish resident agents in order to regularise trade with regions further south (Sofala and Waq-waq). Early connections with the Persian Gulf were particularly marked: Siraf traders regularly visited and settled on islands off the Zanj coast (Ricks 1970: 345), there is considerable similarity between a tenth-century mosque at Shanga and family mosques in Siraf, and between floriated and plaited Kufic inscriptions on *mihrabs* at Kizimkazi and Tumbatu in Zanzibar and eleventh to twelfth-century Sirafi inscriptions. Again, Arabic tomb inscriptions at Mogadishu dated 1217 and 1268–9 concern two Persians.[25]

As in other Indian Ocean Africa regions, the first local converts were members of the political and merchant elite. Islamisation accelerated between the twelfth and fifteenth centuries but was chiefly confined to the Swahili – those who inhabited the port cities and their immediate island hinterland (Eaton 1993: 24–25; Mgomezulu 1981: 448; Trimingham 1964: 1–2). Most of the Swahili elite mastered at least basic Arabic which they used when travelling overseas for business and when performing the *hajj* which, because of ease of maritime travel, they indulged in more often than, for example, African Muslims from sub-Saharan West Africa (Robinson 2004: 33). Of Kilwa, Barbosa commented:

[…] the Moors of Sofala, Zuama, Anguox [Angoche], and Mozambique were all under obedience to the King of Quiloa [Kilwa], who was a great king amongst them […] These people are Moors, of a dusky colour, and some of them are

---

25 Horton, M. 'East Africa, Persian Economic, Political, and Cultural Relations Through 1900' – *http://www.iranica.com/articles/v7/v7f6/v7f655.html* (accessed on 16th June 2006).

black and some white [...] The speech of these people is Arabic. (Barbosa quoted in Hasan 1928: 137–38)

As in North-East Africa, Arabicisation was not an automatic concomitant of conversion. Kiswahili, a language with a Bantu structure that had emerged in the port cities by about the eighth century, became the mother tongue of local Muslims and non-Muslims, while foreign merchants and hinterland Africans in regular commercial contact with the Swahili ports often adopted Kiswahili as a second language. Moreover, Muslim holy men and scholars used Kiswahili when teaching – to the degree that Islamisation in East Africa was associated with the spread, not of Arabic but of Kiswahili (Robinson 2004: 27–8, 43).

The European Impact

Indian Ocean Africa attracted European merchants initially for three principal reasons: the flow of spices from the East to the Mediterranean via the Red Sea, its allegedly unlimited gold resources, and as a provisioning base for fleets to and from the East (Pearson 2003: 120). The traditional wisdom is that following their intrusion into the Indian Ocean World from the early sixteenth century, Europeans drove Muslim merchants from the main arteries of maritime commerce, imposed monopoly control over the most valuable commodities, and diverted commercial traffic from India and the East directly to the Cape route with the result that Indian Ocean Africa maritime commerce stagnated (Boxer 1968: 16; Godinho 1996: 103–4, 109–10; Pearson 2003: 148–9; Pires 1990: 10–12; Scammel 1981: 139–40, 272; Tuchscherer 2003: 52–3; Wake 1996: 161).

By *c.* 1515, the Portuguese had diverted about half of all spices to Europe around the Cape and continued to do so until the early 1560s (Ashtor 1996: 69; Lane 1996: 85, 91; Wake 1996: 161). Also, they attempted to regulate all other Indian Ocean World maritime trade through a system of passes and taxes (Boxer 1968: 16–17; Pearson 2003: 121). Nevertheless, the European impact has been exaggerated. First, Europeans suffered high losses. Thus the momentum of Portuguese attacks on Muslim shipping and trading communities quickly faded as the cost of maintaining a large armed presence was very high in the face of heavy losses; of ships (due to storms and enemy attacks); and of men (due to shipwrecks, disease and warfare). Losses along the way were as high as 50 percent for some fleets (Boxer 1968: 20). In 1677, about 2,000 Portuguese emigrants sailed for Sofala, but most died of disease, probably en-route or shortly after arrival (Elkiss 1981: 51–52). Of the 171,000 Portuguese who left for the Indian Ocean World between 1497 and 1590, some 17,000 were lost to disease and shipwrecks on the way out, and 11,000 on the return trip (Pearson 2003: 138) – a high attrition rate for a country with a population of about one million (Boxer 1968: 20). Disease was also a major killer on land. For example, malaria decimated Portuguese, Dutch, French and English settlements in tropical East Africa (see Elkiss 1981: 20–1; Sleigh 1980: 22). High soldier mortality forced the Portuguese and other Europeans to rely increasingly on Creoles and locally recruited auxiliaries to maintain their military presence in the Indian Ocean World (Arnold 1991: 5–6).

In addition, despite the initial onslaught on Muslim ships and communities by the Portuguese, Muslims remained a vital military and economic force in the region. In 1505, the Ottomans sent naval assistance to the Mamluks to secure the Red Sea route, while Portuguese defeat in 1509 of the Egyptian fleet was a principal reason for the 1517 Ottoman conquest of Egypt and extension of Ottoman naval power in the Red Sea, from which they excluded the Europeans (Badger 1863: cx; Barbosa 1918: 21; Barendse 2002: 16–17; Brummett 1994: 9–10, 12; Elkiss 1981: 51; Pearson 2003: 130; Scammell 1981: 392). As inadequate resources ensured that no European power could dominate Indian Ocean sea lanes, indigenous merchants were able to divert traffic from the Portuguese-dominated route along the northern rim of the Indian Ocean, to the southern equatorial route running from Indonesia through the Maldives and subsequently direct to Aden and the Red Sea. This ensured that the Ottoman-Egyptian regime (that lasted with variations up to the British takeover of 1882) continued to dominate trade between Europe and the Indian Ocean World (Brummett 1994: 14–15; Godinho 1996: 110; Wink 1989: 51).

Euro-centric histories concentrate on the territorial ambitions in Europe of the Ottomans, who are traditionally perceived as having neglected the Egyptian economy. However, from the start Ottoman attention focused on the Indian Ocean World which experienced a seventeenth-century boom in trade as the large Muslim states of West and South Asia (Ottoman, Safavid, Mogul and Deccan) imposed peace and security, costs of production fell, and European demand for eastern goods was stimulated by profits from the Atlantic economy (sugar and slaves) and American precious metal imports (Brummett 1994: 10–12; Vérin 1999).

By 1670, the Dutch East India Company had imposed a virtual monopoly over certain spices such as Indonesian nutmeg, mace, cloves and Sri Lankan cinnamon (Pearson 2003: 146–7; Prakesh 1994: 187– 89, 194–95). However, the Dutch could not maintain too high a price in Asia – the market for approximately one-third of fine spices – lest demand there fall (Pearson 2003: 147), as it did in Europe in the latter part of the seventeenth century (Prakesh 1994: 193) when spices were challenged by other high status exotic 'oral consumables' like coffee, chocolate, cocoa, alcohol and tobacco from tropical regions (Pearson 2003: 148). Muslim-dominated Indian Ocean Africa trade befitted directly from this change as the Ottomans developed a highly lucrative trade in coffee, originally from Kaffa in Ethiopia, which was introduced to Turkey as a beverage in the sixteenth century.[26] By the eighteenth century, coffee was the chief source of wealth for the *tujjar* (the long distance merchants) just as spices had been for the *karimi* in the Middle Ages (Marsot 1990: 2). The *tujjar* possessed a monopoly over its flow from Mocha, which under the Ottomans replaced Aden as the chief southern Red Sea port (Pearson 2003: 132), to the Mediterranean.

The Ottoman-Egyptian regime also promoted local agriculture, manufacturing and trade. It countered the depopulation that characterised the preceding Mamluk period by promoting immigration from neighbouring countries, especially North Africa (Dols 1977: 169),

---

26 Turkoglu, S. 'Traditional Turkish Coffee' – *http://www.koffeekorner.com /turkish.htm* (accessed on 10th March 2005).

and encouraged soldiers based in Upper Egypt to settle, produce families and cultivate the surrounding land.[27] In addition, it stimulated craft manufacture. Artisans, who enjoyed considerable status, comprised probably between 20 percent and 40 percent of the population. Most were engaged in small-scale cloth production (about one third of artisans were textile workers) but larger scale manufacturing units also existed, notably oil presses and sugar refineries.[28] In return for a tax on production, Egyptian textiles and other crafts were protected by the local elite. Initially protection was granted by janissaries of foreign origin up to *c*.1700, from which time they were recruited locally and from the mid-eighteenth century by Mamluk Beys (Marsot 1990: 5). Craft and specialist agricultural activity was stimulated by regional elite and European demand (Vérin 1999).

By the eighteenth century, Egyptian long-distance trade was conducted chiefly with the Ottoman Empire and Syria, followed by the Red Sea region, Europe, North Africa and the Sudan. Because of Egypt's key position on major commercial routes, much of this was transit trade: Some two-thirds of trade flowing to Egypt from the Red Sea was re-exported (to Europe and Turkey); 20 percent of Syrian imports were re-exported (to Europe, North Africa and the Sudan); as were one-sixth of European imports, to the Red Sea and the Sudan (Marsot 1990: 1–2). In order to tap Sudanese gold and slaves, ivory and other tropical produce from equatorial regions, the Egyptian Ottoman regime expanded its imperial frontiers in Indian Ocean Africa. Egyptian rule steadily advanced into Nubia and the Sudan, from Aswan to the second Nile cataract in the 1550s, and by 1583 to the third cataract, 600km from Khartoum. Beyond lay the independent land-locked Funj (or Fung) and Tajur sultanates, the most easternly of a chain of Islamic states that stretched westwards to the Atlantic through the Sahel and savannahs, marking the *Dar al-Islam–Dar al-Kufr* frontier. At its peak in the seventeenth century, Funj controlled the trade of the entire region from

27 Anon. 'The Ottoman Turkiyya in the Sudan AH 930/1553 AD – 1200/1823' – *http://www.dur.ac.uk/justin.willis/alexander.htm* (accessed on 10th March 2005).
28 Elbendary, Amina. 'When Crafts were Industry' – *http://weekly.ahram.org.eg/2001/ 534/cu2.htm* (accessed on 16th June 2006).

the Red Sea westward to Kordofan. However, Ottoman Egypt also expanded along the Red Sea. Its forces seized Suakin (1524) which controlled the caravan trade in gold slaves and ivory from the Funj sultanate, Zeila (1548) and Eritrea (1557) – where Ottoman rule lasted until the 1880s – although attempts from the 1580s to subdue the Ethiopian highlands failed (Tuchscherer 2002).[29] In the seventeenth century, Ottoman control was also imposed over the Somali ports of Saylac and Berbera. Prior to Napoleon's invasion of Egypt in 1798, the Ottoman Empire in Africa covered some seven million square kilometres.[30] Finally, in the nineteenth century, the Egyptian trading frontier broke through the Sudd marshlands and into East Central Africa (Brummett 1994: 6).[31]

The destructive impact of the Portuguese on the east coast of Africa has been similarly exaggerated. In Madagascar, in 1506, they sacked the Muslim ports of Sa'da, Langani (Nosy Longany in Mahajamba Bay) and Kingani, but Portuguese rule was never imposed and Muslim trade quickly recovered, while Vohimara was untouched and continued to prosper until the eighteenth century. A gradual decline of foreign commerce along the northeast coast between the sixteenth and eighteenth centuries was due to the concentration of Muslim trade on the northwest coast and from there, with the plateau interior (Vérin 1986: 7–8).

In East Africa the mercantilist obsession with 'bullion' underpinned the Portuguese quest to capture the famed trade in Sofala gold, and use it to pay for spices, Indian pepper and other valued Indian Ocean World commodities (Elkiss 1981: 30, n. 67). In 1505, they established a factory on the Sofala coast and subsequently moved inland, by 1531 establishing forts at Sena and Tete on the Zambezi, from which trade routes ran to

29 Anon. 'Ottoman Turkiyya in the Sudan' – _http://gurukul.ucc.american.edu/ted/ice/eritrea. htm_ (accessed on 10th March 2005).

30 Anon. 'The Future of Oromo/Kush and Abyssinia' – _http://www.warmafrica.com/index/ geo/9/cat/1/a/ff/thrid/49/sa/d/topic/288_ (accessed on 10th March 2005).

31 Anon. 'A Brief History of The Ottoman Empire 1299–1923' – _http://www.atmg.org/ OttomansSynopsis.html_ (accessed on 10th March 2005).

Mozambique Island, and later to Quelimane (Elkiss 1981: 14–22, 35). Nevertheless, Muslim and African traders diverted most of the East African import-export trade to other ports, while in 1631 Arab forces recaptured Mombasa from the Portuguese (Pearson 2003: 132; Shirodkar 1988: 39). Moreover, by the 1530s it was evident that Sofala was not an Eldorado and although gold exports remained significant until the early eighteenth century (Elkiss 1981: 45, 47–8; Shirodkar 1988: 44), the Portuguese henceforth concentrated on the lucrative trade in ivory, and secondarily ambergris and slaves, to India; initially to Chaul, 60km south of present-day Mumbai, until its conquest by the Moguls in 1601, and subsequently Goa, 350km to the south (Elkiss 1981: 22–3, 36; Huffman 1986: 92; Shirodkar 1988: 38, 47, 191). In the sixteenth century, the India-East African trade was the most important maritime connection in the Portuguese Indian Ocean World, sustaining a large export trade in Indian textiles and victuals (Mathew 1990: 143).

Limited resources and regional disdain for European manufactures obliged Europeans to continue to ship bullion to the Indian Ocean World, to enter 'country trade', and hence to seek accommodation with regional, including Muslim, authorities. Such collaboration was assisted by the relatively open system of indigenous trade in the Indian Ocean World, whereby different ethnicities and religions had in mercantile contexts long been tolerated (Segal 2001: 6). Thus, the Moguls granted the Portuguese access to the Gujarati cotton goods required to pay for Goa's East African purchases and their cargoes to Europe, in return for the right to trade with, and carry *hajj* pilgrims to the Red Sea (Pearson 2003: 131, 133–34). Europeans also increasingly relied on indigenous commercial networks for access to sources, for local services, and often for funds. The Portuguese in Goa, for example, sought credit from Hindu and Jain financiers in Gujarat (Pearson 2003: 134; Prakash 1994: 198). Such collaboration also encouraged Europeans to tolerate Indian Ocean World merchants. For instance, the foreign merchant community in Portuguese-controlled Goa included Indians (chiefly from Malabar, Kananar and Gujarat), Persians, Arabs and Ethiopians. Should European powers overly tax or otherwise impose inordinate burdens on Indian

Ocean World traders, the latter would simply switch to alternative routes
and entrepôts (Mathew 1990: 141).

Moreover, the Portuguese military hold in the western Indian Ocean
and therefore on the East African coast quickly weakened. In 1538 the
Ottoman fleet captured Aden and attacked the Portuguese stronghold of
Dui in Gujarat, and in the 1580s assaulted Portuguese posts on the East
African coast (Brummett 1994: 28; Pearson 2003: 114, 130, 132).
Although the Ottomans failed in their bid to dominate the Persian Gulf,
they opened the way for an Omani resurgence in the western Indian
Ocean: in the 1660s, Omani ships also attacked Portuguese posts along
the East African coast, in 1689 captured Mukalla in Yemen, and from
1690 re-established Muslim trading dominance in the southern Red Sea,
Gulf of Aden, and East African coast north of Mozambique as well as
constructing a series of fortified warehouses on the west coast of India
(Badger 1863: cx; Barbosa 1918: 21; Barendse 2002: 16–17; Brummett
1994: 9–10, 12; Elkiss 1981: 51; Fadiman 1973: 15; Pearson 2003: 130;
Scammell 1981: 392).[32] From 1700, the Portuguese presence in East
Africa was largely restricted to Mozambique where, however, their
defences were so weak that in 1632 the Viceroy had entertained the
possibility of an alliance with Madagascar (Shirodkar 1988: 40). Again,
in 1722, there were only twenty-six Portuguese (almost all Creoles) at
Sofala where the fort was garrisoned by a small group of Creoles and
degredados,. criminals despatched to unhealthy parts of the Empire
(Elkiss 1981: 54–5).

One result of Portuguese weakness and resurgent Muslim trade was
the continued expansion of Islam in East Africa, and in this the *tariqa*
(Muslim brotherhoods) and the Muslim traders often associated with
them, played a key role. Martin (1976: 1) estimates that from 1500 to
1800 possibly 60 to 80 percent of all African Muslims became members
of a Sufi order. Those affecting Indian Ocean Africa mainly derived from
spiritual bases in Iraq, Syria, Iran and Central Asia. Most moderate Sufi
movements also had a profound economic and social impact. The

---

32 Lodhi, A.Y., and D. Westerlund, *African Islam in Tanzania* – *http://www.islamtz.org/
hist.htm* (accessed on 5th March 2005).

influence of the *tariqa* and larger Muslim traders was augmented by ordinary Hadhrami and other Arab migrants to the Swahili coast where they engaged in overseas trade, agriculture and craft production. Thus Martin notes that:

> [...] there are hints that the Muslim commercial empire partly destroyed by the Portuguese after 1500 was in part established by *sharif* migrants throughout the Indian Ocean, and that their social and religious prestige helped them very considerably in expanding trade. (1976: 279)

This was the case, for example, of the Ba 'Alawis in Lamu, Pate and the Comoro Islands (Martin 1976: 279). Similarly, some of the Jamal al-Layl Sayyids, and its sub-lineage the Al- Qadri, the first of whom reached East Africa in 1543–4, the year of Ahmad Gran's defeat in Ethiopia, settled at Pate and Lamu as craftsmen. Their descendants spread along the coast, by 1650 possibly reaching the Comores (Martin 1976: 384–5).

The decline of Portuguese influence from the mid-seventeenth century, and an increased relationship with the Hadhramaut led to the transformation of the decayed Shirazi culture by that of the Hadhrami Shi' Islam. Islamic influence in the East Africa region was further bolstered by the development from *c.*1700 of Kiswahili as a written language, and the expanding Omani political and economic power that reached a peak in the nineteenth century following the transfer of the Omani court to Zanzibar in 1840 (Robinson 2004: 3). The *'ulama'* (Islamic scholars) helped spread literacy, in nineteenth-century Indian Ocean Africa, while brotherhoods with Hadhramaut links, such as the 'Alawiyya, also played a major role. Moreover, although most Muslim publications emanated from Cairo, East African branches of *tariqa* became increasingly Swahili in ethnicity and language (Bang 2003: 21–22; Becker 1969: 51).

Islam and the Scramble for the Indian Ocean World

It is generally assumed that Muslim influence in Africa declined sharply as a result of the expansion of Western capitalist and imperialist forces in the region from the late eighteenth century. However, European expansion also provoked a sharp reaction in the form of Islamic revivalism, and while European political pressure mounted on indigenous authorities, the expanding international economy offered enhanced commercial opportunities eagerly grasped by Muslim merchants and financiers.

The Napoleonic invasion of Egypt shook Muslim political confidence and religious pride, triggering a major Sufi revival with the aim of defending Islam. This gained momentum with the steady nineteenth-century advance of European influence, formal and informal, over Muslim territories in Indian Ocean Africa. The British occupation of Egypt in 1882 and invasion of the Sudan helped foster an emerging pan-Islamic consciousness and visits to the Ottoman ruler by influential Muslims from all over the Islamic world, including Indian Ocean Africa (Martin 1976: xvi–xvii, 4–5). It also revived Mahdism, a millenarian movement that in Sudan, under Muhammad Ahmad ibn ʿAbdallah, rebelled against the European-Egyptian authorities (Martin 1976: 6–7).

However, in East Africa, the major form taken by resurgent Islam was Sufi brotherhoods. The Uwaysiyya, founded in the mid-nineteenth century, was first centred in Somalia and subsequently in Zanzibar. It created hundreds of deputies (*khalifa*) across the region including Zanzibar, the Comoros, other coastal regions, and Islamised Somalis from the interior, and was the first movement to adopt the Arabic script for Somali (Becker 1969: 34–5; Nuotio 2000: 6–7). Similarly, the Shadhilyya movement, founded on the Comoros, made its headquarters at Zanzibar where close and profitable links were established with sultans Barghash (to 1888), Khalifa (1888–1890) and Hamid bin Thuwaini (1893–1896). In the late 1880s, it expanded rapidly on the African mainland (Pangani and Bagamoyo, Dar es-Salaam, the mouth of the Rufiji, Lindi, Mikindani and probably the Yao region of northern Mozambique), and in the first decade of the twentieth century into the hinterland, where the Qadiriyya helped the Islamisation of Uhehe and Unyamwezi (including Tabora and Ujiji) and part of the Manyema region of eastern Congo (Nuotio 2000: 7; Martin 1969: 472–74). Again, the Uwaysiyya branch of the Qadiriyya, founded in *c.*1881 in Somalia by Shaykh Uways, after he had studied in Baghdad, and performed pilgrimages to Mecca and Medina, worked actively in Somalia and in the Zanzibar region, subsequently spreading to the Comoro and Bajun islands, the Hadhramaut and even Java (Becker 1969: 50; Martin 1969: 471–73).

Following the establishment of a *Pax Britannica* in the Indian Ocean World at the end of the Napoleonic Wars, the transplanting of the Omani court to Zanzibar, and the huge commercial boom that accompanied the development of the international economy in the nineteenth century, there was a resurgence of Hadhrami emigration to, and of Indian Muslim and Hindu commercial influence in, East Africa. The Hadhrami established family networks that spanned the Indian Ocean World. Thus the Al Bā Hārūn branch of the Jamal al-Layl lineage of the 'Alawiyya *tariqa* established itself in Mogadishu at the end of the sixteenth century, from where it spread to the Comoro Islands and to India (Bang 2003: 25). By the nineteenth century, the Jamal al-Layls had branches in Somalia (Mogadishu) and Indonesia (Achin, on the northern tip of Sumatra), while the al Qadris had relatives in Borneo and in the Sunda group (Martin 1975: 384–85). Again, Abū Bakr b. 'Abd Allāh of the 'Alawiyya *tariqa* migrated from the Hadhramaut to the Comoro Islands in the 1850s. He was already an experienced sea captain and merchant having travelled widely in the Indian Ocean World, including Java and the Persian Gulf. His sons in the Comoros kept close contact with the family in the Hadhramaut and branches in South-East Asia. Abū Bakr had seven dhows on the Comoros which he used to trade all over the Indian Ocean World. His son, Ahmad b. Sumayt received an education in the 'Alawiyya *tariqa* and continued his father's trading reaching up to Madagascar. He was also a skilled navigator and astronomer. Like his father, he operated a dual scholastic and trading network from their base in Itsandraa in Grand Comore (Bang 2003: 47–52).

At the same time, traditional histories have under-estimated the growth of international and intra-regional trade in the Indian Ocean Africa from the mid-nineteenth century and the role in it of British Indian traders, both Muslim and Hindu – although the latter

predominated as, unlike their Hindu counterparts, Muslim traders
tended to settle permanently in East Africa and take African wives.
Indian traders established a large commercial network across the region.
This omission is in large part due to the hidden dimensions of the trade,
much of which flowed via indirect channels or bypassed Europe
altogether. One example is ivory, the main source of which had long
been East Africa. Traditionally, India constituted the chief ivory market,
but with the rise of 'bourgeois' demand for ivory products in Europe and
America from mid-nineteenth century, ivory was increasingly re-exported
from India to the West. Only from the mid-1880s did European
merchants start shipping ivory directly from East Africa, with the result
that the re-export trade from India declined sharply. Rising demand and
finite stocks of elephants pushed the ivory frontier rapidly into
hinterland Africa, helping to expand commercial links between the East
African interior and the coast throughout the second half of the
nineteenth century (Sheriff 1986). Similarly obscured have been the
dimensions of the regional traffic in slaves. Traditionally, historians have
focused on the slave export trade from the Swahili coast to offshore
plantations and to Muslim countries to the north, which declined rapidly
following the 1873 treaty with Zanzibar (Beachey 1976: 113; Toussaint
1971: 85). However, it is now clear that there was also a vibrant slave
export trade south of Cape Delgado (essentially from Mozambique to
Madagascar and Transvaal, and from Mozambique and Madagascar to
the French islands) continuing into the 1890s (Campbell 2005: ch. 10).

Taking full advantage of the new conditions of liberty of commerce
and the security emanating from *Pax Britannica*, Indian traders expanded
their maritime commercial network and trading colonies from the 1820s,
both across the Persian and Arabian coasts and, under the protection of
the Omani power, down the East African coast. In the 1840s, the first
Europeans attracted to the commercial rise of Zanzibar found British
Indians there playing a pre-eminent role as capitalists, wholesalers and
retailers (Frere 1873; Owen 1833; see also Gilbert 2004). Moreover,
although the Swahili coast, notably Zanzibar, remained the centre of
Indian trade and investment, their influence spread rapidly south of
Zanzibar from the 1840s, into Mozambique, to the Comoro Islands and

North-West Madagascar. In these regions, they supplemented long standing colonies of Indians (Haight 1967: 22–3). By the 1860s, Indians, whose trading structure embraced most of Indian Ocean Africa from the Red Sea to Natal and the islands, dominated regional trade, as middlemen, financiers and as shippers. They were largely responsible for stimulating East African exports, not only of ivory and slaves, but a vast range of animal and forest products, as well as cash crops (from sugar to spices), and imports dominated by cotton cloth, arms, alcohol and ironware (Campbell 1993, 2005: ch. 8; Sheriff 1987).[33]

By the 1880s, a fleet of Indian-owned dhows, of 60–100 tons each, sailed annually from Bombay and other western India ports directly to Maintirano and Manambolo on the independent west coast of Madagascar before crossing to East Africa.[34] There, these 'British' Indians joined the established Indian community which, in Delagoa Bay, largely comprised Portuguese Indian merchants from Goa, Diu and Damão (Harries 1994: 14, 88). Although sailing vessels offered low freight rates for intra-regional trade, Indian merchants increasingly took advantage of steamship services for their trade to Europe (Campbell 2005: ch. 8). From the mid 1880s the Indian commercial frontier rapidly moved south. By 1895, Nosy Ve, the main *entrepôt* on the southwest coast of Madagascar, boasted twenty-seven Indian traders who dominated the foreign trade of western Madagascar. Indians traders there maintained regular commercial contact with their counterparts on the Swahili and Mozambique coasts. Through them, even prior to the 1883–1885 conflict, they had forged strong trading links with Cape Colony and with Natal. From the late 1860s, a mercantile community of Indians, known locally as 'Arabs', emerged in Natal, most of whom represented family firms from Surat and Bombay. As elsewhere in Indian Ocean Africa, they possessed access to capital, making them important sources of credit and established trading relationships with both petty Indian traders and with larger European concerns – including McCubbin of Natal. In a very real

---

33 See also Frere (1873), especially Frere to Granville, 27th February, and 10th and 12th of March.

34 Stanwood (1886). 'Commercial Situation', Andakabe, 31st December 1886 – United States National Archives, Washington, DC.

sense, therefore, the Indian mercantile empire in the western Indian Ocean World formed the basis for British economic influence in Indian Ocean Africa (Campbell 1993, 2005: ch. 12).

Summary
Traditional Euro-centric histories have tended to portray Islam as a monolithic politico-religious institution with a Middle-Eastern core and a wide-flung periphery that included most of Muslim Africa. Islam dominated much of the Indian Ocean World for some thousand years before being eroded by the technologically superior and more adaptable modernising forces of Europe. In Indian Ocean Africa, the chief economic impact of Muslim intervention was the creation of a heinous slave export trade.

By contrast, the material in this chapter strongly suggests that the economic role of Islam in the Indian Ocean World and Indian Ocean Africa needs to be reconsidered. Islamic armies, government institutions and law created a *Pax Islamica* over vast regions providing a hitherto unparalleled degree of security and protection in which merchants of all nationalities and religions prospered. Moreover, conventional assertions that the advent of Europeans in the Indian Ocean World from the end of the fifteenth century undermined Muslim influence and restricted the indigenous commercial sphere to small-scale peddling are largely unfounded. The high cost to Europeans of maintaining a significant military and commercial presence in the Indian Ocean World and the indifference of indigenous consumers to European manufactures obliged European traders to forge regional alliances and to enter the country trade. Even so, Europe was obliged to export bullion to the Indian Ocean World until the nineteenth century (Prakesh 1994: 186–7, 189).

Indian Ocean Africa, comprising most of eastern Africa from the Cape to Cairo and the islands of the western Indian Ocean, formed an integral part of the Muslim trading world, commercial and religious linkages being promoted between Indian Ocean Africa regions and with the rest of the Indian Ocean World. The Ottoman-Egyptian regime excluded Europeans from the lucrative Red Sea trade and steadily expanded its commercial frontiers into the Horn and south into the

Sudan and beyond. Ottoman and Omani naval attacks formed the basis for the expulsion of the Portuguese from the east coast north of Mozambique. Even there, the Portuguese hold was tenuous; limited to a few ports, and Muslims dominated most foreign trade, forging close links with African traders and, in the nineteenth century, expanding their frontier deep into the East African interior.

As Muslim holy men worked closely with merchants, Islamisation generally advanced with the Muslim trading frontier. Sufi orders were particularly important in spreading Islam in sub-Saharan Africa (Robinson 2004: 19). Arabic became the political and commercial *lingua franca* over much of the Western Indian Ocean World but Arabisation did not necessarily follow Islamisation: In most of North-East and East Africa, Muslims spoke local languages, while Kiswahili developed as the *lingua franca* of the East African littoral and in the nineteenth century in much of the East African interior. Also, vibrant commercial relations were generally maintained with non-Muslim communities, assisted by linguistic and cultural communalities.

Moreover, western capitalist and imperialist expansion in Indian Ocean Africa from the late eighteenth century, while resulting in mounting European political pressure on indigenous authorities, did not totally undermine Muslim influence, as traditionally thought. Muslim political power in Indian Ocean Africa declined decisively from the 1870s, but European expansion provoked a major Islamic revival throughout the region, while the expanding international economy offered enhanced commercial opportunities that Muslim merchants and financiers seized and developed. A reflection of this is the spectacular resurgence of 'British' Indian trade and finance that formed the basis for much of the British economic influence in the region.

In sum, Indian Ocean Africa constituted an integral and dynamic part of the Indian Ocean World and its Muslim commercial and religious networks from the rise of Islam in the seventh century until the European Scramble for Africa in the late nineteenth century.

Bibliography

Abu-Lughod, J.L. 1989. *Before European Hegemony. The World System A.D. 1250–1350.* New York, Oxford: Oxford University Press.

Adas, M. (ed.) 1993. *Islamic and European Expansion. The Forging of a Global Order.* Philadelphia: Temple University Press.

Adler, M. (ed. and trans.) 1993. *The Itinerary of Benjamin of Tudela.* London: Henry Frowde.

Ahmad, N. 1947. *Muslim Contribution to Geography.* Lahore: Muhammad Ashraf.

Ali, S.S. 1996. *African Dispersal in the Deccan: From Medieval to Modern Times.* New Delhi: Orient Longman.

Alpers, E.A. 1975. *Ivory and Slaves in East and Central Africa to the Later Nineteenth Century.* London: Heinemann Educational.

—— 1967. 'The French Slave Trade', *Historical Association of Tanzania* 3.

Badger, G.P. 1863. 'Introduction', in L. di Varthema. *Travels in Egypt, Syria, Arabia Deserta and Arabia Felix, in Persia, India and Ethiopia AD 1503 to 1508*, (trans. J.W. Jones). London: Hakluyt Society.

Bang, A.K. 2003. *Sufis and Scholars of the Sea. Family Networks in East Africa 1860–1925.* London: RoutledgeCurzon.

Barbosa, D. 1918. *An Account of the Countries Bordering on the Indian Ocean and Their Inhabitants (c. 1518),* Vol. I. London: The Hakluyt Society.

Barendse, R.J. 2002. *The Arabian Seas. The Indian Ocean World of the Seventeenth Century.* Armonk, New York & London: Sharpe.

Beachey, R.W. 1976. *The Slave Trade of Eastern Africa.* London: Rex Collings.

Becker, C.H. 1969. 'Materials for the Understanding of Islam in German East Africa', *Tanzania Notes and Records.*

—— 1999. 'The Fātimid City, Misr al-Kāhira, and the development of Cairo till the end of the 18th century', in *Encyclopaedia of Islam*, CD-Rom Edition, Vol.1.0, Leiden: Koninklijke Brill.

Boxer, C.R. 1968. *Four Centuries of Portuguese Expansion, 1415–1825: A Succinct Survey. Johannesburg:* Witwatersrand University Press.

Brummett, P. 1994. Ottoman Seapower and Levantine Diplomacy in the Age of Discovery. Albany: State University of New York Press.

Bryson, R.A., and C. Padoch 1981. 'On the Climates of History', in R.I. Rotberg and T.K. Rabb (eds), *Climate and History*. Princeton: Princeton University Press.

Cain, P.J., and A.G. Hopkins 1992. 'Gentlemanly Capitalism and British Expansion Overseas, I: The Old Colonial System 1688–1850', *South African Journal of Economic History*, 7.1.

Campbell, G.1988a. 'Madagascar and Mozambique in the Slave Trade of the Western Indian Ocean, 1800–1861', *Slavery and Abolition*, 9.3.

—— 1988b. 'The East African Slave Trade, 1861–1895: The "Southern" Complex', *International Journal of Southern African Studies*, 21.4.

—— 1993. 'Indians and Commerce in Madagascar, 1869–1896', *University of the Witwatersrand, African Studies Seminar Paper*, 345 (23rd August).

—— 2005. *An Economic History of Imperial Madagascar, 1750–1895: The Rise and Fall of an Island Empire*. Cambridge: Cambridge University Press.

Casson, L. (trans. and comment.) 1989. *The Periplus Maris Erythraei*. Princeton: Princeton University Press.

Catlin, A., and E.A. Alpers 2004. *Sidis and Scholars – Essays on African India*. Delhi: Rainbow Publishers; Lawrenceville, N.J: Africa World Press.

Chami, F.A. 1999. 'Roman Beads from the Rufiji Delta, Tanzania: First Incontrovertible Archeological Link with the Periplus', *Current Anthropology*, 40.2.

Chaudhuri, K.N. 1985. *Trade and Civilisation in the Indian Ocean. An Economic History from the Rise of Islam to 1750*. Cambridge: Cambridge University Press.

—— 1992. *Asia Before Europe. Economy and Civilisation of the Indian ocean from the Rise of Islam to 1750*. Cambridge: Cambridge University Press.

Christides, V. 1999. 'History of the Islamic Province and Modern State of Egypt', in *Encyclopaedia of Islam*, CD-Rom Edition, Vol.1.0, Leiden: Koninklijke Brill.

Coquery-Vidrovitch, C. 1989. *Africa: Endurance and Change South of the Sahara*, (trans. D. Maisel). Berkeley: University of California Press.

Devic, L.-M. 1883. *Le Pays des Zendjs ou la côte orientale d'Afrique au moyen-âge*. Paris: Libraire Hachette.

Dols, M.W. 1977. *The Black Death in the Middle East*. Princeton: Princeton University Press.

Donham, D. 1986. 'Old Abyssinia and the New Ethiopian Empire: Themes in Social History', in D. Donham and W. James (eds), *The Southern Marches of Imperial Ethiopia*. Cambridge: Cambridge University Press.

Donini, P. 1991. *Arab Travelers and Geographers*. London: Immel.

Duyvendak, J.J.L. 1949. *China's Discovery of Africa*. London: Probsthain.

Eaton, R.M. 1993. 'Islamic History as Global History', in M. Adas (ed.). *Islamic and European Expansion. The Forging of a Global Order*. Philadelphia: Temple University Press.

Ehret, C. 1998. *An African Classical Age: Eastern and Southern Africa in World History, 1000 B.C. to A.D. 400*. Charlottesville: University Press of Virginia.

Elkiss, T.H. 1981. *The Quest for an African Eldorado: Sofala, Southern Zambezia, and the Portuguese, 1500–1865*. Los Angeles: Crossroads Press.

Fadiman, J.A. 1973. 'Early History of the Meru of Mt Kenya', *Journal of African History*, 14.1.

Fahny, A.M. 1950. *Muslim Sea-Power in the Eastern Mediterranean from the Seventh to the Tenth Century A.D.* (s.l) :Tipografia Don Bosco.

Fanon, F. 1968. *The Wretched of the Earth*, (trans. C. Farrington). New York: Grove Weidenfeld.

Fisher, A. 1967. 'Zanj', in Finkelman and Miller (eds), 1998. *Macmillan Encyclopaedia of World Slavery*, Vol. 2. New York: Simon & Schuster.

Francis (Jr.), P. 2002. *Asia's Maritime Bead Trade 300 B.C. to the Present*. Honolulu: University of Hawai'i Press.

Frank, A.G. 1998. *ReOrient: Global Economy in the Asian Age*. Berkeley, Los Angeles and London: University of California Press.

Frere, B. 1873. 'Correspondence Respecting Sir Bartle Frere's Mission to the East Coast of Africa, 1872–73', in House of Commons Parliamentary Papers, London: House of Commons, no.51, Inclosure 1.

Gilbert, E. 2004. *Dhows & the Colonial Economy of Zanzibar, 1860–1979*. Oxford: James Currey.

Godinho, V.M. 1996. 'Le repli vénitien et égyptien et la route du Cap, 1496–1533', in M.N. Pearson (ed.), *An Expanding World. The European Impact on World History II. Spices in the Indian Ocean World*. Gateshea: Variorum.

Gran, P. 1980. 'Political Economy as a Paradigm for the Study of Islamic History', *International Journal of Middle Eastern Studies*, 11.4.

Gray, A., and H.C.P. Bell 1890. *The Voyage of François Pyrard of Laval to the East Indies, the Maldives, the Moluccas, and Brazil,* Vol. 2, part 2. London: The Hakluyt Society.

Haight, M.V.J. 1967. *European Powers and Southeast Africa; A Study of International Relations on the South-east Coast of Africa, 1796–1856.* New York: Praeger.

Harries, P. 1994. *Work, Culture, and Identity. Migrant Laborers in Mozambique and South Africa c.1860–1910.* Portsmouth, NH, Johannesburg & London: Heinemann.

Harris, J.E. 1993. *Global Dimensions of African Diaspora.* Washington: Howard University Press.

Hasan, H. 1928. *A History of Persian Navigation.* London: Methuen.

Hodges, R., and D. Whitehouse 1983. *Muhammed, Charlemagne & The Origins of Europe.* London: Duckworth.

Hopkins, A.G. 1977. *An Economic History of West Africa.* London: Longman.

Hornell, J. 1946. *Water Transport. Origin and Early Evolution.* Cambridge: Cambridge University Press.

Horton, M. 1996. *Shanga. The Archaeology of a Muslim Trading Community on the Coast of East Africa.* London: British Institute in Eastern Africa.

Huffman, T.N. 1986. 'Cognitive Studies of the Iron Age in Southern Africa', *World Archeology,* 18.1.

Hunwick, J. 1995. 'Africa and Islamic Revival. Contemporary and Historical Perspectives', *Sudanic Africa: A Journal of Historical Sources,* 6.

Ismail, O.S.A. 1968. 'The Historiographical Tradition of African Islam', in P.E. Mveng and T. Ranger (eds), *Emerging Themes of African History.* London: Heinemann.

Jayasurya, S. de S., and R. Pankhurst (eds) 2001. *The African Diaspora in the Indian Ocean.* Trenton: Africa World Press.

Kapteijns, L., and J. Spaulding 1982. 'Precolonial Trade between States in the Eastern Sudan, ca. 1700–1900', *African Economic History,* 11.

Lane, F.C. 1996. 'Pepper Prices Before Da Gama', in M.N. Pearson (ed.). *Spices in the Indian Ocean World, An Expanding World,* Vol. 11. London: Variorum.

Leur, J.C. van 1967. *Indonesian Trade and Society,* The Hague: The Royal Tropical Society, Amsterdam.

Levine, D.N. 1974. *Greater Ethiopia. The Evolution of a Multi-Ethnic Society*. Chicago: University of Chicago Press.

Levtzion, N., and R.L. Pouwels (eds) 2000. *History of Islam in Africa*. Athens: Ohio University Press.

Lo, J.-P. 1955. 'The Emergence of China as a Sea Power during the late Sung and early Yüang Periods', in *Far Eastern Quarterly*, 14.4.

Marsot, A.L.al-S. 1990. *Egypt in the reign of Muhammad Ali*. Cambridge: Cambridge University Press.

Martin, B.G. 1969. 'Muslim Politics and Resistance to Colonial Rule: Shaykh Uways b. Muhammad al-Barāwī and the Qādirīya Brotherhood in East Africa', *Journal of African History*, 10.3.

—— 1975. 'Arab Migrations to East Africa in Medieval Times', *International Journal of African Historical Studies*, 7.3.

—— 1976. *Muslim Brotherhoods in Nineteenth-Century Africa*. Cambridge: Cambridge University Press.

Marvazī, S.al-Z.T. 1942. *On China, the Turks and India*, (trans. and ed. by V. Minorsky). London: Royal Asiatic Society.

Mathew, K.S. 1990. 'Trade and Commerce in Sixteenth Century Goa', in T.R. de Souza. (ed.), *Goa Through the Ages, An Economic History*, Vol. 2. New Delhi: Concept Publishing Company.

Meilink-Roelofsz, M.A.P. 1962. *Asian Trade and European Influence in the Indonesian Archipelago between 1500 and about 1630*. The Hague: Nijhoff.

Mgomezulu, Gadi G.Y. 1981. 'Recent Archeological Research and Radiocarbon dates from Eastern Africa', *Journal of African History*, 22.4.

Mills, J.V.G. (trans.) 1970. *'Introduction, Notes and Appendices'*, in Y.-Y.S.-I. Ma Huan [1433]. *The Overall Survey of the Ocean's Shores*, Cambridge: Hakluyt Society.

Modelski, G., and W.R. Thompson 1996. *Leading Sectors and World Powers. The Coevolution of Global Economics and Politics*. Columbia: University of South Carolina.

Mollat, M. 1971. 'Les relations de l'Afrique de l'est avec l'Asie: essaie de position de quelques problèmes historiques', *Cahiers d'Historique Mondiale*, 13.2.

Nuotio, H. 2000. 'Islamic Mystical Orders on the East African Coast', *University of Helsinki, Seminar of African Studies* (27th March).

Nurse, D., and T. Spear 1985. *The Swahili. Reconstructing the History and Language of an African Society, 800–1500*. Philadelphia: University of Philadelphia Press.

O'Fahey, R.S., and J.L. Spaulding 1974. *Kingdoms of the Sudan*. London: Methuen.

Oliver, R., and J.D. Fage 1988. *A Short History of Africa*. New York: Penguin.

Owen, W.F.W. 1833. *Narrative of Voyages to Explore the Shores of Africa, Arabia, and Madagascar*, Vol. 2. London: Richard Bentley.

Panikkar, K.M. 1945. *India and the Indian Ocean*. London: George, Allen and Unwin.

Pearson, M.N. (ed.) 1996. *Spices in the Indian Ocean World, An Expanding World*, Vol. 11. London: Variorum.

—— 2000. 'The Indian Ocean and the Red Sea', in N. Levtzion and R.L. Pouwels (eds), *The History of Islam in Africa*. Athens: Ohio University Press.

—— 2003, *The Indian Ocean*. London: Routlededge.

Pires, T. 1944. *Suma Oriental (1512–15)*, Vol. 1, (trans. and ed. by A. Cortesao). London: The Hakluyt Society.

—— 1990 [*c*. 1512]. *The Suma Oriental of Tome Pires (1512–15)*, I. New Delhi & Madras: Asian Educational Services.

Prakesh, O. 1994. *Precious Metals and Commerce. The Dutch East India Company in the Indian Ocean Trade*. Hampshire: Variorum.

Rashidi, R. 1993. *The Global African Community: The African Presence in Asia, Australia and the South Pacific*. Washington DC: Institute for Independent Education.

Reid, A. 1988 and 1993. *Southeast Asia in the Age of Commerce, 1450–1680*, Vols I & II. New Haven: Yale University Press.

Reid, S. 1993. *The Silk and Spice Routes. Exploration by Sea*. London: UNESCO.

Ricks, T.M. 1970. 'Persian Gulf Seafaring and East Africa: Ninth-Twelfth Centuries', *African Historical Studies*, 3.2.

Robinson, D. 2004. *Muslim Societies in African History*. Cambridge: Cambridge University Press.

Scammell, G.V. 1981. *The World Encompassed. The First European Maritime Empires c.800–1650*. London & New York: Methuen.

Schoff, W.H. (trans. and ed.) 2001. *The Periplus of the Erythraean Sea*. New Delhi: Munshiram Manoharlal.

Segal, R. 2001. *Islam's Black Slaves. The Other Black Diaspora*. New York: Farrar, Straus and Giroux.

Sheriff, A. 1986. 'Ivory and Commercial Expansion in East Africa in the Nineteenth Century', in G. Liesegang, G.H. Pasch and A. Jones (eds), *Figuring African Trade*. Berlin: Dietrich Reimer Verlag.

———— 1987. *Slaves, Spices and Ivory in Zanzibar*. London: James Currey.

Shirodkar P.P. 1988. 'India and Mozambique: Centuries old interaction', *Purabhileck-Puratatva*, 6.1.

Sleigh, D. 1980. *Jan Compagnie. The World of the Dutch East India Company*. Cape Town: Tafelberg.

Stanwood 1886. 'Commercial Situation', Andakabe, 31 December 1886 – United States National Archives, Washington, DC.

Strathern, P. 1993. *The Silk and Spice Routes. Exploration by Land*. London: UNESCO.

Tibbetts, G.R. 1971. *Arab Navigation in the Indian Ocean before the coming of the Portuguese*. London: Royal Asiatic Society of Great Britain and Ireland.

Toussaint, A. 1971. *Histoire de l'île Maurice*. Paris: Presses Universitaires de France.

Trimingham, J.S. 1964. *Islam in East Africa*. Oxford: Clarendon Press.

Tuchscherer, M. 2002. 'Trade and Port Cities in the Red Sea-Gulf of Aden Region in the Sixteenth and Seventeenth Century', in L.T. Fawaz and C.A. Bayly (eds), *Modernity and Culture. From the Mediterranean to the Indian Ocean*. New York: Columbia University Press.

———— 2003. 'Coffee in the Red Sea Area from the Sixteenth to the Nineteenth Century', in W.G. Clarence-Smith and S. Topik (eds), *The Global Coffee Economy in Africa, Asia, and Latin America, 1500–1989*. Cambridge: Cambridge University Press.

Varthema, L. di 1863. *Travels in Egypt, Syria, Arabia Deserta and Arabia Felix, in Persia, India and Ethiopia A.D 1503 to 1508*, (trans. J.W. Jones). London: Hakluyt Society.

Vérin, P. 1999. 'Madagascar', in *Encyclopaedia of Islam*, CD-ROM Edition, Vol.1.0. Leiden: Koninklijke Brill.

—— 1986. *The History of Civilisation in North Madagascar.* Rotterdam, Boston: A.A. Balkema.

Wake, C.H.H. 1996. 'The Changing Pattern of Europe's Pepper and Spice Imports, ca. 1400–1700', in M. N. Pearson (ed.), *Expanding World*, Vol. 11. London: Variorum.

Wallenstein, P. 1998. 'Cheng Ho', in P. Finkelman and J. C. Miller (eds), *Macmillan Encyclopedia of World Slavery*, I. New York: Macmillan.

Wink, A. 1989. 'Al-Hind. India and Indonesia in the Islamic World-Economy, *c.*700–1800 A.D', in n.p. *Comparative History of India and Indonesia III. India and Indonesia during the Ancien Regime.* Leiden: E.J.Brill.

—— 1996. *Al-Hind. The Making of the Indo-Islamic World*, Vol. 1. Leiden, New York and Köln: Brill.

Zewde, B. 1991. *A History of Modern Ethiopia, 1855–1974.* Athens: Ohio University Press.

Internet:

Anon. 'The Role of Islam in African Slavery' – *http://africanhistory.about.com/library/weekly/aa040201a.htm* (accessed on 16th June 2006).

Anon. 'The Advent of Islam in East Africa' –*http://baobab.harvard.edu/narratives/islam/EastTrade.html.* (accessed on 5th March 2005).

Anon. 'The Ottoman Turkiyya in the Sudan AH 930/1553 AD –1200/1823' – *http://www.dur.ac.uk/justin.willis/alexander.htm* (accessed on 10th March 2005).

Anon. 'Ottoman Turkiyya in the Sudan' – *http://gurukul.ucc.american.edu/ted/ice/eritrea.htm* (accessed on 10th March 2005).

Anon. 'The Future of Oromo/Kush and Abyssinia' – *http://www.warmafrica.com/index/geo/9/cat/1/a/f/thrid/49/sa/d/topic/288* (accessed on 10th March 2005).

Anon. 'A Brief History of The Ottoman Empire 1299–1923' – *http://www.atmg.org/OttomansSynopsis.html* (accessed on 10th March 2005).

Anon. *http://www.mudulood.com/PageMudbefore1960.html* (accessed on 21st April 2005).

Anon. *http://www.collectornetwork.com/article_postal_br* (accessed on 10th March 2005).

Anon. *http://www.usc.edu/dept/MSA/fundamentals/hadithsunnah/* (accessed on 16th June 2006).

Egziabher, T.B.G., assisted by Y.G. Egziabher and S. Edwards 'Firearms in Rural and Traditional Ethiopia and Humanrights' –. *http://www.unu.edu/unupress/unupbooks/uu08ie/uu08ie0n.htm* (accessed on 10th March 2005).

Elbendary, A. 'When Crafts Were Industry' – *http://weekly.ahram.org.eg/2001/534/ cu2.htm* (accessed on 16th June 2006).

Horton, M. 'East Africa, Persian Economic, Political, and Cultural Relations Through 1900' – *http://www.iranica.com/articles/v7/v7f6/v7f655.html* (accessed on 16th June 2006).

Lodhi, A.Y.and D. Westerlund. 'African Islam in Tanzania' – *http://www.islamtz.org/hist.htm.* (accessed on 5th March 2005).

Mujani, W.K. 'The Economic Decline of Circassian Mamluks in Egypt, 1468–1517' – *http://www.ehs.org.uk/ehs/conference2004/assets/mujani.doc.* (accessed on 16th June 2006).

Spooner, B. 'Indian Ocean: Cradle of Globalization' –*http://www.accd.edu/sac/history/keller/IndianO/Spooner.html* (accessed on 16th June 2006).

Turkoglu, S. 'Traditional Turkish Coffee' – *http://www.koffeekorner.com/turkish.htm* (accessed on 10th March 2005)

2

THE HISTORY OF BHUJ
AS TOLD BY ITS OWN HISTORIANS[1]

Edward Simpson

There are many historians in Bhuj. I have not consulted them all. This shortcoming notwithstanding, this chapter is about contentious and competing distortions of the past and the theoretical difficulties of dealing with reinvented facts and traditions designed to fit contemporary needs. In other words, it is about invented traditions as well as the inventive power of traditions and competing traditions. It is also about the problems of writing historically informed anthropology and touches on the problems of writing ethnographically informed history. I contrast two provincial expressions of well-known meta-narratives on history, identity and authenticity drawn from Kachchh District, the westernmost part of Gujarat, India. The first narrative assimilates Kachchh linguistically and culturally to the ruling and religious traditions of Rajasthan and northern

1   I am indebted to Dilip Vaidya for assistance and guidance during this research and to Farhana Ibrahim for sharing notes from her own fieldwork in Kachchh, although I have not used or reproduced them here. I am also grateful to Umiyashankar Ajani, Chris Fuller, Aparna Kapadia, Mohamedhussein Khatri, Pramod Jethi, Isabella Lepri and the participants in the 'Struggling with History' Workshop at the University of St Andrews for commenting on this material. It will be obvious to the reader that this work owes its existence to the thinking of Gafoor Jamadhar, an historian of Bhuj. But I stress over and above the usual disclaimers that any errors and opinions, other than those in quotation, are my doing. Fieldwork on which this chapter is based was conducted between August 1997 and May 1999, and between September 2003 and March 2004. The earlier fieldwork was supported by the Economic and Social Research Council (RO0429634237 and TO26271189), the later period by a Nuffield New Career Development Fellowship (NCF/00103/G). Gafoor and I painstakingly went through the text together in Bhuj during December of 2006.

India and to the Hindu nation to which it is seen as being inextricably bound. In this view, Kachchh is on the vulnerable periphery of a clearly defined cultural unit, India, the boundaries of which need to be shored up against predation from the Indian Ocean and from Islam. The second narrative assimilates Kachchh to Sind, the Indian Ocean, to Islam and to patterns of knowledge, language and material culture that migrated with people from the lands to the west. Both narratives lay claim to religious legitimacy and territorial supremacy, the former for Hinduism and the latter for Islam. However, far from simply being modern conveniences, such narratives have long and politicised histories relating to the colonial presence in India, and, more recently, to territorial competition between Pakistan and India. The two types of narrative I focus on here also present pasts of different characters: the former being largely self-referential and suggestive of stasis, the latter focusing on movement, conquest and social transformation, and a drift of people and things from west to east.

The tone and assumptions in the following quote, from a recent Government of Gujarat publication, exemplify the first narrative.

The State of Gujarat is fortunate in having abundant and varied source material for its history. Gujarat had long and continuous historical traditions because, of all the people of India, except Kashmiris, Gujaratis had greater historical sense.' (Gujarat State Gazetteer, Vol. I, 1989: 119).

Implicit here, as I discuss later, is a sense of infringed primordial rights and privileges. In contrast, the second type of narrative feeds from the assumption that historical consciousness is at its most intense on the margins, precisely where Hindu India has been threatened by invasion.

You must excuse my English as I cannot talk like Gregory Peck. History is my subject, I thank the almighty I am a Muslim. Politically, I cannot publish my book because in India we are supposed to be second-class citizens from the word go. Now this Hindu *Rastra* [nation] is coming into practice its historians and politicians are doing their utmost to project this country as a Hindu nation in terms of history, rewriting the truth. So, naturally, at this time we cannot publish our writing and our research.[2]

---

2   Interview with Gafoor Jamadhar, Bhuj, February 2004.

At the most general level, the first narrative belongs to Hindu nationalism, although it clearly has a much longer history than the modern forms of political nationalism that have come to the fore in independent India. The second narrative was told to me by a Muslim and reflects the flows of people in the Indian Ocean that are central to the history of Islam in the region, but this is also a narrative found in writing of the nineteenth century concerned with the diffusion of peoples through empires.

Both types of narrative are deployed in a variety of contexts to explain a variety of phenomena ranging from caste origin myths to political and racial affiliations. In this chapter however, I wish to focus solely on how such narratives are given shape in the foundation myths of Bhuj, the administrative centre of Kachchh. The main body of the chapter is divided into four sections. The first describes the dominant Hindu foundation myths and the geographical and intellectual conditions of their emergence against the backdrop of contemporary Hindu nationalism in western India. The second section outlines equivalent foundation myths from the perspective of a Muslim. This section draws heavily on an intelligent and enchanting tale told to me by Gafoor Jamadhar, an engineer by trade and amateur historian by vocation, which links the rise of Islam in the western Indian Ocean to the foundation of Bhuj. His seemingly innocuous narrative condenses the significant events leading the foundation of Bhuj into a span of around a century from the death of the Prophet in AD 632. In many ways however, the tale is rather daring, offering a dramatically different account to the foundation myths and intrigues of the ruling dynasties, essentially the prevailing 'history' of the region, in which Bhuj is founded in 1549 by a Hindu ruler. The third section looks at the reason and purpose behind the structure of Gafoor's narrative in relation to the narratives of Hindu nationalism and assesses the examples he provides in support these aims. The final section explores the implicit theory of sociality in the Indian Ocean underlying Gafoor's narrative and outlines some of the complexities of doing anthropology in a place that has such a long, important and contested history as the seaboard of western India.

The Past in a Hindu Nationalist Frame

To the south and east of Kachchh stretches the long coastline of India towards the ancient Gulf of Khambhat (Cambay), the Western Ghats and eventually the Malabar Coast. To the west, are the Mouths of the Indus, the Makran, the Gulf of Oman and the Arabian Peninsula. Today, Kachchh is a somewhat peripheral administrative district of Gujarat, but for centuries before India's Independence it was a reasonably successful tributary, first of the Moguls and later of the British. Prior to that, the area does not seem to have had a separate political existence, and was regarded as part of the dominions of whatever dynasty chanced to rule over the lands now known as Sind and Saurashtra. The semi-island territory is bordered by sea to the south, by the Kori Creek to the west and to the north and east by desert-like salt flats, known as the Rann, which flood with monsoon waters. Thus, until relatively recently, the only reliable method of transport to and from the territory was by sea. Unsurprisingly, given its geographical position and the fact that monsoon winds allow seasonal ingress and egress of ships to the ports of Kachchh, the district developed healthy traditions of maritime activity in the Arabian Sea and beyond.

During the nineteenth and twentieth centuries Kachchhi people migrated to East Africa and the Arabian Peninsula in large numbers. The enduring legacy of large-scale movement and migration is firmly reflected in the contemporary social, architectural and religious fabric of Kachchh (see Simpson 2003, 2006). In my view, as with other chapters in this book, what movement and migration there was tended to create new or modified divisions in the population both at home and away rather than creating a unified cosmopolitan society. In a general sense, movement is a symbolic and creative resource which may be turned into status and prestige at home. In the Kachchh case, movement in the Indian Ocean plays a central role in how the past is represented, commemorated and constructed. This 'ethno-history', in the form of family, caste and regional fables, uses texts, oral tales, geographical features in the landscape, real and putative ancestry, well-known gods, saints and religious traditions and received and fabricated wisdoms as narrative devices, legitimising agents and status-bestowing strategies. From an almost fixed repertoire of components a whole variety of tales can be told, truths born anew and old wisdoms elided. Undoubtedly, over the course of the last two centuries, the structural conditions in which such micro-narratives are produced have periodically transformed. The late nineteenth century, under British rule, saw a wave of linguistic and cultural revivalism in western India. New literary journals came to the fore, extolling the virtues of vernacular poets, authors of fiction and the region's historical grandeur and prowess (see Desai 1978). In part spawned by technological innovations such as the printing press, the tone of the period hailed local traditions through the idioms and techniques of the colonial power (also see Blackburn 2003). By the 1930s, the mood had changed and traditions in Gujarati literature and scholarship began to openly resent the presence of the British. Economic textbooks turned to Japan as an example of how to create a strong and self-sufficient economy, anticipating the departure of the British overlords. Such were the foundations for popular history in the post-Independence era. In the 1960s, extolling the virtues of the region took on renewed importance as Gujarat fought for separation from Bombay State on linguistic grounds. In the last few decades, various kinds of regionalism and nationalism have moved squarely into the arena of party politics and the 'production' and 'quality control' of 'history' has, in part, become the task of the state and its shadows.

At the precious core of representations of the past in Kachchh lies material compiled by British administrators schooled in Latin and Greek, their memoirs, gazetteers and journals. Simply, much of the contemporary Gujarati writing on seafaring traditions repeats a well-rehearsed list of sources, first enlivened in India as the seminal texts of colonial scholars. Thus, vicariously, works of the classical world such as *Periplus Maris Erythraei*, Pliny and Ptolemy are brought to bear as somewhat optimistic evidence for the early success of Kachchhi trade. There is however much more to innovating the past than stressing the importance of Kachchhis on the world stage because the notable biases of religious nationalism, with one foot in the history summarily sketched above, have begun once again to play a role in the creation of a fitting past.

Although Hindu nationalism has had a long career in Gujarat, the new forms are perhaps more populist and aggressive than their forbearers. In the nationalist view, 'Hinduism' and 'nation' equate. The nationalists are thus attempting to redraw the country's history and address the perceived ills of the past by redefining the divine landscape of the continent. India has become the Hindu motherland, weakened by Muslim infiltration which culminated in the partition of the sub-continent at the hands of the British. In Gujarat, the epic Ramayana text plays a key role in the nationalist political imagination. The primary character is Ram, an incarnation of the god Vishnu who embodies the ideal characteristics of a king. In the epic, Ram is sent to restore the order of the world after it is threatened by Ravana, an ascetic of nearly invincible qualities. As Pollock (1993: 264) suggests, the unique imaginative instruments offered by the text allow on the one hand a divine political order to be conceptualised, narrated, and historically grounded, and, on the other, a fully demonised 'other' can be categorised, counter-posed and condemned. Thus, the nationalist preoccupation with ruler-ship and xenophobia is given legitimacy by supposedly ancient scripture and is readily articulated if needs be in politically motivated confrontations with minority groups.

India's most enduring political crises take place, by and large, within the majority Hindu community over the rights and privileges of minority communities. It strikes me as a convenient illusion to suggest, for example, that the war of attrition over the Babri Masjid site in Ayodhya, the birthplace of Lord Ram, is simply a battle between Hindus and Muslims for control of sacred space. The sides are too ill-matched for this to be a battle: one side has the full weight of the state behind it, while the other, the minority community, has little recourse to an audience for their protests. No, here the principle battle lines are drawn more clearly between the forces of nationalism and secularism within the Hindu fold. Similarly, Gujarat has become firmly associated with the articulation of 'Hindutva' (a series of Hindu nationalist philosophies) agendas in party politics and through other kinds of nationalist organisations. Consequently, in Gujarat, life is being given to these texts as rivers, mountains and whole regions are being inscribed with the sacred past. Lying behind the gaudy colours of the new cartography are battles and defeats at the hands of the 'invading' Muslims. The achievements and grandeur of Hindu civilisation are viewed as having fallen at foreign hands. The ruins and archaeological traces throughout the region are being reinvented as either sites of wrongdoing and injustice or as evidence of former glories. As the landscape is reanimated by temples dedicated to the heroes of the epics, and religious symbolism is invested with new meanings, the history of religious contest and dispute is also being redrawn in order to reclaim the past and the land. The most recent government gazetteer of Gujarat (1989. Vol. 1: 139–140), for example, recounts the life of Lord Krishna as a central and apparently undisputed part of the history of the state.

At a local level, there are other identifiable narratives which similarly influence popular perceptions of what the past was, what it means and how it is to be commemorated. This past is also produced by clearly identifiable people and institutions and has been given a new lease of life following the devastating earthquake of 2001. The earthquake destroyed vast swathes of Kachchh, including the towns of Anjar and Bhachau and Bhuj, where many of the history makers live. In the aftermath, there has been considerable soul searching about what the District was and how it should be rebuilt. Much of this nostalgia has come from prominent citizens; much more has been generated by the outside agencies that came to assist in the enormous task of reconstruction. In the countryside, damaged temples and ancient monuments have come under the spotlight as people turn to mourn their dead and to find some form of solace in the past. The reconstruction of a number of temples has been accompanied by the parallel production of revisionist history. Some pamphlets proclaim that the temples in question were previously destroyed by invading Muslims and were splendidly rebuilt, a triumph equal to overcoming nature's fury and rebuilding the temple after the earthquake. The 'Muslim invaders' listed in such publications are Mohammed of Ghazni and Ala-ud-din Khilji, two names commonly attributed in the Hindu nationalist canon with all manner of destruction and mayhem in western India. Simply, there is no evidence to suggest they or their armies ever visited Kachchh, let alone destroyed its temples, but to be concerned about such facts is perhaps to miss the point.

In Bhuj, following guidelines established by international development banks, some of the reconstruction agencies have been working to promote a cathartic sense of heritage and identity encapsulated by the traditional architecture and morphology of the town. Some townsfolk have responded enthusiastically to these initiatives and have implemented their own forms of commemoration and memorialisation (see Simpson and Corbridge 2006). Emerging from this process is a clear 'history' of Bhuj, regularly articulated by local print and visual media, museum curators, local experts and in letters of protest written to town planners and departments of Government.

Albeit something of a caricature, the dominant chronology of the development of the town through dominant Hindu eyes is as follows. Bhuj was founded in or around 1549 when the first ruler, Kengarji, drove a *kili* (peg, nail or stake) into the ground around which palaces, walls, the town and the kingdom developed concentrically. This stake, which is still existent, marks the centre of the kingdom and the moment of its foundation. According to the legend, as the future ruler was passing what was to become Bhuj he saw a hare fighting with a dog.[3] Impressed by the courage and strength of the hare, he concluded that the people of this place must also be abnormally able, and so decided to build his capital on the site. As he hammered the stake into the ground, as part of the rituals to purify the land, it bounced back, its tip covered in blood. The attendant priest believed the king to have injured a subterranean serpent and ordered a temple be built to propitiate its wrath. In other versions of this tale, the king is said to have been attempting to drive the stake into the head of the serpent to harness its power and to prevent it from writhing and causing disruption to the kingdom. Unsure of whether he had found his target, he again removed the stake but, when blood issued forth from the land, he realised he had been successful but when he went to replace the stake the serpent had moved. This time, instead of pinning the hood of the serpent, Kengarji pierced its tale.

---

3 A similar story explains the origins of Ahmedabad.

From that day onwards, the snake has been writhing in its subterranean home causing the earth to quake. In order that the snake would remain quiet, it had to be regularly propitiated and, accordingly, a temple was constructed on Bhujia Hill to the east of the modern town. After the earthquake, new commemorative rituals and structures have been sponsored by the urban municipality to mark the foundation of Bhuj in 1549 as a Hindu kingdom. In this view, the kingdom later amassed the pomp, ceremony, deities and traditions of a full-blown Rajput State. In the centuries that followed, a succession of kings came to the throne, their strength and munificence loyally recorded in eulogistic prose by bards kept in their pay. Each ruler contributed in various ways to the ceremonial and commemorative landscape, constructing city walls, palaces, gates, water tanks, temples and so on. In this image, the king protected his territory and vassals, by guaranteeing their safety, prosperity and well-being. Around the rulers clustered service castes, relationships cemented through particular socio-religious institutions. In this sense, merchants, armies, police, bodyguards, educationalists, craftsmen and so on served the interests of the kingdom, itself synonymous with service to the rulers. The kings and their consorts ideally maintained the hierarchical caste system, protected the privileges of Brahmans and the rights of all the different castes, confirmed their relative rank, and upheld the authority of caste courts.

Within the kingdom there were smaller Jadeja fiefdoms, autonomous tributaries of the state or semi-independent towns under direct rule from Bhuj and under them were tiers of lesser headmen with lordship over particular hamlets. Thus, political authority, although having a centre at the royal courts in Bhuj, was dispersed throughout the kingdom in provincial political centres, which formed ritual and political microcosms of the ruling Jadeja lineages. Rule was associated with a broad collection of people, buildings and institutions connected to the king and protective deity. Together, Jadeja and the goddess Ashapura Mata (Hope-giving Mother) preserved the kingdom. The Goddess is the Jadeja's *kuldevi* (lineage goddess). However, she was also a tutelary goddess, a royal deity and a state deity. An integral part of ruling power, she was the source and representative of *shakti* (power) in the kingdom and was commonly linked to the earth as soil and territory. In this sense, she was identified specifically with the lands of Kachchh and with the rulers, who were literally seen as the sons of her soil. Vital in the relationship between deity and king was the royal lineage, which was also derived from and perpetuated by the powers of the Goddess. This relationship was complex and was informed by other symbols of royal power (throne, sword, turban, horse, palace and city walls) and non-Brahman mediators. As the royal courts in Bhuj were to the lesser fiefs, so the Goddess was to lineage goddesses of fief lineages. Thus, gradations of goddesses and territory were hierarchically ordered, but encompassed by the apical goddess and king.

As with other kingdoms, the post-Independence disintegration of Kachchh as a political entity only partially eroded the power of the Goddess and the significance of kingship as a socio-religious institution. Today, however, the rituals and ceremonies associated with the Goddess are ascendant, replicating traditions of the past in the absence of actual political authority. During Navaratri (nine nights), the Hindu festival most closely associated with kings, hundreds of thousands make *pag yatra* (pilgrimage on foot) to the barren interior of Kachchh to venerate the Goddess. As Tambs-Lyche (1997) has observed for neighbouring Saurashtra, renewed interest in the Goddess has communal and nostalgic overtones. As an evocation of Hindu power within a Hindu kingdom, the rituals of the Goddess have become a rallying cry for Hindu exclusivity. Among the most popular camps providing pilgrims with free food and massage along the route to the abode of the Goddess in Kachchh are those sponsored by Hindu nationalist organisations. The number of pilgrims has grown hugely since the mid-1980s, reflecting the nationalist turn and while taking a rest at a roadside camp in 1998, I listened to a man encourage weary pilgrims to chant the names of the Goddess by saying: 'If we shout loud enough *they* will hear the power of the Mata in Pakistan'. The 'kingdom' thus continues to be a ritualised ordering of gods, people and power, and the land boundary co-terminates with the cosmological construction of the kingdom.

Within this image of state formation are the lesser narratives of the origins of each caste and guild and a chronological history of key happenings. Hindu caste mythology weaves together the social and ritual practices of the present through temples, revered figures and particular places in the landscape. These myths typically identify a divine origin from the Ramayana and the Mahabharata, a human manifestation in a noble descent line and importantly an anti-clockwise arc of migration from northern India to Kachchh via the Indus valley. This kind of mythology also typically shows arrival in Kachchh to have been at the behest of a god, king or holy man, often combined with displacement caused by victory or defeat in battle with Muslims. Once in Kachchh, further miraculous events display the affinity of the new arrivals to particular villages and the ruling families.

The more successful of these myths also connect the caste in question to the kingdom's chronology of significant events. Thus, past battles, invasions, intrigues, successions and so forth became part of the reason for a caste existing in Kachchh. They implicate themselves in the history of the territory and by doing so become indispensable for the narration of the past. The Hindu ethos of the narrative permeates every event, moral and outcome. This ethos is exclusive and attempts to eradicate different geographical origins of the local population, instead presenting them as Hindus of various castes with traceable descent from Hindu deities. The authors of this kind of narrative are tenacious, energetic and often, it seems, genuinely convinced of the truth of their wisdom, or at least of the truth of the purpose it has been drafted in to serve. These authors are inspired by the idea that previous meddling with history by foreign invaders has lessened the potency of Hindu India in historical narrative. They are charged with the responsibility of restoring it.

Patterns of governance in Gujarat have unquestionably turned away from the secular ideals of the Nehuvian government that ruled India in the decades following Independence in 1947. The inauguration of new parliamentary sessions is witnessed by representatives of leading Hindu sects. Buildings, roads and villages are being renamed after the heroes of the Hindu nationalist movement. A significant number of elected representatives at the state-level were groomed by organisations associated with Hindu nationalist ideals. However, many people thought Narendra Modi, the Chief Minister of Gujarat, had gone too far when his Government officially marked the first anniversary of the 2001 earthquake with Hindu chants to appease Hindu deities. He used representatives of local governments to organise this commemoration in hundreds of villages throughout the affected area. The effect was, arguably deliberately, to marginalise the significant Muslim population from the official programmes.

Gafoor's Tale of Jasmine

In some parts of Kachchh, including Bhuj, around thirty percent of the population is Muslim, compared to around twelve percent at an all-India level. The Muslims of Bhuj represent a wide range of sectarian and ethnic interests. Among them are many distinguishable endogamous groups whose origin claims range from 'Gujarat', Rajasthan, Sind and Punjab to Afghanistan, Iran, Turkey, 'Arabia' and 'Africa'. Despite the narratives of Hindu nationalism, Islam has clearly had a constructive and sustained influence in Kachchh, as seen in hagiography and architecture as well as in the ideological and historical diversity among the Muslim population. On one hand, Gafoor's account of the spread of Islam and the foundation of Bhuj is an attempt at reclaiming a stake in dominant patterns of history-making for Muslims; on the other, I assert, it is a way of claiming higher status for his own community in the hierarchy of Muslim narratives that associate people with the territory of Kachchh.

Gafoor told me his well-rehearsed tale through the thick smoke of filter-less cigarettes. I told him I thought Gregory Peck smoked a pipe; he told me I was correct but that unlike cigarettes, pipe smoking was unacceptable for respectable people in India. Occasionally, Gafoor's wife and one of his sons would pass through the room in which we were sitting wearing patient smiles which had clearly seen more genuine days. Gafoor's work takes him the length and breadth of Kachchh. Often on his travels he allocates time to ask those he encounters about the myths, legends and historical sites associated with their villages. He writes notes and tries to see the places he is told about with his own eyes. He also has a keen interest in literary representations of history and has devoted time to tracking down scarce antiquarian books in English and Gujarati about his land and his past. He paused only infrequently during the five or six hours it took to narrate the full version of the story that follows:

One of my people was responsible for the foundation of Bhuj. He is now buried at Shah Bunder near Karachi. A famous Arab book called *Chach Nami*[4] narrates the events from AD 721 leading up to his death.[5] This side was a business route and there is much evidence that vessels from the Red Sea came to Sandan[6] where the Arabs lived before Islam, others lived near Karachi. This can be seen in the *Cambridge History of India*,[7] from Campbell's gazetteer[8] and from ibn Khaldhun.[9] Other writers have noticed our people but these books are now beginning to disappear from our libraries [...] The new generation will not know of these things.

I request you to go to Kari Nadi to the west of Bhuj, this place is connected with the story of the Habasis and in particular with Shruja who camped there for six months. Here there is a marsh, there was a fort. Here a flag was hoisted. Its colours were white, black, white, black, white, black. It was the symbol of Habasi Shruja [or Souza]. He was a clever navigator. He knew many languages including ancient Sindi. He came to trade in the ancient ports of this area. We can see that from the time of Daud, wood from Bombay was being transported to Israel.

[...] Arabs spread all along the trade routes. Some of their returning ships were looted near Pipar on the coast of Kachchh. From this point, there are a number of different stories that need not concern us. All versions lead to the same

---

4   Kufi, Ali ibn, H. 1985. *The Chachnamah: An Ancient History of Sind*, (trans. M. K. Fredunbeg). Lahore: Vanguard Books.

5   Chach was a ruler of Sind in the seventh century.

6   Sandan is a fortified village on the southern shores of Kachchh. Sources relating to the trade and population of the village are scant but it appears to once have been a prosperous port which has dwindled to near extinction.

7   1922–1968. *The Cambridge History of India*, Vols I–VI with supplementary volumes. Cambridge: Cambridge University Press.

8   James Campbell was the official editor of the vast ethnological, historical and archaeological survey undertaken by the British in India in the latter half of the nineteenth century. The gazetteers covering western India, then 'The Bombay Presidency' were published between 1880 and 1914. They are mostly compendia of different sources, sometimes commissioned, but mostly drawn from pre-existent materials – although this debt is not always acknowledged (see Blank 2001: 306–7).

9   Ibn Khaldun, 'abd al-R, 1967. *An Introduction to History: The Muqaddimah*, (trans. F. Rosenthal; abridged and ed. by N.J. Dawood). London: Routledge and Kegan Paul in association with Secker and Warburg.

conclusion that there was a girl, Jasmine, who was most probably from Persia/Iran. She was a clever girl who knew the dangers of travel and piracy. Although she was captured, she used a blade to cut her finger and to write the word '*labaikk*' on a scrap of material torn from her scarf. The word means 'help', 'almighty come to me'. Muslims chant this word on pilgrimage when they are in the presence of God. Jasmine packed the cloth into a Chinese glass bottle, sealed it and threw it into the sea. All those captured were destined to be sold into slavery in Rajasthan, as was the custom in those days.

Jasmine's message was found by a sailor and as was also tradition in those days without considering caste, creed or other things his duty was to find some way of reaching the person appealing for help. The message was written in Kufi the original language of the Quran. The sailor could see that the message was written on Arab-style cloth so he passed the message on to some Arab merchants. They deduced the girl was of such and such an age and because of the type of cloth and because the message was written in blood the situation must be serious.

The message was sent to Bahrain and from there to Hijaj. The year was around AD 710 or *hijra* 96. Under the fourth Caliph, the divisions of the Umayila [Umayyad] and the Abashi [Abbasid] had not yet come and Muslims cooperated with each other. So, Hajjaj, the Governor of Hijaj, ordered the Governor of Bahrain to find out which ships had been looted because they were paying tax to the rulers in Sind and it was their duty to provide security to the ships of Hijaj. They searched the entire Indian Ocean and it was discovered two vessels were missing, so they wrote to the Chachs, rulers of Sind.[10]

The Chachs did nothing to find the girl because they were caught, powerless, between quarrelling Brahmans and Buddhists. The Hajjaj's pride was wounded as the lesser kings had not acted upon his orders. On his instruction, the Arabs went to Sind under the command of his son-in-law, Mohammad bin Qasim. You will find this name underlined in the fifth volume of the *Cambridge History of India*.[11] Mohammad bin Qasim took the help of Habasi Shruja who guided the army along the coast. The Habasi could mix with the people because he knew the language from having come for trade in the past.

The rulers of Sind were in favour of the Buddhists. The Brahmans approached the Habasi and told him that if he favoured them they would show him the way to defeat the rulers in Sind. A bargain was struck between the Habasi and the

10 Chach's son, Dahir, was then ruler and his dynasty carried the name Chach.
11 Dodwell, H.H. (ed.) 1929. *The Cambridge History of India*, Vol. V, British India 1497–1858. Cambridge: Cambridge University Press.

Brahmans; after victory the Brahmans would be given important posts and freedom to practice their religion as well as land and protection. This was an oral promise, a conversation between two parties which is known to a third: the Almighty.

[...] in those days armies used to organise themselves around their flag and if the opposing army was able to destroy or capture the flag it was a sign they were favoured by God, see volumes one and two of Professor Elliot's *History of Sind*.[12] Naturally, the Arabs were using sulphur [as an explosive] for their machines. The Habasi knew the land and with his knowledge they were able to topple the enemy's flag from its position on top of a Buddhist temple. The Sindis then thought that even if they continued to fight, defeat was inevitable because God no longer favoured them [...] it was better for them to retreat. They fled, and the Arabs entered the port of Debal or Dehbal near today's Karachi. There is another famous book recognised by all *The History of the Arab Peoples*,[13] in which you can find this. Mohammad bin Qasim settled his army in Debal and made a plan to advance into Sind as he still did not know just who had looted the vessels and taken Jasmine. He cared so much for the girl because she was an orphan and the Prophet himself was an orphan. That is why Muslims care such for orphans.

As the Arabs continued to search for Jasmine, there was a further war between them and the Chachs in which the Habasi played a central role. He was good with a bow. In those days, elephants were used in war, but this was the first time Arabs introduced technical weapons of war in Sind. The elephants were upset by the explosions and retreated to the banks of the Indus, close to the border with Kachchh. At that time, the Saraswati and Indus valleys were parallel.

Victorious in battle, the Arabs appointed the Habasi as Governor of Debal. He lived up to his promise to help the Brahmans, rewarding them with land in today's Kachchh.

The Arabs allowed the subservient rulers of Sind to maintain their own religious practices. Dahir's son, Jayshiha, was so impressed with their magnanimity that he turned to Islam [...].[14]

---

12 Elliot, H.M. 1954. *The History of India, as Told by its Own Historians: The Muhammadan Period: The Posthumous Papers of the Late H. M. Elliot,* (ed. J. Dowson), Pts 1–2. Calcutta: Susil Gupta.

13 Hourani, A. 1991. *A History of the Arab Peoples.* London: Faber and Faber.

14 Gafoor's account stresses the significance of the politics of the Caliphate in Damascus for the turn of events in Sind and the role of various emissaries sent to Sind to govern and search for Jasmine. I have regrettably omitted these sections because of their length.

The emissary Junaid bin Abdul Rehman and the Habasi continued into Kachchh, pushing up to the east, to Anjar and Adhoi. They passed over the land of today's Bhuj. Then it was a peninsula, mostly surrounded by water. You can see this if you carefully study the geography. They did not find Jasmine.

Later emissaries did not want Jayshiha to have any power in Sind, angrily he threatened to turn his back on Islam. His family did not agree and were threatened [...] It was Junaid and the Habasi's duty to protect them. They had seen Bhuj in their earlier travels and knew that the location offered protection. They shifted the whole family there, some say three to four hundred families, some of them were the original tribes of Sind. They settled on high ground at the spot now known as Thakiya Mosque and became the *murid* [disciples] of Pir Jinda from Baluchistan.

Thus, Bhuj came into existence between AD 725 and AD 735. Today, Negro people go to the tomb of Sidi Sahib [the Habasi] to dance and remember his power. These Hindu thought police have fabricated history, they give credit for the establishment of Bhuj to a king, but really it was the Karmatiya Muslims [Karmati Baluchis] as I have told.

Unfortunately, Gafoor did not know if Jasmine had ever been found, but having searched for clues since the 1960s, and not having any daughters of his own, he gave the name to his younger brother's daughter.

Why the Jasmine Story?
This section explores the reasons and purposes behind the structure of Gafoor's narrative. The story is clearly eclectic and draws on a disparate range of events, epochs and sources. The resources on which it hinges are primarily those of British colonial and post-colonial scholarship, although he is aware of the dangers:

[...] you European people always believe the history you have written, it is but natural. No African or Asian is considered by you, everybody has accepted your scholarship. English people have only narrated the history of the Rajputs in India, you were not allowed to sit with the Brahmans it was considered a crime.

Indeed, the British history of western India, at least in the way it is assembled in endless volumes of memoirs, diaries and records of the colonial administration is essentially a history of the Rajputs. Ethnological investigations and chronicles of the Rajput's mythical origins, tutelage deities, clan and lineage organisation and traditions of rule and justice inevitably emerged from familiarity and curiosity engendered by diplomacy, contact and negotiation. The Rajputs were fiefs and thus it was to them that the British turned for tribute, rule of law and, in many cases, friendship.

Gafoor's story is deliberately positioned against the dominant history of Bhuj outlined in first section of this chapter. His tale has evolved over the last thirty-five years of reading, travelling and thinking – against the backdrop of the changing political climate of Gujarat. He is inspired by the idea that through his efforts to compile and narrate what he thinks of as history, he is helping people to remember or at least not to forget the past. But, more importantly, he sees his work as countering the myths and half truths of the past that have become contemporary facts. The line he takes is a corrective one that addresses the bias inherent in a history of a particular group of elites that purports to be a general history. Obviously, it is a narrative that focuses on Muslims and on Islam rather than on Brahmanical Hinduism: the tale's centre of gravity is the Arabian Peninsula rather than northern India, and the foundation of Bhuj is associated with Arab militarism and not with the territorial expansion of Rajput polity or with the consolidation of their power.

The feats of imagination and creativity required to produce an alternative history for Bhuj are not to be underestimated. Punches were thrown at the 2003 meeting of the Kachchh History Society over less startling and contentious claims. It is Gafoor's belief that the truths and convictions of prevailing patterns of Indian history are largely erroneous, designed for the ends of political and xenophobic nationalism. However, Gafoor does not see the rise of Hindu nationalism simply as a populist conspiracy against Muslims or other minority communities. To him, the outright lies of nationalism have their origins in party politics and the greed of politicians seeking election for personal gain.

These lies, he suggests, started with Sadar Patel, a notable leader of post-independence India from Gujarat, and have been perpetuated by the work of local historians some of whom have links with organisations that design and promote a grand vision of Hindu civilisation. As Gafoor explained:

I am a man of limited capacity but I cannot accept the current political mentalism [sic.] in my country. There is no liberty of speech, if someone writes something wrong here we will be imprisoned. In India, Muslims are put in jail, imprisoned and abused. In 2002, 2,000 Muslims were burned alive and no one has been punished because of the Hindu *Rastra*.[15]

Again, this is not a claim for conspiracy but to suggest that the nationalist agenda, building firmly as it does on some British scholarly traditions, has also become a way of thinking outside the realm of party politics. If in the past the Hindu nationalist agenda was a stance, an option, or a platform then now it has moved into the mainstream as a staple way of thinking and has brought its myths with it. Gafoor ironically observed that a historian from the University of Oxford who had written a history of Kachchh from the perspective of its rulers had chosen his words carefully:

Rushbrook Williams knew all this; that is why he named his book 'In Myth and Legend' because he was a serious historian and did not want to write that Lord Rama did this and this which is why this place is called this and that place is called that.[16]

Quite literally, Muslims are the central demons of Hindu nationalism, the Ravanas of the Mahabharata. They are held to have been aggressive from the outset and arrived and spread into Asia from Arabia through conquest and holy war. Thus, the principal contribution Muslims are seen as having made to Indian civilization is the destruction of Hindu history and temples. In this nationalist frame, in part because of their foreign origins, Muslims in India are supposed not to be loyal to their country and to support rival Islamic powers such as Pakistan. It is a relatively simple task to point out the errors and biases in these views. For example, Islam was brought to India largely as the religion of trade and through the activities

---

15 The reference here is to the widespread religious violence in the east of Gujarat during 2002 in which the victims were mostly Muslims.
16 Rushbrook Williams, L.F. 1958. *The Black Hills. Kutch in History and Legend: A Study in Local Indian Loyalties*. London: Weidenfeld & Nicolson.

of mendicants (see Bayly 1992). It could also be pointed out that periods
of Muslim rule produced many of the monuments, artistic and cultural
traditions for which the country is famous. Similarly, the majority of
Muslims in India are 'converts', and are themselves seen by Muslims from
other countries as peculiarly Indian in their approach to Islamic custom
and practice. However, in Gujarat in the past few years, such anti-Muslim
rhetoric has grown noticeably more sophisticated and elaborate. Muslims
are now commonly blamed for the historical fragmentation of Hinduism
into Buddhism, Sikhism and Jainism, which apparently formed, or at least
gained popularity, as defence strategies against Muslim incursions and
predations. To anyone with a slight knowledge of conventional religious
history in India this will appear to be ludicrous in the terms in which it is
stated but plausible at least in as far as these religious movements gained
credence during particular political epochs.

However, in Kachchh, unlike other parts of Gujarat which saw large
scale organised religious violence in 2002, the relationship between
Hindus and Muslims is generally not openly confrontational or
antagonistic; rather, the communities simply tend to avoid one another,
albeit within a framework of political and economic inequality. Despite
this however, Muslims are being written out of the past. As we have seen,
the dominant Hindu history of Bhuj is essentially the story of the
emergence of a Rajput kingdom. Although Muslim influence has largely
been written out of this narrative, two characters have escaped erasure.

The first is the ruler Rayadhanji II who came to the throne in 1778
and supposedly converted to Islam in the 1780s under the influence of
the Muslim fakir, Mohammed Saiyed. His adoption of Islam was a clear
break with what would be now called 'Rajput tradition' in a court that
clearly patronised both Hindu and Muslim religious figures and
institutions. The 'legend' states that the ruler began to roam the streets of
Bhuj accompanied by a band of Pathan followers and demanded that
everyone he met should profess Islam, regardless of their position or
creed. Later, he turned his attention towards the coastal town of Mandvi:

He first began by slaughtering animals in large numbers; he then announced his
intention of smashing all the images in Rameshvar's [an incarnation of Shiva]
temple [...] But he had underestimated the temper of the citizens of Mandvi.

They collected in large numbers and attacked the *Maharao* [King], and his Pathans so fiercely with stones, sticks and other improvised weapons that Rayadhan[17] had to ride for his life, while two of his followers were killed and a number were wounded. (Rushbrook Williams 1958: 170)

Today, most Hindus consider Rayadhanji's adoption of Islam a sign of insanity, witchcraft or both. During his reign, attempts made by other fiefs to quieten him led to a disintegration of order. In the ensuing chaos, the second Muslim figure, Jamedhar Fateh Mohammed, emerged as a strong political leader who restored the peace. In previous decades, he was a widely respected figure within the dominant historical narrative, and was affectionately known as 'the Cromwell of Kachchh'. However, today, most artistic depictions of him show him bending down in respect before Lord Swaminarayan, a god-like Hindu saint whose cult first spread into Kachchh during Jamedhar Fateh Mohammed's overlordship.

The references are hardly flattering, one Muslim is a convert inspired by insanity or driven by malicious intent and the other is a supplicant to a powerful Hindu religious cult. Gafoor's uphill struggle to reinstate Muslim contributions to the history of the land he loves and to integrate it into a broader international history involves the search for examples that counter prevailing ideas. In his view, Sindi is more ancient than Sanskrit, yet, after Independence, again building on the work of colonial British scholars, Sanskrit has been promoted as the 'mother language' and a Hindu language from which other, lesser, regional languages were derived. Why does this matter? According to Gafoor, there are many Arabic and Persian loan words in the Kachchhi language, which, he suggests, migrated with people from the west, via Sind, and not from the plains of northern India. Similarly, he also turns to dress to support his thesis that the people of Kachchh came from the lands to the west and not from northern India as the typical Aryan/Hindu myths suggest. It is his contention that sewn cloth came to India from Sumeria via the Arabian Peninsula and that its design was inspired by 'Islamic principles of sexual segregation'. According to him, the indigenous people of Sind

---

17 Here, interestingly, the author drops the respectful suffix 'ji' he otherwise consistently uses throughout the book for the names of other Rajput rulers.

wore only the bark of a tree over their genitals in the same way that Lord Rama is depicted in the televised serialisation of the Mahabharata. However, after his arrival in Sind, Mohammad bin Qasim ordered the social separation of men and women and the covering of female bodies in line with Muslim principles. The people of Sind wanted to please the Imam and avail of his protection but they could not afford the clothes that the Arabs wore. Instead, they thought of an ingenious solution mimicking the stitches they had seen in their ruler's clothes by joining pieces of material together with the long thorns of the local vegetation. In Gafoor's view, the kinds of clothes and ornaments worn by a number of castes in Kachchh today can be traced back to this time and to the edicts of Mohammad bin Qasim.

He also highlights the role of Persian and Sumerian styles of dress to support more general thesis about the origins of Hinduism, Indian forms of social organisation and the ancient nature of the Arab presence in India. According to Gafoor, the bank of the Sarbamati River, where Mahatma Gandhi established his first ashram in 1915, was an ancient home to Arabs. The place was called 'Kochrab', which Gafoor says is a corruption of the words 'Kuch o Arab', meaning 'the people of Chach, or Arabs'. He also recalls how the famous chronicler of the nineteenth century, James Tod, suggests people came to western India from the Red Sea by ship and how in Diu they constructed Greek and Egyptian temples.

Similarly, Gafoor claims wars in Greece and Egypt forced people to flee for safety. The soldiers of Cleopatra escaped to western India; Pryas (Somnath) was built by people from Thebes who later became the Hindus with Rajput names such as Chaura and Parmar. Those who came from Iran later became subjects of Kshatriya kings and were also called 'Raj-Puts' (lit. the sons of kings) and the Semitics and Indo-Scythians became Hindus and Brahmans. Likewise, there is a small port on the Kachchh-Sind border known as Ramkibazar or Rahimkibazar, which according to Gafoor is properly called Romkibazar, (the Roman's bazaar) because it was a free port in those times for all vessels within the Roman Empire. Furthermore, he suggests in the pre-Islamic period, a people called Bhumini from Bhuminabad in Iran came and settled in India. In time, the name of their original settlement was corrupted to Brahmanabad, they became the Brahmans of India. Finally, Gafoor suggests:

Iran was a great empire that used to fight with the Greeks via Iraq and Alexandria and vice versa. This came to an end when Alexander or Shikundar as we call him, a leader of Macedonia, invaded Persia and conquered Punjab, Afghanistan and Central Asia. He died at the age of 32 near Mosul, where the day before yesterday an American helicopter was hit by an Iraqi rocket. His kingdom was divided. Kachchh became part of Iran, for that you must see a Greek author who mentions a King of Persia who surveyed his entire territory up to Samiyarkiyari in eastern Kachchh. His knights or chiefs were Chatrubs or Shatrabs, they later also become Kshatriyas [members of the second or military caste among Brahmanic Hindus] in India. They were Aryans [Indo-Europeans]. The Rigveda [the first of the four *veda*] came from them. I say that because there is no difference between their philosophy and the inequality of the Rigveda.[18]

These claims taken individually are not unique and many of them can be traced back to Victorian diffusionist and ethnological scholarship; other ideas can be traced back as far as the political commentaries written by ibn Khaldun (1967). Simply put, Gafoor believes that Muslims are being written out of Indian history. He also believes that the modern Hindu population are migrants from the lands lying to the west and that the true history of western India and its people is much more entwined with Islamic social history than the current ideologues suggest.

Behind the grand aims of Gafoor's story there is also another and rather more self-interested reason for its existence. Gafoor is himself a descendent of black Africans. In his own words:

They used to call us 'Siddis'. It is a bad word, like 'Nigger'. In India, we are properly called 'Habasi' or black. My ancestors came from Eritrea [...] Other Habasis here are Maasai, some are Swahili, not a linguistic group but a

---

18 For an illuminating illustration of what Gafoor may have had in mind compare Louise Marlow's (1992) discussion of hierarchy and egalitarianism in ancient Persia with some of the classic anthropological literature on caste in India (Dumont 1970). The social hierarchy described in Persia has more than passing resemblance to the hierarchy in India as characterised by Dumont, albeit without the same stress on purity and pollution.

community. In Bhuj, two centuries ago there were more than seven hundred Habasi houses. We came as warriors, fighting alongside the Maratha and Mogul armies. Many of my people have since left this place because of 'political' reasons.

I have no doubt that Gafoor is interested in the truth of the past and in generating public debate. However, it seems to me that he is also attempting to place his own community at the centre of local history. He may have a number of reasons for wanting to do so aside from making the general point that Kachchh owes its identity to the lands lying to the west and not primarily to northern India. His own community are of lowly rank and often the source of ridicule among other Muslims and the Hindu population. They are something of a social anomaly in the sense that they are quite noticeable in a region where most skins are generally much fairer, and, as Gafoor points out they are also derogatorily called 'Siddis'. His story is thus an attempt at social elevation through claims made to prestigious and important origins. Habasis are also associated with ritual practices condemned as un-Islamic by various sections of the local Muslim orthodoxy, musical performances, spirit possession, the patronage of Hindu shrines and so forth (see Basu 1998, and in this volume). Claims to have played a part in the historical development of Islam are thus also claims for being a part of the origins of Islam. And, more generally, the story puts his community at the centre of the wider Islamic world with Habasis playing a sagacious and integral role in the spread and development of religion and culture in the western Indian Ocean.

At the turn of the nineteenth century, a young Scot, Lieutenant James MacMurdo, was sent with a flotilla to investigate the affairs of the ports of Kachchh and Sind. He later became the British Political Agent, first in the town of Anjar and later in Bhuj. He is generally remembered as having a keen interest in the affairs of Kachchh which did not always correspond with the interests of the East India Company. He apparently learned to speak both Gujarati and Kachchhi languages and was intimately interested in the ethnology of the kingdom. He was also, apparently, a shrewd negotiator. He is reported to have died of cholera, but, according to Gafoor, his meddling in the affairs of Kachchh was put to an end by Habasis who were acting in the interests of a local ruler, a

Muslim woman named Kesurbai.[19] They deliberately poisoned him, his body turned to soup and he was buried along with his bed where he lay. In Gafoor's words: 'The British Empire was not ready to disclose at the time, that a woman could kill a leading soldier. She poisoned him because of his ugly politics. He attempted to weaken the armies of Kachchh by oppressing people'. Gafoor's account of these events suggests that if the Habasis could exert so much influence in favour of a Muslim, then the Hindu ruler of Bhuj must have been impotent. Moving back in time, many centuries, Gafoor also claims that under Habasi rule in Debal the land was peaceful and the rights of different religious groups were respected. Furthermore, local rulers were allowed to maintain their seats of power even in the presence of the Habasi Governor:

[...] they were even allowed to sit on golden thrones in the presence of the Governor. Ibn Khaldun says that when Alexandria was conquered, Greek kings could bring their own golden thrones to sit before their new masters. The same happened in Sind. Nowadays everybody hates and abuses Islam of course, but in those days we were responsible for people. Kings could no longer dispense local justice, but they could enjoy their position and wealth. The aim was to treat the old rulers as decently, giving them time to reflect on the might of their conquerors. That way the defeated kings would come to Islam.

In Gafoor's view, Habasis were as important in the history of Kachchh as they were magnanimous in Sind. Yet, according to him, they were even wiser when it came to the grand narrative of Islamic history:

There were quarrels between Umiyyad and Abbasid Muslims, two sects of one origin. They were struggling for power after the death of the Prophet, the messenger and king, peace be upon him. After his death some people differed as to whether his nephew or his son-in-law should come to power. But it was

---

19 The colonial records are somewhat ambiguous as to the cause of his death. A translation of a letter from Aanandjee Narrainjee to Seth Hansraj of Mandvi addressed to the Chief Secretary to the Government in Bombay on May 1st 1820 simply states: 'Captain MacMurdo marched from Hakwad to Teiker (or Leiker) where the whole of the remaining villages were settled with, and marching from there came to Warrarwar where he died about 10 or half past 10 o'clock am. Melancholy indeed is the circumstance but the will of God be done.' Maharashtra Government State Archive, Political Department. 1820–21. Mixed Vol. 25/1.

democracy, and some wise men chose the Caliph Abu Bhakr Siddiq to be the deputy messenger of almighty God.

Under the first Caliph there were those who spoke out against Islam, others turned to Christianity. There was a fight and many who knew the Quran by heart were killed. The power hungry thought it was the turn of Hazrat Ali [the Prophet's nephew] to lead Muslims. Under Umar [the second Caliph], when Islam was being spread, he saw the meaning of the Quran was changing as it was transformed linguistically. Thus, controversy started. He ordered a draft of the Quran to be written. Soon, as Arabs travelled so extensively, everyone knew the Quran was to be written down.

The Arabs here in the ports of Kachchh knew this as they had known about the Prophet in Arabia. Now we have letters and telephones, but in those days it only took a few years for everyone to know about the Quran. Of course, there were heretics and deviants and *jihad*. You might not know the real facts of *jihad* but in the Quran it is written: do not do wrong and do not allow wrongdoing. If you are brave fight him. If you are wise advise him but do not be cowardly and keep silent.

The Caliph tried to keep human words away from the Quran. There was checking and cross-checking but some wrong things crept in. Before the work was completed, the Caliph was slain by a man from Alexandria. Under the next Caliph, the Quran was finalised and no changes were allowed. They divided the book into thirty chapters and gave each one a name. It starts from the daily prayer to God.

Later, conflict came between Umiyyad and Abbasid. Earlier I told you that the flag of the Habasi was white, black, white, black, white, black. Generally, green is used for Islam. Habasis have their own religious places in Kachchh with black and white flags because Umiyyad had a white flag, Abbasid black. Sunnis had white and a king from the Abbasid sect had a black flag. So, while they were fighting for power, the Habasis, the first people to embrace Islam, were wise enough to say: 'Do not fight with yourselves because there are only three things of importance: the Almighty, the messengers and the Quran'.

Gafoor draws on many of the same colonial and vernacular sources as the dominant Hindu narrative. In this sense, his tale is also a claim for the truth derived from what he considers to be the correct interpretative method of historical artefacts and documents. The truth as he sees it is that for many centuries Kachchh was part of what he calls the 'Muslim sphere'. As we have seen, he draws on supportive evidence that suggests people, customs and material culture arrived in Kachchh by land and sea routes to the west. He is also keen to suggest that Muslims generally, and Habasis in particular, also played significant roles under Rajput rule. Yet, to my mind it is notable that there is nothing in Gafoor's tale that contradicts the dominant notion of Hindu history and this, I suggest, is a claim for a wider social acceptance in arenas beyond local Muslim status politics. Gafoor places a different emphasis on some of the key events of Rajput rule, he also changes some of the terms of reference and places less stress on the significance of some happenings, but in his view the general structure and pattern of the narrative remains intact. His tale is thus a claim for having more ancient roots in the history of the city than the Hindu narrative and this far from being an idle claim, has recently taken on a significance Gafoor could not have dreamed of when he started his investigations.

The years following the earthquake of 2001 have hosted vociferous public debates about the history of the town and the significance of parts of its heritage. The dominant narrative has been grafted on to new traditions sponsored by the local administration to nostalgically reaffirm the emergence of a Hindu kingdom. Rather like the tale of two narratives told here, post-earthquake Bhuj has also become more geographically polarised along religious lines than it was before the earthquake. Generally, Muslims have concentrated in the northern areas of the town and Hindus have taken to Government sponsored housing societies to the south. However, there is little legitimate space in the town to ask the following types of questions: If Bhuj was founded by a Hindu ruler in the sixteenth century then why is it surrounded by Muslim graveyards that are clearly older? It is reputed that the water tanks in the centre of the town were one of the earliest engineering projects undertaken by the Hindu kings but why is there a Muslim shrine, often known as Jalal Pir, below the high water line?

Sociality in the Indian Ocean
This chapter has outlined two versions of the past, one oriented towards the political demands of Hindu nationalism; the other is Muslim-centric, focusing more on the Indian Ocean and the chains of events that drew people into Kachchh. The dominant narrative starts in the sixteenth

century, following the development of a Hindu kingdom. The second narrative, inspired by Islam, places the key events that led to the foundation of Bhuj in the eighth century. The former links Kachchh and its traditions to Hindu India, the latter to the rise of Islam, trade and rise and fall of empires. Despite such differences, these narratives are derived from different readings of similar texts and resources and are designed to testify to the largesse of the central characters.

The tale of two pasts narrated here also has implications for the anthropology of history and the history of anthropological subjects. To pose the central question of this chapter in a different way would be to ask whether Bhuj resembles Barth's (1984) interpretation of the Omani town of Sohar, a sort of ethnic diversity in social unity view informed by travel and trade in the Islamic Indian Ocean; or, whether, Bhuj conforms to patterns of classical Hindu thought, a sort of indigenous and idealised microcosm of the religious and bounded nation. To my mind, the real truth of the matter will never be known, primarily due to the spectacular lack of empirical historical evidence – if indeed it is desirable or possible to know such truths – but also because both are largely projects of the imagination.

Historical sources for Kachchh are few and far between. The main archive in Mumbai catalogues most of the Kachchh records as having been transferred to 'Kathiawad' in the first half of the twentieth century. Kathiawad, the ancient land of the Kathis, is today synonymous with Saurasthra, the main bulk of land forming the Gujarat peninsula to the east of Kachchh. I searched, to no avail, for the transferred records in the archives of Jamnagar, Rajkot, Amreli and Gandhinagar. Living representatives of the old ruling family in Kachchh told me that their copies of the political and administrative records were burned by an over-enthusiastic administrator shortly after India's Independence. The largest collection remains in the India Office of the British Library in London. There, the ancient references are vague and as improbable as the events they describe. The colonial references are acerbic and written with one eye on the policies and technologies of the Empire. The Gujarati materials tend to be eulogistic and self-satisfied, yet more intimate and revealing than the Rajput-centric literature of the British. All are inevitably riddled with political machinations, the logic of which is not always possible to reconstruct.

The issue here of course is not what was or was not true in the past but what claims people make for it. Kachchh exists not only as an administrative district but also, in the imagination of its people, as a territory, an idea and a homeland with a history and a culture. Because the image of Kachchh, with Bhuj as capital, is primarily the work of the imagination is it open for contest and debate. The past is one of the most effective resources available to the socially mobile and competitive. The quote from the most recent Gazetteer with which I opened this chapter states that 'Gujarat is fortunate in having abundant and varied source material for its history. Gujarat had long and continuous historical traditions because, of all the people of India, except Kashmiris, Gujaratis had greater historical sense.' I have often wondered why the region with an undoubtedly ancient history of maritime activity, commercial endeavour and, more recently, international labour migration should now play host to one of the more successful manifestations of intolerant and xenophobic political Hindu nationalism and what the author of this section of the Gazetteer might have meant. In short, I suspect that this is a comment on the national struggle with Pakistan and with Muslims more generally, Gujarat's position at the crossroads of Asian and Indian Ocean travel and the fact that Islam and Muslims have had a long and successful presence. Gafoor suggests that there was a mosque in Bhadreswar on the southern shores of Kachchh during the life of the Prophet. It is beyond my competence to assess the accuracy of this claim against the inscriptions on which it is based; however, it underscores the general point that Islam has been an active social force in the region for many centuries. It also emphasises the general point that the contemporary boundaries of nation states and the myths and legends that sustain them can successfully elide truth.

The perception that Islam and Hinduism are monolithic and antagonistic faiths in South Asia has become so deeply ingrained that the complexity of the historical relationship is often overlooked or ignored. In a sense, many Hindus and Muslims have also absorbed this image and explain these differences by using the resources of the past. But there is another point here: the construction of both Hindu and Muslim pasts occurs within certain limitations and within certain logical frameworks oriented around particular goals. The meta-narratives around which these more localised tales revolve tend to be the central history of either Islam or Hinduism, which are then conjoined with other lesser elements taken from secondary sources. In some cases, such bricolage passed into print and became the secondary sources for other later writers who went on to interpret them selectively. Some of these caste or region-specific narratives were widely read and, to a significant degree, became *the* oral traditions through which people imagine themselves in legend and myth. These days, the fact that the past is open to debate is taken for granted in the social sciences as much as the acceptance of the 'invented traditions' canon of writing. However, as Appadurai has illustrated, there is 'an assumption that the past is a limitless and plastic symbolic resource, infinitely susceptible to the whims of contemporary interest and the distortions of contemporary ideology' (1981: 202). In order to counter this tendency, Appadurai shows that all societies have some substantive provisions to determine how the past is authorised, given continuity, consistency and interdependence with other pasts.

Thus, treatments of the past are aspects of politics involving competition, opposition and debate. I have attempted to flesh out some kinds of politics and competition involved in creating pasts in western India. However, implied by this is the idea that in any given context there are ways of structuring narrations of the past that only make sense locally. Or, in other words, the resources, techniques and styles of presenting the past can vary from time to time and from place to place. The same is of course true of some forms of academic history which have their own various methods, styles of presentation and obsession with certain kinds of facts such as chronology or, in the case of the Indian Ocean, spatial theory. I suspect very few professional historians would take at face value either version of the past presented in this chapter. Indeed, they may well dismiss them as fanciful and hopeful, or, perhaps even more dismissively, as 'ethno-history'. There may well be some genuine methodological incompatibility between the professional concerns of the historian and the myths and legends that are commonly told of the Indian Ocean which invariably bolster the reputation of the community doing the narration. But to simply dismiss such traditions is surely to miss the point of them, and I would suggest there is much to learn from them. At one level, the alternate views of the past presented here reflect just how much Hindus and Muslims in western India have embraced the idea that their religions are almost naturally opposed and at perpetual loggerheads. At another level, the two tales offer competing visions of the social realities that have shaped sociality in western India and indeed what and how we can know about it. The Hindu nationalist ideals stress the uniquely Indian conditions that led to the development of a Rajput kingdom, within the confines of ideally inviolate national boundaries. Gafoor's tale stresses movement and fluidity within the Ocean; he also attempts to show specifically the influence of Islam on the direction of past events rather than attributing the spread of Islam to a *jihad* propelled by organic and self-referential principles. Here, to my mind, history can and should speak of how these ways of thinking developed.

The differences between these tales are also evocative of a broader debate in the study of the Indian Ocean and the allegations of cosmopolitanism generally levelled against the region. Historians have generally paved the way for general theoretical discourses on Indian Ocean sociality. Most have been keen to erode the hegemonic influence of the boundaries of nation states and continents from the way the academy thinks about this space. This project is well and good, but solely emphasising movement, voyages and overlapping cultural zones disguises the fact that many people in the region consider differences given by nationality, religion and race as the fundamental facts upon which they act. Of course, boundaries and borders have histories and their meanings shift over time, but they also have presents and a great many people, such as the Hindu nationalists, invest considerable effort in producing the past in which it is precisely the 'natural' territory of the nation state and its indigenous characters which define all significant events. If India had been part of a cosmopolitan Indian Ocean in a broader sense then many of the nationalist claims would be utter nonsense.

Bibliography

Appadurai, A. 1981. 'The Past as a Scarce Resource', *Man* (n.s.), 16.2.

Barth, F. 1983. *Sohar, Culture and Society in an Omani Town*. Baltimore: Johns Hopkins University Press.

Basu, H. 1998. 'Hierarchy and Emotion: Love, Joy, and Sorrow in a Cult of Black Saints in Gujarat, India', in P. Werbner and H. Basu (eds), *Embodying Charisma. Modernity, Locality and the Performance of Emotion in Sufi Cults*. London: Routledge.

Bayly, S. 1992. 'Hijacking History: Fundamentalism in the Third World Today', in A.W. Van den Hoek, D.H.A. Kolff and M.S. Oort (eds), *Ritual, State and History in South Asia*. Leiden: E.J. Brill.

Blackburn, S. 2003. *Print, Folklore and Nationalism in Colonial South India*. Delhi: Permanent Black.

Blank, J. 2001. *Mullahs on the Mainframe. Islam and Modernity among the Daudi Bohras*. Chicago & London: The University of Chicago Press.

Desai, N. 1978. *Social Change in Gujarat. A Study of Nineteenth Century Gujarati Society*. Bombay: Vohra and Co. Publishers Pvt. Ltd.

Dumont, L. 1970. *Homo Hierarchicus: The Caste System and its Implications*. Chicago: University of Chicago Press.

Hollingsworth, L.W. 1960. *The Asians of East Africa*. London: Macmillan & Co.

Hourani, G.F. 1951. *Arab Seafaring in the Indian Ocean in Ancient and Early Medieval Times*. Princeton: Princeton University Press.

Ibn Khaldun, 'abd al-R. 1967. *An Introduction to History: The Muqaddimah*, (trans. by F. Rosenthal; abridged and edited by N.J. Dawood). London: Routledge & Kegan Paul with Secker & Warburg.

Marlow, L. 1997. *Hierarchy and Egalitarianism in Islamic Thought*. Cambridge: Cambridge University Press.

Miller, B.S. 1991. 'Presidential Address: Contending Narratives – the Political Life of the Indian Epics', *Journal of Asian Studies*, 50.4.

Pearson, M.N. 2000. 'Consolidating the Faith: Muslim Travellers in the Indian Ocean World', *UTS Quarterly: Cultural Studies and New Writing*. 6.2.

Pollock, S. 1993. 'Ramayana and Political Imagination in India', *Journal of Asian Studies*, 52.2.

Rushbrook Williams, L.F. 1958. *The Black Hills. Kutch in History and Legend: A Study in Local Indian Loyalties*. London: Weidenfeld & Nicolson.

Sakarai, L.J. 1980. 'Indian Merchants in East Africa Part One: The Triangular Trade and the Slave Economy', *Slavery and Abolition*, 1.3.

Schoff, W.H. 1912. *The Periplus of the Erythræan Sea*. New York: Longmans & Co.

Simpson, E. 2003. 'Migration and Islamic Reform in a Port Town in Western India', *Contributions to Indian Sociology*, 37 (1 and 2).

—— 2006. *Muslim Society and the Western Indian Ocean: The Seafarers of Kachchh*. London: Routledge.

Simpson, E., and S. Corbridge 2006. 'The Geography of Things that May Become Memories: The 2001 Earthquake in Kachchh-Gujarat and the Politics of Rehabilitation in the Pre-Memorial Era', *Annals of the Association of American Geographers*, 96.3.

Tambs-Lyche, H. 1997. *Power, Profit and Poetry. Traditional Society in Kathiwar, Western India*. New Delhi: Manohar.

van der Veer, P. 1994. *Religious Nationalism. Hindus and Muslims in India*. Berkeley and Los Angeles: University of California Press.

Vincent, D.D. 1805. *The Periplus of the Erythrean Sea* (Parts 1–3). London: A. Straham for T. Cadwell Jnr. & W. Davies.

Government Publications

Gazetteer of the Bombay Presidency. 1896. *History of Gujarat*, Vol. I, Part I. Bombay: Government Central Press.

Gazetteer of the Bombay Presidency. 1880. *Cutch, Pâlanpur, and Mahi Kântha*, Vol. V. Bombay: Government Central Press.

Government of India Gazetteers. 1989. *Gujarat State Gazetteer*, Vol. I. Government of Gujarat: Gandhinagar.

3

SAINTS, REBELS AND BOOKSELLERS: SUFIS IN THE COSMOPOLITAN WESTERN INDIAN OCEAN, *ca.*1780–1920[1]

Nile Green

> It is He who conveys you
> on the land and the sea;
> and when you are in the ship –
> and the ships run with them
> with a fair breeze,
> and they rejoice in it,
> there comes upon them a strong wind,
> and waves come on them from every side,
> and they think they are encompassed;
> they call upon God.
>
> (Quran 10: 22)[2]

The seaboard of western India has a long history of contact with Iran, the Arabian peninsula and East Africa that in addition to facilitating commerce has contributed to the formation of migrant communities on both sides of the ocean. In India, these communities include the Indo-African Sidis of Gujarat and the Arab-descended Mappila Muslims of

---

1 Although based largely on textual sources, parts of this chapter also contain ethnographic data collected in Maharashtra and Andhra Pradesh (India) between 1999 and 2005 and more general historical reflections on field trips to the ports of Hadhramaut, Oman, Makran and Iran.

2 Quoted from the translation of Arberry (1964).

Malabar (Basu 1995; Catlin-Jairazbhoy and Alpers 2004; Dale 1980), both of which revere the shrines of saintly migrants regarded as ancestor figures or personifications of their community histories. While shrines of saints of African descent are limited in number, the western coast of India contains scores of saints regarded as early Arab migrants and in turn related to local traditions of genealogy and ethnogenesis. These traditions of ethno-history among India's coastal and maritime communities often include accounts of the miraculous migrations of holy men from across the sea. One example is seen in the legend of the creation of the Muslim community of the Lakshadweep Islands, attributed to ʿUbaydullah, a purported grandson of the first caliph of Islam, Abu Bakr, who ruled from 632 until 634 C.E. (Gabriel 2003). Having dreamt of being sent to the islands by the Prophet Muhammad, the ethno-historical tradition of the Lakshadweep describes ʿUbaydullah being shipwrecked on the islands before converting their inhabitants to Islam. The traditional hereditary leaders of the islands' influential Sufi orders in turn trace their family genealogies to this founder figure.[3] In the eighteenth century Indo-Persian travelogue *Shigarf-namah-ye-wilayat* we read several aetiological narratives concerning the foundation of the Muslim communities of the Indian Ocean through the arrival of seafaring *sayyids*. The Muslims of Malabar Island in the Seychelles were said to owe their existence to a Companion of the Prophet who came to settle there; his renunciation of the world and wayfaring was described by the author of the *Shigarf-namah* in a typically Sufi idiom. Having brought knowledge of the Prophet and the Quran to the islanders, the Companion returned to Medina to seek permission from the first Caliph, Abu Bakr, to bring his entire family to settle on the island (Iʿtisam al-din 1995: 28–9). In Kadalundi on the Malabar coast of India, the *sayyids* (known locally as *tannals*) claim descent from the son of a

---

3 Whatever the historicity of this tradition, we can be more certain about Sufis travelling to the islands of the western Indian Ocean during the colonial period. Saʿid ibn Muhammad al-Maʿruf (d.1904) is one example, having been initiated at Acre in Palestine before travelling to the Comoros Islands, where he introduced the Shadhili Sufi order. In the years after his burial in the islands' capital of Moroni, the Shadhiliyya went on to become the dominant *tariqa* on the Comoros.

sultan of Acheh, Sayyid Muhammad Jamal al-Layl, who quit his home city in disgust at the excesses of court life to cross the Indian Ocean on a prayer rug and so reach Malabar (Dale 1997: 182). In their echoes of the Breton tradition of founder saints that describes Irish monks sailing in stone troughs to Brittany, such narratives demonstrate the ways in which historical memory has often fused with the religious imagination among communities connected to the sea.

In many cases, of course, Muslim religious figures did cross the ocean to reach India, with the memory of actual events later being embroidered with accounts of the miraculous that possessed important meanings and functions in their communities. While typically arduous, for centuries such travel was supported by the maritime networks of the western Indian Ocean, which were in turn sustained by trans-oceanic ties of mercantile, genealogical and religious kinds. Encouraged and sustained by these networks, Sufis travelled between various points around the western Indian Ocean, often settling far from their homelands. For much of the pre-colonial era, like the Indonesian archipelago beyond it, India formed an important destination for migrant Sufis. During the Mogul period in particular, the opportunities of wealth and promotion offered to Muslim migrants to India led to one of the most significant periods of Sufi migration. Data from biographical dictionaries and court histories shows that migration from Iran (often between the ports of Bandar Abbas and Surat) was as important a feature of the period as the overland movement of Sufis from the Mogul homelands in Central Asia (Dadvar 1999). The latter was particularly encouraged by the strong bonds of identity that tied many Mogul notables to the shrine cities of Transoxiana (*Mawara al-nahr*) and their holy families. But Sufi migration to and from India also continued under British colonial rule. Just as the Mogul Empire had earlier served to draw together India and Central Asia through its networks of overland trade, in some cases such mobility was encouraged by the new travel routes opened up by the maritime colonial geography of the *pax Britannica*.

Whatever the incentives to travel to India, it was naturally the Hijaz that always formed the focal point for Sufi travellers from all around the ocean. Despite the Wahhabi capture of Mecca and Medina, throughout the nineteenth century the holy cities continued to host semi-permanent communities of Sufis from all corners of the western Indian Ocean. As in earlier cases of Sufi migration, such colonial Sufi *hajjis* reflected the wider movement of Muslim travellers. For in the decades after 1850, the number of Indian Muslims making the *hajj* increased dramatically, in considerable part through the greater travel opportunities offered by British shipping (Peters 1994: 266–315). Notable nineteenth century representatives of Indian settlement in the Hijaz include the great Sufi reformist Shah ʿAbd al-Aziz (d.1824) and the last of the Indo-Afghan Bangash *nawwabs*, the former moving into self-imposed exile beyond the indignity of infidel rule and the latter being forced into exile for his support of the Rebellion of 1857.[4] Beyond the reach of British power, Mecca in the nineteenth century acted as a pious refuge for a range of moral, militant and intellectual rebels, who included a community of Indian Sufis and their followers from across the Indian Ocean. Among these Indian Sufi refugees was Shaykh Ahmad Saʿid, a descendent of the great Naqshbandi 'renewer' (*mujaddid*) Ahmad Sirhindi (d.1624). Like many of the Muslim notables of Delhi, Shaykh Ahmad had been forced to flee the city when the British recaptured it after the Rebellion. Escaping first to Punjab then Dera Ismaʿil Khan on the Afghan frontier, he subsequently crossed the Arabian Sea to Bombay, before taking a ship from there to the holy land; he died in Medina in 1860 (Fusfeld 1988: 206–7). A more influential figure was the major nineteenth century Chishti Sufi, Hajji Imdadullah (d.1899), who similarly sought pious exile in Mecca from British rule and taught there a large body of Indian, Arab and Ottoman disciples (Thanawī 1317/1899).[5]

---

4   *En route* to Bombay and thence into exile, the journey of the last Bangash *nawwab* was observed at Nasik by the appropriate figure of Captain Henry Raverty (1825-1906), the colonial scholar of Pashto. Raverty would later describe the *nawwab* as having been 'conducted, on foot, with fetters on his legs [...] on his way to undergo perpetual banishment at Makka [...] He had been sentenced to death; but his punishment was commuted to perpetual exile, in any place he might select. He chose Makka in Arabia, where, I have since heard, he subsists on alms' (Raverty 1862: 326).

5   Some decades earlier, the trans-oceanic networks of the Naqshbandiyya had seen the great Kurdish Naqshbandi shaykh, Mawlana Khalid Shahrazuri (d.1827), initiated in

Despite the cultural and political autonomy of the Hijaz, the nineteenth century saw the wider expansion of British power all around the western Indian Ocean, from Muscat to Aden, along the Somali coastline and the Swahili-speaking littoral to eventually incorporate Natal in the far south. Concurrent with this imperial and administrative expansion was the consolidation of ties of maritime transport. With the introduction of steamships on routes such as those connecting Bushire, Muscat and Bombay, the experience of travel itself took on new forms stamped with the imprint of British power; commentaries on such new technologies became a common feature of nineteenth century Muslim travelogues. At the same time, the specific geographical connections fostered by the British Empire opened a new chapter in large-scale migration in the western Indian Ocean. Just as the maritime empire of Oman had dispersed Baluchis, Africans and Arabs between Makran, Zanzibar and Muscat, so Britain's imperial administration and markets saw the migration of Tamil bonded labourers to Natal and Sikh militiamen to British East Africa.

While these new maritime networks often overshadowed older patterns of migration – it is perhaps not too trite to picture a dhow in the shadow of a passing steamship – they by no means brought them to an end. Merchants, pilgrims and scholars continued their journeys around the western Indian Ocean throughout the colonial period, at times hampered by British administrative strictures, at other times aided by the greater security of travel and the opening of new routes. Sufis, and the ritual practices and learned traditions that they carried with them, likewise continued to move between different points of the western Indian Ocean. The remainder of this chapter examines some of the different ways in which Sufism, both as a discursive system and as a network of men of influence, continued to engage in oceanic travel in the nineteenth and early twentieth centuries. In an Indian context, the term Sufism is also used here to refer to the tradition of devotional Islam predominant in South Asia before the rise of the nineteenth century

---

Delhi before being sent to initiate hundreds of deputies (*khulafa*) in Kurdistan and Damascus; see Hourani 1981.

reform movements and which, as we see below, was in many cases able to utilise the same conditions of modernity (such as improved transport and print culture) that fostered reform. The next section discusses the continued significance of the Sufi saints as the supernatural protectors of colonial Muslim travellers, while the following section assesses patterns of continuity in Sufi travel between India and Iran during the nineteenth century. A final section examines ways in which Sufis took advantage of new colonial travel routes in the context of indentured labour migration between India and Natal. While the chapter in this way focuses on various points around the western Indian Ocean, it is argued that the maritime cosmopolis of Bombay assumed an increasingly important role as both staging post and destination for Sufis and countless other Muslim travellers of the late-colonial period.

The Saint and his Dependents: The Sufi as Protector of Sea Travellers

Amid the vagaries of ocean travel, long before the rise of British influence Sufi holy men had for centuries played important roles in the experience of travel in the western Indian Ocean by acting as the supernatural protectors of sea travellers. The connection between sea-borne travel and ties to the saints on dry land back home is best seen in ritual customs and miracle stories concerning the role of holy men as the patrons of sea travellers. Here seafarers reflected a wider *modus operandi* of travel in which the supernatural insurance of saintly protection played an important role. An interesting example is seen in the overland travels of the great Ottoman admiral, Sayyidi ʿAli Raʾis (d.1562), who after the wreck of his ship returned from India to Anatolia by land via an itinerary punctuated with visits to the shrines of the saints. In several cases these pilgrimages of convenience resulted in dreams in which Sayyidi ʿAli was assured of a safe passage home (Sidi Ali Reïs 1899: 33, 84–5, 91).[6] The cult of the Sufi saints was in this sense integral to the experience of travel.

---

6   The most interesting of these dreams appeared to one of Sayyidi ʿAli's companions after they had visited the famous shrine of Bayazid (d.875) at Bistam in Iran: 'Bayazid Bestami with 40 Dervishes had appeared unto him and spoken thus: "Let us pray for the safe return of Mir Sidi Ali." The Sheikh [Bayazid] moreover had written a passport and sealed it, "that we might not be molested by the way"' (Sidi Ali Reïs 1899: 91).

The single most important figure in this respect was Khizr, the eternally youthful culture hero whom the Sufis regarded as their own especial patron but who, in narratives and ritual practices from many parts of the Muslim world, was more generally associated with the protection of sea travellers (Franke 2000). Such customs, long prevalent in the maritime and riverine regions of India, persisted throughout the colonial period; numerous nineteenth century accounts describe popular devotion to Khizr in Bengal, for example. Travelling towards Dacca in 1824, the missionary bishop Reginald Heber described boatmen on the Ganges making offerings to Khizr for a safe passage (Heber 1873: vol. 1, 84–5). A few decades later, the Deccani Muslim Ja'far Sharif ('Jaffur Shurreef') described similar devotion to the Chishti Sufi Qadir Wali of Nagore among sailors and fishermen on the Coromandel Coast, whose vows sometimes included the offering of silver and golden model ships (Shureef 1991 [1863]: 161–62). Here India echoed wider patterns across the Muslim maritime world. These ranged from the association of the Moroccan shrine (*qubbah*) of Sidi 'Abdullah ibn Hassun at Salé with the protection of (and later from) pirates (Brown 1976: 89–91) to the similar roles of the Muslim saints of Acheh among sailors in the Indonesian archipelago (Hurgronje 1906: vol. 2, 297–302). So closely associated were the saints of Acheh with the sea that they were regarded as being personally protected by whales and sharks. Saintly shrines on the coast of Eritrea, including those in the former pirate settlements on the Dahlak Islands, were similarly maintained by clients involved in a range of maritime activities (Insoll 2003: 52).

The very commonality of such traditions points to the tenacious association of the saints with the pre-modern Muslim experience of sea travel. Reflecting these wider patterns, the maritime communities of the western coast of India developed ties to the shrines of their own Muslim saints. A sense of the importance of the shrines of coastal western India on the cusp of the colonial era may be gained from the *Qissah-e-ghamgin* of Munshi 'Abbas 'Ali, completed in 1779. Written in the form of an Urdu *masnawi* poem, this 'doleful tale' (*qissah-e-ghamgīn*) recounted the history of the last *nawwab* of Bharuch (Broach) and his personal and political travails as British power crept irresistibly along the coast of

Gujarat. From Parsi traders to Afghan soldiers and Hadhrami *sayyids*, the personalities who appear in the text are themselves an echo of the cosmopolitan society of the region's port cities. But the text is also of interest for its description of the *nawwab's* pilgrimage to the shrines of the many Sufi saints of Bharuch ('Abbās 'Alī 1975: 37–9), holy men whose names reflected the ethnic diversity of the port. The patronage of India's Sufi shrines by such independent Muslim rulers faded with the rise of British power, but in being able to maintain their connections with maritime trading communities the shrines of coastal India were more fortunate than many similar institutions inland. As the old ports of Gujarat fell into the shadow cast by Bombay, the saintly tombs of the new entrepôt grew incrementally in prestige.

Dating from the period of the medieval Sultans of Gujarat but increasing in importance as Bombay expanded, the shrine of Shaykh Makhdum 'Ali (d.1432) at Mahim (now part of Bombay) stood astride the ages of Islamic and British hegemony of the ocean. The pilgrimage there of the last *nawwab* of Bharuch in the mid-eighteenth century is also described in the *Qissah-e-ghamgin* ('Abbās 'Alī 1975: 77). There, he is pictured reciting the *fatiha* before the tomb as he passed between his own sphere of influence in Bharuch and that of his British rivals in Bombay. As time passed, the shrine of the Arab migrant Shaykh Makhdum became chiefly associated with the Konkani Muslim community, who ascribe their own origins to migrant Arabs and who accounted for the greatest proportion of migrants to Bombay in the nineteenth and early twentieth centuries (Khalidi 2000). Although the saint himself lived during the medieval period, the growth of Bombay increased the importance of his cult through its links to the Indian Ocean world. As a result a new hagiography entitled *Zamir al-insan* was prepared for the saint in 1875 (al-Madanī 1292/1875). Miraculous narratives preserved in a more recent version of Shaykh Makhdum's hagiography place him squarely into the cosmopolitan maritime world of the western Indian Ocean. He is seen helping Hindu merchants recover cargoes previously lost at sea and aiding a poor local boy in a contest to complete the *hajj* more quickly than a wealthy Arab trader with his own ship (Qaisary 1999: 25–32).

Other Indian miracle narratives refer to Sufi saints from well inland helping members of their client communities during dangerous crossings of the ocean. At the Sufi shrine of Mu'iz al-din Abposh in Paithan (modern Maharashtra), the entire identity of the saint has been subsumed into a miracle story that describes him rescuing a merchant captain from Bombay at sea after his own seven year sea journey to India from Iran.[7] To prove to his followers that he had effected this rescue without leaving his inland retreat, Mu'iz al-din wrung sea-water from his shirt sleeve as he sat before them in Paithan, leading them to give him the sobriquet of *abposh* ('water wearing'). Even the architectural presence of Mu'iz al-din's shrine became interwoven with this miracle at sea, for oral tradition relates how the captain subsequently built the complex out of gratitude for the rescue of his ship, before later being buried beneath the shrine's gateway. Appropriately, this rescue story underwent travels of its own, for the same miraculous motif is related to many other Sufi saints in India and elsewhere. For example, the section on the Sufis in Ni'matullah ibn Habibullah's seventeenth century history of the Indo-Afghans *Tarikh-e-Khan Jahani* attributes a ship-saving miracle to the Sufi Shah Bakhtiyar, who similarly proved his role in the rescue by wringing salt water from his clothes (Harawī 1962: vol. 2, 765–66).[8]

Such miracle stories continued to evolve throughout the colonial period and to adapt themselves to the new conditions it presented, at times absorbing elements of the colonial experience to add to the prestige of the saint in question. In 1926 one such account was reported in the *Times of India* with reference to the *hajj* carried out in 1903 by the female Sufi of Poona, Baba Jan (d.1931). In a wonderful meeting of worlds, the report described how during the ocean journey to Mecca, 'she saved the steamer from being dashed to pieces after all the passengers, including the European ones, had promised to garland the

---

7   Interview, *mutawalli* of the shrine of Mu'iz al-din Abposh, Paithan, 10th September 2000.

8   On an earlier Mediterranean version of the similarly widespread motif of the storm caused by the holy man thrown overboard, see Wasserstein (2003).

grave of the Holy Prophet.'[9] A series of similar narratives is preserved in *A'zam al-karamat*, the early twentieth century Urdu hagiography of Baba Jan's Sufi contemporary, Banne Miyan of Aurangabad (d.1921). Here, however, the Sufi's miraculous intervention is described in more vivid terms than the sober account of Baba Jan's miracle in the *Times of India*. According to *A'zam al-karamat*, a devotee called Hasan al-din was saved after 'picturing' (*tasawwur*) Banne Miyan when a storm hit his boat on his way to perform the *hajj* (Khān n.d.: 34). Reflecting the story we have seen associated with Shaykh Makhdum 'Ali of Mahim, another narrative in the same text describes Banne Miyan miraculously finding the means for a poor devotee to complete the *hajj* (Khān n.d.: 70–1). The saint's prediction of the permanent limp that the follower later sustained after falling from his camel on the desert road to Medina is a reminder of the hazards that the *hajj* still involved at this time. The text also matter-of-factly describes the report of a man who, in 1884, came across twenty-five Indian soldiers of the Hyderabad Contingent visiting the shrine of Afzal Shah Biyabani (d.1856), way inland at Qazipeth near Hyderabad. The soldiers described how their ship had been caught in a storm on the way to Jidda. When the ship started to sink, and the captain told the passengers that all was lost, they prayed to Banne Miyan, who five minutes later appeared in the waves, supporting the keel of the ship on his shoulder. When the (English?) captain demanded to know who this madman (*diwanah*) was, in a mixing of classical Sufi and colonial terminology the soldiers replied that he was their 'Sufi master-padre', or *pir padri* (Khān n.d.: 72–3). Here were elements of a kind of negative cosmopolitanism that emerged from the inequalities and discursive competition of the colonial experience. In the oral versions of this story that are still current at the saint's shrine in Aurangabad, Banne Miyan is presented as having proven his presence at the scene by displaying a great bruise on his shoulder where he had carried the ship.[10] The colonial element of the stories is enhanced by explicitly identifying the ship's

---

9   The reports on Baba Jan appeared in the *Times of India* on September 4th and 7th 1926. For more on Baba Jan and the colonial encounters of other Sufis during this period, see Green *forthcoming*.

10 Interview, Seyyid Quddus, shrine of Banne Miyan, 12th December 1999.

captain as an Englishman who, in oral versions of the tale, is said to have later identified Banne Miyan as the madman in the waves after passing through Aurangabad and seeing the saint wandering the streets.

Such stories were a common feature of the cheap print hagiographical works sold at the shrines, markets and fairs of western India during the late colonial period. A further example is seen in a lithographic 'Compendium' (*Majmu'a*) of stories about Shah Wajih al-din 'Alawi (d.1589) of Ahmadabad that was printed in the early twentieth century in Bombay in a parallel Urdu/Persian edition (Anon. n.d.). Among the numerous miracles of Wajih al-din that are described in the *Majmu'a*, we find another version of the sea rescue legend (Anon. n.d. 12–15). In this account, a man from Gujarat decides to make the *hajj* and gives up his home and goods before carrying out a pilgrimage (*ziyara*) to the shrine of Wajih al-din in Ahmadabad *en route*. Later, while he is solemnly sweeping the earth around the tomb of the Prophet in Medina, the thought passes through his mind that he should visit a Sufi in Syria of whom he has heard much. Just then a voice booms from the Prophet's grave telling the pilgrim that he has not yet even begun to discover the depths of Wajih al-din's wisdom and commanding him to return to India. However, on the return journey his ship sails dangerously close to a mountain looming out of the water and all of his fellow passengers begin to weep and wail. The pilgrim has the presence of mind to concentrate (*tawwajuh*) on Wajih al-din and the dénouement of the tale unfolds as the passengers all feel the sensation of someone lifting the foundering ship from the waves and hurling it beyond the mountain to safety. In its emphasis on loyalty to the saint, the narrative illustrates the central theme of the devotional Islam of the saints that was coming under reformist threat at this time. The pivotal point of the story in the pilgrim's near decision to turn to a saint in Syria instead of Wajih al-din from back home also underlines the cosmopolitan cultic temptations provided by travellers' experiences of a wider world. But it is also clear from the content of such stories that the writers of saintly chapbooks aimed to provide a kind of licit entertainment to an audience brought up on such tales of wonder. Termed as 'tales' (*hikayat*) in the *Majmu'a*, the narrative voice of the storyteller is apparent throughout; without such enticements the chapmen who dealt in these unpretentious pamphlets would presumably have found scarce custom. Embedded in such forms of entertainment, the stories of the miraculous deliverance from the waves helped give shape to perceptions of travel in the popular imagination.

Yet it is still important to grasp the rhetoric of factuality in such narratives, for in them we hear authentic voices of the experience of Indian Ocean travel in the colonial era and of the dangers that caused travellers to place their faith in the saints on dry land. Even on *hajj*, the orientation of a Muslim spirituality anchored to Indian *terra firma* was strong enough to make pilgrims call on the patron saints of their home communities rather than on the prophet whose tomb in Medina they were visiting.[11] These facts notwithstanding, we should neither fail to recognise that these are after all narrative clichés, the kind of motifs that feature all over the Muslim or even maritime world. This is amply illustrated by a Christian perspective on saintly interventions in travel at sea. For in the ports of the Christian Mediterranean similar legends were connected with the cults of such figures as San Nicolá of Bari and San Andrea of Amalfi, the latter re-arranging the motif in actually summoning a tempest to thwart an attack by the pirate Barbarossa in 1544. For their part, Portuguese Catholic sailors in the western Indian Ocean regularly begged for the intercession of the Christian saints of Goa during storms, and the Indo-Portuguese hagiographical tradition is no less replete with stories of sea-borne miracles than its Persian and Urdu counterparts (Županov 1998: 147–49). The history of narrative tropes and clichés is therefore important, for like a mutually intelligible language such tropes denote a shared underlying worldview born from the sense of insecurity that has in all ages plagued the imagination of

11 Nonetheless, other Muslim sea-travellers during this period only recommended recourse to the recitation of the Quran to bring about a safe journey. While aboard ship in the Mediterranean *en route* to Mecca, the nineteenth century Mauritanian pilgrim Ahmad ibn Tuwayr al-Jannah (d.1848–9) thus recited the suras referring to ships (Quran 10:21, 17:66–9, 42:32). He noted with great disapproval how after one powerful storm a fellow pilgrim had claimed that the boat had been saved by the *baraka* of a saint; see Norris (1977: 24).

sailors. For those abroad and at sea, the saints were able to embody the security of not only dry land but also perhaps of homeland. This is a pattern that we see repeated below in the migration of Sufis to Natal as part of a larger movement of Indians to new homes in Africa.

Old Bushire and New Bombay: Colonial Travels between Iran and India
An important aspect of the ongoing tradition of religious, commercial and cultural exchange between India and Iran during the nineteenth century was the way in which India served to re-export older elements of Iranian religious tradition that had survived among former diaspora communities in India.[12] Sufism was central to this process, for after almost two centuries of state suppression in Iran the last years of the eighteenth century saw the Sufi orders reintroduced to Shiʿite Iran through the migration of Sufis of the Niʿmatullahi order, whose ancestors had moved from Iran to the Deccan in the fifteenth century (Graham 1999; Royce 1979). According to the main Persian source on these events, this Sufi 'homecoming' began when the head of the Niʿmatullahi order in India Riza ʿAli Shah Dakani (d.1799) sent his follower ʿAbd al-Hamid Maʿsum ʿAli Shah to the Iranian province of Fars in around 1776 (Shīrāzī 1339–45/1960–6: vol. 3, 332–34). Although Maʿsum Shah was ultimately murdered in Iran in 1798 by powerful clerical opponents of the Sufis, with religious and mercantile travel routes overlapping, his preaching tours of the trading cities of central Iran were effective enough to gain a following that spread quickly through the work of his successors. Due to the ties that the Niʿmatullahi order had long had with India, many members of the order continued to travel between Iran and India throughout the colonial period. Reflecting the trajectory of these journeys, the extensive early twentieth century Persian history of the Niʿmatullahi order *Taraʾiq al-haqaʾiq* contains numerous references to Iranian members of the order who travelled to, or settled in, Bombay during the late nineteenth century (Shīrāzī 1339–45/1960–6: vol. 3, 117, 328, 373, 399, 434, 438–39, 464–66, 471, 510).

---

12 For an earlier period of Iranian trans-oceanic migration, see Subrahmanyam (1992).

In many respects, the greatest changes in the world of the western Indian Ocean during the nineteenth century were symbolised by Bombay: as nodal point of trade and transport; as centre of technical progress; as Asia's cosmopolis. The massive re-construction of Bombay's docks saw the city emerge as the principal focus of shipping in the western Indian Ocean, and with such technical developments as the opening of the first rail service in Asia during the 1860s it heralded a strange new age of travel. As the century wore on, as a result of the growing British hold over maritime transport in the region Iranian, Indian and other pilgrims increasingly found their itineraries to Mecca incorporating a journey to Bombay, the colonial equivalent of the role assumed in more recent times by the commercial stop-over in Dubai. For all of these reasons, Bombay assumed a central role in the travel itineraries of Sufis and countless other Asian travellers during the nineteenth century, so becoming the first cosmopolis of the modern era.

Bombay played an important role in the travels of one of the later Iranian Sufis connected with the Niʿmatullahi order, Mirza Hasan Safi ʿAli Shah (1835–1899). Born into a merchant family in Esfahan, during the 1860s Safi ʿAli Shah journeyed to India as part of what turned out to be a rather unhurried pilgrimage to Mecca. The Indian leg of his travels included a lengthy stay in Bombay as well as a visit to the former headquarters of the Niʿmatullahi order in Hyderabad. While in Bombay, he found a patron in the leader of the Ismaʿili community, Aqa Khan Mahallati (d.1881), whose own journey to India a few decades earlier had heralded the beginning of the consolidation of the Ismaʿili diaspora that has continued to the present day. Probably the most significant Iranian exile of the nineteenth century, Aqa Khan had earlier been connected to the politics surrounding the appointment of the head of the Niʿmatullahi order, which by the middle of the nineteenth century had gained considerable influence at the Qajar court in Iran.[13] In an example of the blending of the Sufi discourse and practice of travel, Safi ʿAli Shah later related a picaresque account of his travels and shipwreck while travelling between Bushire, Muscat, Jidda and Bombay (Green 2004;

---

13 On Aqa Khan and the Niʿmatullahis, see Algar (1975).

Homāyūnī 1371/1992: 246–74). Claiming to have been washed up on a desert island populated only by wild men and no less ferocious animals, Safi ʿAli Shah was quite correct when he wrote that he feared his audience might think him a mere spinner of travellers' tales (*afsanah-ye-siyahatgaran*).[14] Alongside this hoary account of adventurous shipwreck, Safi's travelogue is replete with accounts of his encounters with a variety of Hindu and Muslim holy men in India, and also contains another maritime yarn of being washed overboard and rescued by a supernatural sailor off the coast of Jidda. Yet through its defence of the spirituality of Hindus and Ismaʿilis, the travelogue also contains echoes of an older tradition of regional cosmopolitanism that is seen in the writings of the somewhat earlier Persian Sufi, Zayn al-ʿAbidin Shirwani (d.1837).[15]

Born in Shamakhi in 1780 but brought up from the age of five in the holy Shiʿi city of Karbala, Zayn al-ʿAbidin later embarked upon a prolonged series of travels that took him to Kabul (where he met his Sufi master, Hasan ʿAli Shah (d.1801)), Delhi, Bengal, the Deccan, and thence across the Indian Ocean to Yemen and the Hijaz before then visiting Egypt, Anatolia, Greece and the Maghrib. Zayn al-ʿAbidin's profuse travel narrative, *Riyaz al-siyahah* (1821–1827) reveals a writer fascinated by religious diversity and possessed of a keen eye for ethnographic detail (Shīrwānī n.d.). Echoing the travel narrative of Safi ʿAli Shah, one of the most striking features of the *Riyaz al-siyahah* is its discussion of the beliefs of the various religious communities whom its author encountered, including Zoroastrians, Hindus and Ismaʿilis (Shīrwānī n.d.: 179–83, 494–96, 681–83). With their worldly sense of humour, such texts are an important testament to the cosmopolitanism that was at times fostered by the combination of travel with the more humane aspects of Sufi doctrine.

---

14 On earlier legends of strange Indian Ocean islands, see Toorawa (2000).

15 Both the travelogues of Safi ʿAli Shah and Zayn al-ʿAbidin in this sense reflect the ethnographic curiosity of the well-known seventeenth century Central Asian traveller, Mahmud ibn Amir Wali. As well as describing a range of encounters with Hindus, Mahmud was a keen visitor to the Sufi shrines of India. Like that of Safi ʿAli Shah, his travelogue also contains an account of shipwreck, though in his case rescue came from the more terrestrial hands of European merchants; see Balkhī (1980: 6, 13, 63–64).

Of course, such curiosity was by no means limited to Sufi or Iranian authors and several Indo-Persian travel narratives demonstrate similar interaction with the wider world accessed by the ocean. An interesting Indian parallel to the *Riyaz al-siyahah* is the somewhat earlier travel narrative of the Bengali Muslim, Munshi Iʿtisam al-din (d. unknown), detailing a journey made from India to Britain on behalf of the Mogul emperor Shah ʿAlam II between 1767 and 1769. While primarily devoted to a description of Britain, the Munshi's *Shigarf-namah-ye-wilayat* ('Book of the Rarities of the Motherland', 1785) is also of interest for its accounts of the islands of the Indian Ocean (Iʿtisam al-din 1995: 22–36).[16] Yet despite the itinerary of the journey, the *Shigarf-namah* remained a pre-colonial text demonstrating a series of encounters with Europeans which were not yet shaped by the power relations of empire. The *Shigarf-namah* is typified by a spirit of scientific curiosity, containing summaries of intellectual and geographical discoveries alongside its accounts of the customs and mores of the peoples its author encountered. As the Munshi conceived it, the Indian Ocean remained part of an Islamic world system in which the civilisational standards of its island inhabitants were measured in such terms as their ability to discriminate between *halal* and *haram*, or their submission to the legal restraint of the Shariʿa. A supplementary measure of 'development' was demonstrated by reference to the islanders' commercial engagements and maritime prowess. Yet among his descriptions of the principal trade items, sailing practices, and geography of such islands as Mauritius, the Maldives and Ceylon, Munshi Iʿtisam al-din also included sailors' tales of a more exotic kind. One of these concerned an island of cannibals, who lure ships close to their shores with false fire signals. However, what is most interesting about the Munshi's account of the cannibals' island is the prominence given to the fate there of an English sailor called Captain Murray (Iʿtisam al-din 1995: 29–30). Given that the Munshi's travelling companion was a British employee of the East India Company sailing on a European ship, it seems likely that there was a British source for the

16 I am grateful to Carl W. Ernst for providing access to the *Shigarf-namah*. On another Indo-Persian travelogue of Britain from the same period, see Digby (1991).

Munshi's tale. Such an exchange of maritime folklore represents a cosmopolitanism of a curious but undoubtedly commonplace kind. In his description of the island of Kaf (presumably La Réunion), the island appears as the very limits of the inhabitable world, beyond which lay a more fantastic and medieval domain of treacherous and inhospitable climes. To support this claim he recounted the story of a group of shipwrecked sailors who were cast ashore on an island in this outer sea (I'tisam al-din 1995: 31–32). When the sailors stepped into the waves, the sea suddenly began to boil and all were drowned except for a saint among them who had stayed on the shore and witnessed what had happened. Alone on the island in his misery, the saint prayed to Allah for his delivery and finally heard a voice of guidance in a dream warning him not to step into the sea, but to make a raft to escape instead. In the discrepancy between the matter-of-fact tone of Munshi I'tisam al-din's accounts of the medical schools and museums of Britain and the more fabulous stories of Kaf and the cannibals we see the Munshi standing at the cusp of geographical visions of the world. In such ways, the *Shigarf-namah* represents an important testament of the Indo-Muslim experience of the Indian Ocean in a period in which neither the physical nor the imagined geography of the ocean had been subjected to European control.

It is a very different Indian Ocean world that is seen a century later in the travelogue of another Muslim traveller to Britain, Muhammad 'Ali Na'ini, better known as Hajji Pirzadah (*c.*1837–1904). Hajji Pirzadah's travels in many ways echo those of his fellow Iranian and contemporary, Safi 'Ali Shah and indeed Hajji Pirzadah was an initiate of the same Ni'matullahi order as Safi 'Ali Shah, albeit at the hands of a different master (Vanzan n.d.). He began his travels in 1858 with a journey to Istanbul in the company of his spiritual master Hajji Mirza Safa but, like Safi 'Ali Shah, in the mid-1880s he decided to make the *hajj* from Iran by travelling via Bombay. After visiting Karachi, while in Bombay he too stayed with Aqa Khan (Pīrzādah 1342–43/1963–65: vol. 1, 135–36). The travel diary (*safarnamah*) in which Hajji Pirzadah recorded his experiences is rich in descriptions of his encounters with a variety of Iranian and non-Iranian peoples, as well as in detailed accounts of the curiosities of the places he visited. But while Safi ʿAli Shah's reminiscences of his Indian travels neglected to mention any of the technological marvels of British India, Hajji Pirzadah was less bashful in expressing his interest in European novelties. If this is most evident in his later descriptions of Paris and London, his account of his stay in Bombay also included sections on the city's ice-factory, textile mills and public zoo (Pīrzādah 1342–43/1963–65: vol. 1, 126–28, 138). He also provided accounts of the dress and religious customs of Bombay's Hindus and spoke in defence of the Ismaʿilis, who take up a considerable part of his account of the city. But given the role that Bombay's Parsis were beginning to play in educational and charitable projects among their Zoroastrian brethren beyond the sea in Iran (Boyce 1969), perhaps the most significant aspect of Hajji Pirzadah's account of Bombay is the description of the lifestyle of these earliest of Iranians abroad that he penned for the inquisitive in Iran (Pīrzādah 1342–43/1963–65: vol. 1, 130–31). For in a period in which the Iranian Zoroastrians of the villages around Yazd still suffered from considerable discrimination and were regarded by Shiʿa clerics as ritually unclean, that is as *najis* (Green 2000), Hajji Pirzadah's account of their co-religionists in Bombay emphasised their hygiene and fine appearance along with their wealth and respected status in the great port of the British. Hajji Pirzadah later visited the more distant Iranian merchant communities of Europe (Pīrzādah 1342–43/1963–65: vol. 1, 187), where he also met many leading statesmen and intellectuals.[17] The scale and destinations of Hajji Pirzadah's travels

---

17 While in England, Hajji Pirzadah visited Cambridge where he made the acquaintance of the great scholar of Persian literature E.G. Browne (1862–1926), who was then still a young man. Their encounter, and Browne's evident fascination with this cosmopolitan dervish, has inevitably led to speculation that Hajji Pirzadah initiated Browne as a Sufi, though this seems in fact not to have been the case. Their relationship has been discussed by Īraj Afshār in his introduction to Hajji Pirzadah's *Safarnamah* (Pīrzādah 1342–43/1963–65: vol. 1, xxviii–lv) and more recently in Ridgeon (2004). Both Cambridge and Oxford had also been visited earlier in the nineteenth century by the Iranian traveller Mirza Salih Shirazi (d. unknown), whose travelogue records in detail pleasurable evenings spent dining with dons (*ʿulama*) in the colleges (*madrasas*) of Oxford and Cambridge and days spent visiting the Bodleian library and attending a graduation ceremony (Shīrāzī 1364/1985: 319–29, 349–53). A keen observer of

further demonstrate the ways in which Iranian travellers made use of the new itineraries and modes of transport of the colonial era, both in the Indian Ocean and beyond.

Like the hagiographical tales of the previous section, such personal reminiscences were part of a wider tradition of tale-telling through which Indian Ocean travel continued to be vicariously experienced throughout the nineteenth century. Of course, there also existed a tradition of non-Sufi Persian travel writing connected to Indian Ocean journeys and Qajar Iran saw a great blossoming of such travelogues. Once again, however, the description of travel was inseparable from trans-regional cultural categories and specifically local meanings. *Hajj* narratives such as those of the pilgrimages of Sayf al-Dawlah in 1863 and Mirza Husayn Farahani in 1885 were embedded within a value system associating the *hajj* with wealth and social prestige no less than piety (Sayf al-Dawla 1363/1985; Farahani 1990). Yet, as in the case of Hajji Pirzadah, they also served to carry back to Iran reports of new technologies that were observed along the way, such as steam power or rail travel. In such ways, eighteenth and nineteenth century Persian travelogues acted as fields of literary mediation between the experience of the old and new worlds of Indian Ocean travel.

The travelogue was by no means the sole genre connected to travel between Bushire and Bombay. By the mid-nineteenth century, Bombay had attracted a considerable Iranian community, at the centre of which, stepping between the Persian and the British worlds, were Aqa Khan Mahallati and his son Aqa ʿAli Shah, the future Aqa Khan II. Having stayed with Aqa Khan, Safi ʿAli Shah and Hajji Pirzadah nonetheless found themselves among a body of expatriate Iranians several thousand strong that brought political exiles and merchants cheek by jowl with publishers and religious figures (Green 2004, Mohiuddin and Poonawala n.d.). Hajji Pirzadah wrote a short description of a group of Iranian political exiles he encountered in Bombay who had fled the governor of Yazd but were now living on the charity of Bombay's Parsis, whose own

---

political organisation and technological progress, on his return home Mirza Salih established the first short-lived newspaper in Iran, called simply *Kaghaz-e-akhbar*.

ancestral connections with Yazd were being revived at this time (Pīrzādah 1342–43/1963–65: vol. 1, 131). Among the city's other Iranian refugees was the anti-Qajar poet Shaykh Hasan-e-Shirazi, who sought refuge in Bombay during the 1860s. Somewhat later the plight of such political exiles in India was evoked in the famous *Salarnamah* of the pan-Islamist poet Aqa Khan Kirmani (d.1896), whose own years of exile were spent in Istanbul (Machalski 1965: vol. 1, 33–39).[18]

> *Hamah mardom az dast-e-bīdād-e-shūm*
> *gorīzand dar hind ū qafqāz ū rūm*
>
> All the folk escape the cruel hand unjust
> For refuge in Europe, India and Caucasus

Despite the emergence of a Persian poetry of protest, other Iranian *litterateurs* connected with Bombay continued to write in safer, established idioms. Safi ʿAli Shah was one of them, completing the lengthy mystical poem *Zubdat al-asrar* during his residence in Bombay, and publishing it there in 1872 with the encouragement of Aqa Khan, whose own memoirs were also published at one of the city's lithographic presses. Safi ʿAli Shah's blending of travel and literary production helped build a reputation for him on his return to Iran in the late 1860s. With its central focus on the events of the Shiʿa passion, the *Zubdat al-asrar* is a reminder of the continued trans-oceanic character of Shiʿism during the second half of the nineteenth century, after the fall of the Shiʿite kingdom of Awadh that had attracted many Iranian clerics to settle in India (Cole 1988). At the same time, with its repeated evocation of the classic Sufi imagery of the ocean (*bahr*) and its waves (*amwaj*), the *Zubdat al-asrar* represented a mystical appropriation of the semantic power of the high seas (Safi ʿAlī Shāh 1379/2000). Though by this period a longstanding characteristic of Sufi writings, the abundance of this imagery in both Safi ʿAli Shah's *Zubdat al-asrar* and such later poetic writings as his *Bahr al-haqaʾiq* ('The Ocean of Realities') may reflect a

---

18 In more recent times, Bombay acted as an important place of refuge for Iranians fleeing the revolution of 1979. Other connections have also been revived in recent decades by Iranian students travelling to study at the universities of India.

genuine creative response to the experience of ocean travel. However, the discussion of travel (*safar, siyahat*) in these works remained part of a longstanding Sufi logic of the purposes of travel in which outward wayfaring was regarded as a metaphor for the inner journey. It was in this vein that Safi ʿAli Shah devoted two sections of verse in his *Bahr al-haqaʾiq* to outlining the 'real' meanings of being a traveller (*salik*) and of travel (*safar*) itself (Safi ʿAlī Shāh n.d.: 239, 244–45). But aside from such hackneyed imagery, the language of travel continued to be present in the writings of other Iranian poets of the nineteenth century. One example was Qarib Rabbani, erstwhile teacher of literature at the modernising polytechnic Dar al-Funun in Tehran, who visited Bombay during the course of his *hajj* and whose classicising tendencies reflect the poetry of Safi ʿAli Shah (Machalski 1965: vol. 1, 27–29). Echoing the emergence of the nationalist amnesia that would soon all but erase the role of India from Iran's cultural memory, in one verse Qarib Rabbani wrote,

> *Ay pesar, na-āzmūdah ranj-e-safar*
> *natawān bord rah be-ganj-e-watan*

> Hey kid, without being taught the toils of travel
> None tread the track to homeland's treasure

Despite the slow spread of printing in Iran itself during the nineteenth century, Bombay's Iranian community included a considerable number of publishers and book dealers. Like Safi ʿAli Shah, many other Iranians living in or passing through Bombay used the opportunity provided by the city's printing presses to publish poems, tracts and memoirs and Iranian merchants were able to ship books back to Iran exempt from British customs duties. The city's Iranian publishers were part of a wider Iranian diaspora in Calcutta and elsewhere who reinvigorated India's long tradition of Persian literary production through the printing of Persian literary classics (such as the *Masnawi* of Rumi), exile newspapers critical of the government in Iran (such as the influential *Habl al-matin*) and new works (such as the *Zubdat al-asrar*). As a result, many books were printed in Bombay and traded around the western Indian Ocean during the late colonial period.[19]

The book trade was by no means limited to Muslims, and the cosmopolitan character of the ocean's ports meant that other religious or linguistic communities also made use of Bombay's advanced publishing industry. While the publishing activities of Christian groups in Bombay are sufficiently well known, more symptomatic of the continuity of pre-colonial patterns of cosmopolitanism were the activities of Jewish writers and publishers. A diasporic network of Baghdadi Jews was at the forefront of the development of Hebrew printing around the Indian Ocean, with their publishing activities stretching from Baghdad and Basra to the Jewish communities of Bombay, Poona and Calcutta (Hill 2003–04: 53–77). The lingering influence of an older cosmopolitanism was seen in linguistic terms through the printing of Judeo-Arabic works (that is, works in Arabic or Jewish Arabic koine printed in Hebrew script), which developed during this period not only in Baghdad but also in Bombay and Calcutta. Jewish publishers often sent manuscripts from Baghdad and Basra to be printed by the Hebrew presses of Bombay and Calcutta, the printed books in turn being shipped for distribution in Iraq and in many cased being issued under the imprint of local Jewish publishers. Baghdad's printed Hebrew ecumene also included books printed in the Mediterranean port cities of Livorno and Istanbul, which were at times later re-issued in Baghdad or India, such that the trade in books echoed and sustained diasporic connections beyond the western Indian Ocean into the Mediterranean and beyond. An example of this is seen in the life of the printer Ezra Reuben Dangur (1848–1930). Dangur's career encompassed an early life in Burma, where he served as the rabbi of Rangoon, before re-locating to Baghdad where he set up as a printer in 1904 with permission from the Ottoman sultan 'Abd al-Hamid and imported presses and type from Europe. The opposite itinerary was followed by the Baghdadi printer Solomon Twena, who in 1888 migrated to Calcutta to found the last major Hebrew press in the

---

19 For another dimension of the role of traded items in Indo-Iranian cultural exchange during this period, see Zebrowski (1982).

city. Alongside the success of Hebrew printing, the multilingual character
of the publishing industry in the port cities of India is perhaps best
illustrated in the fact that it was in Calcutta between 1814 and 1818 that
the first printed Arabic edition of the *Thousand and One Nights*
appeared, almost two decades before Cairo's famous Bulaq edition of
1835. However neglected, India's ports played as important a role in the
global history of printing as such ports as Venice and Antwerp in the
history of printing in Europe.

The movement of religious ideas during this period was in such ways
intimately connected to the travels of writers, publishers and the books
and tracts that they produced. In the Islamic sphere perhaps the most
influential embodiment of this coalescence of writing and exile during
this period was the Iranian revolutionary Jamal al-din 'al-Afghani'
(d.1897). It had been Jamal al-din's journey to Bombay in the wake of
the Great Revolt of 1857 that had first awoken him to the threat posed
to Muslims by British colonial power, a threat that would subsequently
become the central theme of his life's work (Keddie 1972: 22–32). It was
in the independent Muslim state of Hyderabad that Jamal al-din wrote
his major work, *Haqiqat-e-madhhab-e-naychari wa bayan-e-hal-e-
naychariyan*, whose subsequent Arabic translation as *al-Radd 'ala al-
dhahriyyin* ('The Refutation of the Materialists') would become one of
the most influential Muslim texts of the nineteenth century. While Jamal
al-din's relationship to Sufism has been much debated, there was a strong
Sufi element to his thought and persona during the early part of his
career. The revolutionary doctrines that were the ultimate outcome of his
sojourn in Bombay and his encounter there with the realities of British
power are therefore an important indication of the changes in Islam in
the face of the political pressures of the cosmopolitan experience. Jamal
al-din also demonstrates the continuity of intellectual ties between
Iranian and Indian Muslims during the nineteenth century and the role
that Persian continued to play as one of several languages of educated
discourse around the western Indian Ocean. For here in the Indian
Ocean travels of Jamal al-din we see part of the intellectual genealogy of
pan-Islamism, an ideology predicated on a shared trans-regional identity,
the success of which was born from the increased possibilities of

communication and travel offered by the nineteenth century. A fitting illustration is the influence Jamal al-din later had on the aforementioned poet Aqa Khan Kirmani during their shared exile in that other great port of Istanbul.

Muslims like Jamal al-din 'al-Afghani' were by no means the only Iranian religious figures to travel between Iran and Bombay during this period. For the nineteenth century also saw the resuming of ties between the Zoroastrian community of Yazd in central Iran and their Parsi co-religionists in India, where the Parsis' prominent role in the development of Bombay afforded them the wealth to fund missionary and educational expeditions to Yazd (Boyce 1969). The memory of the Parsis' ancestral connections with Iran had earlier been maintained – and indeed revived – by the sixteenth century Indo-Persian poem, the *Qissah-ye-Sanjan*, which described the journey of the community founders from Iran to Gujarat in epic detail. With the coming of print in the nineteenth century the role of writing in maintaining such trans-oceanic identities received a new impetus. Like the Muslim and Jewish communities of the western Indian Ocean, the Parsi Zoroastrians also made use of Bombay's publishing industry to communicate with their co-religionists across the Arabian Sea. This was principally achieved through the export of religious literature, but by the turn of the twentieth century Parsi publishing ventures also included travel guides helping young Indian Zoroastrians explore their Iranian 'homeland'. More immediately influential in Iran, however, was the dispatching of funds from Bombay for the foundation of new 'fire temples', or *atashkadahs* (Green 2000). In such ways, the renewal of Zoroastrian contact between the ports of India and the trading cities of central Iran played an important part in the re-vitalisation of an older trans-regional Persianate religious culture through the use of a colonial trade network that centred on Bombay. For nineteenth century Bombay provided intellectual, technical and financial resources that could be exported along older travel routes re-invigorated by the Bombay trade to effect far-reaching social change in Iran. The rise to educational, mercantile and briefly cultural prominence of the small Zoroastrian community in twentieth century Iran was only one of the consequences of the Indo-Iranian colonial encounter.

New Colonial Itineraries: Sufi Migrations to Natal

The links between Iranian and Indian Muslim religious forms, and India's role as the refuge of an older Persianate religious culture, are also relevant to the spread of Sufi models of Islam from India to South Africa.[20] Once again, here India exported religious forms that, though in no sense 'un-Indian', were nonetheless the legacy of an older and wider Persianate culture that in the pre-colonial era connected India to Anatolia and Central Asia no less than Iran. In contrast to other regions of the Indian Ocean littoral, the introduction of Islam to southern Africa occurred through the movement of people under the influence of the European colonial powers. The earliest Muslim community in southern Africa emerged through the transport of political exiles from the Indonesian archipelago and the settling of slaves of African, Indonesian and Indian origin by the Dutch East India Company (Bradlow and Cairns 1978; Shell 2000). Settled around the Cape, this early community developed its own patron saint in the figure of the exiled Indonesian scholar Shaykh Yusuf al-Maqasari (d.1699). Shaykh Yusuf's connections with Sufism are unclear, though he may have had links with the Khalwati order. Nonetheless, his tomb (*kramat*, from Arabic *karama*, 'miracle') outside Cape Town came, along with other lesser shrines in the region, to form a local geography of pilgrimage for the Muslims of the Cape (Greyling 1980; Tayob 1999: 23). Along with pilgrimages to these shrines, the Cape Muslims also developed a tradition of ecstatic rituals (known as *ratiep* or less often as *khalifah*) involving the piercing of the body with skewers or swords. The terminology and form of these rituals bear strong similarities with faith performances in other Muslim regions, particularly the ritual displays of Rifaʿi and Hamadsha dervishes.[21] Like the Sufi ritual forms that Ghulam Muhammad would later introduce to Natal from India, the popularity of the *ratiep* among the 'Malay' Muslims of the Cape reflected the way in which rituals acted as a palimpsest of migration. A corruption of the Arabic term *ratib* denoting

---

20 On the introduction of Sufism to Malawi by Zanzibari Arabs during the same period, see Thorold (2001).

21 For an early description of the *ratiep* ritual in Cape Town, see Cole (1852: 44–6).

supererogatory prayers or the chanting of litanies, *ratiep* rituals were a popular part of Muslim practice in the Indonesian archipelago where the ancestors of most of the Cape Muslims originated. Several such performances in Acheh were described at the turn of the twentieth century by Snouck Hurgronje; these included musical gatherings centring on ecstatic self-mutilation with daggers or swords of the kind also associated with the Cape Muslims (Hurgronje 1906: vol.2, 251– 57).[22] In this way Indonesian Muslims introduced to southern Africa elements of Islam that had earlier been brought to South-east Asia through trans-oceanic contacts with Arabia.

While reflecting some of the broader patterns of the Cape Muslim experience, the introduction of Islam to Natal came through the migration of indentured labourers under British control during the 1860s and then, in a second movement, from the 1870s onwards (Argyle 1986; Kuper 1960; Rochlin 1940–42). The largest number of early labourers was shipped from Madras, with between seven and ten per cent of the first shipments of 1860–68 consisting of Muslims (Shell 2000: 339). But despite the arrival of small numbers of Zanzibar 'Arab' migrants, the Muslim community that gradually emerged in Natal remained overwhelmingly of Indian origin. Colonial echoes of an earlier Persianate cosmopolitanism are heard in the introduction of the Chishti order to Natal during the 1890s by the Indian Sufi, Ghulam Muhammad Habibi (known in South Africa as Soofie Saheb), and the cult that he initiated around the grave of the earlier Indian – supposedly Sufi – migrant, Shaykh Ahmad. According to the historical tradition preserved by his followers, Shaykh Ahmad sailed to Durban as part of the earliest shipment of labourers from Madras, having traditionally been held to have arrived in Natal on the *Truro* in November 1860 to work in the sugar cane fields around Durban (Soofie and Soofie n.d.: 42). Although a substantial hagiographical tradition has grown up around this figure under his local moniker of Badsha Peer (Urdu *badshah pir*, 'emperor of spiritual masters'), almost nothing is known firmly about his

---

22 The term *ratib* is also used for similar Sufi rituals in the Lakshadweep Islands; see Gabriel (2003).

life. He does, however, appear to have been released early from his indenture due to insanity, a state that was later interpreted through the Sufi idiom of mystical enrapture (*jazb*).[23] Upon his death in 1894 or 1895 Shaykh Ahmad was buried in Durban's Brook Street Cemetery without being accorded any special status among the city's Muslims (Soofie and Essop 2003: 11).

More important in the evolution of the Natal Muslim community was the role of Ghulam Muhammad Habibi, whose own biography and connection to a Sufi order are more clear (Smith 1969; Soofie and Soofie n.d.).[24] Biographical accounts of Ghulam Muhammad claim that he was born around 1848 near to the town of Ratnagiri in the Bombay Presidency to a family of Muslim scholars and judges (*qadis*).[25] Despite this, the Certificate of Domicile with which he was later issued in Durban in 1909 suggests that he was actually born in Bombay around 1863. Since a great many Ratnagiri Muslims migrated to Bombay in the second half of the nineteenth century, we may conclude that Ghulam Muhammad was either a first or second-generation migrant to Bombay from Ratnagiri, who may nevertheless have maintained his connections with the Ratnagiri region.[26] Ghulam Muhammad claimed to be of Arab descent, as testified in a family genealogical document (*shajara*). Such ancestries were not uncommon among the Konkani Muslims, and the

---

23 A similar story of perceived insanity and release from colonial employment occurs in the oral tradition of Shaykh Ahmad's contemporary, Banne Miyan, whom we have discussed earlier. In this tradition, Banne Miyan was released from service in the Hyderabad Contingent after his British officers mistook his state of religious ecstasy for insanity. On other religious aspects of sainthood and madness in colonial India, see Green forthcoming.

24 G.R. Smith's (1969) short study was based largely on oral testimony collected in Durban in the 1960s, while Soofie and Soofie (n.d.) expand upon this oral tradition with documentation collected at the shrine of Ghulam Muhammad in Durban.

25 Soofie and Soofie (n.d.: 45), citing a family genealogical document dated 1185/1771 referring to Ghulam Muhammad's ancestors. During this period Ratnagiri was also the home of a more famous exile, the deposed Burmese ruler Thibaw.

26 On the Ratnagiri District and its people, see Hunter *et al.* (1908–31: 244–58). By 1901, Muslims represented 7 percent of the population of the District, whose main language was Konkani. On the earlier maritime history of this community, see Chakravarti (1986 and 1998).

small ports of the Konkan upheld trading and pilgrimage links with the Arabian peninsula well into the colonial period. Despite their small numbers, the Konkani Muslims were also able to maintain a slender tradition of Arabic learning. According to the official version of Ghulam Muhammad's biography, after the death of his father in 1872 he followed in his footsteps to become imam of his local community in Ratnagiri, before later travelling to Bombay to make the *hajj* in 1892 (Soofie and Soofie n.d.: 47). After completing the pilgrimage, like many other Indian Muslims of the period, Ghulam Muhammad travelled on to Baghdad in order to visit the shrine of 'Abd al-Qadir Jilani (d.1166), where he claimed he was initiated into the Qadiriyya order by the Ottoman Sufi, Ghulam Mustafa Effendi Qadiri.[27] After a short period of residence in Baghdad, Ghulam Muhammad returned to Bombay, where he heard of the circle that had gathered around the Chishti Sufi master Habib 'Ali Shah (d.1906) in the new port district of Mazgawn. After becoming Habib 'Ali Shah's disciple, Ghulam Muhammad moved to Kalyan, a small town lying thirty-three miles to the north-east of Bombay with a well-established Muslim community, where he resumed his earlier role as an imam.[28]

Habib 'Ali Shah had earlier moved to Bombay from his home city of Hyderabad, a move that echoes the migration of other Sufi figures to the colonial metropolis discussed earlier. Habib 'Ali Shah's presence in the

---

27 An account of another western Indian Sufi pilgrim to Baghdad in the same period appears in *A'zam al-karamat*, where the Indian pilgrim Mirza Sahib encounters a Qadiri Sufi of Baghdad called Mustafa Sahib. It is unclear if these two figures in Baghdad with similar names are connected; see Khān n.d: 34. Indian pilgrims to the shrine of 'Abd al-Qadir Jilani in Baghdad were also observed at the beginning of the twentieth century by the great French Islamicist, Louis Massignon (1883–1962). He described them as largely indigent, gathering in small isolated bands, and usually found camping beside the mosque of Shihab al-din Suhrawardi (Massignon 1908: 650). However, Massignon's own journey to Baghdad possessed its religious elements, for it was here in 1908 that he was accused of spying and, in the misery of his brief imprisonment, received the numenous visitation from an otherworldly 'stranger' that would alter the course of his career. On this most curious of colonial escapades, see Massignon (1962: 66-67).

28 On the relationship between Ghulam Muhammad and Habib 'Ali Shah, see Tajam al-Husayn 1331/1912. On Kalyan, see Hunter *et al.* 1908–31: vol. 14, 322–23.

city, however, is of special interest in that he represented one of the most important Sufi lineages active in colonial India, having been the follower of the North Indian Chishti Sufi Hafiz ᶜAli Shah Khayrabadi (d.1850) (Nizāmī 1405/1985: 667–84). Hafiz ᶜAli Shah had established a Sufi lodge and madrasa in his home town of Khayrabad near Lucknow in imitation of those founded by his own master Sulayman Tawnsawi (d.1851) in Punjab (Nizāmī 1405/1985: 608–66, Phillott 1908). Habib ᶜAli Shah's move to Mazgawn and his establishment of a lodge and large circle of followers there is an illustration of the continuity of traditional Muslim religious activity in colonial Bombay.[29] In turn, Ghulam Muhammad's own relocation to the hinterland of Bombay during the early 1890s reflected a much larger migration of Konkani Muslims into the city during his lifetime, a period in which his home district of Ratnagiri was regarded as 'the great recruiting ground of the Bombay Presidency'(Hunter *et al.* 1908–31: vol. 21, 250).[30] Reflected in Ghulam Muhammad's journey to Mecca and Baghdad was Bombay's role in the re-establishment of contacts between Konkani Muslims and the Arab homelands of their ancestors. Elements of such sea journeys remained associated with Habib ᶜAli Shah even after the return of his cadaver to Hyderabad for burial in 1906, despite the location of his shrine hundreds of miles from the coast. The oral tradition of his shrine contains several miraculous legends of Habib ᶜAli Shah helping sailors and merchants. In one of these tales Habib ᶜAli Shah issues a warning to a merchant not to set sail on a voyage, but the advice is ignored and when the ship sinks, as Habib ᶜAli Shah had foreseen, the saint is forced to miraculously rescue his merchant follower from the waves. As in the story of Muᶜiz al-din Abposh recounted in the first section, back on dry land Habib ᶜAli

---

29 On Habib ᶜAli Shah, see Chishti 2004. On the shrine of Makhdum ᶜAli in Bombay, where in the early twentieth century Church Missionary Society volunteers preached to the mixed Muslim and Hindu pilgrims, see Qaisary 1999.

30 In 1872, there were 71,000 people registered as born in Ratnagiri District resident in Bombay, a figure that by 1901 had risen to 145,000.

Shah's sleeve was seen at the moment of the rescue to be dripping with seawater.[31]

As a follower of Habib 'Ali Shah during his years in Mazgawn, Ghulam Muhammad's residence in the Bombay region played a central role in the journeys that would ultimately render him a saint in his own right. For in 1895, Ghulam Muhammad travelled from Bombay to Durban to bring the Sufi message to its Indian population in the wake of the earlier migration of indentured labourers and the more recent movement of the 'Passenger Indian' migrants who travelled to Natal from the 1890s to set themselves up in small businesses. Ghulam Muhammad seems to have been unsuccessful on his first journey, and over the next two decades returned to India several times, eventually persuading other male members of his family to join him in classic migrant strategy. As with the other Sufi sea journeys we have described, those of Ghulam Muhammad to Durban are similarly connected with miraculous events, including the saint purifying water and curing dysentery on board (Smith 1969: 274; Soofie and Soofie n.d.: 76).

Echoing the role of the shrine of Shaykh Yusuf among the Muslims of the Cape and the shrines of numerous other saintly community founders in India, one of Ghulam Muhammad's earliest activities was to locate the tomb of the earlier 'Sufi' migrant Shaykh Ahmad in Durban and encourage local Muslims to regard it as a place of pilgrimage. The tradition of Shaykh Ahmad's arrival on the first vessel to bring Indian labourers from Madras further emphasised his role as a community founder. Ghulam Muhammad seems to have been responsible for the construction of an early wood and iron shelter above the grave soon after his arrival in Durban, and by 1919 this was replaced by a concrete domed mausoleum in the style of the Sufi shrines of India (Soofie and Essop 2003: 12–13). Around this new saintly geography, Ghulam Muhammad began to organise the rituals of the death anniversary ('*urs*) of Shaykh Ahmad in reflection of the popular festivals that had been celebrated at the shrines of the Sufi saints of India for the previous six

---

31 This narrative was recounted to me at the shrine of Habib 'Ali Shah in Hyderabad on 26th July 2005 by Faisal Yar Khan Habibi.

centuries. While Ghulam Muhammad was himself a Konkani Muslim, the ʿurs rituals which he sponsored were no less familiar a ritual and festive idiom for the Tamils who made up so large a proportion of Natal's Hindu and Muslim community.[32] During his own lifetime a mausoleum was also constructed for Ghulam Muhammad himself, where after his death in 1911 his own ʿurs was celebrated under the leadership of the lineage of Sufi successors (*sajjadah nashins*) that was founded from among his family.[33] Along with the ʿurs, Ghulam Muhammad also promoted other aspects of Muslim piety familiar to a constituency of Indian origin. These ranged from formal prayers (*salat*) and meditation (*zikr*) sessions to the celebration of *Muharram* with processions from the Durban lodge bearing representations of the standard (ʿ*alam*) and coffin (*taʿziyah*) of al-Husayn. These processions seem to have been established to counter the popularity of Tamil Hindu *kavadi* processions among the city's Muslims (Soofie and Soofie n.d.: 66–7).[34] Popular processions thus acted as a powerful means of symbolically claiming urban territory for Durban's Muslim community, though in Natal as in India the processions would in turn later dissolve into controversies concerning the maintenance of Shiʿi and Sunni community boundaries.[35]

Ghulam Muhammad introduced to Natal elements of earlier Persian Sufi practices that had been brought to India by Iranian and Central Asian migrants centuries earlier. Having been introduced to Northern India from Iran during the late thirteenth century, the rituals of the ʿurs were themselves a reflection of this older trans-regional Persianate culture that India had in many respects preserved better than Iran. Such traditions nonetheless formed a widely intelligible religious idiom in India and as a consequence of Ghulam Muhammad's efforts a number of

---

32 On the ʿurs and other aspects of popular Muslim piety in nineteenth century Tamil Nadu, see Bayly (1989).

33 Ghulam Muhammad's obituary, which appeared in the *Natal Mercury* (1ˢᵗ July 1911; repr. In Soofie and Soofie n.d.: 76), described the large number of Muslim merchants among the hundreds of other devotees present at his funeral.

34 On the performance of *kavadi* and other trance rituals among Natal's Hindus, see Kuper (1960: 217–35).

35 On *Muharram* processions and the claiming of public space, see Schubel (1993).

Hindus seem to have converted to Islam at his hands (Soofie and Soofie n.d.: 73). Moreover, despite the general maintenance of social boundaries between the ethnically distinct Cape and Natal Muslims during this period, the different ritual practices of the Cape and Natal Muslims did at times move between the two communities. The *ratiep* spread to Natal, where it was incorporated into the *mawlid* as well as Indian wedding celebrations, while in the middle of the nineteenth century it was even reported to have become popular among English Christians at the Cape (Duff-Gordon 1927: 85). Subject to re-appropriation and re-interpretation over time, the multiple journeys of such ritual idioms reflect the easy transferability of this kind of embodied religiosity of holy men and cult practices. The institutionalisation of Ghulam Muhammad's and Shaykh Ahmad's sainthood through architecture and ritual was complemented in 1903 by the establishment of a madrasa in Durban and, over the next eight years, by a wider network of combined *khanaqah*-madrasas that followed the migration of Indian Muslims into the Transvaal and elsewhere. These institutions served as promoters of Urdu learning and the religious curricula that had developed in Indian madrasas during the nineteenth century. The foundation of these religious centres and a number of orphanages for Muslim children was supported by the growing Indian merchant community in Natal, and Ghulam Muhammad was able to attract the philanthropy of Parsi as well as Muslim merchants.[36]

Ghulam Muhammad's journeys to Natal need to be seen within a wider context of religious preceptors and practices moving between India and Natal during this period. Members of the neo-Hindu reformist group Arya Samaj also travelled to Natal at this time, viewing the Hindu community that had developed from the region's indentured labourers as ripe for instruction (Diesel and Maxwell 1993).[37] Ghulam Muhammad's activities should be seen as bringing a similarly modernist, closely defined

---

36 On this merchant community, see Padayachee and Morrell (1991). Fittingly, the signature of Mohandas Gandhi appears on at least one of the legal documents relating to the early purchase of properties by Ghulam Muhammad and his followers.

37 On Sufi-inspired responses to Arya Samaj proselytisation in India at this time, see Sikand (1997).

paradigm of Muslim practice and identity to a disparate and even dispirited Muslim minority, a process that was reflected among East Africa's Isma'ili communities at the same time (Shodhan 1999). Ghulam Muhammad's role in the promotion of Urdu in Natal is in this sense particularly important, sponsoring overseas the role that Urdu was acquiring in India during this period as the proper language of the Indian Muslim. Here Ghulam Muhammad followed more specific currents of linguistic change in his own Konkani community, among whom the use of Urdu in addition to Konkani spread greatly during the early twentieth century, in part as a result of Konkani migration to Bombay (Khalidi 2000: 141–42). Through the promotion of an 'Islamic' language, a sacred geography and the rituals to accompany it, Ghulam Muhammad formulated a distinctly Muslim identity among Natal's predominantly Tamil Indian community that would mark the boundary between different members of a labouring class. Here was an Indian Sufi reform movement setting down roots in African soil.

We remarked earlier upon the significance of accounts of Indian Muslim pilgrims to Mecca praying to their community saints in India rather than to the Prophet for help at sea. The activities of Ghulam Muhammad in Natal reflect this picture of an Islam that was anchored to Indian ground even as it was orientated in the direction of Mecca. Given the centrifugal quality that the Hijaz can easily assume in discussions of Islam in the western Indian Ocean, it is important to emphasise alternative sacred Muslim geographies around this vast region. For in establishing a mausoleum in Durban for Shaykh Ahmad, and then in turn for himself, Ghulam Muhammad was not merely creating a geography of pilgrimage for the Muslims of Natal. He was also creating one that was orientated towards the Indian shrines of his own predecessors in the Chishti order. For over the course of the decades after the death of Ghulam Muhammad, pilgrims from Durban began to travel to the death anniversary of the saint's master Habib 'Ali Shah in Hyderabad. Rather than fading with time, with the coming of affordable air travel in the last decades of the twentieth century these ties of pilgrimage received a new lease of life.[38]

Conclusions

Through the establishment of the Chishti shrines of Natal, Indian Islam had come full circle, from representing the far reach of Sufi traditions originating in Western and Central Asia during the medieval period to itself becoming the focal point of a new geography of pilgrimage on African soil during the colonial era. Occurring at the same time among Indians in Singapore, this process of diasporic sainthood would later be repeated in the development of Sufi traditions of South Asian origin in Britain and the United States (Geaves 2000; Inayat Khan 2003). This process represents neither the straightforward localisation of Islam nor its Arabocentric trans-nationalisation.[39] The journey of Ghulam Muhammad to Natal was only part of a much wider pattern of Sufi migrations in the western Indian Ocean during the nineteenth century through which older modes of circulation were maintained and in some cases renewed. As the cosmopolitan refuge of numerous migrant communities from within and without India, colonial Bombay played an important part in these movements. Here we see Bombay acting as a zone of transit for Sufi no less than other Muslim migrants and so serving to connect trends in Indian Islam with developments in Arabia, Iran and southern Africa.

Amid this focus on circulation as historical process, more individual experiences of the nineteenth century Indian Ocean world are recorded in such Sufi travelogues as those of Zayn al-ʿAbidin Shirwani, Safi ʿAli Shah and Hajji Pirzadah. In their accounts of interaction between members of different communities in the western Indian Ocean and their humane interest in the diverse peoples whom they describe, such personal accounts are testament to the cosmopolitanism that sometimes emerged from the Muslim culture of travel. Yet such writings remained

---

38 Based on interviews carried out at the shrine of Habib ʿAli Shah in Hyderabad, July 2005.
39 On similar issues in other Sufi diasporas, see Gardner (1995), Thorold (1997) and Werbner (1995).

deeply conscious of the weight of tradition, which they deliberately sought to pass on through the colonial era. For in a reflection of the earlier history of migration in Muslim societies, Sufis have always borne a close relationship with travel as both practice and discursive ideal (Brunel 1955; Eickelman and Piscatori 1990; Netton 1996). The early and subsequently classic Sufi manuals presented travel as one of the key duties of the aspiring Sufi, while the language of travel later found myriad expression in the poetry and songs through which Sufism was able to embed itself in the literary cultures of its host societies. While oceanic metaphors occur in several sections of the Quran, in its maritime form this Sufi discourse of travel stretched back at least as far as the tenth century Iraqi writer Niffari (d. after 977), whose *Kitab al-mawaqif* had described the mystical path in terms of a perilous sea journey (Niffarī 1935: Arabic text 7, translation 31). We must therefore recognise the interplay of the practice and discourse of travel in Islamic tradition through which cultural ideals of travel frequently intertwined themselves with accounts of real and imagined journeys. As the stories of miraculous sea rescues demonstrate, Sufis did not necessarily need to leave their homes to vicariously cross the ocean, for they were carried in the hearts of those travellers who relied on them for protection at sea and remembered them on reaching their destinations. Such bonds of devotion, protection and memory in turn knotted the diasporic communities of the western Indian Ocean into networks of pilgrimage and remembrance with the lands of their ancestors across the sea.

Bibliography

ʿAbbās ʿAlī, M. 1975. *Qissah-e-ghamgīn* (ed. S.C. Misra). Baroda: Maharaja Sayajirao University of Baroda.

Algar, H. 1975. 'Mahallati, Aga Khan, Sayyid Hasan Ali Shah', in *Encyclopaedia of Islam* 2, Leiden: Brill.

Anon. n.d. *Majmūʿah: Hālāt-e-Hazrat Shāh Wajīh al-dīn ʿAlawī Gujarātī.* Bombay: Matbaʿa-ye-Shihābī.

Arberry, A.J. 1964. *The Koran Interpreted.* Oxford: Oxford University Press.

Argyle, W.J. 1986. 'The Migration of Indian Muslims to East and South Africa: Some Preliminary Comparisons', in M. Gaborieau (ed.), *Islam et société en Asie du Sud [Purusartha* 9]. Paris: Éditions de l'École des Hautes Études en Sciences Sociales.

Balkhī, M.ibn A.W. 1980. *Bahr al-asrār fī manāqib al-akhyār: safarnāmah-ye-Hind wa Saylān* (ed. Riyāz al-Islām). Karachi: Institute of Central & West Asian Studies.

Bang, A.K. 2003. *Sufis and Scholars of the Sea. Family Networks in East Africa, 1860–1925.* London: RoutledgeCurzon.

Basu, H. 1995. *Habshi-Sklaven, Sidi-Fakire: Muslimische Heiligenverehrung im westlichen Indien.* Berlin: Das Arabische Buch.

Bayly, S. 1989. *Saints, Goddesses and Kings: Muslims and Christians in South Indian Society, 1700–1900.* Cambridge: Cambridge University Press.

Boyce, M. 1969. 'Manekji Limji Hataria in Iran', in N.D. Manochehr-Homji and M.F. Kanga (eds), *K.R. Cama Oriental Institute Golden Jubilee Volume.* Bombay: K.R. Cama Oriental Institute.

Bradlow, F.R., and M. Cairns 1978. *The Early Cape Muslims: A Study of their Mosques, Genealogy and Origins.* Cape Town: A.A. Balkema.

Brown, K.L. 1976. *People of Salé: Tradition and Change in a Moroccan City, 1830–1930.* Manchester: Manchester University Press.

Brunel, R. 1955. *Le monachisme errant dans l'Islam: Sidi Heddi et les Heddāwa.* Paris: Librairie Larose.

Catlin-Jairazbhoy, H., and E.A. Alpers (eds) 2004. *Sidis and Scholars: Essays on African Indians.* Noida: Rainbow Publishers.

Chakravarti, R. 1986. 'Merchants of Konkan', *Indian Economic and Social History Review,* 23.2.

—— 1998. 'Coastal Trade and Voyages in Konkan: The Early Medieval Scenario', *Indian Economic and Social History Review*, 35.2.

Chishti, N.K. (trans.) 2004. *Life History of Khwaja Habib Ali Shah [Zikr-e-Habib]*. Durban: Soofie Saheb Badsha Peer Darbar.

Cole, A.W. 1852. *The Cape and the Kafirs, or Notes of Five Years Residence in South Africa*. London: Richard Bentley.

Cole, J.R.I. 1988. *Roots of North Indian Shi'ism in Iran and Iraq: Religion and State in Awadh, 1722–1859*. Berkeley: University of California Press.

Dadvar, A. 1999. *Iranians in Mughal Politics and Society, 1606–1658*. Delhi: Gyan Publishing House.

Dale, S.F. 1980. *Islamic Society on the South Asian Frontier: The Mappilas of Malabar, 1498–1922*. Oxford: Clarendon Press.

—— 1997. 'The Hadhrami Diaspora in South-Western India: The Role of the Sayyids of the Malabar Coast', in U. Freitag and W.G. Clarence-Smith (eds), *Hadhrami Traders, Scholars, and Statesmen in the Indian Ocean, 1750s–1960s*. Leiden: Brill.

Diesel, A., and P. Maxwell 1993. *Hinduism in Natal: A Brief Guide*. Pietermaritzburg: University of Natal Press.

Digby, S. 1991. 'An Eighteenth Century Narrative of a Journey from Bengal to Britain: Munshī Ismā'īl's *New History*', in C. Shackle (ed.), *Urdu and Muslim South Asia: Studies in Honour of Ralph Russell*. Delhi: Oxford University Press.

—— 1999. 'Beyond the Ocean: Perceptions of Overseas in Indo-Persian Sources of the Mughal Period', *Studies in History*, 15.2.

Duff-Gordon, Lady 1927. *Letters from the Cape*. London: Oxford University Press.

Eaton, R.M. 1993. *The Rise of Islam and the Bengal Frontier, 1204–1760*. Berkeley: University of California Press.

Eickelman, D.F., and J. Piscatori (eds) 1990. *Muslim Travellers: Pilgrimage, Migration and the Imagination*. Berkeley: University of California Press.

Farahani, Mirza Husayn. 1990. *A Shi'ite Pilgrimage to Mecca (1885–1886): The Safarnāmeh of Mirzā Mohammad Hosayn Farāhāni*. (trans. and eds M. Gulzar and E.L. Daniel). Austin: University of Austin Press.

Franke, P. 2000. *Begegnung mit Khidr: Quellenstudien zum Imaginären im traditionellen Islam*. Stuttgart: F. Steiner.

Fusfeld, W. 1988. 'The Boundaries of Islam and Infidelity', in K. Ewing (ed.), *Sharīʿat and Ambiguity in South Asian Islam*. Berkeley: University of California Press.

Gabriel, T. 2003. 'Islamic Mystics of the Lakshadweep Islands', in C. Partridge and T. Gabriel (eds), *Mysticisms East and West*. Carlisle: Paternoster Press.

Gardner, K. 1995. 'Mullahs, Migrants, Miracles: Travel and Transformation in Sylhet', in T.N. Madan (ed.), *Muslim Communities of South Asia: Culture, Society, and Power*. Delhi: Manohar.

Geaves, R. 2000. *The Sufis of Britain: An Exploration of Muslim Identity*. Cardiff: Cardiff Academic Press.

Graham, T. 1999. 'The Niʿmatuʾllāhī Order under Safavid Suppression and in Indian Exile', in L. Lewisohn and D. Morgan (eds), *The Heritage of Sufism. Vol. 3: Late Classical Persianate Sufism*. Oxford: Oneworld.

Green, N.S. 2000. 'The Survival of Zoroastrianism in Yazd', *Iran: Journal of Persian Studies*, 38.

—— 2003. 'Migrant Sufis and Sacred Space in South Asian Islam', *Contemporary South Asia*, 12.4.

—— 2004. A Persian Sufi in British India: The Travels of Mīrzā Hasan Safī ʿAlī Shāh (1251/1835–1316/1899)', *Iran: Journal of Persian Studies*, 42.

—— forthcoming. 'The *Faqir* and the Subalterns: Mapping the Holy Man in Colonial South Asia', *Journal of Asian History*.

Greyling, C. 1980. 'Schech Yusuf: The Founder of Islam in South Africa', *Religion in Southern Africa*, 1.1.

Harawī, Khwājah Niʿmat Allāh ibn Habīb Allāh 1962. *Tārīkh-e-Khān Jahānī wa Makhzan-e-Afghānī*, vol. 1&2. (ed. S.M. Imām al-dīn). Dacca: Asiatic Society of Pakistan.

Heber, R. 1873. *Narrative of a Journey through the Upper Provinces of India, from Calcutta to Bombay, 1824–1825*, vol. 1&2. London: John Murray.

Hill, B.S. 2003–04. 'Hebrew Printing in Baghdad', *Report of the Oxford Centre for Hebrew and Jewish Studies*.

Homāyūnī, M. 1371/1992. *Tārīkh-e-silsilahā-ye-tarīqah-ye-niʿmatullāhiyyah dar īrān*. London: Bonyād-e-ʿIrfān-e-Mawlānā.

Hourani, A. 1981. *The Emergence of the Modern Middle East*. London: Macmillan.

Hunter, W.W., J.S. Cotton, R. Burn and W.S. Meyer (eds) 1908–1931. *Imperial Gazetteer of India*, 25 vols. Oxford: Clarendon Press.

Hurgronje, C.S. 1906. *The Achehnese*, vols 1&2. (trans. A.W.S. O'Sullivan). Leiden: E.J. Brill.

Inayat Khan, Z. (ed.) 2003. *A Pearl in Wine: Essays on the Life, Music and Sufism of Hazrat Inayat Khan*. New Lebanon, NY: Omega Publications.

Insoll, T. 2003. *The Archaeology of Islam in Sub-Saharan Africa*. Cambridge: Cambridge University Press.

I'tisām al-dīn, M. 1995. *Shigarfnāmah-e-wilāyat*. (Urdu trans. A. H. Nūrānī). Patna: Khoda Baksh Public Library.

Keddie, N.R. 1972. *Sayyid Jamāl ad-Dīn 'al-Afghānī': A Political Biography*. Berkeley: University of California Press.

Khalidi, O. 2000. 'Konkani Muslims: An Introduction', *Islamic Culture*, 74.1.

Khān, Muhammad Ismāʿīl. n.d. [*c*.1921]. *Aʿzam al-karāmāt*. Awrangābād: Muʿīn Prēs.

Kuper, H. 1960. *Indian People in Natal*. Pietermaritzburg: University of Natal Press.

Lawrence, B.B. 1982. 'Islam in India: The Function of Institutional Sufism in the Islamization of Rajasthan, Gujarat and Kashmir', *Contributions to Asian Studies*, 17.

Machalski, F. 1965. *La Littérature de l'Iran contemporain*, vol. 1&2. Wrocław: Zakład Narodowy Imienia Ossolinskich.

al-Madanī, Sayyid Ibrāhīm al-Hussayni. 1292/1875. *Zamīr al-Insān*. ms. Bombay University Library: vol. 56, no. 99.

Massignon, L. 1908. 'Les pélerinages populaires à Baghdad', *Revue du Monde Musulman*, 6.12.

—— 1962. *Parole donnée*. Paris: Julliard.

Mohiuddin, M and I.K. Poonawala n.d. 'Bombay: Persian Muslim Communities', in *Encyclopaedia Iranica*.

Netton, I.R. 1996. *Seek Knowledge: Thought and Travel in the House of Islam*. Richmond: Curzon Press.

Niffarī, Muhammad ibn ʿAbd al-Jabbār. 1935. *The Mawáqif and Mukhátabát of Muhammad Ibn ʿAbdi 'l-Jabbár al-Niffarí*. (ed. and trans. A.J. Arberry). London: Luzac.

Nizāmī, Khalīq Ahmad 1405/1985. *Tārīkh-e-Mashā'ikh-e-Chisht*. Dilhī: Publik Āfset Prēs.

Norris, H.T (trans.) 1977. *The Pilgrimage of Ahmad, Son of the Little Bird of Paradise: An Account of a 19th Century Pilgrimage from Mauritania to Mecca*. Warminster: Aris and Phillips.

Padayachee V., and R. Morrell 1991. 'Indian Merchants and Dukawallahs in the Natal Economy, *c*.1875–1914', *Journal of Southern African Studies*, 17.

Peters, F.E. 1994. *The Hajj: The Muslim Pilgrimage to Mecca and the Holy Places*. Princeton: Princeton University Press.

Phillott, D.C. 1908. 'Note on the Shrine at Taunsa', *Journal of the Asiatic Society of Bengal*, 4.1.

Pīrzādah, Hājī Muhammad ᶜAlī. 1342–43/1963–65. *Safarnāmah-ye-Hājī Pīrzādah*, vol. 1&2. (ed. Hāfiz Farmān-farmā'iyān). Tehran: Dānishgāh-e-Tihrān.

Pourjavady, N., and P. Lamborn-Wilson 1975. 'Ismāᶜīlīs and Niᶜmatullāhīs', *Studia Islamica*, 41.

Qaisary, M.A.M.P. 1999. *The Life History of Hazrat Shaikh Makhdum Ali Paro*. Mumbai: Ghazali Typesetters.

Raverty, H.G. 1862. *Selections from the Poetry of the Afghans, from the Sixteenth to the Nineteenth Century*. London: Williams and Norgate.

Ridgeon, L. 2004. 'Ahmad Kasravi's Criticisms of Edward Granville Browne', *Iran: Journal of Persian Studies*, 42.

Rochlin, S.A. 1940–42. 'Aspects of Islam in Nineteenth-Century South Africa', *Bulletin of the School of Oriental and African Studies*, 10.

Royce, W.R. 1979. *Mir Maᶜsum ᶜAli Shah and the Niᶜmat Allahi Revival, 1776–77 to 1796–97*. Unpublished PhD dissertation. Princeton University.

Sayf al-Dawla, S.M. 1363/1985. *Safarnāmah-ye-Makkah*. (ed. A.A. Khudāparast) Tehran: Nashr-e-Nayy.

Safī ᶜAlī Shāh n.d. *Dīwān-e-Safī ᶜAlī Shāh hamrāh bā masnawī-ye-bahr al-haqā'iq*. Tehran: Intishārāt-e-Safī ᶜAlī Shāh.

—— Safī ᶜAlī Shāh 1379s/2000. *Zubdat al-asrār*. Tehran: Intishārāt-e-Safī ᶜAlī Shāh.

Schubel, V.J. 1993. *Religious Performance in Contemporary Islam: Shiᶜi Devotional Rituals in South Asia*. Columbia: University of South Carolina Press.

Shell, R.C-H. 2000. 'Islam in Southern Africa, 1652–1998', in N. Levtzion and R.L. Pouwels (eds), *The History of Islam in Africa*. Oxford: James Currey.

Shīrāzī, Nā'ib al-Sadr. 1339–45/1960–66. *Tarā'iq al-haqā'iq*, vol. 1–3. Tehran: Kitābkhānah-ye-Baranī.

Shīrāzī, M.S. 1364/1985. *Majmūʿah-e-safarnāmahhā-ye-Mīrzā Sālih Shīrāzī*. (ed. Ghulām Husayn Mīrzā Sālih). Tehran: Nashr-e-Tārīkh-e-Īrān.

Shīrwānī, Z.al-ʿĀ. n.d. (c.1985). *Riyāz al-siyāhah*. (ed. Asghār Hāmid Rabbānī). Tehran: Saʿdī.

Shodhan, A. 1999. 'Legal Formulation of the Question of Community: Defining the Khoja Collective', *Indian Social Science Review*, 1.1.

Shureef, J. 1991 [1863]. *Qanoon-e Islam, or the Customs of the Mussulmans of India*. Madras: Asian Educational Services.

Sidi Ali Reïs 1899. *The Travels and Adventures of the Turkish Admiral Sidi Ali Reïs*. (trans. A. Vambéry). London: Luzac.

Sikand, Y.S. 1997. 'The *Fitna* of *Irtidad*: Muslim Missionary Response to the *Shuddhi* of Arya Samaj in Early Twentieth Century India', *Journal of Muslim Minority Affairs*, 17.1.

Smith, G.R. 1969. 'A Muslim Saint in South Africa', *African Studies*, 28.4.

Soofie, A.A., and Essop, O.M. (eds) 2003. *His Exalted Eminence Hazrath Sheikh Sayyid Ahmed Badsha Peer*. Durban: Impress Press.

Soofie, S.M.S., and S-A.A. Soofie n.d. [c.2002]. *Hazrath Soofie Saheb & His Khanqahs*. Durban: Soofie Saheb Badsha Peer Darbar.

Subrahmanyam, S. 1992. 'Iranians Abroad: Intra-Asian Elite Migration and Early Modern State Formation', *Journal of Asian Studies*, 51.2.

Tajam al-Husayn, Mawlana. 1331/1912. *Riyāz-e-Sūfī*. Bombay: Mustafa'ī Steam Press.

Tayob, A. 1999. *Islam in South Africa: Mosques, Imams and Sermons*. Gainsville: University of Florida Press.

Thanawī, Ashraf ʿAlī. 1317/1899. *Karāmāt-e-imdādiyya*. Kanpur.

Thorold, A.P.H. 1997. 'The Politics of Mysticism: Sufism and Yao Identity in Southern Malawi', *Journal of Contemporary African Studies*, 15.1.

—— 2001. 'The Yao Tariqa and the Sukuti Movement in Southern Malawi', in D. Bone (ed.). *Malawi's Muslims: Historical Perspectives*. Blantyre: CLAIM.

Toorawa, S.M. 2000. 'Wâq al-wâq: Fabulous, Fabular, Indian Ocean (?) Islands', *Emergences: Journal for the Study of Media and Composite Cultures*, 10.2

Vanzan, A. n.d. 'Hājjī Pirzāda', in *Encyclopaedia Iranica*.

Wasserstein, D.J. 2003. 'A Jonah Theme in the Biography of Ibn Tūmart', in F. Daftary and J.W. Meri (eds), *Culture and Memory in Medieval Islam: Essays in Honour of Wilferd Madelung*. London: I.B. Tauris.

Werbner, P. 1995. 'Powerful Knowledge in a Global Sufi Cult', in W. James (ed.), *The Pursuit of Certainty: Religious and Cultural Formulations*. London: Routledge.

Zebrowski M. 1982. 'Indian Lacquer Work and the Antecedents of the Qajar Style', in W. Watson (ed.), *Lacquerwork in Asia and Beyond*. London: Percival David Foundation of Chinese Art/SOAS.

Županov, I.G. 1998. 'The Prophetic and the Miraculous in Portuguese Asia: A Hagiographical View of Colonial Culture', in S. Subrahmanyam (ed.), *Sinners and Saints: The Successors of Vasco da Gama*. Delhi: Oxford University Press.

4

COSMOPOLITANISM COLONISED?
THREE CASES FROM ZANZIBAR 1890–1920[1]

Anne K. Bang

The nineteenth century transformation of Zanzibar Town from a small settlement to a real urban environment changed not only a landscape, but an entire society. By the time the reign of Sultan Barghash b. Said was coming to an end in 1888, the political and economic might of the Sultanate was in reality eroded by British power. However, the legacy of the Sultanate was very evident, in the form of Zanzibar Stone Town, its inhabitants and their habits in terms of material consumption, residential patterns, travel, religion and specific mentalities – in short: a society formed by its nineteenth century experience.

This chapter focuses on the first three decades of the colonial era, and will seek to investigate how the colonial takeover affected the cosmopolitan nature of Zanzibari society. It will do so by presenting three cases from three locations: the mosque, the courts and the beach leisure house.

The ability of a population to view its place in a greater, potentially global frame is emphasised by Breckenridge *et al.* (2002), as one of the hallmarks of cosmopolitan society. The discussion here will take as its starting point, that the population of Zanzibar (and specifically Zanzibar Town) by 1890 was very aware of its place in a larger scale. The society had been shaped by the nineteenth century experience and was marked

---

1   Fieldwork for this article was conducted on several visits to Zanzibar and the Zanzibar National Archives between 2001 and 2004, during a post-doctoral research fellowship at the Department of History, University of Bergen. Some of the data used here were collected during archival research funded by the Nansen Foundation of Norway and the Norwegian Non-Fiction Writers' Association.

by a high degree of human influx, lasting trade and family networks with overseas locations, as well as a high degree of awareness of foreign places that shaped its everyday life. In total, the nineteenth century experience had enabled Zanzibar Town dwellers to think and act beyond the local.

The question then remains, whether, or to what degree the colonial takeover represented a 'closure' of Zanzibari cosmopolitanism or perhaps, a transition to a different form of cosmopolitanism? Did the first decades of British rule make Zanzibar 'less cosmopolitan' or even 'uncosmopolitan'? Or, did it merely supply new categories and alter the fields in which cosmopolitanism could be played out?

Background:
Transitional Zanzibar From Bu Saidi Rule to the Protectorate

> 'When I've got a few hundred francs together, I will head down to Zanzibar, where they say there is work to do.'

(Arthur Rimbaud writing home from Aden, 17th of August 1880)

Arthur Rimbaud, author of *Season in Hell* and renewer of French poetry, never reached the shores of Zanzibar. Instead, he spent his last, joyless decade trafficking furs, guns and coffee between the grim furnace of Aden and the dry highlands surrounding Harar. However, many did reach Zanzibar, and many had done so long before Rimbaud had expressed his idea. From the early nineteenth century and particularly from 1832 when Sayyid Said b. Sultan made Zanzibar Town his capital, people kept coming to work in the new trade entrepôt of East Africa. Scholars escorted the Sultan from Oman to become *qadis* and *liwalis* in the East African dominions, while wealthy Omanis came to establish plantations based on slave labour. Omani and Hadrami tribesmen came to work as soldiers, while yet more army personnel were recruited from India and the Sudan. Indian traders, both Ismailis and Sunni Muslims as well as Hindu Banyans arrived, some from India, others from other trading ports in the Indian Ocean, to deal consumer goods and to become money-lenders. People also arrived from the surrounding areas. An unknown number of thousands were brought to the island as slaves. Others came as traders, scholars, dhow captains, sailors and manual labourers from the Comoros, Kilwa, Mombasa, Lamu and the Benadir ports. Finally, Europeans who came as representatives of trading firms, soon gained status as consuls for their respective nations, and sought favourable trading conditions from the Sultan's government. Among these, none were more influential than the British consul, who represented the real naval power of the Indian Ocean.

Following the establishment of the protectorate, trade continued. The trading firms in Zanzibar were granted several concessions. Custom duties were low and soon very low; Zanzibar was made a free port in 1892 (Lyne 2001 [1905]: 166). Consequently, imports to the protectorate increased by 29 percent from 1891 to 1898, while exports increased by 8 percent (Schneppen 2003: 424). The status of Zanzibar as a free port was reversed in 1899, when an import duty of 5 percent was claimed on most goods. However, the pattern remained import-based, while exports stagnated.

The list of administrative, technical and material changes in the early colonial era is long. Said b. Ali al-Mughayri, in his history of Zanzibar, summed up the reign of Sayyid Ali in a tone which indicates a retrospective view on colonialism as such but also points to the immense state of flux under which Zanzibari inhabitants lived during its first decades:

In his days, the British laid their hands on the Government shambas and houses. In his days, taxes were introduced on inheritance and this tax was a great burden to his subjects. In his days, the rest of their possessions in the Bandar Somal was sold to the Italian Government for the sum of 44,000 pounds. In his days, the British Resident's house in Zanzibar was built by General Raikes, engineered by Mr. Sinclair. In his days, the Rupee was introduced as the official currency in Zanzibar in 1908 [...] In his days, the Arabs of Zanzibar established the Arab Association and an official paper, Hizb al-Islah. [...] In his days, Zanzibar got electricity for lights in the houses, the power plant being in Malindi, Forodhani quarter. In his days, the Bububu railway was founded, about 7 miles long, and this was completed by the Americans in 1905. (Al-Mughayri 2001: 422)

Cosmopolitan Zanzibar:
From 'A Place Among Many' To 'Elsewheres Classified'?
Several studies have outlined the nature of Zanzibari society in the latter half of the nineteenth century. These have all marked the 'mixedness', 'heterogeneity' or 'cosmopolitanism' of the society and several have also noted the contradiction or outright incompatibility between the colonial urge to create fixed categories and a social structure which essentially eluded classification. In order to establish the starting point of this chapter – the cosmopolitan nature of Zanzibari society around 1890 – it is necessary to present and discuss some of these findings. In his study of the colonial efforts to establish urban planning in Zanzibar Stone Town, William Bissell (1999) has noted precisely how the very 'mixedness' of the city was a cause for concern and confusion to the early colonial city planners. At the time of the first town survey in 1893, Zanzibar Town had no fixed law courts and residences inter-mingled with burial grounds, cattle and camel sheds, workshops and so forth. The same survey found the city to be extremely heterogeneous. Reflecting the growth of the city in the nineteenth century from huts to stone houses, it is worth noting that even at this late stage, semi-permanent huts still outnumbered stone houses in Stone Town. Here entered the colonial administrator, attempting to create order in what he perceived as chaos.[2] Beyond the division between Stone Town and *Ng'ambo* ('the other side' – residential area mainly populated by people of African or slave descent), there seemed to be no visible residential pattern in the Stone Town itself. Even the Stone Town/*Ng'ambo* division, as Abdul Sheriff (2002: 64) has noted, was the result of a specific historical process, rather than an expression of a cultural characteristic or a specific intention of segregation. In Stone Town, Arabs, Goans, Greeks and Banyans would live within one small cluster of houses. There was, in the words of Bissell, 'no evidence of strict segregation on the basis of neither race nor class' (1999: 185). This heterogeneity was echoed almost everywhere in Stone Town, according to the 1893 survey.

---

2   See for example Bissells (1999) presentation of the efforts of Gerald Portal, the Consul-General of Zanzibar, from 1891 to 1894.

Turning to material culture, Jeremy Prestholdt (2003) has examined the emergence of new consumer patterns in Zanzibar in the second half of the nineteenth century. He argues that this emerging culture relying on the importation of goods from all over the world was not simply a Europeanisation, Arabisation or Indianisation of Zanzibari culture, but a domestication and configuration of globally accessible goods, in order to address local issues. From this perspective, the emergence of Bu Saidi's power is seen as having destabilised older social and political relationships. At the same time, Bu Saidi's rule expanded trade to incorporate a potentially unlimited number of 'elsewheres', which in turn could be incorporated into a new Zanzibari 'global consciousness'. The 'elsewhere' as a concept serves here as a reference point which may be represented either symbolically in the form of stories or objects, or concretely by the arrival and settling of people.[3] Prestholdt demonstrates this point with reference to consumer patterns in East Africa and opens a discussion as to whether the expansion of links may be seen as a formula for cosmopolitanism. He states that: 'The centrality of consumerism to new social relations was a hallmark of Zanzibar's cosmopolitanism' (2003: 195).

Travel patterns, too, had developed under the Sultanate. The monsoon based trading system whereby ships from South Arabia reached Zanzibar around December, was well established even before the nineteenth century. In addition, the Sultanate had expanded widely the idea of travel, sending off naval delegations to India, Europe and as far as Salem, USA. Even to those who did not travel, the very idea of all these 'elsewheres' had a significant influence on the Zanzibari world view.

The emergence of the colonial polities along the East African coast meant limitations where travel hitherto had been subject to very few restrictions. By 1912, Zanzibar was the only territory left in East Africa where immigration remained relatively uncontrolled (Hartwig 2002). However, the First World War changed this. By 1914, passenger lists

---

3 Bhabha in Clifford, J. 1992. 'Traveling Cultures', in L.Grossberg, C. Nelson and P.A Treichler (eds), *Cultural Studies*. London and New York: Routledge; quoted here from Prestholdt 2003: 184.

became mandatory for all ships calling on Zanzibar Harbour. In 1915 the 'Office of Immigration and Embarkation' was established, which in turn issued a series of regulations referring to the issue of travel passes and other documents. In 1922, the wartime rules were transformed into the 'Immigration Regulation and Restriction Decree' which operated with visas, employment rules, and the classification of travellers.

As Friedhelm Hartwig (2002) has shown, one of the most far-reaching reforms came on the issue of passports, and, implicitly, on the issue of nationality. Identification of person and origin was something new in East Africa at this time, and caused endless headaches for both administrators and the travellers it was supposed to control. Who should carry British passports and who should not? If not eligible for British passports, what should the traveller use as a means of identification?

The issue of passports touches directly on issues of identity. While the Sultanate had few classification categories beyond the free/slave, Muslim/non-Muslim and Ibadi-Omani/other Muslim dichotomies, the British administrators were more prone to closely categorise the governed peoples. As has been demonstrated by Laura Fair (2001), the British administrators placed much emphasis on where people came from (literally, *where people arrived from*). Not only were the British more prone towards categorisation. They were also, as has been described by both Laura Fair and Jonathon Glassman (1995), more prone to translate these categories into access to political representation, housing, food rations, education and employment.

Colonial ideas of ethno-racial origin are particularly clearly expressed in memorandums on education.[4] These documents convey glimpses of British views on education, and the supposed suitability of the various 'races' to schooling and later occupations. The 'Arabs' were envisioned as suitable for business, teaching and certain types of civil service, the 'Indians' purely for civil service, whereas the 'natives' were to have their natural place in industrial and agricultural courses.

---

4   A good example is ZA-AB6/1: Report by committee for education, 1921.

British racial labels were also used in information leaflets, supposedly celebrating precisely the very heterogeneity administrators were struggling to organise:

> In the narrow streets of a typically Eastern Town [...] may be seen the stately, long-robed Arab – a well-bred, courteous gentleman – his cousins from Muscat and the Persian Gulf, Shihiris from Makulla [sic.] and Southern Arabia, Turks, Egyptians, Persians and Baluchis, Europeans of all countries, Goans, occasional Japanese and Chinese, tall, lean, fuzzy-headed Somalis from the Benadir coast and African natives of all types and from every part of the continent.[5]

The persistent emphasis on origin, expressed in a language of ethnography, caused new organisations to emerge which were based precisely on origin. Examples of these are the Arab Association and the Comorian Association (both established in 1911).

It may be argued that the Arab Association was founded more in the spirit of Islamic modernism and budding Arab nationalism, which were emerging in Cairo, Damascus and elsewhere in the Middle East, rather than in a direct 'response' to colonial pressure towards classification in Zanzibar (Glassman 2004). While this is not the place for a prolonged discussion on the origin of Arabism in East Africa, it should be noted that early Arabism in East Africa certainly owed at least part of its inspiration to the Middle East. However, it should also be noted that the two motives are not mutually exclusive. Certain aspirations, even aspirations under colonialism, were expressed in the language of 'Arabism', but in the Zanzibari context its rhetoric would encompass specifically the Arab landowning (or former landowning) class and the recent immigrants from Yemen/Hadhramaut, rather than for example, the people of Cairo or the Levant.

What is certain, is that these associations often took on the role of educators of their own communities (or what they perceived as their communities), or what in modern parlance would be called 'awareness raisers', a good example being the efforts of the *'alim* and influential teacher Burhan Muhammad Mkelle. Under the auspices of the new Government schools and the Arab Association, Mkelle (who was of

---

5   Notes for Officers Appointed to Zanzibar, 1916, ZA-BA97/2.

Comorian origin, thus presumably not eligible for membership in the
Arab Association) in 1918 took it upon himself to teach Arabic to the
young Arabs of Zanzibar. In the preface to his grammar for 'Arab
children', Mkelle wrote:

> The non-existence of a book of grammar and easy pronunciation has caused great
> difficulties for *Arab children* [my emphasis]. Since they speak Swahili during their
> childhood [*mundhu saghrihim*], they are not able to fully understand their
> grammar lessons. Egyptian or Syrian grammar books of various sorts have been
> present in Zanzibar but have not been put to beneficial use except with the
> children who speak Arabic and they are few. Concerning the children who do not
> speak Arabic, they are in the majority and they have very great difficulties.[6]

In other words, if the 'Arabs' were to continue being Arabs, they had to
be taught. Whether or not this meant that the children were also to think
of themselves distinctly as Arabs (as in Middle Eastern Arabs) and not
Zanzibaris of Arab decent, is matter for further research.

In general, it must be emphasised that the colonial process towards
new lines of identity did *not* necessarily mean that people started to think
of themselves in new ways. As has been pointed out by Jonathon
Glassman, the origins of racial thought (and implicitly, racial or ethnic
ideas about oneself) did not *only* originate in colonial hegemony
(Glassman 2004). The Sultanate, for example, distinguished sharply
between the coastal, 'civilised' culture and the 'barbarian' interior.
However, the arrival of the British introduced new division lines, or –
useful for the discussion of this chapter – new formulas for
cosmopolitanism.

In sum, Zanzibari urban society by 1890 was marked by a high
degree of heterogeneity, a population with a high awareness of a
potentially infinite number of 'elsewheres' and a consumerism which, in
combination with the first two factors, made for a distinct

---

6 Mkelle B. and Ali S. bin 1918. *Al-Tamrin. Book of Primary Lessons on Grammar, Part I.
   Containing Parts of Speech.* Zanzibar Government Print. The book was co-authored by
   Saleh bin Ali who was employed by the British residency. The quote is from the Arabic
   preface. There is also an English preface in which the text is slightly different. Amongst
   others, the passage about the very few children who speak Arabic is omitted, as is the
   statement that Swahili speakers are the majority.

cosmopolitanism. In the following, three cases from the early colonial era will be presented, whereby established patterns were challenged by new, colonial structures. The focus here is on how these structural changes affected established formulas for cosmopolitanism.

The Mosque in the Era of Transition

On the 27th of *Sha'ban* 1322/6 (November 1904), the Shadhiliyya Sufi brotherhood at Zanzibar found it necessary to petition the young sultan, Sayyid Ali b. Hammud b. Muhammad (ruled 1902–1911) to reverse his order to cease *dhikr* (prayer recitation) sessions in Zanzibar mosques:

> Your instruction obeyed by us was to stop *dhikr* over all, so we stopped our *wird* (prayer formulas for recitation) and awaited your instruction. We shall never stray from our path, nor leave our tradition, like some people have done as they lack knowledge. Our way is that of our shaykhs, and we have received it from them. In this, we have the witness of our *tuqat muslimin* (holy Muslims, 'friends of God' – the *awliya*) on every night that we read in the Qahwa Mosque after *'isha* (evening) prayer for one hours time. So we thank you for what you gave us, and pray that God prolong your life and increase his beneficence.
> Salaams to you from Ahmad b. Khayr b. Hasan and his brothers of the Shadhiliyya-Yashrutiyya.[7]

There are a number of problems with this document. First of all, one might ask why the Shadhili brothers would direct their letter to the still under-age Sultan, instead of to the British minister, A.S. Rogers, who ruled in his place. Secondly, and more importantly, why should the Sultan – or the British regent, for that matter – have instructed Sufi orders in general to cease *dhikr* rituals? It is known that during the reign of Sayyid Barghash (1870–1888), steps were taken to limit the influence of the Sufi orders – the activities of the *mutawwa* (religious overseers) faction of the budding Ibadi reform movement.[8] However, after thirteen

---

7 ZA-AA5/9-25 (previous ref. ZA-AA5/9-60). Letter to Sayyid Ali b. Hammud b. Muhammad from the Shadhiliyya brotherhood, dated 27th *Sha'ban* 1322/6 November 1904.

8 This, amongst others, seem to have been one of the reasons why the later Chief *Qadi* and Alawi Sufi leader Ahmad b. Sumayt left Zanzibar during most of Barghash' reign. See Bang, 2003. See also Pouwels (1987: 204–6) and Bennett (1978: 90–1).

years of British Protectorate rule, Sayyid 'Ali – with his secular Harrow education – seems to have had neither the grounds nor the ability to implement restrictions on Sufi activities in the mosques.

Mirroring the nineteenth century urban growth of Zanzibar Town, the mosques constructed reflected closely the origins of their founders. (Sheriff 1992: 2001–02). However, the proliferation of mosques reflected not only urban expansion, but also a specific development within Islam itself, and specifically in the East African context. The nineteenth century, and especially the latter half, had seen the emergence of Sufi orders as mass organisations. Between 1870 and 1890 both the Qadiriyya and the Shadhiliyya had recruited numerous followers in Zanzibar (Bang 2003; Farsy and Pouwels 1989; Glassman 1995; Pouwels 1987). In the same period, the orientation of the already established Alawiyya had shifted its attention more towards the public sphere, focusing on Islamic education (Bang 2003). The orders introduced new rituals, prayers, grave visitation cults and ultimately became new *foci* for social organisation, both for established residents of Zanzibar Town and newcomers.

By the late nineteenth century, individual mosques, and particularly some of the Sunni-Shafi'i mosques, had come to be closely associated with Sufi orders. The Mnara Mosque of Malindi, for example, was regarded as a Qadiri mosque, closely associated with the Brawan community in Zanzibar.[9] The Gofu mosque, founded by the Jamal al-Layl family, became known as a centre of teaching linked to the Alawiyya *tariqa*. The Ibadis and Shi'as too, built mosques in their neighbourhood, and by 1890, about fifty mosques dotted the urban landscape in Zanzibar Town (Sheriff: 1992).

We may speculate that the final and real takeover by the British opened up wider contests within the religious field than had been possible under Sultanic rule. This was at a time of strong religious reform currents in the Islamic world, both within the Sufi orders and in the

---

9 Personal communication, Maalim Muhammad Idris Muhammad Saleh, Zanzibar, 2003–2004. The Mnara Mosque was associated with such influential names as the Amawi family, including Abd al-Aziz and Burhan al-Amawi (see Bang 2003).

emerging Islamic modernism (Bang 2003). It was also a time in which Muslim intellectuals in Zanzibar (as elsewhere) sought new expressions through which to express moral guidance (Reese 2004: 244–56). Given the degree of interconnectedness between Zanzibar and the outside world, it is not surprising that some of these debates were played out locally. Some indications for this may be found in the account given by Pouwels (1987). Although in vague terms, the period from 1903 to 1911 is here described as one of religious strife and rivalries, and while these seem to have been more of a personal than of ideological or theological nature, it seems clear that the religious field in Zanzibar, in the first decade of the Protectorate era, was becoming a highly contested one. The question to be raised is whether this contestation was in fact a series of claims being staked in new formulas for cosmopolitanism.

The letter is also an indication that the new regime, in the spirit of creating order, took an interest in the events taking place in the mosques. The main thing worth noting is that the Shadhili brothers absolutely contested any decision banning their practices ('… we shall never stray from our path'). Furthermore, the letter indicates that some other unspecified people had strayed from their path, but how and in what direction, we can not know. The Shadhilis may have been referring to orders practicing transgressing *dhikr* sessions or to religious scholars verging on secularism – either one is possible. Finally, steps taken to limit the activities of these particular Shadhili brothers may have had a more mundane reason, originating for example from scholars of other orders, who were more centrally positioned within the new regime. Whatever our speculation, the letter indicates the state of flux existing in the religious realm during the early colonial years, while also revealing the will of individual groups to stake their claim in the new order.

Qadis and Courts: A Legal System Under Colonial Reorganisation
A similar development can be found if we turn to the courts. The courts of Zanzibar were fully re-organised in the period from 1890 to 1908. From being marked by a relatively informal hierarchy of *qadis* appointed by the Sultan, they were brought into a system of higher and lower courts, presided over by British judges and selected *qadis* of both the

Sunni and Ibadi persuasion (Bang 2003). This restructuring of a system which had previously relied on the prestige of each individual *qadi*, opened up new hierarchies in terms of prestige and power. Who actually had the final say on a case? The British judge? The *qadi* of your choice? The *qadi* who agreed with you – although he might be of a different sect? One person who did *not* have a final say was Sultan Sayyid Ali himself, having been stripped of his traditional role as ultimate appellate authority, by the British. Since the establishment of the Zanzibari Sultanate, the Sultan himself had functioned as the fount of justice. Sayyid Said, Sayyid Majid and especially Sayyid Barghash often delivered verdicts themselves. Sayyid Barghash in particular is noted to have spent two hours every day on legal matters, either delivering verdicts directly, or discussing particular cases with his *qadis* (al-Mughayri 2001: 420–22). The removal of this right by the British was highly controversial, and part of the controversy among the Zanzibari *'ulama'* of the time.

As an example, the case raised by one Bashir b. Nadhir in a letter to Sayyid Ali b. Hammud in 1903 can be mentioned.[10] Complaining to the Sultan about what he perceives as unfair treatment at the courts, he gives the entire sequence of events and his wandering from *qadis* to British judges and back, before finally resorting to a direct appeal to the Sultan – despite the fact that Sayyid Ali no longer had any rights to deliver verdicts. The original court case concerned an alleged debt of 700 Rupees, claimed from Bashir by a man named Amani. Initially, Bashir denied that he owed any money, but in the court of *qadi* Burhan b. Abd al-Aziz al-Amawi, he was ordered to pay the amount in full. In order to raise the amount, Qadi Burhan ordered the sale of a *shamba* belonging to Bashir. Bashir, not amused by the ruling, complained to the Ibadi judge Nasir b. Sulayman al-Rawahi, who in turn agreed with Burhan. Not easily defeated, Bashir hired a lawyer and put his case before Judge Green

---

10 Letter from Bashir b. Nadhir to Sayyid Ali b. Hammud, dated 10 Dhul-Hijja, 1320/10th of March 1903, ZA-AA5/9-91 (previous ref. ZA-AA5/11-82). There is a problem with the dating of this document, as the date actually reads 10th *Dhul-Hijja*, 1310, which would correspond to 25th June 1893. This is almost a decade before Sayyid Ali b. Hammud became Sultan. In all likelihood, it was a simple error on behalf of the letter-writer.

in the British court system. The judge considered the case to fall under the jurisdiction of the Sultanic Court System and sent him back to the *qadis* Tahir al-Amawi and Ahmad b. Sumayt, both Sunni *qadis* of the Zanzibar court system since the early 1890s. Unfortunately for Bashir, the two *qadis* upheld the ruling of Shaykh Burhan and ordered the auction of Bashır's *shamba* for the purpose of raising money for the debt. The case then continued as a dispute over the actual ownership of the *shamba*, which Bashır now claimed was at least partly owned by his wife. The case was eventually solved in the Sultanic courts in 1906, after a prolonged dispute.[11]

What should be emphasised here is the way in which Bashir contests the ruling of the Sunni *qadi* and moves on via an Ibadi *qadi* directly to the British legal system. At the time when the letter was written, the Zanzibari legal system had not yet fully been transformed into the dual legal system which came to be its hallmark in the inter-war years. (It was only implemented in the Zanzibar Courts Decree of 1908 and finally settled in 1923). His Britannic Majesty's Court had been established in 1897 to hear cases involving European, British, or British-protected subjects. However, given the flux in population categories and the open state of self-identification at this point in time, the lines where hazy as to who was actually a British-protected subject and who was a Sultanic subject. In other words, the court system was still relatively open, and discontent members of the public could – to the degree of their means – use the system of informal courts of appeal to its full extent.

Chwaka – The 'Brighton of Zanzibar' 1895–1930:
A Colonised British Beach?

About 30km directly east of Zanzibar Stone Town lies the village of Chwaka, which until the 1890s, was inhabited mainly by the Hadimu people who made their living from fishing in the wide Chwaka lagoon. By the mid-1890s, a new breed of settlers arrived in Chwaka – British colonial officers, the retinue of the Bu Saidi Sultan, as well as men of other nations who came to take advantage of the sea breeze and healthy

---

11 ZA-AA5/9-90 (previous ref. ZA-AA5/11-81)

climate. According to Sir Lloyd Matthews, the opening up of Chwaka as a resort area and the construction of a road across the island would, make a 'sanatorium or health resort' in 'Chwaka with its land coral reef of five miles' accessible within 'an easy drive'. He acclaimed the village for 'being completely open to the Indian Ocean' and regarded its climate 'as the most salubrious'.[12] This enthusiasm about the resort is also reflected in the words of an 'occasional correspondent' of the *Zanzibar Gazette*, who found himself moved to rephrase an ode by Lord Byron, after having visited the upcoming 'Brighton of Zanzibar':

> And if, through the course of the years which await me
> Some new scenes of pleasure should open to view
> I will say while with rapture the thought will elate me
> Oh! Such was the land which at Chwaka I knew.[13]

In the original, 'On a distant view of Harrow' of 1806, Lord Byron refers to the land of his infancy. The choice of ode by the *Gazette* correspondent makes Chwaka not only truly English, but also a paradise, long lost, but now revisited.

The first Government 'rest house' was a small chalet, brought in parts from Norway in 1895. It was completed in 1896 on a plot of land a few hundred meters north of Chwaka village. The building was conceived to be used 'along the lines of the Indian Dawk Bungalow, so that town residents after giving notice and on payment of a suitable fee could 'have the privilege of residing there for several days at a time.'[14]

In 1898, the foundation stone was laid for a large 'summer palace' for Sayyid Hammud b. Muhammad Al Bu Saidi.[15] By that time, the British Resident had already commissioned a separate bungalow in Chwaka, situated about a hundred meters south of the two other villas.

---

12 ZA-AC4/2.

13 *Zanzibar Gazette*, 26th June 1895.

14 *Zanzibar Gazette*, 29th May 1895.

15 *Zanzibar Gazette*, 2nd April 1900. The ceremony where the foundation stone was laid included speeches and Quran recitation by the honourable *shaykhs* Hilal b. Muhammad al-Barwani, Sayyid Mansab b. Abd al-Rahman al-Husayni (Qadi of Chwaka) and Ahmad b. Salim. A photo of the three *shaykhs* reciting on the occasion can be found in ZA-AV28/48.

Reflecting the British tendency towards categorising people into ethno-racial groups, it was understood that Chwaka should be a 'European' retreat. In this case, the definition included the retinue of the Sultan. However, it was not only a British beach. Among those in need of a 'change of air' were the Germans in Zanzibar. The German community was among the most well-established foreign trading communities in Zanzibar, some of them having been established on the island since the 1840s. Their influence on Zanzibar declined following the Anglo-German treaty, where Helgoland was exchanged for Zanzibar, which resulted in the proclamation of the British protectorate of Zanzibar (Schneppen 2003: 403–8). However, the German firms established on the island (the most prominent being the Hamburg firms Hansing and Oswald Co.) were privy to liberal trade conditions, although the Deutsche Ost-Afrika Linie was to continue to call on Zanzibar on its way to the German mainland ports. Although dwindling, German presence in Zanzibar remained influential. So influential, that when the British started to turn Chwaka into what was persistently referred to in the *Zanzibar Gazette* as 'the Brighton of Zanzibar', the Germans, too, threw themselves into the search for suitable beach resorts. The 'Chwaka Verein'[16] was established in 1901, for the purpose of building a beach bungalow in Chwaka to be used as a rest/holiday house for German trade firms in Zanzibar. The bungalow was duly built – on a cliff on the southern outskirts of the village, at a polite distance from two British villas and the Sultans beach palace.

Thus, by 1905, four prominent villas dotted the Chwaka beach. The German one was open for lease to Germans, the one termed 'Norway Bungalow' was open to British and other Europeans, while the Sultan and the British Resident had their respective villas, which could also be rented on occasion by British and prominent Arabs, mainly of the Bu Saidi family. Here, relaxing leave periods were spent eating, drinking, fishing and exploring the surrounding landscape.

A description of one Christmas spent at the Norwegian Bungalow at Chwaka can be found in the correspondence of the Norwegian timber-

---

16 ZA-AE2/784.

trader, O. Chr. Olsen.[17] He spent the Christmas of 1903 in the bungalow, together with one Mr. Robinson of the Eastern Telegraph Co. The two men arrived on the 24th of December and found the bungalow to have two bedrooms, one dining room and a wide terrace. Here they sat down to a Christmas dinner of lobster, fish, steak, chicken, pudding and fruit, accompanied by whisky, claret and punch. Two servants were at hand throughout the stay for the comfort of the holiday makers. The next day was spent canoeing and fishing and making a courtesy call to the *wali* of Chwaka, with cigarettes as a present.[18]

Upon the outbreak of the First World War, the German villa was left empty as all Germans were ousted from Zanzibar. The villa was confiscated, and an inventory was held in 1915. The inventory list makes for entertaining reading and gives another glimpse of the high life led in these early beach resorts. The German villa was found to contain amongst other things: soda tumbler glasses, eighteen champagne glasses, thirteen wine glasses, thirteen light green sherry glasses, twenty vermouth glasses, nine plates, eleven soup plates, one gun, twelve cheese plates, eight cups and diverse cutlery.[19]

The lease of the land and the building was then sold to the bishop of Zanzibar. He in turn leased the villa to another influential trading community in Zanzibar – the Parsis.[20] Shortly thereafter, the former German villa in Chwaka was re-named 'Cowasjee and Dinshaw Villa' after the rich merchant brothers Cowasjee and Dorabjee Dinshaw. Originating from the Parsi merchant community of Aden, the brothers Cowasjee and Dorabjee Dinshaw set up their business in Zanzibar in 1884, after having been urged to do so by the relatively small Zanzibari Parsi community (Salvadori 1997). Shortly thereafter, the brothers, in an echo of the migration of Sayyid Said, transferred their business

---

17 O. Chr. Olsen was a trader and an agent for the Norway East Africa Trading Company, established in Zanzibar in 1895. Olsen lived in Zanzibar from 1896 to 1918, interrupted only by a few periods in Norway. His correspondence consists of about 3000 pages in Norwegian, English, German and Swahili.
18 Olsen Correspondence (in family possession), Book II, 227–35.
19 ZA-AE2/170.
20 ZA-AE2/170.

headquarters to Zanzibar, to a building which until then had been the American Consulate.[21] In 1890, Dorabjee's son died in Zanzibar. In his memory, Dorabjee built the first Parsi fire temple in Zanzibar Town, built on the land of the Parsi *Anjuman* (the Parsi religious assembly). The connection between the Dinshaws and the Parsi *Anjuman* grew so close that they practically merged. By 1910, the *Anjuman* was run by Cowasjee & Dinshaw Bros. Cowasjee died in 1901 and Dorabjee in 1907. The company (and the *Anjuman*) was continued by cousins, and eventually by Cowasjee's son. The latter also became known as a philanthropist in the East African Parsi community, sponsoring book-publishing and financing a Chwaka holiday house.

The lease to the Parsis was not unproblematic for the British, who until then had held Chwaka as their 'private beach', shared only with the Sultan. Initially, the lease to the Parsis was only approved on the strict condition that no Tower of Silence should be built on the premises.[22] By 1918, one British administrator concluded with an air of resignation:

The idea of reserving the whole of Chwaka for Europeans (by which I understand that the Indians be èxcluded) is not only impolitic but not practicable. There are Indians now at Chwaka and far nearer the Government Quarters than the Bungalow.[23]

The Indians were close and closing in further, as more Indian communities were taking an interest in Chwaka. In 1920, the Ismailis leased a plot of land slightly south of Chwaka village, although it is not clear whether a building was ever constructed on the plot.[24] By 1926, Mr

---

21 Under Dinshaw ownership, the building came to be known as *Nyumba ya Tembo*, meaning 'Elephant House' or 'Tembo House', due to the almost full-size carved elephant by its door. The house is today a hotel with the same name. A replica of the elephant is to be found in the front yard.

22 Tall structures upon which the Parsis laid out their dead to be consumed by birds. The British were opposed to this practice throughout the Empire.

23 ZA-AE2/170.

24 ZA-AE2/830. The lease was valid to the end of 1920. It appears that the lease was a confirmation of a previous agreement, thus it may be possible that the Ismailis had interests in Chwaka even before that time. However, it is unclear whether a building was constructed, and if it was, whether it was left standing.

Kanji on behalf of the trading firm, Moloo Brothers, made an offer to lease a plot of land next to the Norwegian Bungalow. The initiative was not viewed favourably:

> I consider that the erection of a Bungalow in these circumstances would have a very deleterious effect on the amenities of HE's bungalow. I further consider that the leasing of land to private individuals in the middle of the area which has hitherto been reserved for the government is highly undesirable.[25]

In other words: If the Indians were to be at Chwaka, they should stay south of the village, at a proper distance from the 'Government Beach'. In the end, the Moloo Brothers built their villa near to the 'Cowasjee & Dinshaw' building. However, the building constructed was an imposing one, bigger than the Parsi villa, rivalling both the British Residents house and the Sultans palace.

The history of the development of the 'Brighton of Zanzibar' reveals the blatant contest for the prestige of beach houses and sea air. Zanzibar Town, described in officers' information leaflets as 'diverse' and 'cosmopolitan', was to be less so when transplanted to the beach, where officers were to relax. The British persistently sought to keep the area 'to themselves', thus revealing a distinct view of what their 'Brighton' should be. Neither Germans nor Indians were allowed to build on the northern side of the village, where the strip of beach was to be reserved for British or Bu Saidi guests. Typically, the need of the native residents of Chwaka for access to the sea is nowhere mentioned. Also evident, is the urge to classify according to race and religion rather than money – which eventually was what decided access to Chwaka beaches.

As the British Protectorate of Zanzibar had grown more administratively complex, its staff became accordingly ethnically diverse. This led to debates over who had access to which houses and whether or not non-European staff should be allowed to use all buildings for leave and vacations. The Norwegian Bungalow was by the 1930s also periodically used as leave bungalow and picnic spot for non-European (Indian and Arab) staff. However, the right to the use of other bungalows

---

25 ZA-AE2/174. Lease of Land in Chwaka.

was undetermined, causing Mr C.M. Patel to raise the question in the Legislative Council on the 27th of December 1934, 'whether the Government buildings, except the Norwegian Bungalow, [...] are exclusively reserved for Europeans.' The answer was simply yes.[26]

The history of the Chwaka resort shows the initial colonial quest to create separateness out of the apparent lack of racially based residential patterns existing in town. This separateness was based on power and status, as the inclusion of the Sultanic retinue demonstrates. However, it also shows the gradual albeit grudging inclusion of others, as various Zanzibari communities had become attentive to the niceties of a beach resort. The Germans were the first, but the Indian communities soon caught on. By the time colonial Zanzibar had settled into its lasting form in the 1930s, it was only a matter of time before the Government Rest House was opened to all employees. This happened in the 1940s.

Conclusion: Creating Order or Creating New Formulas?

For the issues raised in this chapter, fruitful discussion points have been proposed by Ackbar Abbas (2003) in the form of a series of questions. Defining cosmopolitanism as the will and ability to engage with the Other, he stresses the fact that in the ideal situation, these engagements take place in circumstances where the encounters are voluntary – a matter of choice. However, this is clearly not always the case. The colonial encounter is precisely a case where the Other is 'forced upon us'. What constitutes cosmopolitanism in this case, and where is the line between a cosmopolitanist stance and a compradorist one? When does cosmopolitanism become cultural imperialism? Referring to the examples of Shanghai and Hong Kong, Abbas describes two different modes of cosmopolitanism under colonialism. Shanghai, in the period between 1880 and 1930, with its numerous concession holders ruling sections of the city, can be likened to the situation in Zanzibar under Bu Saidi rule – or to what Abbas calls a 'cosmopolitanism of extraterritoriality' (2003: 214). Similar to the British, French and Japanese in Shanghai, the British, Germans and French – but also the Ismailis, Omanis and

---

26 ZA-AB 39/80.

Banyans held stakes in the development of Zanzibar Town. Here, cosmopolitanism is understood not necessarily as foreign domination (as in the Zanzibar case: by the Bu Saidis, and behind them, in turn, the British), but as a process of local appropriation of elements of the foreign (Prestholdt 2003, on the issue of local appropriation in Zanzibar).

Hong Kong, on the other hand, was a different story. What developed here, according to Abbas' analysis, was a 'cosmopolitanism of dependence' (2003: 218), which only fully blossomed after the announcement of the return of Hong Kong to mainland China. Here, the analogy with colonial Zanzibar is evident. By 1930, the institutions and hierarchies were established that were to remain functioning until independence in 1963. All the groups who previously had held stakes in society were redefined (or had redefined themselves?), now taking up a clearly subaltern place in the social order. This, however, does not mean that colonialism 'closed' cosmopolitanism.

Our concern here is with the 'in-between' – the development of cosmopolitan Zanzibar between Shanghai and Hong Kong, so to speak. This was the period when new formulas for cosmopolitanism emerged, but the question remains as to what these were and how they came to have an impact. Referring to the cases presented here, it seems that the colonial take-over led to a period of re-orientation, whereby each group tried to find its new place and also its new relationship to the various 'Others' (including those 'forced upon' them, to use Abbas' phrase). The Shadhili brothers in the first example are appealing to the 'old', in the sense that they seek out the Sultan as the addressee for appeals. On the other hand, they also emphasise their intention to stick to their ways, thus staking their claim *as a group* in the new political order. Not only would they continue to say *dhikr*, but they would do so as the Shadhiliyya order. In the second example, Bashir's journey through the court system, demonstrates both local appropriation (of the new legal system and the use of lawyers) and the emergence of a system of dependence, in which individuals and groups were assigned to certain positions, also within the court system. Finally, the contest for beach space not only demonstrates the blatant racial bias of the colonisers, but also the appropriation of the niceties of beach retreats by the locals (in this case, by Parsis and Ismailis – local in the sense that they had been part of the previous extraterritorial cosmopolitan system).

In that sense, the cases presented above demonstrate the transition from one formula of cosmopolitanism to another, moving towards dependency and a system of sub-alternity. In other words, the transition was really one from a pre-colonial Indian Ocean port city cosmopolitanism to what may be referred to as a more universal 'colonial cosmopolitanism.' However, the question remains whether Zanzibari cosmopolitanism really was fully 'colonised'. If we take as a general observation that cosmopolitan societies are best studied either in the abstract or in minute detail, the conclusion must be that more cases are needed before we can arrive at a periodisation of Zanzibari cosmopolitanism.

Bibliography:

Abbas, A. 2003. 'Cosmopolitan De-scriptions: Shanghai and Hong Kong', in C. Breckenridge, S. Pollock, H.K. Bhaba and D. Chakrabarty (eds), *Cosmopolitanism*. Durham, NC: Duke University Press.

Bang, A.K. 2003. *Sufis and Scholars of the Sea. Family Networks in East Africa c. 1860–1925*. London: RoutledgeCurzon.

Bennett, N.R. 1978. *A History of the Arab State of Zanzibar*. London: Methuen & Co.

Bissel, W.C. 1999. City of Stone. Space of Contestation. Urban Conservation and the Colonial Past in Zanzibar. PhD Thesis, University of Chicago.

Breckenridge, C., S. Pollock, H.K. Bhabha and D. Chakrabarty (eds) 2002. *Cosmopolitanism*. Durham, NC: Duke University Press.

Clifford, J. 1992. 'Traveling Cultures', in L. Grossberg, C. Nelson and P.A. Treichler (eds). *Cultural Studies*. London and New York: Routledge.

Fair, L. 2001. *Pasttimes and Politics. Culture, Community and Identity in Post-Abolition Urban Zanzibar, 1890–1945*. Oxford: James Currey.

Glassman, J. 1995. *Fiests and Riots. Revelry, Rebellion and Popular Consciousness on the Swahili Coast, 1856–1888*. Portsmouth: Heinemann.

——— 2004. 'Slower than a Massacre: The Multiple Sources of Racial Thought in Colonial Africa', *The American Historical Review*, 109.3.

Hartwig, F. 2002. 'The Segmentation of the Indian Ocean Region. Arabs and the Implementation of Immigration Regulations in Zanzibar', paper presented to the International Conference on Cultural Exchange and Transformation in the Indian Ocean World, University of California, Los Angeles.

Lyne, R.N. 1905 [2001]. *Zanzibar in Contemporary Times*. Zanzibar: The Gallery Publications.

al-Mughayri, Said b. Ali, 2001. *Juhaynat al-Akhbar fi ta'rikh Zinjibar*, Fourth Edition. Muscat: Ministry of National Heritage and Culture, Oman.

Pouwels, R.L. 1987. *Horn and Crescent, Cultural Change and Traditional Islam on the East African Coast, 800–1900*. Cambridge and New York: Cambridge University Press.

Prestholdt, J. 2003. *East African Consumerism and the Genealogies of Globalization*. PhD Thesis, Northwestern University.

Reese, S. 2004. 'The Adventures of Abu Harith: Muslim Travel Writing and Navigating the Modern in Colonial East Africa' in S. Reese (ed.), *The Transmission of Learning in Islamic Africa*. Leiden: Brill.

Salvadori C. (ed.) 1997. *Two Indian Travellers in East Africa, 1902–1905*. Mombasa: Friends of Fort Jesus. (Private publication).

Schneppen, H. 2003. *Sansibar und die Deutschen. Ein besonderes Verhältnis, 1844–1966*. Munster: LIT Verlag.

Sheriff, A. 1992. 'Mosques, Merchants and Landowners in Zanzibar Stone Town', *Azania*, XXVII.

—— 2001–2002. 'The Spatial Dichotomy of Swahili Towns: The Case of Zanzibar in the Nineteenth Century', *Azania*, XXXVI–XXXVII.

Primary Sources:

Zanzibar State Archives. Sultanic correspondence (correspondence to Sayyid Ali, AA5/9). Land Records.

Zanzibar Official Gazette.

Correspondence of O. Chr. Olsen from the period 1895–1925, in family possession, Norway.

5

THE 'RESPECTABLE CITIZENS' OF SHAYKH UTHMAN: RELIGIOUS DISCOURSE, TRANS-LOCALITY AND THE CONSTRUCTION OF LOCAL CONTEXTS IN COLONIAL ADEN[1]

Scott S. Reese

It was a scandal, really. Muhammad Ali Isma'il Luqman, journalist, President of the Arab Reform Club and an ethnic Indian,[2] simply stood up during the Friday prayer and began to read a newspaper article condemning the Italian invasion of Ethiopia as the *khutba* (sermon). Awadh Abudllah Sharaf, ex-*qadi* of Shaykh Uthman, appalled by such an overtly political sermon stood up and walked out. But even more distressing, when he signalled to his nephew, Abdullah Umar the serving *qadi* (Muslim judge), that he should do the same, he just sat there and listened to Luqman speak! If you couldn't count on your kin, who could you depend on?!

The Muslim community of Aden, where this incident took place in 1931, was one of the most ethnically and socially cosmopolitan in the British Empire. Arabs, Indians and Africans; Sunni, Shi'i and Isma'ili –

---

1 The research for this chapter was conducted primarily in the India Office records contained in the British Library, London between 2003 and 2006, as well as a brief field visit to Aden in 2005. Support for this work was provided by generous grants from the American Philosophical Society, the British Academy and the American Institute for Yemeni Studies as well as internal funding from Northern Arizona University.
2 Luqman's ethnicity is still somewhat open to speculation. While a seemingly native speaker of Arabic, his family maintained close ties with Bombay making it likely that his family were 'Arabised' Indians who had lived in Aden for several generations.

189

all resided within the Settlement perimeter. Some belonged to families who had lived there for generations while others were recent, and sometimes temporary, immigrants. The social and economic profile of the Settlement's Muslim residents was equally diverse. From labourers, shop owners and large scale merchants to policeman, doctors, lawyers and clerks, Muslims could be found throughout the colony's socio-economic structure. To the casual observer, the Muslims of Aden might have appeared to be the nearly ideal Muslim community. Issues of race and class seemed to have been minimal concerns. Within neighbourhood mosques, rich prayed with the poor, Indian with Arab and African. The wealthy looked after the spiritual needs of the less fortunate through the endowment of mosques and schools, while numerous social welfare organisations looked after the physical and health needs of the population. As the uproar surrounding the so-called 'Italian sermon' demonstrates, however, this was nothing more than a veneer that covered serious divisions within the community. These fissures were due, however, not to differences in race or class or discrepancies in wealth. Instead, they were about belief, ideology and differing views of how one should live life as a good Muslim.

As a window on to the dynamics of social construction among Adeni Muslims, this episode might be interpreted in a number of ways. Certainly, one reading might be a demonstration of the desire of various parties to outline particular (and ultimately competing) moral frameworks for the community. Another could be as naked posturing by these same parties to substantiate their authority to construct and define such frameworks. While both interpretations would on some level be valid, I would argue that incidents such as this represent a much broader social process – that of creating the community itself.

Unlike most Muslim communities, the believers of Aden were an ethnically heterogeneous group of diverse socio-economic backgrounds thrown together largely by colonial happenstance. Occupying a crossroads of the British Empire linking the Mediterranean, Eastern Africa and India, by the 1920s the Muslims of Aden had hammered out a distinct, though obviously contested, communal space. This chapter examines the role of Islamic religious discourses in the construction of what Arjun Appadurai (1996) refers to as the 'neighbourhood' within the Aden Settlement. In part it explores how individuals, who were themselves inherently 'trans-local' (coming from and maintaining connections with locations throughout the *'umma*), constructed new Muslim communities that cut across other social constructs such as class, ethnicity and economic status in favour of ones premised on an adherence to common ideological beliefs (e.g. pro-Salafi and anti-Salafi). It examines how individual local intellectuals engaged various trans-local discourses of religious reform (i.e. ideological discourses having as their point of origin places outside of Aden such as Salafism) and adapted them to fit their own communal needs creating new contexts in the process. By the same token, it suggests that, in the process of being placed in the local context, the meanings of these trans-local ideologies themselves become transformed. In short, it looks at religious or reformist discourse that exists as part of a larger web of discursive interactions that ultimately play an active part in the construction of new contexts.

Aden: A Muslim 'Melting Pot'

From its founding as early as the first century B.C.E., the port of Aden served as a cross-cultural epicentre for virtually all of the trading civilisations of the Indian Ocean and Mediterranean worlds. With the evolution of maritime technology it was there that Romans, Egyptians and Greeks traded gold and silver for Indian spices, African ivory and Chinese silks. The cosmopolitan nature of the town continued with its increased commercial prominence during the Islamic period. So, it should come as little surprise that when the British occupied 'the Crater' for use as a coaling station in 1839 it continued to host a diverse population of Arab, African and Indian Muslims, Sephardic Jews and even a small community of Parsi merchants. (Gavin 1975 1–38, 59–61) This was a diversity that accelerated under British rule. By the 1850s, as one modern historian of Aden has noted, the British settlement was home to an 'exceedingly mixed and shifting' population comprised largely of Indians, Arabs, Jews and Somalis. The proportional strength of these communities shifted greatly over time. During the 1850s, for instance, Indians constituted over 40 percent of the Settlement's population.[3] By the 1930s, however, Arabs from both the inland Sultanates and Hadhramaut as well as Somalis were predominant among the non-European population (Gavin 1975: 291–92).[4]

The social and economic standing of individuals also varied greatly. While prominent merchants such as the Cowasjee Parsis could still be found in the Settlement in the 1930s, most Indians were employed within the ranks of government bureaucracy as mid-level police officers, clerks and translators or with private concerns such as the Anglo-Persian Oil Company.[5] Members of the sizeable Somali community inhabited a similar array of socio-economic positions. Of the nearly 4,000 Somalis living in Aden at the time of the 1931 census many were casual or unskilled labourers who found work as stevedores, sweepers,[6] boatmen and carriage drivers. Others, however, were prominent local merchants, court interpreters and relatively high ranking non-commissioned officers in both the civil and armed police (Alpers 1986).[7]

Somewhat ironically, it was the Arabs of Aden who seem to have been the most occupationally constrained – at least in relation to their overall numbers. By 1930 Arabs were probably the least well represented of all colonised peoples within the British administration. During the first decade of the protectorate Arabs, mostly former functionaries of the Sultan of Lahij, predominated within the Aden petty bureaucracy. From

---

3 See footnote 2.

4 In 1931 out of a total population of 46,638 inhabitants 29,820 were recorded as Arabs, 3,935 Somalis, 4,120 Jews and 9,452 Indians. See also Gavin (1975: 445, Appendix B) who notes that the census numbers include those belonging to the garrison. However, in 1929 he also notes, the Indian garrison was removed indicating that the numbers listed for the Indian population account primarily for the 'civil' population.

5 See various references throughout the Aden records.

6 Somalis appear to have been a minority in this profession with most sweepers belonging to what the British referred to as *'Jabarties'* which they seem to have considered a distinct ethnic group; see R/20/A/2700. Examination of Aden police files, however, indicate that in fact the 'African sweeper class,' consisted of individuals from a variety of ethnic backgrounds including Sudanese, inter-riverine Somalis and Ethiopians; see R/20/A/2766 'Tamboora in Aden'.

7 See India Office records R/20/A/2700 and R/20/A/3648 which detail the various occupations of Somali residents.

about 1850, however, they were pushed aside in favour of Indian bureaucrats and the only official office that remained in Arab hands consistently over the next 80 years was that of *qadi,* or Islamic court judge (Gavin 1975: 60). Aden's Arab residents only started to regain ground in the Settlement's governing institutions in the late 1920s when a policy of 'Arabisation' was adopted, beginning with the recruitment of Arab men for the civil and later the armed police (Gavin 1975: 290–91).

Though the least represented within official institutions, the Arabs of Aden were hardly an insignificant part of local Muslim society. Certainly, the overwhelming majority of Arabs in Aden were un-skilled seasonal labourers who found work either on the docks or as day-labourers on various public works projects. Others, however, were long term residents, whether immigrants or locally born, who occupied positions of both economic and social prominence. Police and Residency records – while far from comprehensive – provide at least anecdotal evidence for Arab social and economic importance. As already noted, the position of *qadi* was reserved for Arab residents. However, this included not only the Chief Judge of the Settlement but government appointed judges for each district.[8] In addition, most Imams, muezzins and *nadirs* (referred to as 'mosque managers' in the Settlement records) appear to have been Arab residents of the Settlement. Economically, Arab residents were no less prominent. Thus far I have not uncovered any formal statistics on the economic status of Arab residents; however, various police reports and petitions by residents suggest that they were at least as economically well off as any other community.[9]

---

8 A fact that clearly rankled the sensibilities of at least some non-Arab residents evidenced by Somali demands in 1914 and 1920 for the appointment of their own *qadi* on the grounds that the Arab officials did not understand Somali custom and were prejudiced against them. These demands, I should add, were largely ignored. India Office, R/20/A/1396 40/1 Pt. II Kazi of Aden: Complaints made by Somalis 1914–1920.

9 Thus we find many of the Arab residents involved in the disputes of the early 1930s occupying prominent economic positions within the community. Sayyid Ali Isma'il for instance has made substantial money as a butcher while the preacher Ahmad al-Abbadi had amassed considerable wealth as a landlord.

Life in the Suburbs – Shaykh Uthman

The Muslim community of the Aden Settlement was certainly one that was ethnically diverse. It was not, however, one that was in any way self segregating – at least not along ethnic lines. A few of the town's Muslims lived in the original old town known as the Crater while those employed in government service generally lived within either the civil or military 'lines.' By the 1930s, however, the overwhelming majority of Muslims resided in one of the Settlement's two major non-European neighbourhoods, Tawahi and Shaykh Uthman. Originally home to labourers employed in bunkering ships, Tawahi was a natural outgrowth of the coaling station located at Steamer Point. Shaykh Uthman, on the other hand, was a village that originally lay on the outer edge of the Settlement's perimeter. Host to a number of wells that supplied the British enclave with water the village was considered to be of great strategic importance and was purchased from the Sultan of Lahij in 1882 (Kour 1981: 106). Laying five miles inland on the edge of Settlement territory the British also viewed Shaykh Uthman as a possible solution to overcrowding in Tawahi and Crater. In the hopes of relieving crowding in the harbour area, the British set out to remake Shaykh Uthman as a 'modern town' building 150 houses, a school and a dispensary along a pre-planned grid of streets (Gavin 1975: 189). Located far from the Settlement's centres of employment Shaykh Uthman proved at first unpopular with workers whose jobs were in Crater or the harbour area. However, with road improvements and the addition of public transportation by 1930 Shaykh Uthman had become almost desirable.[10]

Census data needed to determine the population of Shaykh Uthman and Tawahi and the exact proportions between ethnic communities is not available. Anecdotal evidence from India Office records, however, suggests that the ethnic make up of the two neighbourhoods mirrored the figures for the Settlement as a whole. Using *nisbas*, family names and

---

10 Shaykh Uthman became so popular that by the mid-1960s it had spawned its own
    suburb known as Al Mansura as well as a much smaller neighbourhood located across
    the Settlement boundary in territory that technically belonged to the Sultanate of Lahij;
    see Gavin 1975: 319–320.

names that point to some clear ethnic origin on petitions, we see a clear majority of names indicating Arabian origin (e.g. Ba Junayd, al-Attas and Alawqi) with a smattering of others that indicate African or South Asian origins (e.g. al-Hindi, al-Massawi, al-Suwahil and Luqman).[11] By the same token, there is no evidence to indicate that the various ethnic groups segregated themselves from one another within either Shaykh Uthman or Tawahi. They appear to have lived on the same streets, prayed in the same mosques, belonged to the same clubs[12] and even – in some cases – married one another's daughters.[13] It was also a community that, at least in theory, saw itself as united by the common bond of faith. Thus, a petition calling for a ban on the performance of *zar*, a traditional spirit possession ceremony, in 1923 was signed on behalf of all the 'Arab, Somali and Indian Muslims of Aden.'[14] This solidarity on certain issues deemed of moral concern to the community as a whole is even more apparent nine years later in a petition that called for the continued ban on *zar* which they feared was about to be lifted. The petition of 1932, which outlined in great detail the moral dangers of *zar*, included the signatures of individuals who normally found themselves on opposites sides of the doctrinal divide. Thus it was signed by confirmed Salafis such as the Muhammad Ali Luqman as well as the apparently pro-Salafi Imams of Tawahi the al-Hitari *and* those associated with the anti-Salafi camp including the presiding and former *qadis* of Shaykh Uthman,

11 Certainly *nisba*s can be deceiving and may point to some distant or imagined place of origin. Luckily, the geographic and ethnic origins in some cases may be narrowed down via other evidence. Thus the Salafi patron Zakaria Muhammad al-Hindi regularly signed his name in what appears to be Gujarati and is also identified as 'the Indian merchant,' while Muhammad Ali Ibrahim Luqman and Majid Ali Ibrahim Luqman are identified as the 'Ali brothers of India'; see IOR R/20/A/3390.

12 Membership in the pro-Salafi Arab Reformatory Club, for instance appears to have been determined not by ethnicity but theological predilection. The President of in 1931, for instance, was the local Indian activist Muhammad Ali Ibrahim Luqman; see IOR R/20/A/3390.

13 Again, the evidence for this is so far anecdotal. In one important instance, however, Zakaria Muhammad al-Hindi an important figure in local doctrinal squabbles, married the daughter of a local Arab notable Abdullah Dthaheri; see IOR R/20/A/3465 File no. 921.

14 IOR R/20/A/2906 petition submitted to the Residency, 24th December 1923.

Umar Abdullah Sharaf and Awadh Abdullah Umar Sharaf (who were nephew and uncle) and Ali Ibrahim Luqman (father of Muhammad Ali).[15]

Fissures Within the ʿumma

As already noted, to the casual observer, the Muslims of Aden, on the surface, appeared to be the nearly ideal Muslim community, as issues of race and class seemed to have been minimal concerns. Indeed, the 'respectable citizens' – as they are frequently referred to in colonial documents – could present a decidedly united front when moral dangers were perceived to threaten the community as in the calls for the banning of *zar* in the early 1920s. The wealthy, such as Zakaria al-Hindi, saw to the spiritual needs of their brethren by building and endowing neighbourhood mosques. While the learned saw to the education of the youth either through the auspices of social welfare organizations such as the Arab Reformatory Club[16] or the *qadi*'s school. This seeming tranquillity was nothing more than a veneer covering deep cracks that divided the faithful. These fissures, however, were not due to differences in race or class or discrepancies in wealth. Instead, they were about belief and differing views of how one should live life as a good Muslim.

---

15 The campaign against *zar*, initiated in 1923, seems to have been spearheaded by individuals who would later be at the epicentre of the disputes over sacred space in the early 1930s whose doctrinal leanings might be described as 'pro-Salafi.' Most notable on the 1923 petition are Zakaria Muhammad al-Hindi and Sayyid Ali Ismaʿil both of whom were central figures in both the *dhikr* and Italian sermon incidents to be discussed below. Their absence from any of the 1932 petitions, even that of the Arab Literary/Reformatory Club, may be construed as a desire to maintain a low profile during a period of official scrutiny. See also, Kapteijns and Spaulding (1994: 7–38).

16 British records refer to a number of social welfare organizations in both Tawahi and Shaykh Uthman during the 1920s and 30s. The organization in Tawahi is consistently referred to as the Arab Reformatory Club. In relation to Shaykh Uthman, however, a number of names appear including the Arab Reformatory/Reform Club, the Arab Literary Club and the *Nadi al-Islamiyya*. Though different names they all seem to refer to the same organization.

The Pro-Salafis

By the 1930s the Muslims of Aden were apparently divided into two ideological camps. On the one hand, there were those who seemed disposed towards what can best be described as a Salafi worldview. On the other were those who – while recognising a need for reform within their society – saw many of things that the Salafi party advocated as a threat to important social institutions, especially *dhikr* and *ziyarat* to local tombs that were central elements of the community's moral compass.

Salafism was a 'neo-orthodox' brand of reform dating from the latter part of the nineteenth century. With its intellectual centre in Egypt, adherents of the Salafi movement sought to regenerate the faith by returning to the ideals and traditions represented by the 'pious forefathers' (*al-salaf al-salih*). To be sure, the term 'Salafi' was not one used by any of the parties involved, at least not in their official correspondence with the government.[17] However, it is the term that best describes the thought of those we might term 'modernist reformers.' In a number of petitions, public pronouncements and general correspondence with the colonial authorities, the reformists of Aden echoed many of the sentiments associated with the Salafi school of thought. Their views were best encapsulated in a series of sermons (the so-called 'Italian sermons' referred to earlier) apparently penned by the leadership of the Arab Reformatory Club and delivered at Friday prayers in Tawahi and Shaykh Uthman during April and May 1931 – sermons that would cause a great deal of communal as well as official consternation.

Like their brethren in Egypt, the Aden reformers declared that the troubles of their age (i.e. a faltering economy, unemployment, and colonial domination) were largely of their own making. While European rule was certainly oppressive, it had been brought about as a result of their own sloth, immorality and irreverence:

We wear turbans of different colours and decent clothes, but are like the merchant who behaves arrogantly and then goes about gambling, joking and

---

17 Though somewhat later Ahmad al-Asnag does use the term to identify himself and others in his book *nasib aden min al-harika al-fikriyya al-haditha* published in 1934.

insulting the faith in the coffee-shops and on the street. But if one inspects his
[…] house you will not find a single day's provisions and yet he sticks to his ways
with no work while his family lacks even the most basic necessities. Until when,
oh brothers, will you forsake these habits of laziness and carelessness?

There was a past time when all countries looked upon the Arabs with fear
and awe even the Persian Kisra and Roman Caesar; there was no state greater
than the first Arab state in numbers or in wealth […] But as for now, other
countries have emerged other than that first state; if any state of Europe has
arisen […] it is because every state has millions of men[18] all of whom are of one
heart, each of whom serves himself and his country. They study the sciences and
knowledge, until they reveal things that did not exist in earlier times. European
women, you will find, are learned in the diplomatic arts. If you discuss with her
'knowledge' she will defeat a great *'alim* from among our *'ulama'*. Most of us
know nothing of our religious duties or the other sciences. There pass days and
years and he walks about the coffee houses and lanes fixing his turban over his
eyebrows and raising his sleeves above his elbows with his stick in his hand
visiting from morning to night in the alleys and markets hitting this and cursing
that, abusing the faith and you get nothing from him other than the words 'fuck,
fuck' and the singing of pretty songs as if those were better than religious
learning.

The remedy to their predicament lay in greater attention to piety and
religious duty, the rooting out of *bid'a* or unlawful innovation from local
custom and personal industry and the acquisition of Western learning
which was to be put to the service of the community. 'Awaken and come
round to your senses from this reproachful conduct,' the sermon
continues, 'and exercise piety which is the main guide to good deeds and
protection from sin.'

Would you not fear God and change these circumstances into a life of progress
which would raise you to the degree of your ancestors? Will you not awaken from
this foolishness [*ghafila*] and follow what God has commanded and shun what
God has forbidden? Will you not fear God so that he may increase your wealth
and enable you to conquer your enemy, strengthen your power [*shawkah*] and

---

18 Curiously the Residency translator who was most likely of South Asian origin chose to
   translate the word *rijal* literally 'men' as 'soldiers'. The mistranslation of such a simple
   and unambiguous word suggests that even the civil servants of the Residency sought to
   influence the official view of communal politics.

your faith? If you remain in this state, know that your enemy will overpower you and disaster will befall us [...] Exercise piety and work for bettering yourselves, your country, your faith in this world and the next. Learn sciences so that you rise to the level of your forefathers and lead prosperous lives. May God extirpate our enemies and enable us to conquer them with His grace and mercy and enable us to learn useful knowledge to provide us with legitimate livelihoods.[19]

While pro-Salafi reformists appear to have been active in both Tawahi[20] and Shaykh Uthman, it was the latter which seems to have served as the epicentre of their activities and, indeed, conflicts with other Muslims. The India Office files identify three centres of pro-Salafi activity in Shaykh Uthman – the Arab Reform Club, the Zakaria or 'Zakoo' mosque and the Ahl al-Khair mosque. They also identify a number of individuals who were associated with each of those places who British officials regarded as the leaders of the reformists: Muhammad Ali Isma'il Luqman, Ahmad Muhammad al-Asnag, Zakaria Muhammad al-Hindi, Sayyid Ali Isma'il and Shaykh Ahmad al-Abbadi. Each of these men was linked by the British to both the reformist ideals associated with the Salafi movement and with one another. Shaykh al-Abbadi, for instance, was the Imam of the mosque supported by Zakaria Muhammad and taught in the school operated by the Arab Reform Club of which Muhammad Ali Luqman was president. Sayyid Ali Isma'il the *muttawali*, or patron, of the Ahl al-Khair mosque was a contributor to the Arab Reform Club and received religious instruction from Shaykh al-Abbadi. Ahmad Muhammad al-Asnag though seemingly having no official position within the community was cited as an active figure in both the Zakoo and Ahl al-Khair mosques.[21]

---

19 The Settlement authorities obtained a copy of one of these sermons delivered in the Ahl al-Khair mosque in Shaykh Uthman, 8th May 1931 through Awadh Abdullah, a former *qadi* of Shaykh Uthman and opponent of the Salafis. The full text of the sermon is contained in the appendix to this chapter.

20 The original sermon that sparked protests from the Italian Consul and subsequent British inquiry was read in a Tawahi mosque; see IOR R/20/A/3390 File 795, Note of Protest from the Italian Consul.

21 These connections are sketched out across various Indian Office Record files, the most important of which are IOR R/20/A/3390 File 795, R/20/A/3465 File no. 921 and R/20/A/2906.

These men were an odd collection, to say the least. Of the five, only one, Sayyid Ali Isma'il, was a native Arab resident of Aden. Zakaria Muhammad was an Indian merchant who had married into Shaykh Uthman society[22] and Muhammad Ali Luqman, though born in Aden, was the son of a senior Indian civil servant. Shaykh al-Abbadi was a Hadhrami born in Ibb and Ahmad al-Asnag was from Mukalla, the principle port of the Hadhramaut. Furthermore, with the exception of al-Abbadi (and possibly al-Asnag) none were trained religious scholars. Zakaria Muhammad and Sayyid Ali Isma'il were well-off merchants and landlords with penchants for endowing religious institutions. Muhammad Ali Luqman had a purely secular education in the Settlement government schools and in addition to serving as a president of the Arab Reform Club was a some-time journalist. Finally, al-Asnag while possibly having some religious training (the India Office Records files are vague on this count), was better known as a confident of the Sultan of Mukalla and apparently 'his man in Aden.' What they had in common, however, was a shared Salafi-esque view of the world and an open disdain for anyone who did not. Particular ire seems to have been reserved for those they regarded as the guardians of all that was backward and decadent in contemporary Muslim society, namely the serving and former *qadis* of Shaykh Uthman.

The 'Anti-Salafis' and the Shape of Local Confrontation

Because the British obviously considered the pro-Salafi reformers as potential sources of trouble there is much more about them in the official record. Intelligence was collected, their movements were watched and their public pronouncements monitored.[23] We have far less detailed information on those whom we might term the 'anti-Salafi' faction. The two most vocal, and therefore most visible, opponents of the pro-Salafis were the presiding and *qadis* of Shaykh Uthman, Shaykh Abdullah Umar Sharaf and his uncle Shaykh Awadh Abdullah Umar. Given the nature of

---

22 See footnote 17.
23 It is no coincidence that most of the biographical information on these individuals is garnered from police reports contained in IOR R/20/A/3390 and 3465.

the documentation it is much easier to distinguish what (or who) these individuals were against, rather than what they were for.[24] What we do know about them is that they shared a deep antipathy towards the individuals discussed above – if not, as we shall see, all of their ideas – and certainly seemed to speak for at least some of Shaykh Uthman's Muslims.

At first glance, the conflict between the pro-Salafis and the Shaykh Uthman *qadis* seems to a certain extent rooted more in a deep personal animosity towards one another than in any deep ideological differences. This is certainly how the British Commandant of Police characterised the problem when he wrote in the midst of the squabbles that 'the root of the present trouble is personal jealousy.'[25] And there is certainly evidence to support such a view. In the two years preceding the Commandant's comment in 1932, the *qadi* and his uncle had certainly lost public 'face' if not actual influence to the newly emergent reformists. The former *qadi*, Awadh Abdullah, had seen two mosques that he tried[26] to fund taken over and completed by the deep pockets of the Salafi-minded Zakaria Muhammad al-Hindi and Sayyid Ali Ismaᶜil.[27] Similarly, his nephew's own *madrasa* was steadily loosing students to the school of the Arab Reform Club with the arrival of Shaykh al-Abbadi who – as a result of his travels many seem to have regarded as more learned than the *qadi*.[28] While tempting, such a simple explanation belies the fact that all of the disputes contained in the Settlement files had at their root a

---

24 Also due to the nature of the records we have far less information on their lives than any of the pro-Salafi figures, these are hopefully gaps that will be filled in as research continues.

25 IOR R/20/A/3465 File no. 921 Memo 2362 from R.H. Haslam, Commandant of Police.

26 The Ahl al-Khair and Zakoo mosques.

27 There also existed a third benefactor, Abdul Rahim Khan whom we are told funded the bulk of the Ahl al-Khair construction. The fact that he is only mentioned in the past tense implies that by the time of the events related here he had either left the Settlement, died or otherwise refrained from involving himself in communal disputes; see IOR R/20/A/3390 letter from Awadh Abdullah Umar to the First Assistant Resident, 25th May, 1931.

28 IOR R/20/A/3465 File no. 921 Memo 2362 from R.H. Haslam, Commandant of Police.

conflict over religious authority. In particular, the authority to decide what was and was not permissible within public sacred space.

The first hint of dissension between these two parties emerged at the end of April 1931 when the Italian Consul lodged a complaint regarding the supposedly libellous sermons delivered by members of the Arab Reform Club in several mosques and quoted above. The Italians charged that during ʿId al-Adha a sermon was delivered in a Tawahi mosque 'in which references were made to alleged massacres and atrocities committed by Italian troops in Tripoli.'[29] On each successive Friday through the end of May similar sermons were reportedly given in mosques in Shaykh Uthman, in particular at the Ahl al-Khair, during the communal prayer. On each occasion the sermon was delivered by the president of the Arab Reform Club, Muhammad Ali Ibrahim Luqman. And on each occasion the sermon was duly reported to the Settlement authorities by the former *qadi*, Awadh Abdullah.[30] According to Qadi Awadh, at the beginning of May, Muhammad Ali accompanied by members of the Arab Reform Club – including Ahmad al-Asnag – began attending Friday prayers at the Ahl al-Khair mosque even though they had never 'been accustomed to offering their prayers there.' Following the prayer, Luqman stood and delivered the *khutba*,[31] and on each occasion, Qadi Awadh stood up and objected both to the topic and the right of an unlearned individual such as Luqman to preach. On the last of these, May 29th, before the prayer he went to the Imam of the Mosque – Ahmad Nu'man Qudsi – and asked him not to allow this to continue. The former *qadi* was then confronted by Sayyid Ali Ismaʿil and Ahmad al-Asnag and the situation degenerated into a shouting match. Qadi

---

29 IOR 20/A/3390 Note to First Assistant Resident 30th April, 1931. A reading of the full text in the Appendix at the end of this chapter will, indeed, show this to be true.

30 There are distinct references to three different occasions May 3rd, 8th and 29th. IOR 20/A/3390 Awadh Abdullah to First Assistant Resident, 25th May 1931 and Police report 5th June, 1931.

31 Qadi Awadh claimed that these were all the same sermon, it is more likely what he meant was they all followed the same formula as the one contained in the appendix, *i.e.* Luqman read excerpts from *al-Shura* or some other newspaper and then preached a lesson on moral probity and the need for reform.

Awadh stormed out (or was thrown out, it's not clear which) and went to say his prayers at the Aydarus mosque in Crater.[32]

Qadi Awadh's objections to Luqman's sermons, noted in a subsequent letter to the Resident, were twofold. First, the mosque, he noted, was a place of worship and not a venue for 'politics or abuse of other religions.' Second, simply because they had money did not give the reformers the right to throw their weight around and implement changes on their own initiative. 'The people, Sir [sic.],' the former *qadi* wrote, 'are going out of their bounds to the extreme and it is high time to set an example in their case in the interest of the general peace of the protected public in Aden.'[33]

Up to a point, the British authorities seem to have agreed with Qadi Awadh. H.M. Wightwick, the Acting Political Resident, ordered Luqman, Sayyid Ali, Ahmad al-Asnag and Shaykh al-Abbadi to appear before him.[34] Al-Asnag was conveniently away accompanying the Sultan of Mukalla on a tour of Europe. The others, however, were brought before the Resident on 15th June, 1931, and told in no uncertain terms to cease and desist. Luqman was told that 'he had no business whatever to go to Sheikh Othman [sic.] to deliver sermons in Mosques without the permission of the Imam.' Sayyid Ali, for his part was reminded that he was simply a 'butcher' and 'not one of the leaders of Sheikh Othman.' Leadership, he was told, was in 'in the hands of the Mansab, the Kadi [sic.] and the leading men of Sheikh Othman [sic.],' and 'he was to have nothing to do with it.' Shaykh al-Abbadi was sternly reminded that he was a guest in the Settlement and might face deportation if he was connected with future disturbances.[35] The 'anti-Salafi' Qadi Awadh would seem to have won the first round. However, this dispute over who

---

32 IOR 20/A/3390, Police Report 5th June 1931.

33 IOR R/20/A/3390, Letter from Qadi Awadh to Wightwick, 16th July, 1931.

34 It is certainly curious that al-Abbadi was included on this list. Neither the police nor Qadi Awadh implicated him in the sermons. It is likely the Resident called him in simply because he was seen as the ideological leader of the reformists.

35 IOR R/20/A/3390, A note of warning given by the Acting Resident Wightwick to (1) Mohamed Ali Ibrahim (2) Sayed Ali Ismail (3) Sheikh Ahmed El Abbadi.

had the right to determine what was preached during the Friday prayers was only the first of many public disputes among the Muslims of Aden.

Disagreements between the parties – which now expanded to include the former *qadi's* nephew Abdullah Umar, other custodians of the Ahl al-Khair mosque and Zakaria Muhammad – appear to have continued through the rest of year. The nature of these disagreements is unknown but they were apparently serious enough to merit a *sulha* or reconciliation council that took place on the 26th January, 1932 which also happened to be the middle of Ramadan. The gathering was convened by Sayyid Fadhl al-Aqrabi[36], in the presence of a British police inspector, E. Raynor. After considerable discussion the parties agreed to 'remove whatever ill there was in their hearts against the other' and that none should act to harm the other. In particular, Sayyid Ali and the *qadi* Abdullah Umar agreed that in future they would discuss in writing any disagreements they had and would refrain from involving the authorities in their religious disputes.

The truce was very short-lived and was essentially broken on a February evening near the end of Ramadan in 1932, when the head of the Ahmadiyya Sufi order, Shaykh Muhammad al-Rashid, was visited by two men in his Shaykh Uthman home. The two, Abduh Haydar and Abdullah Muhammad Hattim were followers of Ahmad al-Abbadi. They questioned the Ahmadi *shaykh* about his theological beliefs and then issued a stern warning (some would say threatened). He was to stop performing *dhikr* and disseminating, what they believed were, his misguided teachings. If he failed to do so, there would be trouble. This, according to Shaykh Muhammad, was only the first of a number of warnings which grew increasingly ominous.

Not one to be cowed by threats, the harassed Sufi leader decided to take the fight to the enemy. On the evening of February 24th, following the *'isha* prayer, he and his followers entered the Zakaria mosque. When the prayer had ended, and as worshippers filed from the sanctuary, Shaykh Muhammad and his supporters began to recite their *dhikr*. Not

---

36 Nothing is thus far known about this individual other than the fact he appears to have been agreeable to all parties as a mediator.

surprisingly, an altercation quickly developed. One of the followers of al-Abbadi began to swear and verbally abuse the praying Sufis. In an effort to stop the worshippers, the caretaker of the mosque dowsed the lights hoping the darkness would prevent them from continuing. Undeterred, Shaykh Muhammad and his followers continued their remembrance of God and left only when they were finished. Upon leaving the mosque, however, rather than return home they proceeded to the house of the *qadi* Abdullah Umar and then to the police station to file a complaint. As individuals under 'the protection of the British Flag,' they declared, their right to freedom of religious expression had been violated by the Salafis. They demanded satisfaction and filed a formal complaint.[37]

The goal of the Ahmadiyya Sufis in performing *dhikr* in the Zakaria mosque on the 24th February seems to have been a statement meant more to defend their right to perform *dhikr* at all rather than to celebrate it any place they chose.[38] For a while Zakari Muhammad claimed that he only objected to *dhikr* being held within the precincts of the mosque he had constructed and endowed, the Sufis held that the pro-Salafi adherents (which included Zakaria Muhammad) were engaged in a systematic attempt to prohibit *dhikr* and other public displays of spirituality within Aden.[39] In support of this contention, they cited not only the threats made against the Ahmadiyya but another incident less than a week later. On February 29th a group of Shadhilis were holding *dhikr* in the Sayyid Hashim Bahr mosque, a place that all agreed regularly hosted such rituals.[40] In the midst of their prayers a group led by Abdullah Hattim, Abduh Haydar and Ahmad al-Asnag burst in and threatened the Sufis if they continued. Despite the provocation, the Sufis refused to rise to the bait and continued their prayers. In light of the past weeks of

37 India Office Records [IOR] R/20/A/3465 File no. 921.
38 Their claim to this is given greater credence by the fact the Ahamdiyya adherents held their *dhikr* not in the Zakaria mosque itself but in a smaller adjacent structure known as the Dhahiri mosque constructed by Zakaria Muhammad's father-in-law and, as far as the Sufis were concerned, not subject to the ban.
39 IOR R/20/A/3465 File no. 921 letter from Zakaria Muhammad to H.C. Fleming, Magistrate, 10th March 1932.
40 A list of Mosques in Shaykh Uthman compiled by Residency officials notes the Sayyid Hashem mosque as one where *dhikr* was regularly performed; see footnote40.

harassment, however, the unnerved Shadhilis petitioned the Resident for help. Noting the increasingly aggressive pattern of pro-Salafi behavior they begged protection from the authorities against 'the revolution of Muhammad Ahmad al-Abbadi and his followers,' before 'very harmful things happen in mosques among Muslims in Shaykh Uthman.'[41]

The Shadhili's warning, it would seem, was not just about *dhikr.* There were other flashpoints among the suburb's Muslims regarding acceptable ritual. As early as 1926, for instance, Sayyid Ali Isma'il and others had sought to restrict observances during the annual *ziyarat* at various tombs throughout the Settlement. In particular, they wished to ban the performance of *tamburra*[42] which Sayyid Ali argued promoted licentious mixed dancing, sorcery and debauchery.[43] *Tamburra* was, in fact, banned from the *ziyarat* though, unlike *zar*, its performance in private ceremonies was not outlawed. Nevertheless, this did not stop the performers and devotees of *tamburra* continually petitioning for its reinstatement. As late as 1931, they begged the Residency to consult the *'shams al-'ulama"* Sayyid Abdullah Aydrus on whether or not it was a permissible practice.[44] Sayyid Ali, for his part, complained to the authorities that Qadi Abdullah Umar was conspiring against him because of his opposition to *tamburra* and other immoral activities associated with the local 'fairs'.[45]

The ban on *tamburra*, in fact, takes up its own entire file in the Aden records.[46] However, quite possibly because the majority of people whom it affected were Sudanese and Somali sweepers living on the margins of

41 See footnote 39, Letter from the Shadhilis to the Resident, 3rd March 1932.
42 A kind of spirit possession ceremony associated with the Sudan but commonly found in Aden during this period. It appears very similar to *zar* except that its practitioners were mainly men and it was closely associated with the annual pilgrimage to the tomb of Sharif Aydarus.
43 IOR 20/A/3390 letter from Sayyid Ali Isma'il to Wightwick, 20th July 1931.
44 Aydrus consistently argued that is was indeed permissible within the bounds of religion.
45 IOR R/20/A/2766 Tamboora in Aden, petition to perform Tamburra at the Ziyara of Shaykh Ahmad Tawahi, 16th November 1931; IOR R/20/A/3390 Letter from Sayyid Ali Isma'il to Wightwick, 20th July 1931.
46 IOR R/20/A/2766 Tamboora in Aden.

Shaykh Uthman society, it seems to have generated no open conflict.[47] Indeed, even the Sufi dispute over *dhikr* would seem to have involved only a limited segment of society. This was not the case with an issue that had a more direct impact on all believers, the ritual performance of prayers and the 'proper' *adhan* (call to prayer).

Within the file on *dhikr* a peculiar set of reports and affidavits appear from approximately the same time period. On January 5th 1933 a near riot erupted outside the Awadh Salem mosque following the evening prayer. The *nadir* or 'manager' of the mosque, Abd al-Majid Ahmad had suddenly declared that the *fatiha* (opening *sura* of the Quran) was no longer to be recited at the end of the *adhan*. To insure that his order was followed, Abd al-Majid dismissed the Imam of the mosque who usually recited the call to prayer and ordered one of his own companions to utter the call omitting the 'offending' verse. Not surprisingly, this caused a stir among the regular attendees who, encouraged by the Imam, demanded an explanation. Abd al-Majid responded angrily, shouting that he was the one responsible for this mosque and that the *fatiha* would not be recited. If anyone disagreed, he would fire the Imam and shut the mosque. Violence, according to the Shaykh Uthman police, was only averted by their timely arrival and dispersal of the crowd.[48]

Once again, the Muslims of Shaykh Uthman were at one another's throats; this time over proper ritual. Within Aden, it seems to have been commonplace to recite the *fatiha* at the end of at least the *maghrib* or evening *adhan*. The pro-Salafis seem to have regarded this as a dangerous innovation and resolved that it should be stopped. It was already omitted from the *adhan* in the Zakaria and Ahl al-Khair mosques, of course, and it would seem by early 1933 they had decided to try and extend this to the other mosques in the neighbourhood. Their first attempt, as we have just seen, nearly caused a riot. Naturally, it spawned retaliation.

Salih Mahdi Habashi had been filling in for the regular muezzin at the Ahl al-Khair mosque since 4th January. Since the Ahl al-Khair was

---

47 See IOR R/20/A/2766 Tamboora in Aden for details.
48 IOR 20/R/A/3465 file no. 921 Report from Shaykh Uthman police station, 5th January 1933.

under pro-Salafi control the *fatiha* was not read at the end of the call to prayer. On the 9th, after he'd been reciting the call for five days, Salih Mahdi suddenly added the *fatiha*. The leadership of the mosque was furious and a complaint was filed with the police. When questioned as to why he had recited the verse when on previous occasions he had left it out, Salih Mahdi replied, 'I recited this verse, because I'd forgotten all about it' on the other evenings.[49] The next evening, needless to say, Salih Mahdi was not asked to recite the *adhan* and the verse was omitted. This did not mean there was not trouble. As Abdullah Hatim began the evening prayer, another individual Mahmud Hasan appeared on the mosque's porch and began to lead another group in prayer. As the police inspector reporting the incident noted, 'two imams are never allowed to say prayers at the same time in the same mosque.'[50] Mahmud Hasan stated that the reason he and his followers began reciting their prayer separately was that as the *fatiha* was not recited after the *adhan*, prayer had never started. The only thing that prevented another potentially violent incident from erupting among the worshippers was the quick action of the unnamed police inspector. Expecting trouble, he had stationed plain-clothes policemen in and around the mosque who quickly intervened before trouble could begin.

The administration had had enough. On the 17th they ordered all the Imams and *nadirs* of Shaykh Uthman to appear before the district magistrate. In addition, as the suspected instigators of discontent, Qadi Umar Abdullah, Shaykh Ahmad al-Abbadi and Sayyid Ali Isma'il were each called in separately. The Imams and *nadirs* were informed that they were responsible for keeping the peace within their mosques and could only make changes in ritual with the consent of the congregation. Umar Abdullah, Ahmad al-Abbadi and Sayyid Ali Isma'il were informed that the authorities were at their wits end and that further disturbances would not be tolerated. If further breaches of the peace occurred that could be traced to any one of them, dire consequences (i.e. deportation from the

---

49 See footnote 50. Report from Shaykh Uthman police station, 10th January 1933 and statement by Salih Mahdi Habashi, 10th January 1933.

50 Ibid., Report from Shaykh Uthman police station, 11th January 1933.

Settlement) would swiftly follow. Overnight the disturbances ceased and this is the last record in the file. It can only be presumed that this was the end of the leaders' open disputes.

Communal Faultlines

British officialdom in Aden tended to view all of these disputes as essentially personal squabbles among elites that spilled over into the public sphere. Police reports and notes from the Residency are unanimous in their conclusion that public disruptions caused by these disputes were in fact a result of the machinations of elites intent on serving their own venal ends. Certainly, a strong odour of personal dislike permeated these quarrels. Muhammad Ali Luqman, for instance, attacked the character of the ex-*qadi* Awadh Abdullah in a piece in the Egyptian newspaper *al-Shura*. At the same time, Muhammad Zakaria in an affidavit to the Residency accused the former *qadi* of embezzling mosque funds and Sayyid Ali Isma'il formally requested that charges be brought against him for slandering his good name.[51] Those on the other side acted no better. The ex-*qadi* referred to Muhammad Ali Luqman as a boy meddling in the affairs of men while Zakaria Muhammad was viewed disdainfully as 'that foreigner' who thought he could simply buy his way into the leadership of the Muslim community. The worst slurs were reserved for al-Abbadi who was vilified as a 'Wahhabi' bent on forcefully imposing his teachings on the faithful.[52]

However, is petty political bickering and nascent factionalism all we are able to discern from the example of colonial Aden? If we move beyond the name-calling we can see that these disputes were about very real issues of authority, ritual and practice that were of concern to all

---

51 IOR R/20/A/3390 'What Kind of Man' article in *al-Shura*, 1st July 1931; IOR R/20/A/3465 File no. 921 Letter from Zakaria Muhammad to the Assistant Resident at Shaykh Uthman, 15th March 1932; IOR R/20/A/3390 Letter from Sayyid Ali Isma'il to Wightwick, 20th July 1931.

52 See various letters and note in IOR R/20/A/3390 and IOR R/20/A/3465 File no. 921. I should add that during the late nineteenth and early twentieth centuries the label 'Wahhabi' was the favourite charge to throw at any individual whose views you did not agree with. As such, it was used more as a swear word than a designator of one's actual theological beliefs.

Muslims. At the heart of these disputes was the desire of all parties to shape and define the identity and boundaries of their community. These 'petty squabbles' were, in part, disputes over who had the right to define what it meant to be a 'good' Muslim in Aden. But at the same time, they represented a struggle to build a strong social consensus regarding exactly what these defining elements should be. For this reason it should come as little surprise that all of these disputes had at their core not only the definition of acceptable ritual but the control of sacred space where 'proper conduct' could be publicly inscribed: the neighbourhood mosque. If 'space', as Akhil Gupta and James Ferguson have argued, is '[…] a kind of neutral grid on which cultural difference, historical memory and social organization are inscribed' (1997: 34) then, in Aden, the mosque was the natural site for identity to not only be shaped but contested.

Mosques formed the backdrop of almost every factional dispute of the early 1930s. Pro-Salafis, such as Zakaria Muhammad and Sayyid Ali, believed that their financial support of mosques in Shaykh Uthman (e.g. the Zakoo and Ahl al-Khair mosques) gave them the right to determine what was said and done within those sanctuaries.[53] Others, including *qadis* of Shaykh Uthman as well as the Ahmadi and Shadhili Sufis, disagreed. From their perspective, an individual could not simply buy their way into a position of spiritual authority. This is surely their greatest complaint against the likes of Muhammad Ali Luqman who, they held, felt his right to preach to the community derived from his

---

53 In 1929 Zakaria Muhammad purchased the site of an unfinished mosque from the former Qadi Awadh Abdullah, for Rs. 6,000 which he then completed for an additional investment of Rs. 31,000. This was what became known as the Zakoo Mosque. He supported the mosque with a *waqf* that generated Rs. 100 of income per month. Built into the endowment was the stipulation that the site should be used strictly for prayer and that non-orthodox activities such as *dhikr*, which seems to have offended his reformist sensibilities, were explicitly forbidden. In addition, he engaged Shaykh al-Abbadi as the imam who used the *minbar* to advocate Salafi style reforms. Similarly, Sayyid Ali contributed Rs. 3,000. to finish construction work on what became known as the Ahl al-Khair mosque, coincidentally another mosque the former *qadi*, Awadh Abdullah, supposedly started but never finished; see IOR R/20/A/3390.

father's status as a 'great landlord' in the Settlement.[54] Communal leadership was not something that was for sale. Neither could it be obtained through mere learning. Both Luqman and Ahmad al-Abbadi were educated, the latter with impeccable religious credentials, but neither was considered to have any local standing. Authority, they would have argued, meant not only being able to talk knowledgeably about religious matters, but more importantly it meant representing the needs and respecting the beliefs of the wider community. To them, the likes of Zakaria Muhammad, Sayyid Ali, Ahmad al-Abbadi and the rest were crass *parvenus* interested not in protecting the beliefs and views of the community but in imposing their own ideas from above. The question of whose authority was more 'authentic' or representative of the community is largely beside the point as *both* parties obviously had some widespread support. What is of interest, however, is the nature of support for the opposing parties frequently defied easy characterisation and that the mosque served not only as a mouthpiece for elites to push their own agendas, but also as a stage for the articulation of genuine popular opinion and communal concern. It was the stage upon which local identity was defined.

The backgrounds of many of those expressing support for the pro-Salafi line are hardly surprising. Zakaria Muhammad, Muhammad Ali Luqman and Ahmad al-Abbadi were all well-educated and well-travelled individuals who were clearly in touch with the wider currents of Islamic religious and political discourses of their age.[55] Likewise, it should come as little surprise to find Muslims employed in the colonial civil service (including the Head Clerk of the Port Health Office, the Senior Boat Fare Clerk, the Head Postal Clerk and an unnamed Police Inspector of Crater) among the supporters of the pro-Salafi camp.[56] The pro-Salafi

---

54 IOR R/A/3390, Confidential note Awadh Abdullah to Wightwick, July 1931.
55 In particular, al-Abbadi, though from Ibb, is said to have travelled widely and studied in Persia and India.
56 The first three, named as Ali Asef, Ali Ahmad and S.A. Bari, respectively were signatories of the 1924 anti-*zar* petition along with the pro-Salafi Hitaris of Tawahi. The loyalties of the unidentified police inspector of Crater were demonstrated in a report filed with his superiors on 6th May 1931 in which he praised al-Abbadi and

camp, however, also drew support from quarters that, at a glance, would seem to be less than natural allies. These included individuals who are listed on various petitions as shopkeepers, butchers, artisans and even labourers. Most striking of all is the presence of a number of *Sayyids*. Foremost among these, of course, was Sayyid Ali Isma'il a self-described illiterate butcher whose social standing as a Yemeni descendant of the Prophet – one might have reasonably assumed – would have given him more in common with the Sufis and adherents to the Cult of the Saints than the Salafis with whom he allied himself.[57]

The anti-Salafi camp was similarly diverse. While including the 'usual suspects' such as many of the local '*ulama*' and the Sufi community, the anti-Salafi camp also included at least two employees of the Anglo-Persian Oil Company and a Havildar of the Mounted Police. The first two were South Asian clerks listed as petitioners for the re-establishment of *tamburra* as part of local *ziyarat*. The Havildar, Ali Husayn Murkashee whose ethnicity is unclear, took it upon himself to write a note to the Resident warning that al-Abbadi was spreading dissension among the Muslims of Aden by 'provoking the people who refused to obey his orders through sermons which consist [of] a prayer to God to ruin those who do not follow his doctrine.'[58] While none of these were directly involved in either the 'Italian Sermon' or *dhikr* incidents, their actions make clear with which party their sympathies lay.

Neighbourhood mosques certainly provided a venue for elites to push their own communal agendas. But they also provided a setting for non-elite individuals to voice their stake in the community. Local practitioners of *dhikr*, for instance, quickly took matters in to their own hands in order to defend their right to perform what they viewed as an essential Muslim ritual. More importantly, they sought not only to

---

denounced the Shaykh's detractors. A further note was appended to the report by his superiors who worried that he had become too closely associated with the pro-Salafi camp; see IOR R/20/A/2906, Petition against re-legalisation of Zar, 17th September 1932; IOR R/20/A/3390, Confidential report, Police Inspector, Crater, 6th May 1931.

57 For social importance of the cult of the saints and the Yemeni Sada, see Knysh (1997).

58 IOR R/20/A/3390, Letter from Havildar Ali Hussain Murkashee to First Assistant Resident, 6th July 1931.

protect this right within their own spaces but carried the fight to the ground of their opponents in the Zakaria mosque. By doing so, they were able to lay claim to *dhikr* as not simply a local custom, to be performed within spaces dominated by Aden 'tradition' but as a perfectly respectable Islamic ritual that could be carried out in any Muslim space. A claim they sought to reinforce by seeking the backing of both religious (i.e. the *qadi*) and civil authorities. The dispute over the *adhan* can be viewed as a similar dynamic one in which both sides attempted to exert authority over all sacred space in an attempt to inscribe their own definition of proper Muslim ritual and conduct across the entire community of believers.

On their own, the disputes among the Muslims of Aden constitute an interesting case study in the construction of a local community's sense of self. This process, however, did not emerge in some sort of local vacuum. While the boundaries of community were disputed within the confines of the neighbourhood mosque, the debates themselves were always informed by – and often in dialogue with – the intellectual currents of the wider *'umma*. As such, the resolution of local identity in Muslim Aden was, almost by definition, part of a broader trans-local process.

The term 'trans-local,' is one that has been in vogue for a number of years, but whose meaning continues to remain slippery. Though it has been used to describe physical movements or pluri-cultural spaces, in theoretical terms trans-locality is probably most usefully perceived as a state of tension between moment and consolidation out of which many processes of change result (von Oppen 2004). On the social level, such tensions lead to what Appadurai (1996) refers to as the production of localities and neighbourhoods. Localities, in this sense are not necessarily physical spaces but are more intangible spaces of social identity and interaction that are being re-produced again and again via practice and perception (see von Oppen 2004). As such, they are 'primarily relational and contextual rather than [...] scalar or spatial' (Appadurai 1996: 204). Following this line of thought, communities – what Appadurai refers to as 'neighbourhood' – emerge from the continuing interaction between social actors and the ideological constructs associated with the larger 'locality'. So, communal identity in Aden emerges not simply as a result of interactions between its Muslim inhabitants, for example, but also as a consequence of their interactions with the ideas present within the wider community of believers.

The structure of a community or neighbourhood within the trans-local paradigm is heavily influenced, if not out rightly dictated, by its interaction with what might be termed 'trans-local flows' i.e. the spatial movements of people, goods, ideas and symbols that connect places and regions (von Oppen 2004) and, I might add, communities. In Appadurai's view, however, the 'flow' itself is merely a vehicle which in turn creates *contexts* (i.e. social, political, intellectual or economic spaces) that are perceived, analysed, debated and reacted to by individuals and the interpretations of which ultimately result in the construction of neighbourhood/community boundaries. Such flows, however, are hardly a one-way street, thus the construction of contexts within a given community conversely affect both the trans-local flow and its point of origin. In the words of Appadurai, 'neighbourhoods are contexts and at the same time require and produce contexts' (1996: 209). The trans-local process, therefore, is a dynamic one in which the 'target community' has as much potential impact on the wider discourse as the wider discourse has on the individual community. The idea that cultures are neither fixed in space nor naturally occurring primordial phenomena is one that has been widely accepted in anthropological circles for more than twenty years (Gupta and Ferguson 1997). The problem for historians has often been the ability to demonstrate this process within a historical context.

The Muslims of colonial Aden provide insight into this process via the fortunate confluence of a number of circumstances. First, they constituted a paradigmatically trans-local community. This was due not simply because they were an ethnically and socially diverse group thrown together as a result of British colonialism. Rather, it resulted from the tension created through their interaction with a number of broader 'trans-local flows' including the world of Islamic ideas; the economic networks of the Indian Ocean trade; and the growing and diametrically opposed political networks of colonial service and anti-colonial resistance. It was the interaction amongst all of these in concert with local social issues that worked to define and redefine the boundaries of their own community. More importantly, we are able to gain entry into this process due to the highly public stage on which these issues were debated, i.e. the neighbourhood mosque as well as affiliated institutions. The colonial record demonstrates that to one degree or another each of these flows had an impact on the socio-religious context of Aden's Muslims. It was Indian Ocean commerce, for example, that not only brought the Indian Zakaria Muhammad to Aden, but enabled him to bankroll pro-Salafi activities. Muhammad Ali Luqman's emergence as a local leader, as well as his own colonial education, was due at least in part to the colonial civil service career of his father Ali Isma'il who was the Residency's chief interpreter. However, the most important flows were the intellectual currents emanating from throughout the *'umma* that were clearly at the heart of communal strife and debate.

The Muslims of Aden were well acquainted with contemporary currents of reformist thought through their own travels or the growing print media that was available to inhabitants of the Settlement. Ahmad al-Abbadi, for instance, studied in Iran, the Hijaz and India, while Ahmad al-Asnag travelled on at least one occasion to Egypt and continental Europe in the company of the Sultan of Mukalla.[59] Muhammad Ali Luqman and his brother Abd al-Majid, for their part, were well connected with at least one highly politicised Egyptian newspaper, *al-Shura* whose masthead declared it to be 'An investigative newspaper in the affairs of Arab countries and other tyrannised lands.' As for the wider community, British reports asserted that newspapers such as *al-Shura* were easily available within the Settlement and, despite an apparently low literacy rate, widely disseminated. In the words of one *'alim*, there were as many newspaper readers in Aden as mosque attendees. From the tone taken by the British administration, it seems

---

59 The fact that al-Asnag's travels were reported in the July 1st, 1931 edition of *al-Shura* on the same date as articles appearing by the Luqman brothers – including the one which allegedly slandered Awadh Abdullah – would seem to indicate that he had a more than passing acquaintance with the publishers of the reformist paper.

clear that at least they believed that such connections had an impact on the local community and played a role in 'stirring' things up.[60]

Whether one supported or opposed them, reformist issues occupied the minds of many Adeni Muslims; ideas that – whether supported or resisted – played a role in shaping local identity. Aside from the affidavits, interviews and police reports concerning the activities of the community's leading actors, the Residency files of Aden are filled to overflowing with letters of protest and petitions opposing or defending supposedly anti-Islamic activities such as *zar*, *tamburra* and Sufi *dhikr* bearing the signatures of literally hundreds of Muslim residents. Prior to the 1920s, none of these issues appear as divisive. It was only after 1920 and the emergence of the Salafi movement that they became the focus of social conflict. As the practitioners of *zar*, for example, noted in their complaint to the authorities after being banned, the ritual had been practiced in the city for over a hundred years and thus could hardly be unlawful. Even the acknowledged leader of the *'ulama'*, Sharif Abdullah Aydrus, noted that it was a long standing social institution in Aden and even though not explicitly condoned by religious law it was also not forbidden.[61] The initial complaint in late 1923 prominently bore the signature of Zakaria Muhammad suggesting that the anti-*zar* campaign was initiated by those with a pro-Salafi orientation. By the early 1930s, however, *zar* was no longer seen as socially acceptable by many, if not most, of Aden's male Muslims. Petitions appearing through the 1930s calling for a continuation of the ban include signatures of many associated with anti-Salafi activity. Even the heretofore supportive *shams al-'ulama'* Sharif Abdullah Aydrus joined his voice to the chorus of those calling for its prohibition. Salafi thought, as an ideological flow, thus had a clear impact on the inscription of Adeni Muslim identity. This is not, however, a history of how Salafism challenged and ultimately eliminated 'traditional' forms of the faith. Rather the importance of such an ideological flow is that it provides a window through which we can

---

60 They indicated that at least two other papers – *al-Fath* from Egypt and *al-Iqbal* published in Beirut – were also easily obtained.

61 R/20/A/2906; see note of meeting between First Assistant Resident and Sharif Aydrus, 10th January 1924; and petition by practitioners for removal of the ban on *zar*.

observe the contextual realities of the Adeni Muslims. What we see is a social-religious reality that was both complex and continually shifting. Such shifting realities are also reflected in the complex political lives of Muslim Adenis. As we have already seen, adherence to any one ideological school appears to have cut across what are often viewed as traditional social, ethnic and economic boundaries. Thus, it seems not uncommon to find a high level Indian civil servant devoted to the veneration of saints while one of the most vocal proponents of the Salafi camp was a Hadhrami Sayyid with an abhorrence of local *ziyarat*. By the same token, total dogmatic loyalty to any one set of ideals – aside from certain members of the identifiable leadership – appears relatively rare. Thus, the Qadi Abdullah Umar seems to have sided with the pro-Salafi faction over the permissibility of politicised Friday sermons, but actively opposed their condemnation of local Sufi practices as *bid'a*. Similarly, while a prominent figure in the debate over the 'Italian' sermons and an open opponent of *zar*, Muhammad Ali Luqman's name is conspicuously absent from the controversies over Sufi practice and ritual prayer. While his absence should not be construed as a sign of tacit support for the Sufi or 'traditionalist' position, it may indicate that his Salafism was somewhat selective in nature and that he may have chosen not to embroil himself in all aspects of their reformist activities. At issue, it seems, for individuals was not necessarily adherence to an abstract set of ideas, but rather the best way to arrest the moral, economic and social decay of their community. Beliefs that may, nevertheless, have begun to erode and change their relationships across communal boundaries and social contexts.

The second half of Appadurai's position (the notion that the local context in its turn informs and ultimately impacts the broader discourse) is at the moment more difficult to demonstrate. The journalism career of Muhammad Ali Luqman, however, certainly supports the image of Aden's Muslims as active participants in the intellectual currents of the period, rather than passive recipients of reformist ideology. Luqman regularly published in the Egyptian newspaper *al-Shura*, including pieces detailing Italian incursions across the Ethiopian border in the early 1930s and a shorter contribution, accusing the ex-*qadi* Awadh Abdullah of being a corrupt collaborator. While it's impossible to say what impact writers such as Luqman had on Egyptian political/social discourse, his was a voice from the so-called periphery that certainly had its place.

This chapter is a preliminary foray into the social and religious world of Aden's Muslims. It suggests an avenue of inquiry that takes us beyond the traditional categories used for social history. Namely, faith and its use in the construction of local contexts. Certainly, issues such as ethnicity, wealth, gender and social standing remain important in any examination of a community's social history. However, as the case of Shaykh Uthman demonstrates, other – more personal – factors may also play a role in determining where an individual's loyalties lie within communal discourse as well as the construction of communal space. As the episodes presented above demonstrate, the Muslims of Aden were hardly a monolithic community. Like many Muslims around the world, the believers of Aden were divided over how best to engage modernity and the question of religious reform. An individual's attitude toward such issues, however, is not easily predicted simply by their membership in a particular socio-economic or ethnic category.[62] Rather, other far less tangible factors need to be made part of the equation if we hope to construct a more nuanced image of Islam's encounter with the colonial or the 'modern' world. As the evidence from Aden suggests, while education, profession and social standing certainly played an important role in how one viewed the world, the much fuzzier realm of personal spiritual belief also had its place. More importantly, the construction of local Muslim space was deeply impacted by currents within the broader Islamic world. Contemporary reformist debates had a clear affect on local intellectual and communal contexts. However, as we have seen, the emergence of these debates was always shaped by local context itself as realized by local actors. In the end, while Adeni Muslims were part and parcel of the larger ʿumma the boundaries of their community were constructed by personal choice and personal piety.

---

62 Although, it should be pointed out, such categories are not completely useless as predictors of an individual's attitudes.

Bibliography

Alpers, E. 1986. 'The Somali Community at Aden in the Nineteenth Century', *Northeast African Studies*, 8.2 and 8.3.

Appadurai, A. 1996. *Modernity at Large: Cultural Dimenions of Globalization.* Minneapolis: University of Minnesota Press.

Gavin, R.J. 1975. *Aden Under British Rule, 1839–1967.* New York: Barnes and Noble Books.

Gupta, A., and J. Ferguson (eds) 1997. *Culture, Power, Place: Explorations in Critical Anthropology.* Durham: Duke University Press.

Kapteijns, L., and J. Spaulding 1994. 'Women of the Zar and Middle-Class Sensibilities in Colonial Aden, 1923–1932', *Sudanic Africa*, 5.

Knysh, A. 1997. 'The Cult of the Saints', in U. Freitag and W.G. Clarence-Smith (eds), *Hadhrami Traders, Scholars, and Statesmen in the Indian Ocean, 1750s–1960s.* Leiden: E.J. Brill.

Kour, Z.H. 1981. *The History of Aden, 1839–72.* London: Frank Cass.

von Oppen, A. 2004. 'Translocality – espace, relation ou mode d'action?', in L. Marfaing and S. Wippel (eds), *Relations Transsahariennes aux 20 ième et 21 ième Siècles [Réorganisations et Revitalisations d'un Espace Transrégional].* Paris: Karthala.

Appendix:

Sermon delivered in Shaykh Uthman, 8ᵗʰ May 1931

Oh brothers! God the Almighty has said 'if you espouse the cause of God, He will grant you success and strengthen you.' God has also said, 'Make preparation as much as you can by displays of strength and the possession of horses in order to horrify the enemy of God and your enemy as well.

The Apostle of God—may the peace and blessing of God be upon him, said 'The son of Adam can only be prevailed upon by those whom he fears and had he feared no one other than God, no one would have prevailed over him.' Similarly the son of Adam is made to rely upon those whom he sought for help and had he sought no one's aid other than that of God, God would not have made him rely upon other than Him.' He also said, 'Verily God is most forbearing.' Had not there been youngsters who entertained fear from God, aged people who worshipped Him, animals that grazed the pastures and sucking babies as well, He would have cast his severe chastisement upon you, Know, oh brothers, that each and every incident which takes place and each and every calamity or serious catastrophe that God has wrought upon us are on account of our wrongful deeds, non-cooperation and the jealousies we carry against one another' in that a man envies his brother for the clothing he wears or for a gift bestowed upon him by God. Jealousy is considered one of the most abominable sins which God has forbidden. The Prophet, (Peace Be On Him), said, 'Jealousy eats away good deeds as fire eats away firewood.' I see that in the present time in which we live dissension and bad manners amongst ourselves increase. Similarly drunkenness, sodomy, adultery and scandal are rife amongst us. A man sees his brother committing adultery, taking liquor or perpetuating misdeeds without checking or dissuading him as if the doing of wrong has become permissible. As if the Prophet, may the peace and blessing of God be upon him, had not given us the Holy Quran ... or as if God will not ask you to account for your misdeeds ... Do you scoff at the religion of your Prophet and play with the Holy Book of God taking it as an object of ridicule? Do you ignore the commandments of your Lord and the traditions of Your Prophet and act upon your desires as if the Holy Book were not in existence [...]? The Holy *shariᶜa* has been cast aside and replaced by [mere] laws and false sayings [traditions]. Where is our religious fervour[63] and Islamic zeal? Where have all the adherents of good morals gone?

We wear turbans of different colours and good clothes, but are like the merchant who behaves arrogantly and then goes about gambling, joking and insulting the faith in the coffee-shops and on the street. But if one inspects his... house you will not find a single day's provisions and yet he sticks to his ways with no work, while his family lacks even the most basic necessities. Until when, oh brothers, will you forsake these habits of laziness and carelessness? Awaken and come round to your senses from this reproachful conduct and

---

63 Interestingly, the word used here is '*ghayra*' literally meaning 'zeal' or 'fervour'; however the British translator chose to render it as 'fanaticism.'

exercise piety which is the main guide to good deeds and protection from sin. God said in the sixth chapter revealed to the prophet Moses, 'Oh worshippers of the *dinar* and the *dirham*, I did not create these for any purpose other than that you might eat My provisions and wear My clothing and thank My graces and use them as an aid for obedience and a way of leading you to paradise and away from hell. On the contrary you have used *dinars* as a means for disobedience and raised it upon your heads and worshipped it and kept My Holy Book under your feet. You have raised up your house and lowered Mine [...]

[Repetitive paragraph omitted]

Look at this noble address which shakes the mountains and frightens the hearts of the inhabitants of both worlds. There are many who deliver such speeches but where are those who will comply with them and there are many interdictions, but where are those who will be checked? Whenever we hear any admonition, we never take heed of it. What are these hearts which are harder than stone? What of these eyes that plead blindness from the right and reasonable path? As if you did not hear of your brethren in Tripoli who have been treated by the enemy as boys playing with a ball, they seek help but none is received, they call out, but no one gives them reply. He inflicted upon them various punishments and made them targets and subjected them to serious chastisement. Had you seen them, you would have heard the cries of the babies at the top of their lungs and your heart would have burst and your liver would have torn. They separated infants from their fathers while both were crying and weeping like animals in their fields. They could find no one to support them against their enemy. The Italians sent airplanes to drop bombs on their houses so that entire villages were raised. They threw people from planes laughing and saying 'where is your Bedouin Prophet, let him come and release you from our hands.' They went to the *Jabal al-Akhdar* and removed 80,000 Muslims—men and women—and drove them like cattle for thirteen days to a barren desert where there was no pasture or water. There they incarcerated them and surrounded them with iron bars while the people read the Quran and wept until most of them died... They took 300 women of the *Sayyids* and ordered them to be kept in the prostitute's lines, their soldiers saying they wished to enjoy the daughters of Muhammad. They took children and put them in schools to be taught Christianity so that they might be converted. Many other calamities befell them that would shake the earth and make the heavens rain blood. The received no help against their enemy. They [the Italians] ordered the burning of the Holy Quran and trod them underfoot. Some were thrown in dust-bins, others in road ways to be trampled under the hooves of horses and still others used for fuel. Is there any more serious calamity than this?

There was a past time when all countries looked upon the Arabs with fear and awe even the Persian *Kisra* and Roman Caesar, there was no state greater than the first Arab state in numbers or in wealth [...] But as for now, other countries have emerged other than that first state, if any state of Europe has arisen... it is because every state has millions of men[64] all of whom are of one heart, each of whom serves himself and his country. They study the

---

64 Again, a curious choice of words on the part of the translator who chose to translate this as 'soldiers' when the Arabic is clearly '*rijal*' or 'men'.

sciences until they reveal things that did not exist in earlier times. European women, you will find, are learned in the diplomatic arts. If you discuss with her 'knowledge' she will defeat a great *'alim* from among our *'ulama'*. Most of us know nothing of our religious duties or the other sciences. There pass days and years and he walks about the coffee houses and lanes fixing his turban over his eyebrows and raising his sleeves above his elbows with his stick in his hand visiting from morning to night in the alleys and markets hitting this and cursing that abusing the faith and you get nothing from him other than the words 'fuck, fuck' and the singing of pretty songs as if those were better than religious learning. Would you not fear God and change these circumstances into a life of progress which would raise you to the degree of your ancestors? Will you not awaken from this foolishness [*ghafila*] and follow what God has commanded and shun what God has forbidden? Will you not fear God so that he may increase your wealth and enable you to conquer your enemy, strengthen your valour and your faith? If you remain in this state, know that your enemy will overpower you and disaster will befall us... Exercise piety and work for bettering yourselves, your country, your faith in this world and the next. Learn sciences so that you rise to the level of your forefathers and lead prosperous lives. May God extirpate our enemies and enable us to conquer them with His grace and mercy and enable us to learn useful knowledge to provide us with legitimate livelihoods.

6

THE USES OF HISTORY:
RHETORICS OF MUSLIM
UNITY AND DIFFERENCE ON THE
KENYAN SWAHILI COAST[1]

Kai Kresse

This chapter is concerned with the uses of history in Swahili Islamic discourse. It looks at three accounts of the past that are presented in circumstances of a socially contested present, by two prominent Swahili Islamic scholars. In different ways, these two can be seen to represent recent historical pathways of transformation for the East African Muslim community. I describe this below, and I suggest how the particular concerns about history and its uses here can be linked back more generally to the relevance of history and the past within Islam, where it is central for the social establishment of normative orientation and religious authority. In this respect, Mohamed Qasim Zaman has recently taken up

1 Field research upon which this article is based was conducted in East Africa, mostly Mombasa, over thirteen months between 1998 and 1999, and for several weeks in 2003 and 2005. Funding by the German Academic Exchange Service (DAAD, HSP3 Doktorandenstipendium), SOAS, and the School of Philosophical and Anthropological Studies at the University of St Andrews is gratefully acknowledged. I am particularly grateful to Sheikh Abdilahi Nassir, for the invitation to attend his lectures, and for many subsequent conversations. My thanks for useful comments and discussion go to the participants of the 'Struggling with History' workshop in St Andrews, particularly to Mohamed Bakari. I also thank Anne Bang, Louis Brenner, Mark Harris, Edward Simpson, Roman Loimeier, Hassan Mwakimako, Joy Adapon and particularly Scott Reese, for comments on previous drafts. An earlier version of this chapter was also presented as the fourth of six Evans-Pritchard Lectures given at All Souls College, Oxford, in November 2005. I am most grateful to John Davis and David Parkin for their hospitality and comments.

the idea of a kind of flexible 'traditionalism' at the core of Muslim society, pointing at 'the recurrent effort by Muslims to articulate authority and evaluate claims to such authority by positing and reaffirming a connectedness to the past', an effort which he says 'is nowhere more pervasive than in Islam' (2002: 3–4).

Below, I explore how this connection to the past is addressed and maintained by the two selected Islamic scholars in lectures and publications. Shaping a sense of continuity within the community hereby seems an important rhetorical strategy for sustaining (and reshaping) communal identity in times of social change and contestation. In contrast, the forceful and resourceful claims to predominance by (an externally steered) Islamic reformism seem disconnected from the regional past and pose the threat of social alienation. With increasing loss of continuity and connectedness to the past (in a religious and social sense) comes the decrease of mutual respect and a common social vision. This characterises the contemporary scenario among Muslims on the Kenyan Swahili coast. In a situation of doctrinal competition and factional squabbles, the past continues to be a prominent and fundamental reference point.

The Swahili coast, as is well documented, has been part of Indian Ocean trading networks for at least two millenia (Pearson 2000: 37); and it has been part of the Muslim world for well over one millennium, as archaeological research has proven the existence of mosques in the area from around 800 C.E. (Horton and Middleton 2000). Portuguese sources of the sixteenth century attest to a wide range of ethnic background of the urban citizens (Strandes 1961). This reflects cultural influences and social interactions throughout history, comings and goings that had long been at work throughout the western Indian Ocean region; it also reflects the social networks that developed inward on the African mainland. The same sources also testified to the well-established urban grandeur of the coastal stone-towns which consisted of elaborate multi-storeyed houses. These features indicate flourishing trade relations, economic strength and vibrancy of a kind of multicultural society built around city states and their dependencies, already five hundred years ago.

Indeed, the period before the invasion of the Portuguese has been qualified as the 'golden age' of Swahili civilisation (Berg 1972). By that time, the Swahili towns were long integrated into the Muslim world through networks of religious, mercantile, and kinship nature. The Swahili coast was connected to others along the Indian Ocean, and Islam had been a major catalyst in the formation of these urban centres. Swahili networks of trade and kinship were expanded far into the African continent as well, taking Islam with them and making Kiswahili the *lingua franca* for traders and travellers all over East Africa.

The internal dynamics of the coastal Muslim communities, in terms of tensions, divisions, and activities of reconciliation, have been the focus of some recent studies (e.g. Hirsch 1998, Yassin 2004, Loimeier and Seesemann 2006) and will also be at the centre of this chapter. I look at the present and recent past, to describe and discuss the uses of history, or historical narratives, by two Islamic scholars based in Mombasa. Sheikh Abdallah Saleh Farsy (1912–1982) and Sheikh Abdilahi Nassir (*1932) use historical narrative to shape a sense of unity and solidarity within a community (and a particular audience) experiencing strong tensions between rivalling Islamic factions. I examine three historical accounts of different character and purpose, their interconnections and their relevance. These accounts also represent ways of negotiating history in a demanding situation for the Muslim community in Kenya during the post-colonial period.

Sheikh A.S. Farsy, originally from Zanzibar, moved to Mombasa after the Zanzibari revolution and, as Chief Kadhi of Kenya (1968–1980), is commonly seen as a decisive figure for the subsequent establishment of Salafi-inspired reformism along the Swahili coast.[2] Several of his followers visited Middle Eastern centres of Islamic higher education, and returned as advocates drilled for the reformist cause. Overall, Farsy, who is probably the most prolific writer of Islamic pamphlets in the history of the Swahili coast, played a crucial role in establishing this reformist ideology regionally (see Lacunza Balda 1990,

---

2 Along the Kenyan coast, the (more correct) term 'Salafiyya' for the Islamic reformist movement now mainly based in Saudi Arabia is rarely used among ordinary people.

1993). Sheikh Abdilahi Nassir, a politically engaged Islamic scholar and
former politician and publisher, on the other hand, changed alliances in
the early 1980s and turned from a pro-reformist orientation to Shi'ism,
becoming one of the first prominent Muslims with a Swahili and Shafi'i
background to declare himself Shi'a. Since then, he has become an
influential figure for the promotion of Shi'ism in East Africa, helping to
open it up to a new constituency of Swahili and upcountry Muslims.
Over the last two decades, he has also defended Shi'ism against
ideological attacks by so-called 'Wahhabi' reformists.[3] In speeches and
booklets addressing a wider regional Muslim public, he has presented
arguments for the commitment of Shi'ism to the Quran, the hadith, and
the companions of the Prophet; in the same vein, he has argued in
defence of *maulidi* celebrations[4] and the Shi'a traditions of *taqiya*[5] and
temporary marriage (Nassir 1989a, 1989b, 1990, 2002, 2003a, 2003b).
In this way, he has been making a case for a respectful relationship
between Shi'as and Sunnis in the region, and against what he saw as
common prejudices about Shi'ism within the Sunni community.[6]

Notably, both scholars were, at different stages and for different
reasons, denounced as 'outsiders' by proponents of the local Islamic
faction opposing them: in Farsy's case, by members of the Sufi-oriented
masharifu faction,[7] the Alawiyya, with its main stronghold around the
Riyadha Mosque in Lamu; in Nassir's case, by influential members of the
Swahili-Shafi'i community in reaction to his conversion which they

---

3 Following the local conventions of language use, this chapter will, when following
   internal references by local actors, use the term 'Wahhabi' to refer to Salafi-oriented
   reformists. For clarification on the background meaning of these terms, see entries
   'Salafiyya', 'Wahhabiyya', and 'Rashid Rida' in the *Encyclopedia of Islam*.
4 These are ritual celebrations of the birthday of the Prophet Muhammad, performed
   mainly through the recitation of praises. They may also mark or commemorate events
   in the life cycle of family or community members.
5 This refers to the practice of hiding one's true faith in order to guard oneself and one's
   life, borne out of a history of persecution of Shi'as.
6 Elsewhere (Kresse 2004, 2007: Chapter 6) I have written more extensively on Sheikh
   Abdilahi's life and the Ramadan lectures referred to in this chapter.
7 *Masharifu* (singular, *sharifu*) is the common Swahili expression for the descendents of
   the Prophet (Arabic, *ashraf*).

regarded as betrayal. Intellectually, both were allied to Sheikh Muhammad Kasim Mazrui (1912–1982), who was a teacher and mentor of Sheikh Abdilahi and a close friend and companion of Sheikh Abdallah Saleh Farsy in the mission for Islamic reform (see Kresse 2003). Mazrui and Farsy had been students of Sheikh al-Amin Mazrui, the initiator of 'modernist' Islamic reform in East Africa.[8] Farsy and Nassir were both educated within the same regional system of Islamic scholarship and education on the Swahili coast, which was integrated into global networks of the Muslim world but had its own distinctive character (see below). This chapter is about the presentation of history, mainly by these two figures. In the way that they present their historical narratives, both convey to their audiences the impression of historical continuity between themselves and a unified yet internally pluralistic system of Islamic scholarship. This is expressed against the background of social tension and ideological battles that characterises the present and recent past, where such a unity has been lost.

The points of discussion here are closely connected to the historical shifts and transformations within East African Islam in post-colonial Kenya, first towards and later against 'Wahhabi' reformism – processes in which both of these figures have played a significant role. Against the background of the current situation (presented first, below), the historical narratives each emphasise a particular take on the use of history. Sheikh Abdilahi Nassir, in his Ramadan lectures from January 1999 provides a sketch of the historically established Islamic groups and schools of Islamic law (*madhhabs*) in the region, and positions the incoming strand of reformism within it; this also includes an account of the historically grown system of East African Islam (presented in part two). Some of the most influential scholars of these networks have been described by Sheikh Abdallah Saleh Farsy (1972, 1989), and his description is summarised and discussed against the background of his own position within East African Islam at the time (in part three). Reference to Sheikh Farsy becomes crucial in Sheikh Abdilahi Nassir's discussion of a series of 'open letters to the Wahhabi' in 2003. Here,

---

8 On Sheikh al-Amin Mazrui, see Pouwels (1981), A. Salim (1987) and S. Salim (1985).

Sheikh Farsy, as a pinnacle of regional reformist scholarship, is centrally invoked in the construction of an outspoken counter-discourse, defending Shiʿas – and with them, it is argued, all other local Muslims – against 'Wahhabi' attacks (part four).

History and the Current Situation
Over the second half of the twentieth century, Islamic reformism, supported predominantly from Saudi Arabia, attained a prominent and possibly dominant position within the Muslim community of the Kenyan Swahili coast. In terms of doctrinal orientation, this marked a change from what was generally accepted as 'mainstream' Islam on the coast. Simply summarised, East African Islam turned from a self-sustaining system to one reliant on external support and direction. The reformists seemed to have gained the upper hand in an (ongoing) historical struggle with the previously dominant *masharifu* faction of the Alawiyya and the Riyadha Mosque in Lamu.

Riyadha Mosque and College had been founded in 1901 by Habib Saleh (d. 1935), a Hadhrami sayyid stemming from the Comoros, after a model from Say'un in the Hadhramaut. Sayyid Habib Saleh is commonly credited with opening up the hierarchical system of a rather exclusive Islam dominated by Arabs and Swahili patricians (*waungwana*) to the underprivileged *watumwa* (slaves and former slaves). Their gradual integration into the urban Muslim community proceeded through Islamic education and the communal performance of ritualised Sufi practices, especially the *maulidi* (al-Hibshy) that Habib Saleh had also introduced from Hadhramaut. Thus his efforts during the late nineteenth and early twentieth century led to a social reform in Lamu and beyond (see el-Zein 1974, also Bang 2003). Today, despite strong currents of reformism, Sayyid Habib Saleh continues to be venerated. Thousands of Muslims travel to Lamu every year to celebrate *maulidi*; and for many, the *ziyara* (ritual visit) to his grave is an integral part of the annual celebrations. Yet these events are heavily contested among coastal Muslims because reformist criticism qualifies them as undue religious innovations (*bidʿa*; in Swahili *bid'a*).

This sketch indicates that transformations within the coastal Muslim community occurred due to the interplay of ideological and social factors. The dedicated efforts of individuals who stood for (different kinds of) reform managed to gain popular support, and had an influence on the process of reshaping society. Points of potential transformation were reached through shifts in the doctrinal and ideological orientation of ordinary Muslims in a struggle about what should count as the representative version of Islam for the region – which, for want of a better word, I here call 'mainstream Islam'. In this ongoing process of dynamic renegotiation, the successful recruitment of followers made it possible to press for social changes (in everyday life, politics, and religious ritual) under the banner of a certain interpretation of Islam. In this sense, social change was facilitated, 'made real' and turned into history, ultimately by the ordinary Muslims and their actions.

If this is true, it is also important to look at the ways in which positions are put forward, and how support for them is either granted or denied. Consequently, the historical instances in which a 'mainstream' position is challenged and (seemingly) replaced by another, due to a shift of public support, are potential turning-points within the social history of a Muslim community and as such merit particular attention. The 1970s marked a kind of turning-point for Islamic reformism in East Africa, leading over to a period of external ideological domination (see Kresse 2003). Below, I use a historical narrative presented by Sheikh Abdilahi Nassir as an entry-point to look at the recent situation at the Kenyan coast as another potential turning-point.

There is a difficulty, of course, in using the general expression 'reformists' here. This social environment which hosts a variety of Salafi-inspired reformist groups are partly in competition with each other, linked to different networks, and funded from different parts of the world. Yet for the remainder of this paper, I refer to 'reformists' as those groups whose ideology pushes for a social re-instatement of what they regard as 'pure Islam', as it was practised by the Prophet and his followers, and who are publicly visible in their activism against undue innovative practices (*bid'a*). I also pick up from common local language use among the opponents of such reformism (those criticised or attacked by the reformists) when rephrasing their narratives and portraying their perspectives; they mainly use the term 'Wahhabi' when referring to their adversaries. Strictly speaking, this is somewhat misleading, as these reformists have no direct connection to the historical Wahhabis of the eighteenth century (though they may admire them), nor do they call themselves 'Wahhabi'; yet with its negative connotations the term ethnographically reflects the social reality of local language use.[9] In terms of attitude, project, and agenda, there are reformists of various schools and doctrinal backgrounds, linked to Islamic organisations from outside Kenya, particularly countries like Saudi Arabia, Pakistan, Egypt and Sudan. Local discourse among their opponents somewhat lumps these together, based on general features that these groups share: the rejection of a wide range of practices, in everyday life as well as on ritual occasions, as unacceptable religious innovation (*bid'a*). This includes certain ways of dressing and behaving (including singing and dancing) that are deemed improper, and also other historically developed activities shaping the specific character of regional Islam, such as celebrating *maulidi*.

Despite – and in some ways because of – their strong ideological presence in public Islamic discourse, 'Wahhabi' activists are sometimes (but rarely openly) resented or even derided by ordinary Muslims in everyday life. This may occur in response to the way that they see their established way of life denounced and rejected by reformist ideology. During my fieldwork, I encountered people who resented the existent climate of social pressures to behave according to the strict reformist guidelines in all aspects of their lives. They complained that they were under surveillance by fellow Muslims all the time. On several occasions, I observed reformist demands being rejected, questioned, and even ridiculed or branded as hypocritical expressions of religiosity, ultimately serving the interests of social power and control. Some would even be

9 One important doctrinal influence for these reformist groups is the strand of Salafism, which was developed in the early decades of the twentieth century in North Africa, Egypt and Syria, and actively received in the Swahili region (most prominently by Sheikh al-Amin Mazrui), and we can therefore also call these groups Salafi-like reformists.

able to contest such demands with reference to the Quran (or to a more educated person having made such a reference), and to raise reasoned counterclaims. For instance, I overheard women talking about 'Wahhabi' demands of veiling all skin and hair except for their faces, or even their eyes. They were arguing that this was not necessary, and that a more moderate way of veiling was perfectly acceptable according to Quran and *hadith*. The exclusive claim to truth on the matters by the reformists was rejected. A humorous kind of counter-discourse on veiling has been going on for a number of years, documented for the early 1990s in Lamu (Fuglsang 1994) and still observable today. The way of veiling that covers the whole face except for the eyes is jokingly called '*ki-zorro*' or, more commonly, '*ki-ninja*', adjectives meaning 'Zorro-like' or 'in-a-Ninja-kind-of-fashion', referring to the masks worn by the American rebel and the East Asian warriors, popular through films and television. Such wordplay on matters deemed so serious by reformists naturally undermines the reformist cause. It may also reflect or underline the fact that reformists are often portrayed as notoriously humourless and relentless in their activism to spot *bid'a* products or practices everywhere.

This image is also conveyed by another humorous figure of speech, in which reformist activists are teasingly called *watu wa bid'a*, 'the *bid'a* people'. This seems to portray them going around pointing their finger at things or people around them exclaiming '*bid'a!*' in a kind of offended reflex.[10] Such images indicating anti-reformist counter-discourses may mostly be used confidentially and within a group of more or less trusted equals, when commenting on others. In public, critical comments may be avoided or at least formulated more carefully, using a language that adheres to standards of Islamic piety, so that the speaker may not be seen, or cast, as a bad-mannered or ill-willed opponent of Islam itself, but only of the ideological version advocated by the reformists. In this way, a common argument brought forward against complete veiling of the face is that it makes women unrecognisable and thus provides opportunities for immoral deceit. This point, underlining the ambiguity of veiling –

---

10 For Zanzibar, this has been documented by Purpura (1997: 349ff; 2000: 129).

discussed and negotiated throughout the Muslim world – also raises the suspicion that reformism itself may only consist of a rhetorical layer of piety, a metaphorical veil covering up other activities that it provides opportunity for, while also creating and deepening divisions in the *umma*.

The cases just described indicate a variety of counter-discourses that have emerged in response to the establishment of reformist doctrine in social life – which itself was initially successful in claiming to provide a strategy of safe-guarding what is 'true' and 'valuable' according to Islam. Yet the observed local ambivalence, expressed in both jocular and resentful terms, about the attempts by reformists to implement a new paradigm of regional 'mainstream' Islam (with the help of external funding and ideology), indicates the contentious nature of the issue. What needs to be investigated further, then, are internal accounts and assessments of the historical period in which such a paradigm shift took place – what Mohamed Bakari once called a 'turning point' in Islamic discourse in Kenya (Bakari 1995).

Sheikh Abdilahi Nassir on the History of Islam at the East African Coast (1999)

In January 1999, Sheikh Abdilahi Nassir gave a series of daily Ramadan lectures in which he sometimes responded to questions from the audience. In one such instance he was asked to explain why there were now such pronounced annual squabbles among local Muslims about the beginning of Ramadan.[11] In response, over three consecutive lectures, he chose to provide a historical account of a kind of 'reformist takeover' of East African Islam from within, together with background information and comments about its effect on the established system of East African Islam. His narrative reflects a 'struggle with history' as it recounts the dynamics of fundamental changes for East African (and particularly coastal Kenyan) Islam during the late twentieth century. I will reproduce

---

11 I attended almost all of these lectures, by invitation, and recorded them with permission. Transcriptions of many, including those discussed here, were kindly produced by Swaleh Said. For other details on these lectures, and on Sheikh Abdilahi as a public speaker and thinker, see also Kresse (2004; 2007: Chapter 6).

his main arguments, and connect them later to other interpretations of this history, discussed in the light of his version.

Sheikh Abdilahi Nassir is a notable Swahili intellectual, well-known along and beyond the Swahili coast as former politician, captivating public speaker, and socially engaged Islamic scholar. He was born in Mombasa in 1932, and is of part Indian ancestry. His public switch to Shiʿism in the 1980s, when he was living in Nairobi, transgressed the socially prescribed borderlines of religious identity. It caused some outrage within the Swahili Shafiʿi community, at a time when factional Islamic affiliation was commonly defined by descent and ethnic background. The Swahili community has been overwhelmingly Sunni Shafiʿi for many centuries, while the Shiʿa Ithnaʿashari community was mainly constituted by South Asian and Persian traders immigrating during the nineteenth and twentieth century who intermarried among themselves. Sheikh Abdilahi's decision to convert was rejected by the Swahili- and wider Sunni community who had now lost one of their most popular spokesmen. He had to endure verbal abuse and concerted efforts to isolate him socially within the Swahili community. Being one of the first prominent coastal converts to Shiʿism, his case established a precedent for other potential converts of Swahili and African descent to follow suit, often young people seeking to renew their religious identification. It is to them that Sheikh Abdilahi's lectures are especially but not exclusively addressed.

In the following pages, I discuss three basic aspects about knowledge and use of history in Sheikh Abdilahi's lectures. Firstly, the lectures exemplify the general relevance of historical knowledge for understanding the present. He emphasised that in order to understand the reasons for current disagreements about the beginning of Ramadan (and similar issues) one has to know the basis of the previous consensus about these issues. Secondly, the lectures convey particular historical knowledge about this consensus: how it was based on a unified system of Islamic education and scholarship, which itself was made possible by a unity (or convergence) of underlying principles, as defined by Islamic *madhhab*. Thus, knowing about the historical constellation of *madhhabs* (as legal schools and Islamic sub-groups) in a region is crucial for assessing issues of doctrinal consensus or disagreement, and the corresponding status of social stability. Thirdly, and in conclusion, the lectures convey how change and imbalance in *madhhab* constellation can undermine doctrinal consensus and social unity, and they illustrate how this has been brought about by the introduction of Saudi-led reformism into East African Islam.

To reiterate, Sheikh Abdilahi's three lectures sought to clarify the reasons behind the recent disagreements about the beginning of Ramadan, leading Muslims to start their fast on different days. These kind of squabbles had been recurring for a number of years, leaving ordinary Muslims confused and worried about the correct date for the beginning of the fast, and about the status of their own behaviour. On a national level (where Muslims are a minority), these arguments had become embarrassing for the Muslim community, as their disunity and inability to find a solution to this problem was exposed and commented upon in the media. Now, in order to understand the situation, Sheikh Abdilahi pointed out, it was crucial to look closely at history. There was no short and easy answer, he said, asking people to listen patiently to the long historical sketch he was about to present. He pointed at the necessity to understand how different *madhhabs* were situated in the history of Islam in East Africa, and he presented the four main historically established *madhhabs* in the region as Shafiʿi, Ibadhi, Hanafi, and Shiʿa Ithnaʿashari.[12] Recourse to *madhhab* was needed, he said, as issues about Ramadan were matters of *fiqh* (Islamic jurisprudence), and the different institutionalized traditions of interpretation of *fiqh* de facto constituted the various *madhhabs*.

The point of his overview was to show how a *madhhab* previously alien to the Swahili region, namely the Hanbali one, had been

---

12 It is remarkable that Ibadhi and Shiʿa Ithnaʿashari are listed as *madhhabs* here (Sheikh Abdilahi uses '*madhhabi*' in Swahili), a term usually used for the four Sunni schools only. This may have to do with the trans-sectarian impetus here. The related Swahili term *madhehebu* (derived from *madhhab*) also refers to 'school of thought', 'denomination' or 'sect' more generally. This seems a welcome double-connotation here. – Sheikh Abdilahi also mentioned the Bohoras, Memons, Badalas and Koknis as minor (and for the question irrelevant) regional Islamic factions.

introduced into the Muslim community through the cooperation
between internal (Shafiʿi) and external (Hanbali) reformists. The most
prominent local Shafiʿi reformists were Sheikh Abdallah Farsy and
Sheikh Muhammad Kassim Mazrui. Sheikh Abdilahi noted their role as
facilitators to integrate reformist doctrine from Saudi Arabia, which itself
is based on Hanbali principles. As respectable scholars, they provided an
internal platform for its dissemination. Nevertheless, Sheikh Abdilahi
also stated that it was important to see that, in matters of *fiqh*, they
themselves remained Shafiʿi and stuck to Shafiʿi positions. In this they
differed from incoming reformists and from Swahili Muslims returning
from their higher education at reformist institutions in the Middle East.
Thus the two stood for a continuity of East African Islam, and still
represented a previously established consensus: Shafiʿi interpretation
should prevail in terms of judgements and regulations of public rituals,
based on the majority principle. This principle became undermined,
according to Sheikh Abdilahi, once Hanbali doctrine had quietly
acquired a firm stronghold inside the community, through a system of
scholars and teachers. Yet, Sheikh Abdilahi claimed, this development
had hardly been noticed within the community itself, as it was not
explicitly mentioned by those introducing it. They preferred to declare
themselves generally as 'people of the *sunna*' (*watu wa sunna*), a title
which rejects and overrides the differentiations by *madhhab*.

The following is an extended quote from Sheikh Abdilahi's speech
(in my translation), describing how the Shafiʿi *madhhab* was hollowed
out and substituted from within, with the Hanbali *madhhab*, through the
efforts of the external reformists:

[…] The final thing that led to the Hanbali *madhhab* gaining strength here in
East Africa was that those young men who, after returning from those external
institutions in the Middle East, were now boldly giving public speeches against
our established sheikhs, and had already received their higher education from
there. They were normal young men, just like us or you, but already they had
become part of a *madhhab* that was not the one of their parents and elders. When
they came back, they came back with the *madhhab* followed in Saudi Arabia,
namely Hanbali. This is a *madhhab* that was not around in this area in the past. I
was telling you earlier about the history of those *madhhabs* that were present in

East Africa [i.e. Shafiʿi, Ibadhi, Hanafi, and Shiʿa Ithnaʿashari]; this one was not – but it is a real *madhhab*, of Sunni denomination.

So when they returned, they came with this *madhhab*. People here did not notice that they had returned with a *madhhab* different from their elders, because they used a different label for it, 'Ansaar Sunna' [or also 'Ahlul Sunna']. They said, 'We want to follow the Prophet. We don't want any *madhhab!*' – but still, there in Saudi Arabia and wherever else there are representatives of this school, they are followers of Imam Hanbali. Therefore, this *madhhab* entered our community without people noticing that this was the case, and it entered here by the name of 'Ahlul Sunna'.

From then on people did things differently from the way that they had been done by their elders, and by the great sheikhs in East African history, but they did not notice: 'For what reason did they do such things? They were people like us, and so we were not surprised or frightened – from our point of view we had learned something new!' So now, the known *madhhabs* of Shafiʿi, Ibadhi, Hanafi, and Shiʿa Ithnaʿashari denomination, were complemented by the Hanbali *madhhab*.

So Muslims in East Africa belonged to all these *madhhabs*. And now for some reasons, which I will explain later on, people started to leave the Shafiʿi *madhhab* and became Hanbali, but without it being mentioned that they were actually entering the Hanbali *madhhab*; as far as they knew, they were of the 'Ahlul Sunna *madhhab*.' This gained strength, and what strengthened it were several things. One was that when those who had studied abroad [in the Middle East] returned, their financial status was a lot better than that of those who had stayed. This was because they were earning very good salaries. Their financial status was even better than that of our big sheikhs, the 'original ones' trained here in the region, better than that of our teachers and scholars.

For our teachers and scholars their status remained so-so [tight and difficult], and the system that had been built up long ago, carefully planned to support the teachers when they were in need, the whole system was knocked over, broken down, and crashed to pieces. Now these poor fellows would no more be called to perform a ceremonial reading of the Quran, would not be called for a talk, would not be called for a special reading [e.g. on occasions of specific cosmological constellations]; all of this was now *bidʾa*. In this way, bit by bit, their small sources of income dried out. But the status of their colleagues [who had gone abroad] was fine: at the end of the month they received their salary, and they had no troubles. As this caused those [who had stayed] to become weak financially, those teachers and scholars and judges became weak and severely disadvantaged economically. Their schools began to disintegrate; they had no power, no strength anymore.

And so, Sheikh Abdilahi went on, people preferred to send their children to a cleaner, more 'proper', more 'modern' school, with desks and proper equipment; on top of this, those schools were free, books were supplied (funded from Saudi Arabia), and no debts or gifts had to be paid to teachers (as traditionally was the case); their salaries were also taken care of from abroad.[13]

Thus a social transformation process was set in progress, from a historically Shafi'i-oriented community to one in which principles of the previously alien Hanbali school now have a dominant influence. Now, these changes may have taken place without ordinary Muslims noticing the conceptual issues of *madhhab* denomination involved (as discussed by Sheikh Abdilahi). Nevertheless, they affect numerous aspects of their experience of everyday life, such as the conventions of the call to prayer, sermons, praying, and studying and scholarly orientation. Most prominently though, the ever-present issue of identifying and fighting *bid'a* practices (improper innovations), and the public debates, struggles, and arguments around it, were introduced into local social life as well. In public display of Islamic ideology, such as the rhetorics of sermons and lectures, overbearing emphasis was put on references to the *sunna*, the paradigmatic and unquestionable path of Prophet Muhammad, as a role model for all Muslims.[14] This provided an ideal rhetorical platform on which to rally for 'Muslim unity'. As the label of *sunna*, and not 'Hanbali', was invoked also as the name for this group of activists – 'people of the *sunna*' – social and moral pressure was put on Muslims to adhere to the newly introduced ideology. After all, who could afford to be seen in public to resist following the way of the Prophet? This key

13 These conveniences are similarly supplied by some of the Shi'a networks, also funded from abroad. This reflects the global rivalry between Wahhabism and Shi'ism (and partly, Saudi Arabia and Iran) in spreading 'their' respective versions of Islam on a regional level.

14 See further regional ethnography for this in Parkin (1984), Purpura (1997, 2000) and Fuglsang (1994).

idea of rhetorical strategy, epitomised in the chosen self-denomination of
the reformists, was then socially not recognised for what it ultimately
was: an indirect indicator of factional rivalry, presenting a challenge for
ideological predominance within the Muslim community. Another side
of this self-presentation by the 'Wahhabi', as people of the *sunna*, was to
emphasise again and again that there were no *madhhabs (hakuna
madhhabi)* or that *madhhabs* did not matter; the point was to follow the
sunna and there was only one correct way of doing so. However, Sheikh
Abdilahi took issue with this, in the light of what he had already said,
stating that 'this, saying that there are no *madhhabs*, is indeed the fifth
madhhab' (*hiyo, kusema kwamba 'hakuna madhhabi', ni madhhabi ya
tano)*, much to the amusement of his audience.[15] The point here was to
bring across that this 'fifth' *madhhab*, 'Wahhabism', was illegitimate.[16]

The Second Aspect to the Answer: The Image of the Past
The other major focus of attention in Sheikh Abdilahi's lectures was the
characterisation of a historically grown and well-balanced system of
Islamic education in East Africa. For generations, people from the
relevant schools (such as Lamu, Mombasa and Zanzibar as regional
centres of Islamic scholarship) studied with each other, knew each other,
taught each other, were aware of their respective levels of Islamic
expertise, and were exchanging students. This system was kept running,
and while a very high level of Islamic scholarship was maintained, it also

---

15 Sheikh Abdilahi is delivering a pun here: as everyone knows, there are four *madhhabs* in
  Sunni Islam (Shafi'i, Hanbali, Hanafi and Maliki); stating that the systematic rejection
  of the existence of these doctrinal differences constitutes a *madhhab* of its own, is a
  point well made, and it was duly acknowledged by the audience. The pun that Sheikh
  Abdilahi makes also draws from the fact that *madhhabs* can be understood as ways of
  interpreting and defining what is *sunna*. Each of the four Sunni *madhhabs* developed
  out of the systematic efforts of a particular individual scholar, to provide basic guidance
  for Muslims on how to perform ritual and everyday practices correctly; the basic sources
  of interpretation hereby are Quran and *hadith*.
16 It is interesting to note that historically, this kind of disqualification was already raised
  against the Syrian Salafi reformist Jamal al-Din al Kasimi (1866–1914) who
  emphatically criticised the strict adherence to *madhhab*, making him vulnerable to 'the
  accusation that he wished to found his own *madhhab*' (see Ende's entry 'Salafiyya', in
  Encyclopedia of Islam).

had its internal checks and balances, for instance in making sure that the most knowledgeable person obtained the most responsible position. Furthermore it strengthened the internal solidarity of the (predominantly Shafiʿi) Muslim community. As all relevant scholars knew each other, there rarely was suspicion, and scholars had established the practice of constantly consulting each other. According to Sheikh Abdilahi, *kutambuana* and *kuheshimiana*, to acknowledge one another and respect one another, were key principles that kept this system running. He provided the audience with a beautiful historical illustration of the enactment of these principles that he himself witnessed in the 1940s, when Sheikh al-Amin Mazrui and Sayyid Omar bin Sumayt, who were opponents in a number of doctrinal issues, humbly helped each other into their shoes after attending a lecture at a mosque. Because there was good 'discipline' (*nidhamu*) established, Sheikh Abdilahi said, there were rarely ever the kind of squabbles described above. In fact, the sheikh even used an old British image to illustrate the kind of loyalty within the system of scholarly networking, in comparing it to the college system of the old universities. It was as if students and scholars educated within the system of East African Islam were all wearing 'one and the same *college tie*' (English in the original: 'college tie *moja*'). As with other Old Boys' networks, being a member of the inner circle of Islamic scholarship provided one with all the necessary and helpful links in one's field.

Today, in contrast, there was a lot of confusion, as common underlying principles had become lost, and infighting between various influential factions and positions dominated the scene. *'Kuna dharaudharau'*, Sheikh Abdilahi said: a lot of contempt was now voiced against members of other factions, as public speakers for one group presented themselves as the only knowledgeable ones, casting others as incompetent. According to Sheikh Abdilahi, this would have been inconceivable in the past when all knew each other well, having been students of the same teachers. Also, it violated established conventions of *heshima* (respect) in social interaction. Thus, fundamental disagreements or even spiteful antagonisms did not or could not emerge. The problem today, said the sheikh, is that there was too much freedom and too little discipline: young reformist men without established scholarly credentials spoke publicly on whatever they wanted (and were given opportunities to do so by local *imams* and leaders). Labels and levels of achievement that had previously been useful and respected, were now meaningless, lamented Sheikh Abdilahi: 'These days, everyone is a scholar, everyone is a sheikh' *(Siku hizi, kila mtu ni mwanachuoni, kila mtu ni sheikh)*. A sense of frustration about a socially established pattern of 'everything goes' speaks through here: things are no longer as they should be; rules and principles for decision-making have been overturned. In Mombasa, it seems, decision-making on the right Islamic practice has become a matter of opinion and ideological stance rather than knowledge and reasoning. It is no longer the outcome of qualified scholars' discussion, but largely of public pressure. What can be seen now is chaos, disorientation, and – as he said in English (for the sake of emphasis, it seemed) – a 'complete breakdown of discipline'. He compared this state of affairs to car traffic running without any rules because everyone follows their own. There was no central authority in place, and this was unacceptable.

Linking this back to aspects of knowledge and scholarship within society, Sheikh Abdilahi cautioned his audience not to be naïve and mistake appearance for substance. It has become common to regard people who can speak Arabic well as knowledgeable in Islam, and this boosts the reputation of those people returning from study-visits to the Middle East much more than it actually should. These days, he said, everyone who speaks Arabic, can call themselves as a 'sheikh', and an 'Islamic scholar' (this aroused chuckles from the audience). And, he reminded people, this is similar to how it was in the colonial times – and even up to now – for many in the community who believed that if someone speaks good English, he is very knowledgeable and highly educated. But this was incorrect. It was important to realise that there is a difference between knowing a language and having education *('kuna tafauti ya kuijuwa lugha na kuwa na elimu')*. By implication, he called upon his audience to be mindful of this difference, and to make sure not to be fooled by mere appearance, following someone in matters of Islam because of their fluency in Arabic; it was important to keep these matters separate, and to insist on these differences in public.

Following Sheikh Abdilahi's argument, the current problems of dissent and confusion are caused within the Sunni-Shafiʿi community itself. Within it, rivalling claims to Islamic authority have confused the issues of leadership and orientation.[17] Knowledgeable elders, whether trained scholars or not, were often 'soft', in not defending themselves or failing to respond to frequent attacks, criticisms, and rhetorical dismissals by the assertive (Arabic speaking) reformist juniors dominating public discourse. The result was a popular impression that the youth have 'beaten' the elders and scholars; that they have now taken over the show.

A basic problem that has made this regrettable situation possible, according to Sheikh Abdilahi, is a lack of proper knowledge and education about Islam, leading to insecurity when facing claims made by others. '*Leo sisi, hatuijui dini yetu*', he said: 'Today, we don't know our religion'. And elsewhere, he confirmed to me that, '*Waislamu hawajijui*' (Muslims don't know themselves), referring particularly to Muslims in Kenya, and their lack of knowledge about the history of Islam. His lectures here addressed this problem, and presented an account and discussion of historical developments that led to the contemporary experience of fundamental disagreements and antagonisms in a Muslim community that used to be internally stable, and structured around a system of established rules and principles. Thus these lectures should also be seen as an appeal to his audience, to seek knowledge of history, and use it effectively for the present. Implicitly, they show that historical knowledge is crucial for dealing with the present: after all, ideologies and normative claims in a Muslim context can only be negotiated (confirmed, approved or rejected) with reference to history – social history and Islamic history (see Zaman 2002). This is what Sheikh Abdilahi has done here, while dealing with reformist claims for supremacy. By doing this, he illuminated the reasons for the current differences about the beginning of Ramadan, thus answering the initial question that had been posed to him.

---

17 He states that, in contrast, the Shiʿa Ithnaʿashari has clear principles of decision-making in place.

We can clearly distinguish two main sub-narratives that Sheikh Abdilahi presented as part of his historical account – which, it may be said, altogether conveys the idea of a somewhat unlikely golden age in the past. The first is about the infiltration and transformation of 'mainstream Islam' along the Swahili coast; the second portrays and praises the system of Islamic scholarship and education as it existed in the past, underpinning (and reflecting) the coherence and unity of the Muslim community. In the past, he said, fundamental disagreements about the beginning of Ramadan (for instance) did not occur, as a functioning system of checks and balances – here symbolised by the 'college tie' – was in place. The decision on such matters was taken by a person whose standard of knowledge was known and respected by other scholars, as they were part of the same network of teachers. Thus his judgments would be trusted and followed. If his knowledge was inferior to that of other scholars, he would consult with them and base his decision upon their advice, and again his judgment would find support within the community. So this was a kind of consensus-based model. However, this works only as long as there is social unity, and indeed a consensus on the relevant criteria for the respective decisions. At the historical point when unity had broken down (described above), finding a consensus on such matters became not only difficult but impossible by definition (at least when different basic criteria for Islamic judgments were employed). The squabbles on the ground between different factions reflected their unresolved – and perhaps unresolvable – differences on a scholarly level. For Islam at the Swahili coast, Sheikh Abdilahi claimed, such fundamental internal differences only started to occur recently, 'after entering the teachings of East African people from outside' (*baada ya kuingia usomi wa watu wa Afrika Mashariki kutoka nje*).

The inside-outside axis of qualification is an important one in the narration of this story by Sheikh Abdilahi. The so-called 'Wahhabi' reformists here are clearly qualified as an external group, even adhering to a different *madhhab* from the Muslim host community that they enter and seek to transform. The reformists appear as outsiders, sly and cunning strategists, successful in infiltrating their hosts by veiling their otherness with a rhetorical mantle of overarching unity in labelling themselves as 'people of the *sunna*', a description that no Muslim could seriously reject (as all claim to follow the path of the Prophet). Once established and influential within society – to a large extent also by financial means – they seek to implement fundamental changes demanded from the outside, transforming the East African region into a kind of ally or vassal state of Saudi Arabia. In contrast, Sheikh Abdilahi as the narrator of this account clearly sides with the insider community (represented by the East African 'college tie' system), and tells the story from this angle. He sides with the audience, also by using the first person plural 'we' to shape a sense of unity and solidarity between himself and his listeners, in contrast to 'them', who have entered the community from the outside and brought trouble and confusion. *De facto*, notably, Sheikh Abdilahi thereby implicitly points at another possible alliance through his speech. In the way that he presents his narrative, he invokes common interests between the remaining Sunni-Shafi'i community, troubled by reformist ideology and internal disunity, and the pathway of new Shi'ism in the region, offering support and standing up to reformist attacks. This hints at a possible alliance between these two groups, at least vis-à-vis 'Wahhabi' pressures. For their adherents, this tentatively promises stronger resistance to external pressures, leading to a higher internal stability and one's own free space within it. Simply speaking, then, we would have a tripartite division of the relevant Muslim factions involved here. This is indeed reflected in common usage of terms that I have witnessed in Mombasa: it is not uncommon to hear people speak of 'Wahhabis', 'Sunnis' and 'Shi'as', and the latter two described as under attack by the first. Hereby, the 'Sunnis' notably appear as the somewhat unpronounced faction situated in the middle, its members being wooed in different ways from both sides.[18]

---

18 My impression is that the use of this clear tripartite differentiation has increased, at least in the circles I work with (based on brief visits in 2003 and 2005 in comparison to fieldwork in 1998–99).

Sheikh Abdallah Farsy's Historical Account of Islamic scholars (c.1970)
A clear link can be seen between the historical account of Islam in East
Africa presented by Sheikh Abdilahi Nassir above, and Sheikh Abdallah
Farsy's historical account of twentieth century Islamic scholars (Arab.
ulama) of the East African coast, focusing on Sunni-Shafi'i scholars and
published under two slightly differing titles (see Farsy 1989, 1972).[19] The
link lies in what Sheikh Abdilahi called the 'college tie' above. Indeed
Farsy's narrative, completed in about 1970, conveys an impression of an
overarching unity of Islam. This unity is not simple or homogeneous,
but dynamic and internally diverse, containing a variety of positions,
voices and opinions, within a larger network of scholarship and doctrinal
orientation. This is exemplified by brief accounts of the lives, works, and
teaching influences of Muslim scholars along the whole Swahili coast
(from Somalia and the Banadir coast down to the Comoros), whose
interconnections through teacher-student and kinship relations are
repeatedly flagged up. Farsy's selection is nevertheless personal, and
portrays the scholars in a positive and sympathetic light, transmitting a
good sense of the respective goals and ideals of specific individuals.
Portraying everyone, especially the Sufi scholars too, in sympathetic
terms seems to be in conflict with the way that Farsy's own historical
position is commonly portrayed – as the tireless campaigner against *bid'a*
and the bridge-head to increasing Saudi-dominated 'Wahhabi' reformist
activity in the region.[20] In contrast, Farsy's historical account in *Baadhi
ya mashekhe* is largely fair and balanced, and brings across a sense of the
network of East African Islam that connects the portrayed scholars. In
this sense, it not only underlines Sheikh Abdilahi's image of a 'college
tie', but it also attests to the fact that Farsy did have, and express,
sensitivity and appreciation for the specific regional character of East
African Islam in which, after all, he was raised and trained.

19 The title of Farsy 1989 [c.1970] refers to 'Sunni' scholars (*wa kisuni*) rather than
'Shafi'i' scholars (Farsy 1972). The Swahili text of both publications is identical.
20 This contrast correlates nicely with the description of Farsy's book as a 'hagiographic
account', in the edited edition by Randall Pouwels. Yet of course, this has an awkward
ironic ring to it, as the reformist position that Farsy advocated opposed the veneration
of saints.

Sheikh Abdallah Saleh Farsy's book *Baadhi ya mashekhe* is a unique source, as far as the local (published) historical documentation of twentieth century Islamic scholars along the Swahili coast is concerned,[21] presenting biographical accounts on a selected variety of the most prominent and important scholars. In about 1970, Farsy handed the completed manuscript to the historian Randall Pouwels for subsequent publication, as Pouwels relates (Farsy 1989: preface). Pouwels translated, edited and published this account bilingually in 1989, after his own long-spanning historical account of Islam in the region had come out (Pouwels 1987), a book which draws heavily on Farsy for the description of the twentieth century. Farsy's account was also published locally in 1972 (Farsy 1972). But hardly any of the local intellectuals I worked with in Mombasa seemed to know this or have a copy,[22] and so my own photocopied copy of the edited version that I had brought with me during fieldwork was photocopied again and probably circulated further.

Farsy's account is rich and insightful, and full of personal knowledge and anecdotes about the people he writes about. It covers many relevant Islamic scholars of the Shafiʿi *madhhab* from the late nineteenth century onwards, and has remained a crucial source for their study. To name four of the most famous *ulama*: Sayyid Ahmad bin Sumayt (1861–1925) who was based in Zanzibar for much of his life but also lived and studied in Mecca, Istanbul, and the Hadhramaut (see Bang 2003); his close friend Sheikh Abdalla Bakathir (1860–1925), from Lamu, who also lived in Zanzibar for most of his life, travelled as far as Java, and once went – as requested by the Mufti of Mecca – to reconcile a religious dispute between conflicting Muslim factions in Cape Town in 1913 (Farsy 1989: 131); Sayyid Habib Saleh (d.1935) from the Comoros and of Hadhrami descent, who – as stated above – founded the influential Riyadha Mosque and College in Lamu, opening up Islamic education to the

---

21 Another account, similar in intention and style, has recently been published by Ustadh Harith (Swaleh 2003).
22 See particularly Swaleh (2003: 33). This seems to contrast sharply with the situation in Zanzibar and Dar es Salaam, where, I am told, copies of this book are readily available in Islamic bookshops and vivid discussions continue about the reasons for Sheikh Farsy to select (and omit) those that he did (Roman Loimeier, personal communication).

underprivileged and thereby initiating a process of social reform (see el-
Zein 1974; Bang 2003); and finally, we have Sheikh al-Amin Mazrui
(1891–1947), descendent of the privileged Omani clan that ruled
Mombasa until the take-over by the Omani Sultanate in 1837. He
became the founding father for Islamic reform at the East African coast,
and was a direct teacher and source of inspiration for Sheikh Abdallah
Farsy. The last two, Habib Saleh and al-Amin Mazrui, in fact were the
historical figureheads of the two most distinctly opposed Muslim factions
during the 1970s.

It should be noted that Farsy's *Badhi ya mashekhe* is of a different
category than the bulk of his writings. Fitting into the genre of
biographical dictionaries *(tabaqat)*, it covers a complementary aspect to
his numerous other educational Islamic writings produced over four
decades until 1980, including the first Swahili translation of the Quran
by a mother tongue speaker (Farsy 1969). Sheikh Farsy here produced a
rare document of local intellectual history; indeed, the scarcity of such
written historical documentation is commonly regretted within the
Swahili community.

This text, due to its biographical and personal nature, and by its
focus on teacher-student relationships, conveys the unity of a socially
embedded system of regional Islam that Sheikh Abdilahi characterised
with the term 'college tie'. As mentioned above, this stands in contrast
with a common, more polarised historical assessment of the role and
position of Sheikh Farsy, focusing on his position as major facilitator of
the reformist agenda, and as leading figure in the campaign against *bid'a*
practices that have dominated popular Muslim discourse. In contrast to
the character of subsequent writings of 'Wahhabi' reformists, Farsy
hardly used this account as a platform for pushing the reformist agenda
(though this could be investigated further). Even though throughout the
text there are short comments criticising *bid'a* practices, or commending
critics of such practices for their efforts, the account does not turn into
an ideological treatise, for instance in presenting only the reformist
protagonists sympathetically. Many relevant scholars are mentioned and
described with sympathy and respect, including Sufis and their practices.
This goes well together with the fact that Farsy is commonly

remembered as a man of the people: friendly, flexible, willing to please and respectful in communication.

Sheikh Abdilahi Nassir Defending Muharram (2003)

In 2003, during the month of Muharram and its commemorations of the death of Imam Hussein (Prophet Muhammad's grandson) and his followers at Kerbala – an event of particular relevance for the Shi'a communities – Sheikh Abdilahi gave a series of lectures in which he responded to anti-Shi'a attacks from 'Wahhabi' reformists. They had urged local Muslims not to support or participate in the commemorations, as these were un-Islamic. At the beginning of Muharram, an anonymous letter called 'Open letter to the preachers and imams of the *sunna*' (*Barua wazi kwa wahubiri na ma-imamu wa sunna*), had been distributed in Mombasa. It was signed by the 'Ahlul Tawheed'[23] group. It claimed that Sunnis should not be led astray by 'imitating' Shi'as in these matters; there was, it said, no *hadith* indicating any obligation to hold commemorations. Besides, the accounts of the torturing and beheading of Hussein and his people by the Caliph Yazid and his henchmen at Kerbala were said to be based on lies.

In his lectures, initially called 'Open Letter to the Wahhabi' (*Barua ya wazi kwa Mawahabi*), Sheikh Abdilahi responded to the allegations. Referring exclusively to what he called generally accepted Sunni sources and, most prominently, the regional champion of Islamic reformism, Sheikh Abdallah Farsy,[24] he refuted the 'Wahhabi' claims, showing that

---

23 Referring to the adherents of *tawhid*; *tawhid* is the Islamic doctrine of God's unity which for 'Wahhabi' and Salafiyya reformists is a major cornerstone; their common reproach of other Muslim groups lies in accusing them of violating the principle of *tawhid*.

24 He refers to Abdallah Saleh Farsy, but also to Muhammad Abduh, Allaamah Shawkaani, Abul Hassan Ali bin Muhammad bin Alii at Twabarii, Imam Ibn Hazm, Abul Falaah Abdul Hayy Ibnul Imaad, ibn Kathir, presenting their assessments of Yazid (I am here following the orthography of Sheikh Abdilahi's account). My knowledge of these sources is very limited, but the use of Muhammad Abduh seems striking, and structurally similar to the use of Farsy that I investigate. Here, the prominent historical father-figure of Islamic modernism and fore-thinker to Salafism (developed by Rashid Rida) is turned against the rash and ill-considered attacks by the 'Wahhabi' of

248   *Kai Kresse*

their position (sketched out above) was in fact untenable (Nassir 2003c). This applied especially to their endorsing interpretation of Yazid as 'Leader of the true believers' (*Amirul-muuminin*). All sources cited by Sheikh Abdilahi concurred in their disgust for the barbaric deeds committed by Yazid, thus supporting the point of legitimate grief for Hussein and his people. In this way, Sheikh Abdilahi's lectures aimed to show that, generally speaking, Muharram commemorations of the death of Sayyid Hussein were fully acceptable to Sunnis as well as Shiʿas. Most forcefully, however, the lectures ultimately brought home the point that a position arguing for Yazid as leader of Islam stood against everything that Islam itself stands for, and thus may hardly be called 'Muslim' or 'Islamic'. In this way, the lectures sought to alienate the audience from the 'Wahhabi' position, and in isolating the 'Wahhabis' from the community, outing them as actual opponents of Islam. In terms of rhetoric, both the defence of Muharram commemorations and the general counter-offensive were performed successfully.[25]

Let us have a closer look at the way that Sheikh Abdilahi made reference to Sheikh Abdallah Saleh Farsy in developing his counter-arguments against 'Wahhabi' attacks. Over a sequence of ten lectures, Farsy was invoked centrally in the first six, and mentioned among others in the seventh. He is not mentioned in lecture eight, which is exclusively about *hadith* references, nor lectures nine and ten, which develop conclusions about the 'Wahhabi' position in the context of Mombasa. There are a number of inter-linking reasons why Farsy and his text should feature so prominently in these lectures, but the major reason surely has to do with the overall rhetorical effect mentioned above, namely isolating and alienating the 'Wahhabis' from the social community of local Muslims, by showing how they actually seem to think and act counter to established common standards of what it means to be properly 'Muslim' or 'Islamic'. After all, who in their right mind

Mombasa, who might want to claim to protest in the name of Abduh himself. Sheikh Abdilahi's use and appropriation of 'their' sources, leaves them, it seems, without justified and commonly acceptable basis.

25 I have no ethnographic material at my disposal to assess the actual social success or effect of these lectures, and I was not present in Mombasa at the time.

could, after following the narrative, still champion Yazid and condone his barbaric methods in quenching his blind thirst for power, and then still call themselves a good Muslim? By pointing at the apparent contradictions and untruths in the 'Wahhabi' claims and by indicating the apparent exclusiveness of their position, in isolation from and full of contempt for everyone else, the 'Wahhabi' here are seen to be excluded (or to have excluded themselves) from the common social realm of an existing Muslim community.

Farsy matters a lot here, since reference to him invokes the continuity of a regionally-specific tradition of Islam, an ongoing quasi-'college tie' tradition that is still existent in spirit – or is rudimentarily present so that it can be called back into life. Farsy here is invoked as 'one of us', a local expert from the Swahili realm, indeed a previous Chief Kadhi of Kenya, providing guidance and reliable historical orientation about the matters being discussed here. By emphasising Farsy in this way, Sheikh Abdilahi Nassir re-connects him to the supposed centre of the Muslim community, which in this case consists of Sunni-Shafiʿi as well as Shiʿa Muslims, as both groups have (in indirect cooperation) rejected the wrongful attacks by the 'Wahhabi'. Indeed, Farsy and several generally accepted Sunni sources were involved here as Islamic authorities in the formulation of an argument ultimately protecting the Shiʿa Muslims in their practice of Muharram commemorations. And, by showing a wider Muslim audience that such activities should be protected, Sheikh Abdilahi at the very least pushes for an endorsement of tolerance and solidarity between the local Sunnis and Shiʿas here. In fact, the lectures could also be read as an encouragement for mainstream Sunnis to participate in Muharram commemorations, and possibly to collaborate further.

Claiming Farsy as a figure whose stance, from the inside, is encouraging or supporting such a collaboration, is important for a number of interconnected reasons. Most of all, Farsy was popular with the masses of ordinary Muslims along the coast, and he is known and still held in high esteem by many. He was born, bred and educated on the Swahili coast – thus is not an outsider. And even if he, probably more than anyone else, made the implementation of an externally steered

'Wahhabi' reformist ideology along the Swahili coast possible, reference
to him may also provide the most promising path to reverse that
constellation. If, such as happened in the lectures of Sheikh Abdilahi,
local 'Wahhabi' activists can be shown to contradict Sheikh Farsy, who
represents one of their most important local intellectual corner-stones,
they become vulnerable to lose out in terms of popular support. This
vulnerability becomes all the more of an issue the less they are seen to
have achieved a firm social rooting within the local community. As they
are seen to have fought (and bought) their way in, and have remained
combative toward others, they remain in danger to be re-labelled as
'outsiders' and consequently lose out in terms of local influence and
social control. The most likely and successful way to weaken 'Wahhabi'
reformist doctrine along the coast is to alienate the reformists from their
own support group, and recast them as outsiders who are more of a
danger than an asset to Islam in the region. This, to me, is what Sheikh
Abdilahi has performed in his lectures. And, to conclude these
reflections, one could say that this goal was already indicated in the
opening paragraphs of his first lecture, where he is pointing out that
these reformists 'hide [their true identity,] their "Wahhabi-ness" because
they know that this is opposed by all Muslims' (*kuficha uwahabi wao
wanaojua kwamba unapingwa na Waislamu wote*). By using the name
Ahlul Tawheed for their group, invoking the doctrine of the unity of
God as their label, they seek to expand this to the community of
believers, Sheikh Abdilahi infers: 'they want to cheat Muslims into
believing that they are their friends' (*wanataka kuwavungavunga
Waislamu wawafikirie kuwa ni wenzao*). Both expressions here refer to a
basic otherness of the 'Wahhabi' from ordinary Muslims, including both
Sunni and Shiʿa who, as Sheikh Abdilahi has pointed out in many of his
other writings, do not exist in opposition, but parallel to each other.

As Sheikh Abdilahi shows in his tenth and final Muharram lecture,
their otherness is even emphasised by the 'Wahhabi' themselves, in terms
of claims to an exclusive status over and above all other Muslims, to such
an extent that they do not accept other Muslims as Muslims. This
offensive rejection of the faith of *all* other Muslims, *Sunni and Shiʿa*,
with the ultimate insult of 'unbelief' (*kufr*), is brought home by Sheikh

Abdilahi. He wraps up their position as follows, using the first person plural to signalise a common identity between the 'Sunni' and 'Shiʿa' on the one side, and the 'Wahhabi' on the other: 'in other words, we all (Sunni and Shiʿa) are only infidels for the 'Wahhabi'!' – *kwa lugha nyingine, sote (masunni na mashia), kwa mawahabi, tu makafiri!'* If, for the 'Wahhabi', it is 'us against everyone', for the combined Sunni and Shiʿa force that Sheikh Abdilahi invokes here, it is 'all of us against them'. He closes this set of lectures with a final rhetorical question about the deceiving label that the 'Wahhabi' have used to set themselves up in society, *Ahlul Sunna,* emphasising their commitment to the *sunna.* Sheikh Abdilahi points at the fact that these same people avoid certain historically verified *sunna* practices – not because of rational theological reasons, but because they are performed by the Shiʿas (whom they regard as their enemies). Then he asks who of the two groups, the Shiʿa who follow the *sunna* of the Prophet and the 'Wahhabi' who do not, should be called *'Ahlul Sunna'* and who *'Ahlul Bidʿa'* (linked to the performance of *bidʿa* practices). This is a rhetorical question, and he leaves the answer to his audience.

Apart from the significance of Sheikh Farsy as a historical figure, used to vouch for a widely acceptable position for East African Muslims in the rhetorical and ideological competition for what passes as 'mainstream Islam' in the region, there is of course another, very basic use of history at work here. This concerns the 'truth' of versions of Islamic history put forward to support and underline a certain general claim, in an objective sense, as far as it is demonstrable through recognised sources. After all, the obvious point of using Sheikh Farsy as a reliable scholar and credible source for Sheikh Abdilahi was to show that the basic historical information upon which the 'Wahhabi' built their attacks against the Shiʿa commemorations of the Kerbala events during Muharram, was incorrect. If this could be shown, there was hardly a chance that the 'Wahhabi' claims could continue gaining popular support among ordinary Muslims. In this case, there seems to be little doubt left about who can claim historical accuracy (and thus give wider credibility to doctrinal claims put forward). Sheikh Abdilahi seems to present clear and overwhelming scholarly evidence, by Sheikh Farsy and other Sunni sources, to demonstrate that the barbaric murder of Hussein and his group by Yazid and his men is an accepted historical fact within Islamic scholarship. The attempt to deny this, by reformist activists, can be seen as an attempt to rewrite history. Even if that attempt may look clumsy and incompetent, it is important to recognise the probable impetus and rationale behind it. For what matters most, in terms of a tangible social effect, is the *common assumption of the truth* of a certain account of Islamic history within the Muslim community, a social consensus about the reality of past events, perhaps more than the establishment of such truth itself. So far, and as long as, a majority holds a certain story to be true history, it is possible to push ideological, moral, and political claims somehow building up on it. In case of the so-called 'Wahhabis' in Mombasa, they could have succeeded in their goal of socially isolating (or at least marginalising) the Shiᶜas and their Muharram commemorations from the wider Muslim community, as long as a significant proportion of Muslims could be seen to hold this version to be true. However, this itself can only work as long as a commonly acknowledged basis to publicly support such claims exists. In this sense, there are rules and limits to the game. The basis (for possible popular support) ceases to exist once it has publicly been shown and proven that the historical narrative is incorrect and unjustifiable. This is what Sheikh Abdilahi was doing in his speech, demonstrating that the 'Wahhabi' faction got their basic facts wrong. This of course raises suspicions about other claims and historical accounts by the 'Wahhabi' too. Should Sheikh Abdilahi's run of argument be generally accepted – and ultimately there seems to be little alternative to that – then there is no way back for the reformists to defend their earlier position, nor to retain public support for it. In fact, having lost out on the agenda, they would be vulnerable and even in danger of becoming marginalised or isolated within the regional Muslim community. In that case, they would experience a backlash of their own unsubstantiated attacks. This is another sense in which struggling with history is really at the core of the social dynamics of the negotiation and reassertion of Muslim identity.

Conclusion

We have engaged here with a number of levels on which uses of history in public Islamic discourse are significant for attempts to reshape the Muslim community and initiate social change, or to highlight continuity and encourage a sense of unity and consensus in society. History generally provides a large resource of reference points for the formation and reformation in the negotiation of social identity. This was at work here too, while the particular normative relevance of Islamic history for Muslim believers could also be seen. Historical accounts do not only imply truth claims to the facticity of a certain reality that is recounted, they also have normative implications linked to them and they provide specific role models, which can be expanded upon and used ideologically in factional struggles for dominance over what regionally counts as 'mainstream' Islam. History matters, within these internal dynamics of rivalry and competition, where contestations and counter-discourses emerge in response to dominant narratives, challenging existent truth claims and normative standards while pushing forward others. Knowledge and rhetoric seem to matter most in the way that these discursive contestations are played out. Knowledge, in terms of Islamic scholarship as far as it can confirm (or disprove) the existence, sequence, and nature of historical events that are relevant for the interpretation of Islam, can provide normative directives for Muslims. Rhetoric as the art of convincing one's audience, or of making them believe that the position put forward is true and unquestionable, leads them to act on the basis of their convictions and beliefs. The two axes of knowledge and rhetorics are of course related, and from what we have seen above, it looks like one without the other has little chance of success on a heatedly contested social platform of regionally specific Islamic discourse: knowledge cannot make itself heard, or be acknowledged socially in order to have effect or status without rhetorics; rhetorics alone have no way of keeping social support in the long run without being based on knowledge.

Talal Asad, in a seminal essay on the project of an anthropology of Islam, made a case for the consideration of Islam as a 'discursive tradition'. This conception has proven immensely useful as a starting

point, as it integrates a historical perspective and an insider's perspective
into an engaged discussion of discursive strategies. As Asad says, 'it
should be the anthropologist's first task to describe and analyze the kinds
of reasoning, and the reasons for arguing, that underlie Islamic
traditional practices' (1986: 16). In order to successfully convey a sense
of the internal dynamics of society in terms of debate and discursive
negotiation of Muslim identity, the anthropologist needs to engage with
'the practitioners' conceptions of what is apt performance, and how the
past is related to the present practices' (ibid.: 19). Investigating Islam as
discursive tradition in the sense of Asad means to reproduce and discuss
strands of argumentation for certain ideological or doctrinal positions
within their particular social and historical contexts, and with
consideration for the general Islamic framework prescribing certain rules
of negotiation. The overall task for an anthropology of Islam, as Asad
puts it, is 'to understand the historical conditions that enable the
production and maintenance of specific discursive traditions, or their
transformation – and the efforts of practitioners to achieve coherence'
(ibid.: 20). This chapter has tried to do something along these lines, with
particular reference to history and its uses in the recent negotiation of
Muslim identity in the Kenyan Swahili context. Thereby the
consideration of social tensions and power relations became of central
concern, as part of the overall dynamics to be understood. As Zaman put
it recently, expanding upon Asad's approach: 'This discursive tradition is
constituted not only by an ongoing interaction between the present and
the past, however, but also by the manner in which relations of power
and other forms of contestation and conflict impinge on any definition
of what it means to be a Muslim' (2002: 6).

Perhaps because of the way that social dynamics work in Muslim
contexts, around Islam as a discursive tradition, this provides Muslim
societies with the capacity to create, sustain and potentially expand a
multi-ethnic social network or community that is shaped and defined by
a common core of knowledge and practice (constantly re-interpreted and
re-negotiated), shaping a unity beyond existent ethnic, cultural, and
linguistic boundaries – a cosmopolitan community. History here is a
common reference point for the community and its 'mainstream'

religious identity, constantly to be reconsidered and reconfirmed in the light of, and also for the sake of, public consensus. But this also makes history, in the present and within the flux of social dynamics, a constant source of potential inspiration and normative orientation for social transformation in the future. At the same time – and for parallel reasons – competing and mutually exclusive conceptions of history that exist within the Muslim community and demand authority within it, may also lead to a split and further factionalisation. On the whole, for Muslim communities facing the task of invoking such a public consensus, the rhetorics of history seem inextricably connected to the rhetorics of Islam itself. Whether by shaping a wider unity, or by eroding the existing common understanding even further, reference to history and use of it is part and parcel of public Islamic discourse and the social negotiation of Muslim identity.

For the case of the Kenyan Swahili coast, we have here caught a glimpse of the dialectic back and forth between alternating discourses of Islam seeking to become dominant and establish themselves as 'mainstream' – initially shaped as and later defended against counter-discourses – all of them actively involving Islamic history and invoking Muslim unity. Islamic discourses, here, have made claims to historical truth and spoken out for an envisaged social majority. This is also true for both Sheikh Abdallah Saleh Farsy and Sheikh Abdilahi Nassir, two important figures for social transformation through Islamic discourse in the East African region, during a volatile period of increasing social instability and doctrinal antagonisms. Both were raised and trained within an established system of education, scholarship, and practice of East African Islam, and, through personal efforts, both contributed to its transformation. Farsy pushed for Islamic reformism as a socially liberating force, envisaging a wider unity within East African Islam – a move that ultimately also led to increased internal disunity and dependency on external powers. Within such a situation, Nassir defended regional traditions and continuities of Islam against attacks by uncompromising reformists conceived as 'external'. In an ongoing effort to defend practices and conceptions held both in Sunni and Shi'a circles, Nassir, I think, has been seeking to (re-)create a new, wider sense of

Muslim unity providing a new vision of regional 'mainstream' Islam as a possible foundation for social transformation. He does so by invoking a continuity of peaceful cooperation between these two groups in East African Islam which, he claims, should be restored and promoted. Reference to Farsy plays an important role in this. By invoking Farsy, Nassir is able to address and engage a broader regional Sunni audience by presenting this popular leading figure of East African reformism in support of his own argument. In a way, both examples represent instances of an internal continuity and dynamic renewal of East African Islam, under changing conditions of modernity and post-coloniality.

This connects my reflections to a wider comparative argument recently put forward by Mohamed Qasim Zaman, about the role of the *ulama*, the so-called 'traditional' caste of Islamic scholars within contemporary Muslim societies. Against common preconceptions of the *ulama* as backwardly 'traditionalist', Zaman shows (with reference to Pakistan and Egypt) that 'the *ulama* are often important players in the public and political arena, that they not only compete but also interact with Islamists, and that, in some cases, they may have strategic advantages that the Islamists do not' (2002: 179). These strategic advantages result from their social position, being embedded and rooted within the social dynamics of their communities. In this way, says Zaman, the *ulama* fulfil an immensely important function which the 'Islamists' (reformists) often cannot take on. As 'the custodians of change', the *ulama* are constantly adapting and re-presenting existing Islamic doctrine as accommodating and responding to various effects and needs of life in the modern world. This in itself is a flexible and dynamic activity, making possible what we could call the rootedness of social change locally.

My point for the issues discussed above is along these lines: the externally driven reformist project that affected the coastal Muslim communities in Kenya so fundamentally, could not (so far, at least) be completed successfully because it lacked this crucial instance, the 'strategic advantage' of sustained internal support that Zaman talks about. After the demise of Sheikh Abdallah Saleh Farsy and his companion Sheikh Muhammad Kasim Mazrui, the reformists did not have (and possibly did not seek to implement) another similarly appropriate 'custodian of change' able to convince the Muslim public enough to make it consistently rally behind the reformist project. Without such figures, the (somewhat externally situated) reformists could not establish enough sustained support for such changes. Despite the general success in spreading the reformist ideology, this goal has not yet been achieved. Whether this was due to a lack of attempts in that direction, or due to the lack of key figures from within the community to support such an agenda completely, is open to further investigation.

Anthropological engagement with Islam insomuch as it focuses on discursive strategies, reasoning, knowledge and rhetorics (as Asad claimed long ago, and Zaman has confirmed) seems implicitly concerned with the historical contexts and dynamics that shape Islam as a discursive tradition, and Muslim societies negotiating it. Those Islamic experts who are embedded within these historical contexts and dynamics of their communities, as Zaman argued recently, continue to carry out an important function as 'custodians of change'. As religious authorities and mediators of specialised Islamic knowledge to their communities, they have the responsibility of demonstrating the acceptability of doctrinal change that is publicly advocated – or of their resistance to such change – and thus of vouching for continuity within the changing conditions of social life. Their public appeal, as Zaman says, is 'grounded in their guardianship of the religious tradition as a continuous, lived heritage that connects the past and present' (2002: 180). This characterisation, I think, also applies to the two East African scholars discussed here. Their relative success, in terms of sustained social impact and transformative effects within the Muslim community, seems based on the fact that they managed to present themselves (or were presented by others), through knowledge, rhetorics, and lived example, as guardians of such a regional tradition connecting past and present. As a rule, this may last as long as such presentation is successful.

258 *Kai Kresse*

Bibliography

Asad, T. 1986. *The Idea of an Anthropology of Islam.* Occasional Paper Series, Center for Contemporary Arab Studies. Washington D.C.: Georgetown University.

Bakari, M. 1995. 'The new Ulama in Kenya', in M. Bakari and S.S. Yahya (eds), *Islam in Kenya.* Nairobi: MEWA.

Bang, A.K. 2003. *Sufis and Scholars of the Sea. Family Networks in East Africa, 1860–1925.* London: RoutledgeCurzon.

Berg, F.J. 1971. *Mombasa under the Busaidi Sultanate: The City and its Hinterlands in the Nineteenth Century.* PhD dissertation, University of Wisconsin.

Encyclopedia of Islam. Entries: 'Salafiyya – in North Africa' (P. Shinar), 'Salafiyya – in Egypt and Syria' (W. Ende), 'Rashid Rida' (W. Ende), 'Wahhabiyya' (E. Peskes and W.Ende) Leiden: Brill.

Farsy, A.S. 1969. *Qurani Takatifu.* Nairobi: Islamic Foundation.

—— 1972. *Baadhi ya Wanavyuoni wa Kishafi wa Mashariki ya Afrika.* Mombasa: no publisher given (text is identical with Farsy 1989).

—— 1980. *Maisha ya Sayyidnal Huseyn.* Mombasa: Coronation Printers (reprinted 1999, as *Maisha ya Sayyidna Huseyn.* Mombasa: Adam Traders).

—— 1989 [c.1970]. *The Shafi'i ulamaa of East Africa, c. 1830-1970: a hagiographic account.* 'Baadhi ya Mashekhe Wakubwa wa Kisuni wa Mashariki ya Afrika' (translated, edited, and annotated by Randall L. Pouwels). Wisconsin, Madison: University of Wisconsin Press.

Fuglesang, M. 1994. *Veils and Videos. Female Youth Culture on the Kenyan Coast.* Stockholm: Gotab.

Hirsch, S.F. 1998. *Pronouncing and Persevering: Gender and the Discourses of Disputing in an African Islamic Court.* Chicago: University of Chicago Press.

Horton, M., and J. Middleton 2000: *The Swahili. The Social Landscape of a Mercantile Society.* Oxford: Blackwell.

Kresse, K. 2007. *Philosophising in Mombasa: Knowledge, Islam, and Intellectual Practice on the Swahili Coast.* Edinburgh: University Press for the International African Institute.

—— 2003. '"Swahili Enlightenment?" East African Reformist Discourse at the Turning Point: the Example of Sheikh Muhammad Kasim Mazrui', *Journal of Religion in Africa*, 33.3.

—— 2004. 'Making People Think: The Ramadhan Lectures of Sheikh Abdilahi Nassir in Mombasa, 1419 A.H.', in S. Reese (ed.), *The Transmission of Learning in Islamic Africa*. Leiden: Brill.

Lacunza-Balda, J. 1990. *Islamic Literature in Swahili*. PhD dissertation, University of London.

—— 1993. 'The Role of Kiswahili in East African Islam', in L. Brenner (ed.), *Muslim Identity and Social Change in Sub-Saharan Africa*. London: Hurst.

Loimeier, R., and R. Seesemann (eds) 2006. *The Global Worlds of the Swahili: Interfaces of Islam, Identity and Space in 19th and 20th-Century East Africa*. Berlin: Lit-Verlag.

Nassir, A. 1989a. *Shia na Qur'ani: Majibu na Maelezo*. Mombasa.

—— 1989b. *Shia na Hadith: Majibu na Maelezo*. Mombasa.

—— 1990. *Shia na Sahaba: Majibu na Maelezo*. Mombasa.

—— 2002. *Maulidi: Si Bid'a, si Haramu*. Mombasa: Bilal Muslim Mission.

—— 2003a. *Shia na Taqiya*. Mombasa: Markazi ya Ahlul Bayt.

—— 2003b. *Mut'a : Ndoa ya Halali*. Mombasa: Markazi ya Ahlul Bayt.

—— 2003c. *Yazid Hakuwa Aamiirul-mu'minin*. Mombasa: Bilal Muslim Mission. (Revised version of "Barua ya wazi kwa Mawahabi", lectures, given between March and May 2003, and published via email and internet)

Parkin, D. 1984. 'Being and Selfhood Among Intermediary Swahili', in J. Maw and D. Parkin (eds), *Swahili Language and Society*. Vienna: Afro-Pub.

Pearson, M.N. 2000. 'The Indian Ocean and the Red Sea', in N. Levtzion and R.L. Pouwels (eds), *The History of Islam in Africa*. Oxford: James Currey.

Pouwels, R.L. 1981. 'Sheikh al-Amin b. Ali Mazrui and Islamic Modernism in East Africa, 1875-1947', *International Journal of Middle Eastern Studies*, 13.

—— 1987. *Horn and Crescent: Cultural Change and Traditional Islam on the East African Coast, 800–1900*. Cambridge: Cambridge University Press.

—— (ed) 1989. *The Shafi'i Ulamaa of East Africa, c. 1830–1970: A Hagiographic Account*. (translation of Farsy 1989) Wisconsin, Madison: University of Wisconsin Press.

Purpura, A. 1997. *Knowledge and Agency: The Social Relations of Islamic Expertise in Zanzibar*. PhD dissertation, City University of New York.

—— 2000. 'Portrait of Seyyid Silima from Zanzibar: Piety and Subversion in Islamic Prayer, in D. Parkin and S.C. Headley (eds), *Islamic Prayer Across the Indian Ocean: Inside and Outside the Mosque*. Richmond: Curzon Press.

Salim, A.I. 1987. 'Sheikh al-Amin bin Ali Mazrui: un Reformiste Moderne au Kenya', in F. Constantin (ed.), *Les Voies de l'Islam en Afrique Orientale*. Paris: Editions Kathala.

Salim, S. 1985. *A Modern Reformist Movement Among the Sunni Ulama in East Africa*. MA dissertation, McGill University.

Strandes, J. 1961 [1899]. *The Portuguese Period in East Africa*. Nairobi: Kenya Literature Bureau.

Swaleh, H. 2003. *Chaguo la Wanavyoni*. Mombasa: Bajaber Printing Press.

Yassin, A. 2004. *Conflict and Conflict Resolution Among the Swahili of Kenya*. PhD dissertation, University of London.

Zaman, M.Q. 2002. *The Ulama in Contemporary Islam. Custodians of Change*. Princeton: Princeton University Press.

el-Zein, A.H. 1974. *The Sacred Meadows. A Structural Analysis of Religious Symbolism in an East African Town*. Evanston: Northwestern University Press.

7

COSMOPOLITANISM BEYOND THE TOWNS: RURAL-URBAN RELATIONS ON THE SOUTHERN SWAHILI COAST IN THE TWENTIETH CENTURY

Felicitas Becker

The Indian Ocean world is by definition one of trans-oceanic connections, a site of commercial and cultural exchange. Its shape is traced out by networks and their nodes, rather than by large territorial-cum-political units. In twentieth century history, however, it appears as if the dynamics of regional history falter as colonialism imposes its territorial states. Old connections have withered with the marginalisation of the dhow trade; young nations competed for loyalty with the less territorial networks. To qualify this impression is one aim of this chapter. Its other concern lies with one of the implication of thinking in terms of networks rather than territories: the question of the relation between the nodes of networks and their surroundings. It is one of the strengths of the notion of networks to allow for the possibility of parallel, yet hardly connected social groupings in one territorial and even in one social setting. Towns, the typical nodes of networks, may function as sites for the exchange and elaboration of goods and ideas derived from far away, and resemble other towns far away more than the surrounding countryside. The history of the Swahili coast within the Indian Ocean world has long lent itself to this approach. A string of towns dotted along hundreds of miles of coastline, with a centuries-old cultural unity expressed in language, beliefs, customs and material culture, they appear connected by sea much more than by land. An openness towards influences from across the ocean not matched by the surrounding pastoralist and peasant societies forms an intrinsic part of their identity. Randall Pouwels (1987) has made the relation of the Swahili coast to the Indian Ocean the subject of a long-term study that demonstrates both their persistence and their mutability. Anthropological accounts, too, have given prominence to the connectedness of the Swahili coast (Caplan 1997; Middleton 1992) along and across the ocean.

Still, it has long been clear that the sophistication, the very urbanity of the Swahili towns depended in various ways on their rural environment (Alpers 1975; Caplan 1997). In earlier centuries, some of them had grown rich on the sale of gold obtained from the African interior. At the time colonial observers entered the scene in the second half of the nineteenth century, plantations near the towns, worked by slaves imported from the interior, were the mainstay of this dependence. The hegemonic groups within the towns, though, patricians priding themselves on their membership in family and commercial networks spanning the entire western Indian Ocean, efficiently defined these slaves as outsiders. In their understanding, certainly, the towns 'floated' above surrounding peasant society, sustained by their mutual connections and by their cultural exclusivity. This view begs the question what the 'surrounding' people made of and gained by their relations with these towns, and how clearly the power to define these relations lay on the side of the towns. The best answer we have to this question is found in Jonathon Glassman's description of coastal society on the eve of colonial rule, which has people from the surrounding countryside as one element in the unruly urban crowds, pursuing what he calls their 'struggle for citizenship' in the polities the patricians purported to control (1995: 116 and *passim*).

Glassman emphasises the social, ethnic and cultural diversity of Swahili towns and their role as sites of much fought-over economic opportunity. Allied to but not coeval with economic might, he describes the political power of Swahili patricians as heavily based on conspicuous consumption and public ritual, which people on the outside of the patrician networks continually challenged as well as imitated, or challenged by imitation. Its ritual aspects notwithstanding, patrician power depended on the possibility of enforcement and punishment. It is a portrayal of coastal society that admirably captures its multi-tiered, dynamic nature and brings the mud huts back into its history alongside the patrician palaces. Its implications for the colonial history of the coast, meanwhile, are still to be worked out. Considering Glassman's emphasis on the importance of long-distance trade, the plantation economy and a certain amount of executive power, even if fitful, for the maintenance of the patricians' standing, his account would suggest that a gaping vacuum followed the imposition of colonial rule. Who should struggle for citizenship in their polities, if their economic capacity for patronage and conspicuous consumption, as well as their powers of enforcement, were all gone? In this way, his view echoes the perception arising from the European colonial record, that the Swahili coast lived through a 'classical moment' just before colonialism; that it had then reached an apex from which the colonial period formed a descent. The core of this notion of decline is economic; the coastal regions of Kenya and Tanzania alike have been marginalized in territorial economies focused on cash crop production 'up country'. But it can easily be extended to a loss of cultural and political weight.

The work of a handful of historians of the colonial era, however, as well as that of anthropologists who have traced dialogues between 'town' culture and rural people in the twentieth century, suggests a different emphasis. It indicates that interest in town life and ways remained lively among people from the interior after the passing of the political hegemony of the towns. Justin Willis (1993) has demonstrated the role of rural immigrants in the life of colonial Mombasa. David Parkin's (1991) work in the Kilifi region shows rural dwellers as engaged in an active dialogue with the Swahili towns and Pat Caplan (1997) accords rural dwellers an integral place in Swahili culture. The following account offers another case in point. It focuses on a part of the Swahili coast – the southern Tanzanian section – where the decline of the pre-colonial patriciate after the end of slavery and slave trade was steep. It aims to show that in spite of this, and however marginal the role of the coast in the territorial Tanzanian economy, for the adjacent region it actually became more, not less, meaningful and continued to be the site of negotiations over belonging not only to the towns, but to the wider world they stood for.

The Colonial View of the Distinctiveness of the Coast and Historians' Responses

European observers absorbed a racialised version of the patricians' view of their own cultural distinctiveness. In the most extreme formulation, colonial observers have treated Swahili culture as an extra-territorial 'Arab' culture on African soil. Conversely, when the foundations of the Zanzibar-centred commercial networks of the nineteenth century crumbled, the towns of the coast were seen to, as it were, pay the price for their separate existence. By the time Independence came around, the specific heritage of the coast had become a liability. Reporting on a visit by Julius Nyerere, Prime Minister of soon-to-be-independent Tanganyika, a state-funded regional newspaper on the southern Tanganyikan coast stated that:

Mr Nyerere in his address at Kilwa condemned the complacent attitude adapted by the indigenous population there with the result that their up-country brothers whom they used to deride have out-paced them in development. He advised them to group themselves in villages instead of living singly or in small scattered groups in order that they may be able to develop their resources and energy more effectively.[1]

The town criticized by Nyerere for complacency, Kilwa,[2] had seventy years earlier been one of the hubs of the trade networks in Zanzibar's commercial empire in East Africa. During the interceding years, it had declined from being a major destination for traders from other shores of

---

1 Tanzanian National Archive Acc 593/PRE/2/12 Southern Province News, October/November 1961.
2 The name Kilwa applies to a handful of settlements around Kilwa bay, distinguished by their second names. The most eminent is Kilwa Kisiwani ('on the island'), the medieval town visited by Ibn Battuta in the fourteenth century. Kilwa Kivinje, on the mainland facing Kisiwani, was the nineteenth-century slave-trading hub. Nyerere probably gave his speech in the Kilwa best accessible by road, Kilwa Masoko ('markets'), a planned town built by the British in the 1950s to supplant 'decrepit' Kilwa Kivinje.

the Indian Ocean to a provincial town whose harbour could not even accommodate steam ships.

While Kilwa's decline was exacerbated by regional peculiarities, including the repeated ravaging of its hinterland first during the Maji Maji rebellion (1905–7) and then during the First World War, the transition from hub to minor port was characteristic of many towns of the East African seaboard during the same period. Pangani and Saadani in northern Tanzania, Lamu and Malindi in northern Kenya, and Mikindani in southern Tanzania are other examples. Economic and technological change were the major factors in this decline. The Swahili towns which retained their importance or even grew during the same period, above all Mombasa, Tanga and Dar es Salaam, were the ones with export harbours suitable for large vessels (Iliffe 1979; Willis 1993). They established themselves as ports of exit for the growing quantities of agricultural produce from interior regions of East Africa as well as coastal plantations under European or Asian ownership. The towns that declined were the ones that had exported slaves, ivory and slave-produced agricultural wares, mostly by dhow, and found no replacement for this trade.

But political and social changes accompanied the economic ones. Within Kenya, the political as well as the commercial centre of gravity shifted from the coast to Nairobi in the highlands halfway to lake Victoria. In Tanzania, the coast town of Dar es Salaam kept its predominance, but its internal make-up changed greatly to the detriment of its Swahili patricians. In the market place, they were displaced by South Asian traders. In the administration, they faced successful competition from mission-educated Africans from the interior. The same group out-winged them in developing national politics. At the time of Independence, the Swahili coast appeared economically marginal and culturally retrograde to often mission-educated political leaders; its commitment to trade rather than agriculture 'complacent', amid young nations, made up, according to political rhetoric, of hearty peasants. The statement by Julius Nyerere paraphrased above succinctly expresses this view.

One of most striking elements of this process of change is the shifting
position of the networks of trade, marriage and scholarship that
connected the Swahili towns among themselves and also with many
other parts of the Indian Ocean region. During the late pre-colonial
period and still during the onset of colonialism, members of these
networks formed the mainstay of the politics of the coast. From the
Zanzibari sultan, scion of an Omani dynasty, to his representatives and
allies on the coast, and on to the entire milieu of notables, educators,
clerics and traders that has recently been traced out by Anne Bang
(2003), they held a hegemony that was not unchallenged, but
successfully defended. But in accounts of the rise of national politics, the
role of the same networks is minor or uncertain. In both Kenya and
Tanzania, the coast became the site of movements that detracted from
the demand for speedy Independence during the last years of
colonialism. The Swahili coast, it seemed, was disconnected from the
political current of the day (Salim 1970).

Colonial sources suggest that this disconnection happened quite early
on in the colonial period. Within German East Africa, the
comprehensive disempowerment of the old coastal elites occurred during
the last few years before the First World War. In Kilwa Kivinje, it had
become apparent in 1895, when the capture of a member of the local
oligarchy who had taken up arms against the Germans resulted in a spate
of hangings, banishments and confiscations among his supposed
supporters in the town. The fall of the same groups from the height of
the wealth that the slave plantation economy had afforded them was
similarly precipitous. In the absence of slave labour, indigenous
plantation owners turned instead to the least labour-intensive plantation
crop, coconut palms, which produced copra, a low-value commodity.
Severe indebtedness and bankruptcies were common among the
patricians of the coast by the 1910s. The debts of major Kilwan traders
with the German East African Company amounted to several thousand
Rupees each. In 1925, plantations were reported to be passing into
Indian ownership from 'natives' in the Kilwa area; the impoverished

Kilwan patricians who were selling their plantations no longer qualified as 'Arabs'.[3] The Kilwa District Commissioner reported in 1923:

The merchants are continually in litigation, mostly over debts incurred in the war. A considerable amount of grains is exported from here to Zanzibar. It is a custom for merchants here to liquidate their debts with Zanzibar in this manner.[4]

In the same year, an 'inordinate number of property offences' was said to have taken place in Kilwa town. It appears that the remnants of irrecoverable wealth were being squabbled over. In the 1930s, some administrative correspondence was generated by the question of the refurbishment of decrepit mosques, which wealthy townsmen had donated two generations earlier and their trustees now could not keep up. By 1932, a British official in Kilwa Kivinje, when asked to supply one of the cannons remaining in the town for a museum in Dar es Salaam, said this was like 'stripping the last jewels off a corpse.'[5]

That coastal culture had come to be seen as decadent, meanwhile, is even more evident in the damning attitude of colonial administrators in interior regions, which occasionally described Swahili cultural influence as a sort of pernicious infection. A District Officer in Tunduru, a rural district some two hundred miles west of the coast, had this to say about the people in his charge:

the dominant element is the Yao population, who, unfortunately, are a degraded and immoral edition of the fine people further west: at once cunning and lethargic, they abandoned their old salutary tribal customs, and were [sic.] rapidly sinking into a fatal condition of slothful and dissolute apathy.[6]

Although the District Officer is not explicit about it, the distinguishing feature of the Yao and corollary of their abandoning their 'salutary tribal customs' was their early and pervasive acceptance of Islam (Thorold 1995). This remark, like Nyerere's above, indicates that observers from off the Swahili coast effectively implicated its culture in its economic

3 Kilwa district, annual report 1925. TNA 1733/8.
4 District Annual Report 1923. TNA 1733/14.
5 Kilwa District Officer to Dar es Salaam, 1935, TNA Acc. 16/37/31 'preservation of monuments'.
6 Lindi Province, annual report, 1920/21. 23rd May 21, TNA 1733/5.

marginalisation. The association of 'coast' and 'sloth' recurs in the British colonial record. The decline of the coast relative to areas of successful peasant cash crop production became something of a morality tale, a warning example against the dead weight of the 'Arab', 'Islamic' and slave-trading history of the coast.

In the face of this dismissive attitude, later accounts have since demonstrated the continuity of patrician Swahili culture despite its economic and political displacement and challenged the assumption of cultural decay that characterised the colonial record (Middleton 1992; Pouwels 1987). Relying on ethnographic information gathered in the Swahili towns as well as written records, they have shown that the values, the religious beliefs and ritual practice of 'classical', pre-colonial Swahili towns retained validity to their inhabitants in the colonial and post-colonial period. Rather than giving the impression that the pre-colonial Swahili towns and their networks had crumbled, they describe them as quietly prevailing, even if overshadowed by the bigger and newer associations of national politics. On the other hand, by focusing on the Swahili town as the primary frame of reference, this literature tends to reinforce the impression of the self-contained stability of these settlements, ignoring evidence of outside influence and internal strife. This emphasis on coherence and continuity in turn provoked Jonathan Glassman to develop an interpretation of nineteenth-century coastal history that is much more focused on conflict and competition; on what he terms 'struggles for citizenship' among the multitude of people who for one reason or another kicked the dust in the streets of Swahili towns.

One is left, then, with a number of different ways to state the transition of the Swahili coast from the pinnacle to the margin of the history of the East African region: as a process of inexorable decline according to colonial observers; of cultural persistence in the face of political disempowerment according to Pouwels and Middleton; as the aftermath of the explosive assertion of competing political claims in the pre-colonial period that Glassman describes. The following account, based on oral histories collected in towns on the southern Tanzanian coast and the rural region adjacent to it, will qualify some aspects of this literature and develop others.[7] It will show that in spite of the manifest impoverishment of the old elites, the coastal towns, even Kilwa, did not become irrelevant either economically or culturally from the point of view of villagers from the surrounding region. It will give evidence for the continuing immigration into and engagement with the towns by villagers. These observations form the basis for an examination of post-colonial change, qualifying the suggestion that the coast had been permanently sidelined.

Townspeoples' and Peasants' Views of the
Coastal Towns in the Colonial Period

Oral evidence collected from the districts of the southern Tanzanian coast and those to the west of it suggests that the adoption of Islam in the first half of the twentieth century was partly an expression of a continuing appreciation for coastal culture. People who are old now feel nostalgia for the sophistication and wealth of the coast as they knew it in the 1930s to 50s, when according to colonial observers Kilwa was on its last legs and the coast at large badly suffering from the effects of its 'sloth'. The villagers of this region set the periods of the decline of the coast differently from historians, making of it an entirely post-colonial phenomenon. On the one hand, the coastal towns were, as it were, one-eyed among the blind: their limited economic opportunities stood out against dire poverty up country. On the other, though, their continuing importance stemmed from a continued negotiation among people in the region with the history and culture they epitomised. The recollections of villagers and townspeople also help identify the mitigating factors that made this far more positive view of the coast possible. In spite of the

---

7   I conducted interviews in the region in 2000, 2003 and 2004, totalling around three
    hundred. About half of them come from eight towns and villages on the coast between
    Kilwa Kivinje and Mtwara, the others from a dozen towns and villages in the interior.
    They were semi-structured, conducted in Swahili with the help of a research assistant
    whose first language was Swahili. Swahili-speakers also transcribed the interviews.
    Translations are by myself. Rather than attribute every single observation on salient
    topics to all informants who made it, I will limit myself below to citing by name single
    interviews that made specific points particularly clearly.

negative colonial views of the coast mentioned above, elements of colonial policy actually contributed to propping up the old hierarchies of coastal society. That evidence collected off the coast is crucial in understanding this and suggests that there is something to be said for 'getting off the dhow' and looking at the coast from the other end; from the homesteads of the *bara*.[8]

A different frame of reference from that of colonial observers is an important part of the explanation of peasants' different view of the coastal towns. The parts of the mainland adjacent to the southern Tanzanian coast drew little economic benefit from colonialism (see Becker 2002, for further details). Their experience was one of dire poverty. In the region west of Kilwa, the inhabitants also had to contend with the increasingly aggressive 'game protection' policies of the colonial regime. Some of them became migrant labourers, seeking opportunity in Dar es Salaam and occasionally Kilwa.[9] In these circumstances, small-scale economic opportunities in the towns were better than none. A substantial unregulated trade between Kilwa and Dar es Salaam by dhow, mostly in grain, was noted in 1925.[10] It is likely to have continued, except for the time in the 1930s when economic crisis depleted the purchasing power of Dar es Salaam's residents and depressed prices. Further marginal economic activities in Kilwa during the colonial period included fishing for small fry, *dagaa,* in shallow water – a women's occupation – and the cutting of mangrove poles for use as timber, again exported by dhow. The trade in *dagaa* to the interior has remained important for income generation until now. Another product from mangroves that was introduced during the colonial period was mangrove bark, exported by Indian middlemen for use in the chemical industry.[11]

---

8   The term *bara*, literally mainland, has long been used by people on the coast to refer to the interior of the continent that until recently was considered beyond the reach of civilisation. It is no longer associated with barbarism, but still suggests a lack of amenities and relative isolation.

9   AR W Crosse-Upcott, Report on Migrant Labour in Liwale, 26th April 1954. TNA acc 16/37/105, p. 110.

10 District Annual Report 1925. TNA 1733/8.

11 *Afisa mikoko* (local government mangrove protection officer) Kilwa Masoko, 16th June 2004.

Most former slave plantations were planted with coconut palms, a low-labour crop which nevertheless created some employment for tillers and watchmen, as well as profit from the sale of the nuts. The widespread theft of coconuts limited the profits of the owners, but helped other townspeople.

Further south, peasants from the surrounding region who visited Lindi in the 1930s, 40s and 50s were struck by anything but decline. They found its size, its stone houses and the variety of goods it offered quite impressive. Between the wars, traders were a rarity in the countryside. The itinerant rubber buyers of the early colonial period, who had travelled the countryside on foot with bundles of household goods, had vanished after the collapse of rubber prices. Motorised transport became available in the second half of the 1920s, but remained scarce. Most households therefore obtained all basic necessities that they could not produce from the coast. Typically, peasants carried their grains to Lindi on their backs:

The shops were in Lindi, so we would take the trouble to sleep on the [barely inhabited and lion-infested] Rondo plateau, then to sleep in Ng'apa [on the western edge of the coastal belt]; a round trip to Lindi and back would take six days. We took all this trouble in order to deliver our sesame seed. We would prepare bark cloth sacks to put the sesame in because there were no gunny sacks, there were no bags except our bark cloth sacks, and so we went to Lindi. [...] When we got back here we would have sore feet. [...] One had to go to Lindi, if you had wanted to sell your crops here, who would have been there to buy? [12]

They depended on the town's traders to put them up and sold their grain for a mixture of cash and goods, above all cloth, salt, soap, and other household goods such as pots. 'Gifts' of sugar or salt from the buyers smoothened business. Lindi, then, had retained the status of a commercial centre for the peasants of its outlying districts. As the sale of grain was both more regular and, due to colonial taxation, more widespread than that of slaves had been, it increased the importance of the town as a trade centre for peasants.

---

12 Hamisi Ibrahimu Nangwawa, Mnacho-Ng'au 28th August 2000.

Moreover, sometimes in place of, but more often in addition to, older coconut plantations, sisal plantations grew up, staffed by migrant labour from Mozambique or the Tanzanian interior. The inhabitants of the coast preferred to make money by trading with the migrant labourers rather than by working on the plantations. In 1939, a Lindi Provincial Commissioner said that on Lindi sisal estates wages were

Unconscionable [...] skilled and semi-skilled 12/- to 18/-, unskilled 10/- to 12/- for thirty days' work. [...] 'a day's work' is what the employer likes to make it. Few labourers in any grade complete their thirty tasks in less than six weeks [...] Housing conditions are usually execrable [...] Some estates deduct from the wage the value of the working implements issued to the labourers and some make no allowance for unfinished tasks – in other words, if a task is not completed on the day it is set, the day is 'cut', and the value of the work done accrues to the employer, and not to the labourer. [13]

Given these conditions, it is unsurprising that the workers on the plantations typically came from regions with little or no earning opportunities. The inhabitants of the coast preferred to trade with or provide services for the sisal labourers, providing raw food, beer and cooked snacks.[14] Here one sees the economic rationale behind 'coastal sloth'.

Lindi, home to the Provincial Commissioner, also continued to support a public life. If it had less political drama than in the pre-colonial period, it still gave a fair amount of scope to patricians, and was at the same time less exclusive than it had been. To varying degrees, all provincial commissioners made a show of consulting and liaising with the notables of the town. The ostensibly consultative character of colonial rule was celebrated at public functions for British and Muslim holidays.[15] Behind this show of respect lay a deeply conservative impulse. The preservation of social distinctions was an essential element of the maintenance of societal order to the mind of British administrators. The

13 Southern Province, annual report 1939, section 'Labour', TNA 16/11/170.
14 Mzee Salum Daudi Mbaruku Kigango, Kikwetu 11th December 2000.
15 See e.g. the photos of colonial officials with local notables in various annual reports, including 1947/48. TNA acc 16/11/260.

view of the coast as decadent coexisted with another colonial view of the coast that was more positive, if patronising. This alternative view went back to the coexistence with and partial dependence on Swahili elites by representatives of the European powers in the run-up to colonisation. It looked upon Swahili culture as somewhat closer to European culture than were those of the African interior, due to its urbanity, the presence of literacy and its monotheism. These more positive attitudes came into play where British administrators sought to rely on Swahili notables, for instance in the administration of justice in Swahili towns through *qadis* (Islamic judges).

At the same time, Lindi town centre was shifting from Mikumbi, the quarter inhabited by the old patrician families of the town, to Ndoro, a new area dominated by administrative buildings and the shops of Asian businessmen.[16] The town was growing. The bulk of the increase was due to immigration from the countryside, especially the mountainous region to its Southeast known as the Makonde plateau. These new citizens might go on cultivating fields on the city's outskirts, work as labourers, or become fishermen or petty traders. Moreover, they took a prominent role in the conduct of a new form of public ritual, the *ngoma* or dance societies (Ranger 1975). Notables, especially the ones with religious credentials, viewed their activities with some disdain, but they had no means to act against them.[17] Combining fanciful costume that paraphrased both patrician dress styles and colonial uniforms with the display of physical strength, dance societies drew together young townspeople of non-patrician backgrounds. The fact that their activities took place on Saturdays, at the end of the working week, betrays the influence of labourers among them. There was less at stake in these dances than there had been in the rituals of challenge and conspicuous consumption that characterised the pre-colonial period. Arguably, from the point of view of the protagonists this was a good thing. In particular, the new townspeople involved in these activities no longer had to put a distance between themselves and the threat of slavery.

---

16 Safiya binti Abderehmani Likokora, Lindi-Ndoro 22nd July 2000.
17 Safiya binti Abderehmani; Shehani Mohamed Zaina, Lindi-Ndoro 28th July 2000.

The Role of Islam

During the inter-war period, Islam became the one area of public life to support leaders who were equally accepted by notables and people on the street. The most prominent *shehe* of this period were at the same time *khalifa*, that is, leaders of Sufi brotherhoods or *tarika*.[18] They provided legal interpretations and scholarship for their peers as well as religious education and training in maulidi and other public performances for immigrant Muslims.[19] From the 1930s to the 1950s, Lindi's religious life was dominated by the sometimes tense coexistence and occasional cooperation of two such *shehe*. One of them, Khalifa bin Abdulkarim Jamalidini, was of 'old' Lindi parentage; the Jamalidini family traced its ancestry to Mombasa but had been in Lindi for many generations. He ran a mosque in Mikumbi, the old patrician quarter, and a chapter of the Qadiriyya Sufi brotherhood that practised a relatively austere version of Qadiri ritual.[20] The other one, Muhammad bin Yusuf, known as Shehe Badi, had a Mombasan mother but a Makonde father. An immigrant himself, he was most prominent in the immigrant parts of town such as Ndoro. Like Khalifa bin Abdulkarim, he was a Qadiri, but he had brought a new rite from Mombasa that to Khalifa's dismay included the use of drums.[21] Nevertheless, the British made him *qadi* for a few years from 1936. His religious credentials mattered more than his lack of indigenous status in Lindi town.

Kilwa experienced a duality similar to that in Lindi. Here too it was expressed spatially. In Kilwa Kivinje, the leading *shehe* was Omari bin Farhani, a khalifa of the Qadiriyya *tarika* and member of the town's patriciate. His competitor was Hussein bin Mahmood, who besides running a *madrasa* ('Quran school') on Kilwa Island founded a religious centre or *zawiya* in the hitherto obscure location of Pande at the far

18 I use the Swahili form *shehe* of the Arabic term *shaykh*, religious expert. The Arab term *tariqa*, literally 'way', is routinely used to refer to Sufi brotherhoods; I stick with the Swahili form *tarika* and also avoid the Arab plural *turuq* in favour of the Swahili *tarika*.
19 *Maulidi* are praise-songs for the prophet, performed especially but not only on his birthday, and it is a major ritual occasion in the Swahili calendar.
20 Fadhil Zubeiri, Lindi-Mikumbi 24th July 2000.
21 Safiya binti Abderehmani Likokora, Lindi-Ndoro 22nd July 2000.

south-eastern edge of Kilwa bay, with its back to the open sea.[22] He represented the Shadhiliyya *tarika* with a more lively – and to the mind of the Qadiris under Shehe Omari less dignified – ritual. Although Hussein bin Mahmood had an impeccable pedigree himself, his mother being a native of Kilwa Kisiwani and his father a well-travelled patrician who died in Mikindani, he surrounded himself with people of obscure origins. His disciples in Pande (where he died in 1971) today emphasise that he consulted with and gained the permission of the 'elders' of the location before setting up his *zawiya* here. Difficult to access, sandy and not suited for the production of anything beyond coconuts, fish and some staple foods, Pande was, in the context of inter-war Kilwa, a location for 'squatters', that is, ex-slaves. Greater physical distance notwithstanding, the relationship between Kilwa-Pande and Kilwa Kivinje resembled that between Lindi-Ndoro, the 'new', immigrant part of town where Shehe Badi lived, and Mikumbi, the patrician, now crumbling 'old centre' that was home to Khalifa bin Abdulkarim Jamalidini.

Reminiscences from the rural areas west of Lindi show that many villagers converted to Islam during visits to town. For this purpose, they underwent a ritual in which they were submerged in the ocean. They would also receive minimal instruction, above all on dietary prohibitions, and a new piece of clothing or two:

I had two *wajomba*[23] [who converted to Islam] and my sisters converted too; [they said] let's go to take her [the respondent] to Lindi so that she may convert. I went to Lindi, we walked and walked and bought clothing, [they asked] so now do you accept Kiswahili as is required for conversion, [I said] I want Kiswahili and reject [the ways] of the *bara*, I want those of Lindi, I am going to Lindi to convert. [...] I went to Lindi and I went straight into the water [...] down into it

---

22 Dalini Ahmadi, Kilwa Masoko 18th June 2004; Mwalimu Mfaume, Kilwa Pande 19th June 2004.

23 *Wajomba* (singular *mjomba*) are maternal uncles. In this matrilineal region, they were often as important in households as fathers. The informant, then, was following the lead of authority figures in her family. Notwithstanding the patriarchal nature of Islamic family law, matrilineal networks of uncles and nephews were sometimes involved in the founding of mosques and in teaching the Quran.

three times, while the teacher was reciting, and in this way I became fit to wear the *kikoi*.[24]

The association between Islam and the ways of the town, the coast and the Swahili is very clear in this statement. Informants in the interior west of Lindi state that conversion at the coast was gradually replaced by conversion at home during the inter-war period. Nevertheless, when villagers converted at home, their *shehe* (themselves normally trained on the coast) sprinkled them with water that was mixed with salt, to make it resemble seawater.

These reminiscences offer precious insights into what appear to be paradoxical processes. Islam had been present on the East African coast for centuries and had made very little inroads until the nineteenth century. Then, Muslim communities came into being in settlements along the trade routes in the interior, and in a handful of courts of African rulers off the coast. But only in the twentieth century, after the end of Zanzibari hegemony, and under a Christian colonial government, did large numbers of people in the countryside far away from the coast adopt Islam. The accounts of conversion from southeast Tanzania make clear that this process was driven by the interest of villagers rather than a missionary impetus from the coast. Nevertheless, the coast, inasmuch as it was the repository of Muslim religious knowledge for the region and the way station for the sort of imported clothing and objects associated with it, remained crucial to this process. What the stories of the converts in Lindi, and of the competing *shehe* with their different constituencies, indicate is that at a time when these towns were fading off the map, according to the colonialists' thinking, the combined efforts of visitors from the hinterland, new townspeople and old townspeople gave them new meaning. The decline that the elites were experiencing actually added to the attraction of the towns to less rarefied people. Islam, which had been a marker of distinctions between master and slave, townsperson and villager, now instead became one of the connecting elements of a network that tied town and countryside together in an unprecedented

---

24 Asumini Litanda, Mnero-Mwandila 16th September 2000. A *kikoi* is an imported garment, a gently coloured woven cloth, most often worn by men on the coast.

way. The vibrancy of religious and ritual life in Kilwa Kivinje at the end of the colonial period is attested to by the accounts of the anthropologist Peter Lienhardt, who lived in the town in 1959 (Lienhardt 1966). At the same time, the urbanity of the towns was no longer their exclusive preserve, as the villagers were taking Swahili-ness home with them. In Lindi region, Shehe Khalifa began to tour the countryside extensively in the 1950s, spreading the Qadiriyya *tarika*. Generally, the *tarika* were gaining strength in the countryside in the late colonial period and had their heyday in the first decade and a half of independence.

A curious feature of the developing religious landscape of the southern Tanzanian coast is the low profile of Zanzibar in it. Kilwa and Lindi were clearly the local centres; when it came to seeking learning abroad, Mombasa was the destination of choice. Zanzibar was not absent from the picture; many *shehe* had spent time there. The nevertheless noticeable preference for Mombasa may reflect in part the slight animosity prevailing between Kilwa and Zanzibar, with Kilwans eager to point out that Islam arrived on their island first.[25] It also serves as a reminder that the networked world of the Swahili is multi-polar and multi-layered. Even if a generation of eminent *shehe* who had represented the cosmopolitanism of the late pre-colonial period were dying off in Zanzibar, exchange along the Swahili coast had not come to a halt. But the most crucial Muslim figures of the inter-war period were people who were more 'grounded', more of one particular place on the coast, than the roaming *shehe* of earlier generations. This 'groundedness' enabled them to become catalytic figures for the popularisation of Islam.

In both Kilwa and Lindi, the *shehe* with the less patrician, more immigrant constituencies are the best-remembered ones today. They were the embodiment of a social compromise that had overcome the divisive heritage of slavery. The optimism and dynamism of this compromise are evident also in the run-up to Independence. At a time when Africans felt that for the first time they could bring their own preferences to bear on the state they would live in, Muslims turned to the

25 Mohamed Said Mwichande, Kilwa Masoko 10th July 2000. Villagers from the interior support the same view, see Issa Makolela, Rwangwa-Likangara 3rd September 2003.

soon-to-be independent state to safeguard their orthodoxies, reviving the lingering disagreements over the ritual innovations of the preceding decades.[26] In its way, the state delivered, soliciting judgements from Zanzibari authorities that were used to formulate local compromises.[27] Regarding the political parties that had sprung up, the grand *shehe* did not take sides, but they were on friendly terms with the party of popular choice, TANU (Tanzanian African National Union). As a matter of course, they were among the official guests at the Independence celebrations of 1961. Shehe Badi died in Lindi at around this time. His chosen successor, who was to be the largely uncontroversial head of the Muslim community of Lindi until his death in about 1998, would actually take a number of party offices at local and regional level.[28]

Change After Independence: 'The Coast is not the Coast Anymore'[29]
Thus in 1961, at the time of Independence, the networks that sustained the political life of these Swahili towns had changed greatly compared to the pre-colonial period, but they had neither dissolved nor lost their relevance. On the southern Tanzanian coast at least, the towns had become more 'grounded' without losing their connectedness across the sea. The good relations between TANU and Muslim leaders at this time also give credence to the on the whole positive assessment of relations between Muslims and the state during the first two decades of Independence by various observers of Tanzania's religious scene (Westerlund 1980, Smith 1990, Ludwig 1996). On the other hand, it is clear that the affinity between TANU and the *shehe* of the *tarika* at this time was the outcome of particular social dynamics rather than an active endorsement of TANU's stance on the relations between religion and politics. Most Muslims at the time of Independence believed that TANU was good for them as Tanzanians, but also as Muslims as the party was expected to redress the Christian bias of the education system.

---

26 Hamisi Kidume, Mikindani 28th June 2004.
27 Saidi Ahmad Kilala, Kilwa Masoko 18th June 2004.
28 Mohamed Abdi, Lindi-Mikumbi 13th August 2003, Mohamed Mtoro, Lindi-Ndoro December 2003.
29 Selemani Ali Ahmed, Lindi-Nachingwea 18th July 2000.

Developments since, though, have produced the sentiment that 'the coast is not the coast any more'. Independence, in other words, has not delivered for it. A good part of this change is again economic and very evident when travelling past the abandoned, over-grown sisal estates north of Lindi town. Still, the character of this change is hotly debated. Its causation has become part of the 'blame game' that fuels the increasing alienation of many Muslims from the independent Tanzanian state. No piece of writing could settle this debate given that power is at stake, but while treating the economic changes very briefly, an attempt will be made to give a balanced view of the role of the state in this process.

The demise of the sisal plantations has already been mentioned. Sisal had been the mainstay of the Tanzanian plantation economy on the coast since the German period and, while the centres of the industry were along the northern coast in Dar es Salaam and Tanga, the Lindi area had been significant. There appears to be no doubt that it was the decline of prices in international markets that killed off sisal from the 1960s.[30] Its main use was in producing fibres for use in coarse cloth such as gunny sacks, and during the 1960s alternative products derived from jute and plastics became increasingly available. The speed and pervasiveness of the decline, though, are to the mind of at least some Tanzanian observers also connected with the political context. Around Lindi, many plantations were owned by members of the Indian trading network. Today, the crumbling buildings of Indian trading firms such as Karimjee Jivanjee in Lindi attest to the withering of this network since Independence.[31]

It is also said in the coastal towns that around the time of Independence the last dhows stopped coming. People who, as children in the 1940s, had observed exchanges of clothing, carpets and dates for mangrove poles and dried fish in the old dhow harbours saw no more of this now.[32] Another economic activity came to an end with the cessation

---

30 On the effects of this decline in the centre of Tanzania's sisal industry, Tanga, see Askew (2002).

31 Mohsin Alidina, Mingoyo 14th August 2000.

32 Mohamed Juma Mkalindende, Lindi-Mikumbi 30th July 2000.

of the exploitation of mangroves. As with sisal, buyers' interest in mangrove bark declined with alternative products becoming available. At the same time, the mangrove forests shifted categories in the eyes of administrators, from exploitable resource to protected asset. Mangrove forest reserves were first gazetted in the Kilwa area in the 1970s, ending a minor but viable form of export trade. Another unexpected blow to the economy of the coast came when coconut palms became increasingly unproductive and even began to die off. Partly this was due to the age of the trees, but pests were also involved. In Kilwa-Pande, all coconut palms were killed off by illness in the early 1980s, and all attempts to re-establish the palm groves since have come to nothing as the illness still lingers.[33]

From 1973 onwards, the coast was also affected by the then current policy of 'villagisation': the concentration of the population of small and scattered villages into larger settlements. The immediate effects were ambiguous. The towns became the platform for the distribution of material input – machinery, cars, cattle – intended for the newly established villages, and took fringe benefits out of it. Motorised fishing, cattle-rearing and similar ventures brought some material benefit to the enlarged coastal settlements.[34] On the other hand, the removal of smaller outlying villages made the tending and utilisation of palm and cashew groves more difficult and in some cases trees actually had to be cut down. Moreover, at least in some instances the locations for new villages were chosen without any consultation with the people affected and with little knowledge of local conditions. As a consequence, elementary requirements such as access to water were sometimes served worse in new locations than they had been in the old. Even where this was not the case, the authoritarian style of the intervention rankled and was seen by some as an attempt to destroy the communality and autonomy of coastal villages.[35]

---

33 Mohamed Said Mwichande, Kilwa Masoko 10th July 2000.
34 Muhammad Mtoro; Safiya binti Abderehmani.
35 Shehe Abdulkadir Hassan Bakari Mkoyogole, Dar es Salaam-Temeke 5th June 2004.

By the end of the 1970s, the material inputs into the new villages had generally dissipated. Cars broke down; cattle died off or, some say, were slaughtered to provide hospitality for visiting notables.[36] Moreover, the 'socialist' policies that had accompanied the 'villagisation' policies had unhelpful repercussions. They translated partly into a tendency to victimise private traders, intensifying the exodus of Indian traders to Dar es Salaam or abroad. At the end of the 1970s, Tanzania experienced a general crisis of distribution that left even the towns desperately short of basic goods such as cloth, sugar and soap. In hindsight, observers on the Southern Coast tend to blame this on mismanagement and corruption. At the same time, they mention another, enduring aspect of the crisis: a steep rise in prices for transportation. While this dearth may have been made worse by the economic regime of the period, it is also a reflection of the worldwide 'oil price shock' hitting Tanzania. In the long run, the high fuel, hence transportation, costs were particularly injurious as they not only complicated the moving of goods, but also made it more difficult for people to come together. Combined with the decline in the sisal and coconut trades, they emptied the chests of the Sufi brotherhoods, for whom bringing people together at their annual *ziyara* festivals was the main financial challenge.[37] Muslim villagers from the *bara* reminisce about their annual visits to Dar es Salaam in hired buses; they stopped organising these trips in the 1970s when the costs became prohibitive. The shrinking crowds at the Sufi celebrations are a clear indication to both townspeople and villagers that the coastal towns are not what they used to be.

That the interfering manner of central government in connection with the 'villagisation' campaign led to disaffection has already been mentioned; other actions by government were seen as even more direct attacks on the religious networks of the southern Tanzanian towns. Sometime in the second half of the 1960s, Nuruddin bin Hussein, a son of Hussein bin Mahmood who had begun to take a high profile in the

---

36 Ally Salum Nankomeka, Mingoyo 11th November 2003.
37 Shehe Omari Rashidi, Dar es Salaam 20th May 2004; Hassan Athuman Pachoto, Rwangwa-Likangara 23rd October 2003.

activities of the Shadhiliyya, was arrested and put into prison. Different
reasons were given or imputed for this action: he had smuggled ivory; he
had illegally kept Mozambican refugees at his Lindi home.[38] It is likely
that the arrest was prompted by the ire of the Tanzanian government
over cooperation between members of the Shadhiliyya and the
Portuguese government in northern Mozambique, where the Tanzanian
government was supporting FRELIMO's struggle against Portuguese rule
(Alpers 2000). Here, the international connections of the *tarika* for the
first time became a real liability to them. Nyerere's government was
displaying misgivings against the international, or maybe better trans-
national, character of Muslim organisations also by closing down the
East African Muslim Welfare Organisation in 1968 and replacing it with
an explicitly national central organisation for Tanzanian Muslims,
BAKWATA.[39] Meanwhile, the year 1965 saw a handful of Muslim
scholars from the southern coast leave Zanzibar to settle in Lindi, at least
partly because they found post-revolutionary Zanzibar increasingly
inhospitable to their religious interests.[40] Even if nothing was made
explicit, different aspects of Tanzanian nationalism increasingly
interfered with the religion and networks of the coastal towns and the
surrounding region, which these networks had served to bring closer. In
this situation, it was only to be expected that Tanzanian Muslims would
become more receptive to interpretations of Islam that were more
antagonistic towards the non-religious state than the great Sufi *shehe* had
been.

New Networks and the Changing Place of the Coastal Towns
In the 1990s, a dispute arose among Muslims in Lindi town that serves
to highlight both the weakening of the integrative role of the old Sufi
networks and the history that Sufis had helped to address. After the

---

38 Conversation, Machenza household, Lindi-Mikumbi 2004; Mahmood bin Nuruddin
(Nuruddin bin Mahmood's son), Dar es Salaam, 3rd June 2004.
39 BAKWATA is an abbreviation of its complete name in Swahili: *Baraza Kuu la
Waislamu Tanzania.*
40 Shehe Muhammad Mshangani, Lindi-Ndoro 10th December 2003; Shehe Hassan
Mbwana, Lindi-Ndoro 5th November 2003.

death of Muhammad Shaibu, Shehe Badi's successor, in 1998 there was no designated leader. Rather, Shehe Shaibu had endorsed several people, each one in a limited capacity. Now, these people could not agree among themselves how to distribute the offices that Shehe Shaibu had united in his person, especially those of *shehe* (religious scholar, expert) and *khalifa* (*tarika* leader).[41] Issa Nalinga, the man who at first appeared as the best 'compromise candidate', was hesitant to take on the role of *khalifa* along with that of *shehe*. Long-winded recriminations ensued which resulted in a split among the Qadiris of the town that endures to the present. One party accused the other of racism and elitism, insinuating that they rejected the compromise candidate because he was a Makonde who had no family connection to the 'Arab' milieu of the town. The party thus attacked, albeit led by a man whose partly Arab extraction was undisputed, was adamant that the Arab-Makonde dichotomy had nothing to do with their choices. For them, the association of their leader with the 'old' elite of the town has become a liability. Their position resembles that of a public-school educated Briton who is tempted to acquire a South London accent for street credibility.

Meanwhile, Issa Nalinga's hesitation concerning the role of Qadiri *khalifa* can be taken as an indication of his interest in extending his appeal to a new generation of Muslims. By the time of Shehe Shaibu's death, a reformist faction had begun to form among young Muslims in Lindi town that opposed Sufism.[42] It was endorsed by two members of the older generation, Shehe Hassani Mbwana and Shehe Muhammad Mshangani, who both had lived in Zanzibar in the 1960s. They had formulated a critique of the role accorded to Sufi ritual in current burial practice, based partly on their reading of the translation of the Quran provided by Shehe Abdallah Saleh Farsy, a Zanzibari/Mombasan scholar who maintained a position of eminence from the 1950s to his death in

---

41 Mohamed Bakari and Masoud Japani, Lindi-Ndoro 15th August 2003; Athuman Saidi and Juma Musa Msabaha, Lindi-Ndoro 13th August 2003, Shehe Issa Nalinga, Lindi-Jamhuri 27th August 2003.
42 Fatuma Mohamed, Lindi-Jamhuri 7th November 2003 and in conversation; Maalim Sinani Nabahani, Lindi-Mikumbi 1st December 2003. On opposition to Sufism as a hallmark of Muslim reform in Africa see Rosander and Westerlund (1997).

1981. Their young followers, on the other hand, were inspired also by anti-Sufi sentiment among younger scholars who had made use of the scholarships offered by the Saudi and other Arab governments from the late 1970s onwards to study in various Gulf countries.[43] They form part of a network of young anti-Sufi, reformist – some say Islamist – activists that has established its presence across Tanzania. One characteristic of this movement, known as Ansar Sunna, is that it has a strong presence in 'new' Muslim locations off the coast. Shinyanga in central Tanzania is said to be the site of its foundation. In southeast Tanzania, it is most vocal and best established (with separate mosques and large numbers of mostly – but not exclusively – young followers) not in the old coastal towns but in the towns of the *bara*.[44]

In Lindi, the challenge of the Ansar Sunna, combined with discord among the late Shehe Shaibu's disciples, led to a somewhat paradoxical situation. The so-called 'Arab' faction, initially insistent that the functions of *shehe* and *khalifa* should be combined, now runs its own Qadiri *zawiya* while keeping its distance from Issa Nalinga who has effectively taken over Shehe Shaibu's functions as *shehe*. Issa Nalinga also oversees Qadiri activities at the insistence of some of his poor and little educated 'Makonde' supporters, though he (the 'Mmakonde') takes a more restrictive line on the public performances of the Sufis than the 'Arab', patrician, faction (which in the past had been disapproving of the livelier ritual introduced by Shehe Badi). Still, Nalinga's attempt to appeal to the young anti-Sufis by de-emphasising the role of the *tarika* has failed and the latter are now building their separate mosque in the formerly patrician part of town. The Sufi- and government-friendly BAKWATA, meanwhile, has recently inaugurated a new mosque built with Kuwaiti funding. Its Imam-ship has been given to Shehe Mshangani, one of the two *shehe* that had previously endorsed the anti-Sufi faction (who thereupon relinquished his ties with the Ansar Sunna). In effect, and with some discreet government backing, the *tarika* in Lindi

43 Mwalimu Salim Bafadhili, Tanga 26th July 2004.
44 Fatuma Abdala, Khalima Selemani, Fatuma Mohamed, Lindi-Jamhuri 7th November 2003.

have become the defenders of a local orthodoxy against a younger generation with connections to the Middle East and a critical stance towards the government. In Kilwa Kivinje, meanwhile, the tensions between Sufis and Ansar Sunna were overshadowed by discontent over the government's decision to transport gas extracted nearby by pipeline to Dar es Salaam, rather than use it for the electricity supply of Kilwa. The Zanzibar-based opposition party Civic United Front (CUF) is strong here, leading some locals to observe that the opposition supporters 'want to bring back the Arabs'. Thus even though the 'Arabs', i.e. the immigrant patricians of the days of Zanzibari hegemony, have long stopped being politically relevant, their legacy still is. The factions invoking or refuting this legacy, though, also have to reckon with the Ansar Sunna, a new 'layer' of politico-religious networking that has come into being while the Sufi networks of the mid-twentieth century grew weaker. With its Saudi connections, its anti-Sufi stance, and by recruiting from continental Tanzania far beyond the coastal towns, this latest network is quite new. Still, with its references to Shehe Farsy, the endorsement given by some of his students and a somewhat reified notion of pre-revolutionary Zanzibar as a seat of Muslim learning, it also appeals to the better-known scholarly past of the region (while largely ignoring the older emphasis in local history on the role of Kilwa, rather than Zanzibar, in Muslim learning). Since the end of Zanzibari hegemony, this is the second transformation of religious networks on this part of the coast, one generation after the death of the eminent *khalifa*-cum-*shehe* of the mid-twentieth century.

With the passing of each generation the history of the coastal towns is reassessed. The recent reassessment is connected to a shift in the political place of coastal Islam vis-à-vis the state, towards a more separate, potentially oppositional position. There is also evidence, though, of a rather different kind of relocation of the coast that has occurred in the course of the twentieth century. The following is a quotation from the oral account by Juma Hamisi, an inhabitant of the former town, now fishing village, of Sudi, south of Lindi town:

[The Omani Abdulkadir] arrived when there were already plenty of people living here. That's when this Arab arrived from Arabia, and when he came here he asked for somewhere to live but the place that he wanted was in the part of town belonging to the people from Kilwa, and he said to the people from Kilwa, sell me this area I want to live here, and they said we can't sell to you, but we can welcome you as a guest. They came to an agreement and the Arab lived here and built a two-storey house. [...] and then he built a [yard] to keep slaves in; he had the habit of buying slaves.[45]

The event retold here is the one which German administrators described as the 'founding' of the town of Sudi by an Omani Arab who had fallen out with the Sultan of Zanzibar. A large mosque, now ruined, attests to the presence of an Ibadi community in the late pre-colonial period. That slave exports were their mainstay there is no reason to doubt; Sudi's shallow harbour, well protected by reefs, was like that of Kilwa Kivinje well accessible to dhows but off limits for British vessels trying to enforce the ban on slave exports. Moreover, a well-known warlord on the Makonde plateau, who was on bad terms with the towns of Lindi and Mikindai, used Sudi to export the slaves he captured (Becker 2002: ch. 1). But as Mzee Juma so clearly states, the beginnings of Sudi lay much further in the past.

The way this village started, in the past it was a big *pori* [wilderness, uninhabited place]. There was a dense forest and all the animals were living here, starting with the rhinoceros, the giraffe, the bush pig, the baboon and so on; there wasn't even a single human. But there was one person who governed this *pori* and regarded it as his [...] He lived in that village over there [on] the other shore. [It was called] Mgau. [...] Now one man came from Mozambique and crossed the river [Ruvuma] with his people. He came from Mozambique from a town called Hulo. He was a Mmakonde [...] And this man was a hunter of animals and a specialist for building guns, the sort that shoot one bullet at a time, and he moved on until he arrived here and found this *pori* full of animals, so he liked living here. And this man's name was Mohamed Wauyaya. [...] and he had [with him] his junior relative Binti Uyaya and a junior relative of hers and their children [...] they built little huts here to live in. They would shoot those animals and eat them. Now this man who governed the *pori* was living over there. When he heard that people had come to live here, he came here and asked

45 Mzee Juma Hamisi, Sudi 25th June 2004.

them, 'Who has invited you here?' They said, 'Nobody has invited us, we are just strangers.' He said, 'This *pori* is mine […] give me something as a present and I will welcome you.' They had nothing except iron, because those people were specialists in the building of guns. So they took some iron and gave it to this man. He said to them, 'All this *pori* is yours from now on and if people come, you will welcome them without consulting me again; I have given you this *pori*.' So those people lived there, and after a while they started to clear the forest and build houses. After a long time, other people came from Kilwa. When they arrived here they asked for a place to live. Those people who had been given the village said, 'Give us something as a present and we will welcome you. And those offered cloth 40 meters long and they were welcomed. They were given a boundary: 'from here to there is ours', and this border runs all the way from the beach up the hill.

Mentioning Mozambican place names and personal names, as well as the profession of gunsmith, this account is situated in historical space. Nevertheless, it uses well-known, apparently timeless tropes. The acquisition of the land of a town in exchange for cloth occurs in a version of the origins of Kilwa Kivinje collected by a German linguist in Kilwa a hundred years ago (Velten 1903). Mohamed Wauyaya who first settled in the wilderness, meanwhile, was a hunter-pioneer of a type very common in East African oral history, in spite of his Muslim name. By giving him the most prominent role in the history of Sudi, the narrator places this coastal village very firmly in the history of continental East Africa. On the other hand, the ruler of Mgao who made Wauyaya the rightful owner of the location is a coastal person, and he seems to belong to a pre-Omani, pre-Zanzibari era. 'Mongalo' or Mgao is a location on the southern Tanzanian coast mentioned in Portuguese sources of the sixteenth and seventeenth centuries (Alpers 1975). What this history of Sudi does is to reduce the entire period of Zanzibari hegemony to an episode in a much longer story of encounters between immigrants from the *bara* on one hand and from other coastal locations on the other. It is a reminder of how diverse, how deeply layered and how much part of both African and Indian Ocean history the heritage of the coast is.

Conclusion

Hence while the recent advances of Middle-Eastern anti-Sufi doctrine in southern Tanzania may be interpreted with reference to a contemporary process of 'Islamic globalisation', they do not obliterate the old and subtle forms of negotiation whereby the Muslims of the region have situated themselves between continental Africa and the Indian Ocean. The twentieth-century history of Islam in this region is that of the expansion of ocean-bound networks into the mainland. While it was up to the mainlanders themselves to take Islam back home, the old sites of Islam on the coast provided the information and, at least at first, the ritual expertise. Crucial in mediating this process were the Sufi *shehe* who were willing to accommodate recent African immigrants to the towns into their rituals. They were less cosmopolitan, less ocean-bound than Anne Bang's 'Scholars of the Sea' or Farsy's 'Ulamaa,' but they operated within the same cultural framework, and perhaps even helped increase its reach and relevance. Their prominence in local memory, and relative obscurity in the published literature, highlights one characteristic of these religious networks that shapes every attempt to research them, namely the leeway they give everyone within them to take their particular node of the network as its centre. Networks have a way of appearing complete from any one of their outposts, and it is up to the observer to make sure to identify the limits of their place-specific horizons. In the case presented here, going beyond the coast into the *bara* turns out to be an important step towards understanding events on the coast. As for the effects of national politics on the religious networks, the discomfort each seems to feel in the presence of the other is palpable. But rather than the outcome of natural incompatibility, it is that of the twists and turns in the political and economic history of Tanzania's first five decades of independence. The optimism with which Tanzanian Muslims encountered the state in the mid-twentieth century has dissipated; still, in handling internal disagreements their networks have shown a continuing capacity for negotiation that hopefully can serve them also in their future relations with the state.

Bibliography

Askew, K. 2002. *Performing the Nation. Swahili Music and Cultural Politics in Tanzania.* Chicago: University of Chicago Press.

Alpers, E. 1975. *Ivory and Slaves in East Central Africa.* Berkeley and London: University of California Press and Heinemann.

—— 2000. 'East Central Africa', in R.L. Pouwels and N. Levtzion (eds), *The History of Islam in Africa.* Athens, OH: Ohio University Press.

Bang, A.K. 2003. *Sufis and Scholars of the Sea: Family Networks in East Africa, 1860–1925.* London: RoutledgeCurzon.

Becker, F. 2002. *A Social History of Southeast Tanzania, ca. 1890-1950.* Unpublished PhD thesis, University of Cambridge.

Caplan, P. 1997. *African Voices, African Lives: Personal Narratives from a Swahili Village.* London: Routledge.

Farsy, A.S. 1989 [1970]. *The Shafi'i Ulamaa of East Africa, c.1830–1970: a Hagiographic Account.* ('Baadhi ya Mashekhe Wakubwa wa Kisuni wa Mashariki ya Afrika', translated, edited, and annotated by R.L. Pouwels). Madison: University of Wisconsin Press.

Glassman, J. 1995. *Feast and Riot. Revelry, Rebellion and Popular Consciousness on the Swahili Coast, 1856–1888.* London: James Currey.

Iliffe, J. 1979. *A Modern History of Tanganyika.* Cambridge: Cambridge University Press.

Lienhardt, P. 1959. 'The Mosque College of Lamu and its Social Background', *Tanganyika Notes and Records* 53.

—— 1966. 'A Controversy over Islamic Custom in Kilwa Kivinje, Tanzania', in I.M. Lewis (ed.), *Islam in Tropical Africa.* Oxford: Oxford University Press.

Ludwig, F. 1996. 'After Ujamaa: is Religious Revivalism a Threat to Tanzania's stability?', in D. Westerlund (ed.), *Questioning the Secular State. The Worldwide Resurgence of Religion in Politics.* London: Hurst.

Martin, B.G. 1976. *Muslim Brotherhoods in Nineteenth-Century Africa.* Cambridge: Cambridge University Press.

Middleton, J. 1992. *The World of the Swahili. An African Mercantile Civilization.* New Haven: Yale University Press.

Parkin, D. 1991. *The Sacred Void. Spatial Images of Work and Ritual among the Giriama of Kenya.* Cambridge: Cambridge University Press.

Pouwels, R.L. 1987. *Horn and Crescent: Cultural Change and Traditional Islam on the East African Coast, 800–1900*. Cambridge: Cambridge University Press.

Ranger, T. 1975. *Dance and Society in Eastern Africa: The Beni Ngoma*. London: Heinemann.

Salim, A.I. 1970. 'The Movement for Mwambao or Coast Autonomy in Kenya 1956–63', B.A. Ogot (ed.) *Hadith 2*. Nairobi: East African Publishing House.

Smith, P. 1990. 'Christianity and Islam in Tanzania: Development and Relationships', *Islamochristiana*, 16.

Thorold, A. 1995. *The Yao Muslims. Religion and Social Change in Southern Malawi*. Unpublished PhD thesis, University of Cambridge.

Velten, C. 1903. *Prosa und Poesie der Suaheli*. Berlin: published by the author.

Westerlund, D. 1980. *Ujamaa na Dini. A Study of Some Aspects of Society and Religion in Tanzania, 1961–1977*. Stockholm: Almquist and Wiksell.

Westerlund, D., and E.E. Rosander (eds) 1997. *African Islam and Islam in Africa: Encounters between Sufis and Islamists*. Athens, OH: Ohio University Press.

Willis, J. 1993. *Mombasa, the Swahili and the Making of the Mijikenda*. Oxford: Clarendon Press.

8

DRUMMING AND PRAYING: SIDI AT THE INTERFACE BETWEEN SPIRIT POSSESSION AND ISLAM[1]

Helene Basu

Anthropologists working in Indian Ocean littoral societies such as Gujarat in India are faced with a peculiar dilemma: while the analytical approaches of regional specialists tend to be limited to ideas about the isomorphy of culture and place, the ethnographic settings they encounter are often conceptualised by local people in terms of past relationships of exchange and migrations from places beyond the area studied, as is the case in Gujarat (see also Simpson 2003). Specialists in South Asia are also habitually more prone to relate their findings to pan-Indian structures and themes than to linkages beyond the subcontinent and across the ocean. If, however, anthropologists seek to rectify this limitation by following up the connections that emerge from their ethnographic findings and turn to the Indian Ocean, they encounter specific methodological problems. The Indian Ocean has mainly been constructed and studied as a region in its own right by historians working with archival evidence. While histories of the Indian Ocean region have greatly contributed to the growing awareness of the fictive

1 I wish to express my gratitude to Paul Greenough, Jim Giblin, Meena Khandelwal and others from the University of Iowa for valuable comments when discussing the ideas that have resulted in this chapter. I would specifically like to thank Kai Kresse and Edward Simpson for carefully reading the manuscript at various stages and for many helpful suggestions. The chapter draws on fieldwork carried out in Gujarat between 1987 and 2004. It was made possible by grants of German Academic Exchange Service (1987–89), Free University Berlin (1995, 1996, 1997–98) and the Fritz-Thyssen-Stiftung (2004).

nature of spatial tropes (see Parkin 2000a: 1), their aims are more often oriented towards global designs rather than the detailed descriptions of ideas, values and practices embedded in the localised life-worlds that anthropologists are concerned with. Anthropological research in the Indian Ocean thus requires a methodological approach that allows for the integration of history on the level of ideas and practices while simultaneously focusing upon symbolic linkages across space and time. Such an approach is facilitated by theories of social memory as developed by Halbwachs (1985a, 1985b), Connerton (1991) and others (J. Assmann 1997; A. Assmann 1999). For Halbwachs, social representations are nothing less than past events, persons and relationships that reappear in the form of ideas and values through collective forms of memory. Going beyond the symbolic level of ideas, Connerton stresses the anchoring of social representations in the body through habits, processes of inscription and incorporation through a range of practices.

Since the concept of social memory transcends the dichotomy between history and anthropology, by shifting the focus from actual events to embodied representations of the past in the present, it may be usefully employed when linkages across space and time in the Indian Ocean region are investigated from an anthropological perspective. Working along these lines, I shall analyse ritual practices situated in the wider field of Sufi-Islam and performed by descendants of African slaves and seamen in Gujarat in India, the Sidi. They now constitute a community of about twenty thousand which is associated with the Sunni Muslim community. It has become quite common to apply the concept of diaspora to descendants of Africans in India (Alpers 2003; Jayasurya and Pankhurst 2003). While one may indeed find that Sidi practices are informed by traces of African-derived cosmologies and performance styles, they are at the same time deeply embedded in Sufi discourse. Instead of reducing such phenomena either to notions of local religious syncretism or to African survivals, I want to draw attention to the intertwining of Sufi-Islam and African-derived practices connected to spirit possession that travelled together with forced or voluntary African migrants of the past.

In the history of the culturally diverse Indian Ocean world, Islam has been identified by historians as the most significant unifying feature (McPherson 1995; Risso 1995). The coalescing potential of Islam was not restricted to religious concerns but shaped regional systems of power as much as merchant and maritime activities. Seafaring Muslim merchants not only spread the message of Islam along with their wares, but also took a leading role in the dispersal of African slaves to South- and Southeast Asia by using African seamen and by supplying local elites with military and domestic labour. While in the course of time African slaves in the Indian Ocean accepted the religion of the masters to varying degrees, they still carried with them their own faiths. Thus, in contemporary Gujarat vital manifestations of the latter are encountered in African-derived performances of drumming related to ritual communication with the spirits as practised by Sidi.[2] The dissemination of Islam in the Indian Ocean was therefore not confined to the dispersal of a body of Islamic texts, doctrines and performances of prayer, but included practices of possession by spirits, which, in the words of David Parkin, 'provide the limiting contrasts by which Islam defines itself' (2000b: 143). The historical spread of Islam thus includes the migration of African spirits. In order to clarify this point, I shall first delineate some of the problems involved in the use of a diasporic framework with regard to the Indian Ocean region. In the remaining parts of the chapter, I consider the migration of practices of drumming related to a multi-dimensional healing cult common throughout the Bantu-cultural area of Central and South-East Africa. This is followed by an examination of transformed reconstruction of the cult and its practices in Gujarat through Sufi idioms.

Notions of Diaspora
African presences shaped Indian history from the twelfth to nineteenth centuries in various and by no means unified ways (Basu 2001; Pankhurst 2003). Much more is known of the political and military positions of African slaves in medieval Muslim polities than of the

---

2   See Mirzai (2002) for similar phenomena in Persia.

experiences of people of African origin who came to settle in India up until the late nineteenth and early twentieth centuries and who today form recognisable communities referred to as 'Sidi' in Gujarat, Hyderabad, Karnataka and Sind (Basu 1995; Camara 2004; Minda 2004). [3] In Sri Lanka they are called by the term Kafir which is possibly related to *kufr* (Jayasurya 2003). For quite some time, historians dealing with Africans in Indian history had assumed that the latter had forgotten their African origins and heritages and merged with local Muslim communities. More recently, however, a reverse trend has emerged which stresses 'Africanisms' and attempts to subsume the Sidi presence in different parts of South Asia under the global fold of African diasporas. This trend is fuelled on the one hand by a rediscovery of Harris's work on the 'global African diaspora' (1979; informed by the agenda of pan-Africanism), and on the other by the post-modern call to study globalisation and diasporas defined as 'exemplary communities of the transnational moment' (Toeloelyan 1996: 4).[4] Expanding Harris's approach, Edward Alpers (2003) explores the possible meanings of 'diaspora' by comparing the history of the slave trade and manifestations of slave cultures in trans-atlantic and Indian Ocean settings. Arguing that African diasporas on the American continent and in the Indian Ocean region differ in terms of the scope of the slave-trade but share cultural similarities, he concludes: 'if we focus our attention on cultural manifestations, we can see important innovations and retentions in music, song and dance, spirit possession and healing, medical pluralism and popular religion, all of which are linked and can be compared with

---

3   In the nineteenth century, the term 'Sidi' came to be used for Africans throughout the Indian Ocean.

4   In order to overcome what was perceived as a severe bias of anthropology of previous decades (i.e. the attempt to understand local constructions of sociality) anthropologists turned their attention to the study of diasporas. While anthropologists and other social scientists struggled on the level of theory with 'prizing open a familiar concept' to 'inaugurate new directions for research' (Werbner 2002), on the empirical level people who for a whole variety of different reasons had migrated from one place to another were invariably labelled with the term 'diaspora' (see, for example, Brazil and Manor 2003).

the situation in the Americas and the Caribbean islands' (2003: 30).[5] While this perspective marks a welcome break with earlier assumptions about the obliteration of the African past, it is nevertheless fraught with complications of another kind when situated in the context of theoretical reflections of 'diaspora'.[6] Since the late 1990s, a veritable explosion of interest has led a growing number of scholars to the small Sidi neighbourhoods in Sind, Karnataka, Hyderabad and Gujarat in search of 'African retentions' and/or the 'multiple identities' of diasporic African Indians (see Badalkhan 2002; Catlin-Jairazbhoy 2004; Drewal 2004; Meier 2004; Obeng 2004). This approach has to be positioned in the context of a scholarly debate on the definition of the concept of diaspora in general and African diaspora in particular. With regard to the latter, two approaches come to the fore, of which one emphasises roots, the other processes of creolisation. Those who look for 'retentions', a term coined by Herskovits and the school of Afro-American studies,[7] accept the basic assumptions of the roots approach. [8] This resonates with typological

---

5 In an earlier paper, Alpers (1997) drew attention to the observations made by European and colonial travellers who since the nineteenth century had described 'African slave dances', sometimes referred to as 'gooma', from places all over the north-west sector of the Indian Ocean.

6 From a comparative perspective, structures of rituals and cosmologies in the experiences of displaced Africans in the Americas and India manifest a host of similarities, as well as differences (see Basu 2002).

7 Herskovits was interested in the continuation of African cultural elements despite the disruption of enslavement and subsequent processes of adaptation experienced by African slaves in the New World. Such phenomena he called 'African retentions', which were nevertheless subject to acculturation and social change (syncretism). In the 1950s, the influence of Afro-American studies declined considerably and notions such as 'Africanisms' became disreputable (Whitten and Szwed 1970: 38). Against the perspective adopted by Herskovits, in the 1970s anthropologists shifted their focus more towards problems of adaptation and the great variability to be observed in the cultural constitution of the black Americas in the present.

8 Lovejoy (1997), a vocal proponent of the 'roots' approach, argues for the centrality of real or imagined connections with 'Africa' in the analysis of African diasporas on the American continent. The routes of the slave trade in the past provide ongoing links between the slave-sending (Africa) and slave-receiving continents (America). In the societies of the latter category, African diasporas define themselves by reference to a

theories of diasporas that 'attempt to sort out and create order in the
apparently wild proliferation of new claims to diasporic status' (Werbner
2000: 307) that are arising out of trans-national migrations under the
impact of contemporary processes of globalisation. Thus Cohen suggests
that, while the history and experiences of diasporas may vary greatly, one
may speak of a diaspora 'when members of an "expatriate community"
share several key characteristics' (Cohen 1997: 23f.). These include the
dispersal of the ancestors from an original site to at least two other areas
of the world; remembrance of the location, history and achievements of
the homeland through visions and myths; feelings of non-acceptance by
the host society; and a strong desire to return to and an ongoing
involvement in the politics of the homeland (ibid.). Developing this line
of argument further, Vertovec (1997) lays stress on a 'diasporic
consciousness' expressed in terms of attachment to a homeland.

   In the context of the history of displaced Africans, Gilroy (1993),
Hall (1990) and others reject a view of 'diaspora' based on
'Afrocentrism'. They argue instead for a theory of hybridity that subverts
singular representations of modernity and nationhood by focusing upon
black subjectivities.[9] While there is a general consensus in the literature
that diasporas are historical formations that change over time, Werbner
critically observes the flaws in both approaches (2000, 2002). Instead of
dealing with sentimental attachments to a homeland, she stresses political
vulnerability as a characteristic of diasporic existence. And against
manifestations of hybridity celebrated by diasporic intellectuals as a
subversion of hegemonic constructions of national homogeneity,
Werbner (notably 2000) emphasises the heterogeneity of diasporas and
diasporic identities in relation to social class. Thus, she suggests an
alternative view that attends to how 'the tension between [ethnic
parochial] and [cosmopolitan] tendencies is played out in actual
situations' (2000: 309). So far, the contemporary debate surrounding the

---

boundary that separates those in the host area from those in the diaspora. According to
Lovejoy, the concept of a diaspora is useless unless it includes imaginations of 'Africa' in
terms of an original 'homeland'.

9 See also Clifford (1994) for a de-centred approach to diaspora in terms of political
   identity formation.

notion of 'diaspora' has remained focused upon trans-national migration processes and post-colonial politics of identity in Euro-American contexts. One has to be cautious, however, to extend it without further reflection to the Indian Ocean region and its history. What challenges can be made against a diaspora framework when used to understand the presence of the Sidi in the context of Indian Ocean history?

First of all, notions of diaspora call to mind a host of inter-related phenomena, such as dispersion, exile, ethnicity, nationalism, trans-nationalism, post-colonialism and globalisation, to name just the most common. Furthermore, as Monson notes (2003: 3), putting 'African' in front of them adds the concepts of race and racism. While colonialism left its mark in the Indian Ocean region by administering the Empire from Africa to India through European categories of race (see Fair 2001; Stoler 1997), in Gujarat, African immigrants were assimilated into the local society in terms of indigenous categories of hierarchy, caste (*jamat*) and religion (as Muslim fakirs). These categories also stress difference, but not necessarily in terms of 'race'. Secondly, Africans were not the only people on the move who came to settle in a place other than their 'homeland'. In fact, what is called the Indian Ocean region is to a great extent constituted by criss-crossing movements of people from all over the sea, as, for example, Gujaratis and Baluchis settled in Africa, Arabs landed in Gujarat and elsewhere along the western coast of India, Indonesians made their home in Madagascar, and Chinese settling in Zanzibar. But, as has often been noted before, strangers in diverse Indian Ocean settings were regularly assimilated into the local society, which gave these societies their characteristic heterogeneous compositions. Thus, in Gujarat, ritual patterns developed by Sidi in interaction with Sufism and indigenous traditions go well with notions of creolisation that emphasise the creation of new and unique cultural forms.

Everywhere in the Indian Ocean region, former migrants have been found to identify more strongly with the land of settlement than with the place their predecessors came from. Thus, Gujaratis in Tanzania, many of whom still marry brides from Gujarat, define themselves as 'Tanzanians' rather than as 'diasporic Gujaratis' longing for their homeland. Conversely, Sidi in Gujarat are struggling today for recognition as a 'Scheduled Tribe' with equal rights to those who are classified as autochthonous populations or 'original inhabitants' (*adivasi*). Claiming to be 'African' rather than 'Indian' is as unpromising in attaining this goal in the post-colonial Indian state as it would be to claim to be 'Indian' rather than Tanzanian for Gujaratis in the post-colonial Tanzanian state. The gap between scholarly interests in finding strands of African diasporas in India and the self-perceptions of those concerned can be illustrated by looking into the ways Sidi identify themselves when questioned by strangers.

Even before scholars began to search for the Africanness of Sidi in Gujarat, they were often asked by local people where in Africa they came from. In reply to the suggestion that they were 'Africans' rather than 'Indians', they usually pointed out that they spoke the same language as the person asking the question. This was then followed by an explanation of how their predecessors had come in the distant past to the place where they were settled, and that they themselves, their parents, grandparents and children were living here and were therefore as much 'Indian' as the curious inquirer. Thus, one of the most common experiences of Sidi in India is having to explain why and how they are not 'Africans'. In contrast to local people accepting what they are told by Sidi, foreign scholars who pose similar questions are often not satisfied with what the Sidi consider a convincing explanation. Faced with insistent scholars searching for their 'African roots', Sidi have by now developed ironic strategies to 'give them [the insistent scholars] what they want', as one man explained to me when I visited them in 2004.

During the same visit, I happened to witness a situation in which another foreign scholar who is actively involved in a project to raise 'African diasporic consciousness' in India met a group of Sidi in Gujarat for the first time. His hosts received him with great hospitality and offered him the best chair on the veranda. Since he was not familiar with the local language, a neighbour was called to interpret for him. Soon a group of people consisting of Sidi, other neighbours and myself had gathered to talk about the Sidi's 'African heritage'. One Sidi man, about sixty years old, came forward and spoke some phrases in Swahili (greetings and polite inquiries).

"So you speak Swahili?" the foreign scholar happily asked through the translator. "How come?" "I learned it from my father," the Sidi replied. "Oh, your father came from Africa?" "Yes, my father had gone to Africa." "So you speak Swahili with your family?" "No, we speak Gujarati. My father ran away from home [a harbour town on the coast of Gujarat] and left my mother with we children alone. He worked for a [Gujarati] trader with whom he went to Africa. After fifteen years he came home and taught us these words so that we can show people like you that we are Africans." His Sidi audience, always appreciative of a good joke, was delighted and roared with laughter. The English-speaking neighbour did not translate the last part of the sentence.

This can be taken as an example of the problem, well-known to anthropologists, of how scholarly interest contributes to the construction what is thought to be the object of research. Again, this illustrates the necessity of caution when using a diaspora framework to understand Sidi in Gujarat. Moreover, it should be pointed out that people are quite aware of the difference between citizenship and social memory. What matters is the context in which 'Africa' is evoked as a symbol of Sidi identity. When Sidi refer to 'Africa', they do not have a defined territory, continent or state in mind, but remember the journeys of the ancestors from Africa, their actions in Gujarat or how instruments (drums) were carried by sea to their present location in Gujarat. From amongst a host of African ancestors, Bava Gor, Bava Habash and Mai Mishra are venerated as leading Sufi saints who originally brought their Sidi followers from Africa via Mecca to Gujarat. Each one is said to have travelled by a different route: Bava Gor took the land route while Bava Habash and Mai Mishra followed him later by ship (see Basu 2002, 2005). Saintly ancestors (*bawa* and *pir*) are referred to by the term *dada/dadi* (grandfather/grandmother) or *pardada* (forefathers) from whom contemporary Sidis have inherited curly hair and the black colour of their skin (Basu 1998). When Sidis communicate ritually with their African ancestors, they use performative patterns resonant of spirit possession practices described by anthropologists for East African contexts. To reduce these to African survivals however, carries the danger of essentialising 'African culture' in terms of a 'pure' or 'authentic' origin. Such a perspective would leave little room for understanding the transformations of practices both in Africa and beyond and in different cultural settings in the Indian Ocean region. Moreover, the close intertwinement of cultural practices derived from Africa with the trans-oceanic spread of Islam is easily lost from view. Thus, in Gujarat, the combination of Islamic practices of praying with African-derived forms of spirit possession epitomised by drumming has produced a unique regional cult of affliction practiced by Sidi. Through the agency of displaced Africans, who employed drumming as a means of communicating both amongst themselves and with different sections of the host society, the cult also contributed to the emergence of a collective social identity by binding unsettled individual Africans to a sense of community.

Islam in Gujarat and East Africa

Gujarat and East Africa have been connected for many centuries by the movements of goods and people across the sea. Merchants from Gujarat have migrated to East Africa since at least the sixteenth century (Pearson 1998). Colonial policies reinforced migration in the nineteenth century. Gujarat has remained an important focal point in trans-local and trans-oceanic networks of kinship, trade and religious organisation. Such groups continued to communicate in Gujarati and reconstructed social institutions and customs brought from Gujarat, whereby, in East Africa, distinct and often wealthy diasporic Hindu and Muslim communities emerged, such as, for example, Bhatiyas, Daudi Bohras and Khojas. Conversely, slaves were brought from Africa to India from at least the twelfth century (Alpers 1975; Pankhurst 2003; Sheriff 1987). At the end of the nineteenth century, African slaves entered India mainly through one of the many ports along the coast of Gujarat where they often settled. Here, Sidi served as domestic servants, bodyguards and soldiers. Unlike Gujaratis in East Africa, Sidi could not remain connected to the areas they had been uprooted from. In the nineteenth century, Swahili may still have been used to a considerable extent by Sidi in western India, as demonstrated by a list of terms of possible Swahili roots collected in

Sind by Richard Burton and analysed by Freeman-Grenville a century later (Freeman-Grenville 1971). Today, Sidi communicate in the local vernaculars, in different shades of Gujarati, Kachchhi and a mixture of Gujarati and Urdu, depending on the place of settlement. In the hierarchical set-up of Gujarati society they are assigned a low social status on par with other Muslim servant castes. In contemporary Gujarat, Sidi life is framed by urban proletarian conditions. For at least the last century, a culturally defined ritual role – that of the Muslim fakir who often leads a peripatetic life and mediates spiritual powers of Sufi saints – has provided Sidi men and women with the possibility of an alternative lifestyle and with supplementary sources of income from collecting alms or begging.

In Gujarat, Islam is represented by several different strands of knowledge-traditions and local interpretations that partly overlap with distinctions between social classes and/or sects. Thus, in the social context I am concerned with Islam is shaped by Sunni orientations and understood in terms of Sufism. It is not only through different Islamic 'channels of creed' that Gujarat is connected to the wider Indian Ocean world, but perhaps more so through similarities in practices and in the debates and contestations surrounding them. With Parkin (2000a; also Lambek 2000), these may be understood in terms of prayer as a practice-generating paradigm. This makes it possible to examine the variety of types of prayer existing across the Islamic world in a unified analytic framework. The plurality of terms and types of Islamic prayer can be grasped along a continuum between *salat* as the profession of faith associated with mosque-based prayer on one pole and *dhikr*, 'remembrance of God', a form of prayer in which the worshipper continually utters the name of God whereby he is ultimately filled with the divine presence in a state of trance, on the other (Parkin 2000a: 6–11). Neither type of prayer involves supplication nor intermediaries; in contrast, *du'a'* is a specifically defined supplicatory prayer ('outside the mosque') and *tawasul* as an inter-cessionary prayer transmitted through an intermediary to God. As several case-studies demonstrate (see Parkin and Headley 2000), different practices of prayer serve as useful benchmarks for comparing local arrangements of a globally conceived

Islam across the Indian Ocean. This model also allows for the comparison of Islamic variations along the Swahili coast and in Gujarat. In both regions, the exclusive acceptance of *salat* is characteristic of orthodox Muslims and Islamic reformers of different persuasions. *Du'a'* is much less exclusive. Along the Swahili coast *tawasul* is used in connection with Sufi brotherhoods whereas '*du'a'* shade from those addressed to God as supplication [...] to others addressed to (usually) lesser deities or spirits, who are arguably no longer within the realm of Islam and who, through the voice of human intermediaries [...] engage in mutual verbal negotiation with worshippers' (Parkin 2000a: 6).

In Gujarat, the term *tawasul* is rarely used, the central word for supplicatory and inter-cessionary prayers in Sufi contexts being *du'a'*. *Du'a'* is addressed to living Sufi saints as much as to the souls (*ruh*) of dead saints personifying superior moral qualities and/or Islamic knowledge and who are therefore squarely placed within the sphere of Islam. Muslims generally disagree however, whether it is properly Islamic to approach saints as intermediaries and worship their tombs or whether this is an act of idolatry. Thus, in Gujarat no less than in East Africa, intermediaries mediating communication and bargaining with God, and hosting ecstatic forms of experience, are issues of much disagreement and contestation. But while among Swahili people in East Africa debates about legitimacy revolve around the status of spirits, in Gujarat it is the presumed proximity of Sufi saints to Hindu gods which is the critical issue. Here, reformist Indian-Islamic discourses are more concerned with the purification of Islam by its dissociation from Hinduism. Since spirits are regarded in Hindu cosmologies as impure and forces of the underworld, the matter of praying to spirits usually does not arise. Ironically, the historical dissemination of Islam includes the migration of African spirits and with them the uneasy relationship between Islam and African spirit possession cults.

Drumming and Spirit Possession in East Africa

In order to explore the relationship connecting Islamic traditions and forms of spirit possession of African origins as it is manifested in Sidi practices in Gujarat, the metaphor of the landscape helps to bring into view two overlapping maps. The first outlines the regions where slaves and maritime labourers were drawn in from during the nineteenth century; the second depicts the geography of regional cults of affliction. Through forced or voluntary migrations of Africans, human and spirit landscapes have been recreated in miniature across the sea in Gujarat.

The number of slaves being sold in the ports along the coast of Kachchh and Saurashtra in Gujarat in the late nineteenth century never exceeded more than a few hundred. In Arabic-Persian usage, 'Sidi' denoted black slaves, whereas in nineteenth-century English the term 'Seedi' was used for sailors and port labourers (bonded and/or manumitted slaves) 'who entered the Indian Ocean world from the Swahili coast, especially Zanzibar' (Ewald 2000: 83).[10] Slaves and African seamen who transformed themselves into landsmen by escaping their masters or, if already free, by staying back in Gujarat after the time of rest enforced by the monsoon, originated from a number of parts of East Africa. Although in the Indian Ocean world, trade, travel and maritime labour have been described as having been confined almost exclusively to men, a considerable number of women must have crossed the sea as well, most probably enslaved, as is revealed by the visibly African phenotypes displayed by many Sidi women living in contemporary Gujarat. As Alpers (2003) describes, Zanzibar, having been the hub of the slave-trade in this period, received and dispensed slaves and maritime labourers from the interior of the mainland (Lake Tanganyika), East-Central Africa (notably, Mozambique, Malawi and Zambia) and from South-Central Africa (the deep coastal hinterlands of southern Mozambique and the Zimbabwean plateau).

In the regions that historically supplied slaves, ritual practices epitomised by the symbol of the drum, *ngoma,* are commonly found. The great diversity of religious forms encountered in Sub-Saharan

---

10 For a more detailed discussion of the terms 'Sidi' and 'Habshi' see Basu (2001).

African poses an analytical problem comparable to that faced by anthropologists when they attempt to view the Indian Ocean world in unified terms. In this regard, John Janzen's (1992) ground-breaking study of the historical manifestations and the regional expansion of cults centring on the use of drums has much advanced anthropological understanding of Sub-Saharan African religio-therapeutic formations in terms of a regional discourse (also see van Dijk 2000). In his ethnographic survey of cults of affliction spanning Central, Southern and East Africa, corresponding linguistically and culturally to the wider Bantu region (including the Nguni and Swahili sub-regions), Janzen identifies a cluster of core features that are shared across a wide range of local settings. These are contained in the term *ngoma* (derived from Bantu **-goma*) which has several related meanings: the drum as an object; music, singing and dancing accompanied by drums in ritual performances related to healing; and the performers organised in cult associations or *ngoma* cells. Thus, *ngoma* can be understood as a regional umbrella in terms of practice. In this sense, *ngoma* provides the means to deal with adversity, mainly adversity in the form of diseases afflicted by spirits. Common characteristics of spirit assemblages across the *ngoma* region are manifest in distinctions drawn between spirits (ancestor and alien/foreign, male and female, beneficial and malicious, land and water) as well as in the high mobility of spirit pantheons and their transformations in the process of migration.

As will become more apparent below, the regional theory of *ngoma* as propounded by Janzen also allows for the detection of the cultural baggage carried by migrants beyond Africa, not least to Gujarat. Several scholars have noted, however, that neither African spirit possession in general nor those forms associated with practices of *ngoma* can be fully understood if they are reduced to considerations of illness and health (Lambek 1993; van Dijk 2000). Rather, one is faced with multi-faceted phenomena that involve – among other aspects such as politics and power – distinct traditions of knowledge and practices of remembering. In this way, spirit pantheons and possession practices apparently complement the unifying or hegemonic influence of Islam in the Indian Ocean at the lower levels of the religious hierarchy. Thus, not only may the spread of Islam in the Indian Ocean world be mapped along the routes taken by Muslim traders, scholars and Sufis, but by past movements of African people across the Indian Ocean's coastal regions and islands as reflected and remembered in local spirit pantheons. The Comoran island of Mayotte, for example, had been connected since the eleventh century through Islam, the religion of the mercantile elite, to 'political and intellectual currents that stretched from the Arabian peninsular down to the Swahili coast' (Lambek 1993: 48). Islam in Mayotte coexists with traditions of spirit possession that are partly indigenous and partly reflect the immigration of Africans at different times in history. As Michael Lambek elaborates (1993: 52), in the context of possession one class of spirits (*trumba*) represents the royal elite of Madagascar, another class (*patros*) comprises African spirits indigenous to the island as well as others from places outside the island, such as spirits who are associated with Zanzibar (*rewa*). Conversely, in Zanzibar, as Larsen states, spirits are 'conceived as foreigners [...] The various tribes of spirits come from localities which have, in various ways, been significant to Zanzibar Town in the recent past' (1998: 113). These include spirits who represent the island locales of Mayotte and Madagascar as well as *masheitani ya habshia*, spirits linked to Ethiopia (Larsen 1998: 135).

Along with spirits from Africa there also travelled performances of communicating with and worshipping them, such as *ngoma*. As I have discussed, the term *ngoma* covers a multiplicity of practices in which drums are used and it should not be misunderstood in terms of a single tradition or institution originating in a 'pure core'. In different ethnic contexts in mainland and coastal East Africa, *ngoma* may refer to dissimilar and continually changing observable practices. And yet, the persistence of *ngoma* across East Africa and different societies in the Indian Ocean world allows us to view drumming and possession as things which resemble a deep structure of grammar capable of generating comparable but distinct practices across time and space.

A useful background for comprehending similarities of *ngoma* practices across ethnic and cultural boundaries as well as their transformations through migration is provided by the study of

Nyamwezi *ngoma* in Tanzania by Henny Blokland (2000). Here, it is the names given to different types of drums that, as the names of the spirits mentioned above, often refer to places beyond Unyamwezi and thus reflect historical processes of inland migration (Blokland 2000: 21). And as elsewhere in the region, in Unyamwezi the term *ngoma* denotes (besides the drum) an organisation of performers ('*ngoma* cells', in Janzen's words) as well as drum-song-dance performances enacted by people not joined in a common organisation. *Ngoma* organisations are usually not based on kinship relationships but built around shared tasks or occupations such as hunting, cultivation, smithery and similar activities (Blokland 2000: 29). In addition, drum-song-dance performances play an important structuring role in rituals of transition such as marriage when they are enacted by relatives. In both contexts, different types of drumming performances are used, most noticeably what Blokland calls 'sacrificial' and 'competetive' *ngoma*.[11] Performances of the second type are characterised by an emphasis upon categorical differences such as the ones that exist between bride and groom, male and female, relative and stranger, left and right, and humans and spirits. In sacrificial *ngoma*, though, these distinctions are collapsed in the category of collective ancestral spirits who are 'both relatives and strangers, parents and grandparents, right and left, male and female [...] in sacrificial Ngoma, the unity achieved is absolute, there is no distinction at all any longer [...] between the two parties who are in this case, spirits and humans. The *ngoma* is danced by one party only, that of the spirits' (Blokland 2000: 29). Finally, it should be noted that *ngoma* also includes forms that make no reference to spirits (Ranger 1975).

By following the route of migration of spirit pantheons and *ngoma* from the interior of Tanzania to the coast, Zanzibar and finally to Gujarat, the question of their relationship with Islam arises with greater urgency. Janzen addresses this problem in regard to healers of possession illnesses at the coast of Tanzania. He introduces three types of professional healers, two of them Muslim, who distinguish themselves by

---

11 A comparable distinction is found in 'sacred *ngoma*' and '*ngoma* for entertainment' in Janzen (1992).

the use they make of *ngoma* (drumming, singing and dancing) in healing procedures. Non-Muslim healers of the first type rely entirely on techniques specific to *ngoma*. In therapeutic *ngoma*, different types of drums (small *ngoma* drums, smaller double membrane drums) and rattles (gourd shakers) are used, in addition to collecting and prescribing certain medical plants that provide remedies against spirit induced diseases such as headaches, bodily weakness or loss of appetite (Janzen 1992: 24–5). In this case, the effectiveness of treatment depends on drumming and dancing by the healer and/or his associates. The second type of Muslim healer works with a combination of Islamic and *ngoma* elements. The healer introduced by Janzen had studied the Quran, belonged to a Sufi order and drew his therapeutic knowledge from an Arabic text (Janzen 1992: 27). According to this man, the use of *ngoma* does not violate Islamic norms but epitomises the appropriate and most effective therapy for specific illnesses that are caused by spirits (*sheitani*). Through drumming, singing and dancing the spirit is lured to disclose its identity which ultimately allows for its expulsion from the host's body. The third type of healer involved in the cure of possession illnesses rejects the use of *ngoma* categorically. Such a healer works with texts, purified water and plant roots to draw on the help of beneficial Muslim spirits (*ruhani* and *majini*) which, in this context, are categorised as spirits of the sea. The healer interviewed by Janzen declared himself an adherent of a Sufi order too and relied on Arabic texts for his medical knowledge. His treatment of a person troubled by a spirit consists of readings and recitations of Arabic texts, visits to sacred places and prayers that bring the spirit into the open (Janzen 1992: 30–1). He told Janzen that *ngoma* should not be used therapeutically due to Islamic restrictions 'but also that *ngoma* was just "happiness", not real medicine' (1992: 32). On the basis of his material Janzen concludes that healers are situated along a continuum of practitioners ranging from non-Islamic to those influenced more deeply by Islam; correspondingly, ritual communities such as therapeutic *ngoma* organisations have increasingly come to be functionally substituted by Sufi brotherhoods.

In performances referred to as *ngoma ya sheitani* in Zanzibar, by contrast, 'Muslim' and 'African' identities are not opposed but merged in the medium of possession. This becomes most apparent when shifting the focus to another important dimension of *ngoma* and possession, as demonstrated by Larsen, that consist in acts of remembering and recreating the past through embodiment (1998; see also Lambek 1993, 1996). Unlike Nyamwezi sacrificial *ngoma*, in *ngoma ya sheitani* social distinctions are not transcended; rather, spirit identities are visualised through dress, food, smells, sound and other aesthetic qualities which highlight ethnic divisions based on trans-local origins. The four classes of spirits described by Larsen correspond to four social categories defined in terms of ethnic and/or religious affiliation who formed Zanzibari society in the past and constitute major social divisions in the present. The first class is referred to as *ruhani*, the name given to spirits of the sea at the coast (see above) that in the context of Zanzibar has come to denote Muslim spirits from Arabia (1998: 133). They represent different degrees of Islamic knowledge imparted to those who host them. The second class of spirits, *ruhumba*, consists of non-Islamic spirits of Swahili and Bantu origins. They also impart knowledge of healing, besides sorcery, but both types are ambiguously defined as potentially beneficial and threatening at the same time. The third class, *kibuki*, include Christians and are associated with Madagascar and the Comore islands. They are considered non-Islamic as well as non-African and transmit technical skills in art, craft or other professions which rely upon the techniques necessary to communicate with spirits (1998: 135). The fourth class is constituted by *habshia* spirits already mentioned; these spirits do not seem to be associated with specific types of knowledge. The foremost characteristic of *habshia* spirits is the way in which they recall Zanzibari society of the past, a past dominated by an elaborate social order of high-ranking queens and kings and low-ranking slaves.

The instances of the relationship between Islam and spirit possession considered here reveal two important dimensions of *ngoma*: one is its capacity of healing, the other relates to spirits as vehicles of remembering the past and the creation of ethnically defined religious identities. If we now turn to Gujarat as a further outpost of the migration of African spirit possession performances symbolised by the drum (*goma*), we encounter several of the features discussed which here recur in the guise of Sufism.

Sidi Ritual Practices: Drumming and Praying

Spatially, Sufism is manifested in shrines sheltering the tombs of holy men or spiritual masters. Such shrines are referred to as *dargah*. In Gujarat, many such *dargahs* house 'African saints' and are owned by members of the Sidi community. Quite a few men and women have adopted a ritual role of a fakir. Sidi fakirs carry out a range of activities on behalf of shrine clients deemed as ritual labour (*fakir nu kam*). Ritual labour may include curing rites, divination, the application of ordeals, the reading of the first chapter of the Quran (*fatiha*) at death ceremonies and the performance of devotional Sufi music (*Quawwali*). The most basic types of ritual labour, however, are drumming (*goma*) and inter-cessionary prayers (*duʿa*). The Sidi fakir's claim on the privileged knowledge required for carrying out this kind of ritual labour is based on constructions of common descent from African saints. They are regarded as ancestors from whom Sidi fakirs have inherited the knowledge which they use on behalf of pious people in distress who seek the intervention of a saint in their own personal lives. Through inter-cessionary praying and drumming Sidi fakirs act as intermediaries in the hierarchical relationship of exchange between humans, saints and God (Basu 1998).

In Gujarat, the term *goma* has lost nothing of its multi-vocality: it may refer to drums, to rituals involving drumming, singing, trance-inducing dancing and possession and to local organisations of Sidi performers. The latter are tied to Sidi shrines (*dargah*) which form a network covering Gujarat and extending into Sind in the west and Bombay in the south-east. Each shrine figures as a centre of a local '*goma* cell' based on relationships of kinship and neighbourhood. Next to the tomb drums of various sizes and types are stored. The drum held most sacred is a large-footed drum referred to as *mugarman* which represents the prototype of the East African *ngoma*-drum and which is otherwise unknown in Gujarat. Other drums are of the same type as those used in Gujarat, such as kettle drums (*dhol*) played while sitting and two membrane drums called *dholak*. Another unique instrument stored in

Sidi shrines is the *malunga*, a kind of fiddle made from a gourd. [12] Dusters made from peacock feathers and used for transmitting the blessings of the African saints to their believers complete the picture.

As with East African *ngoma*, Sidi *goma* includes healing of spirit possession without being reducible to therapeutic aspects. The practice also relates to handling the past in the present and to individual and collective identifications and negotiations of identity. The performance of *goma* requires a specific type of musical knowledge as well as body techniques (dancing) which are believed to be only fully accessible to members of the community of Sidi (women and men). Having become something of a caste profession within the pluralistic cultural context of Gujarat, *goma* also signifies relationships of ritual exchange across caste, religious or ethnic lines. These relationships originate in the fact that all aspects of *goma* are ultimately embedded in the socio-religious field of practical Sufism. Here, ritual *goma* organisations do not stand in opposition to Sufi orders but rather are identified as one particular type of Sufi fakir brotherhood, represented by the symbol of the drum. Being enwrapped in the Islamic idiom of Sufi mysticism, one is faced with a code fusing two strands of practices captured in the complementary juxtaposition of 'drumming' (*goma*) and 'praying' (*du'a'* and *jikar* or *dhikr*). The most important sites for the performance of drumming and praying are the sites where Sidi ancestor-spirit-saints are buried, the *dargahs*.

Another word often used for *goma* performances is *damal*. The etymology of *damal* is the Hindi-Urdu term for 'breath' (*dam*). *Damal* surfaces in the vocabulary of various fakir orders in South Asia (such as Madari, Malang and Rifa'i) and refers to a variety of ritual practices that include music and mystical experiences of trance. Each order is seen as a distinct path leading to a heightened proximity to the divine. According to Sufi notions, the divine cannot be approached directly but needs the intercession of pious men or Sufi masters ('friends of God') who, by virtue of their piety and love, are closer to God and thus capable of

---

12 There seems to be an interesting link here to the Eastern Bantu word for God, *mulungu* (Janzen 1992: 65).

mediating divine grace. Holy intermediaries are hierarchically ranked, with *pirs* claiming descent from the family of the Prophet (Sayyid) at the higher level and fakirs of diverse and indistinct pedigrees at the lower level. Many of the high status *pirs* are affiliated with one of the larger Sufi orders (such as Chishtiyya or Qadiriyya). Fakirs may belong to the ritual entourage of such an order or form distinct organisations. Thus, fakir brotherhoods set themselves apart and define their respective tradition or 'path' (*tariqa*) through specific practices such as fire-walking or body-piercing which are accomplished in states of trance evoked by the beat of tambourines or drums. Trance figures importantly in many Sufi fakir traditions, but it normally does not include the idea of being possessed by a Sufi master or holy man. Rather, trance is perceived as a condition for experiencing spiritual closeness in ways that transcend the body, as emotions of ecstasy referred to as *hal* ('mystical condition'). Against this, the Sidi definition of *hal* refers to possession by a specific type of Sufi: those who are classified simultaneously as ancestors of their community. What distinguishes the Sidi fakir brotherhood and defines their charismatic singularity is the association of *damal* with collective possession which is not practiced by other religious traditions present in Gujarat, be it Muslim, Hindu, or aboriginal.

A similar conceptual fusion as in *goma/damal* characterises the identification of Sufi saints with African ancestor spirits, referred to as *pir-dada*; *dada* (grandfather) is the generic term for predecessors and *pir* for Muslim saintly personages. The experience of possession when a person becomes host to an ancestor-spirit during *goma* performances is denoted with the term for Sufi ecstacy, *hal*, which in Sidi discourse is opposed to the Gujarati word for possession, *hajri* (presence). In Hindu contexts, *hajri* denotes the possession of a priest by a goddess whereby he is turned into her medium, thus making her 'present'; by way of contrast, in Sidi-Muslim usage, *hajri* refers specifically to possession by harmful spirits which cause disease and misfortune. Gujarati spirit classifications broadly reflect religious divisions, such as Muslim *jinnat* and Hindu *bhut*. Whereas the category of Muslim *jinnat* is divided into pure and impure spirits some of whom do have a fixed identity, in Hindu cosmologies it is only demons (*rakshas*) that may have a named identity.

The category of Hindu spirits (*bhut* and *pret*) refers to unstable and continuously shifting beings believed to be the unhappy and dissatisfied souls of the dead who cannot find rest until their unfulfilled desires are somehow compensated. Spirits of the dead tend to trouble close relatives or neighbours and only rarely attack strangers. The different types of spirits are often indiscriminately lumped together as 'impure beings'. It is the task of the healer to search for their identity, to find out their wishes and demands for appeasement, and to instruct the relatives of the afflicted person as to what should be done to make the spirit leave. While a class of Hindu priests (*buo*) specialises in therapeutic treatment of spirit possession, many Hindu-Gujaratis are convinced (at least until recently) that Sufi saints command particularly strong powers over evil spirits and that a cure at a Muslim shrine is much more effective than the treatment offered by a *buo*. Thus, in Gujarat a great number of shrines sheltering the tomb of a Sufi saint are not only sacred places where people offer prayers to those closer to God but are also sites of exorcism (Basu 1995; Pfleiderer 1981). This also applies to the shrines dedicated to Sidi ancestor-saints (*pir-dada*). Although the procedures for expelling troublesome spirits from their hosts may vary a great deal amongst Sufi *dargahs*, the actions performed at Sidi shrines introduce an important difference which distinguishes them from all others: they are the only ones where differently evaluated forms of possession – by 'good' (*hal*) or 'bad' (*hajri*) spirits – distinguish healers from patients.

The pantheon of African ancestor-spirit-saints is marked by the fusion of fragments of symbolic constructions of spirits found in East Africa with Sufi concepts of spiritual genealogy and spiritual allegiance to *pirs*. First of all, Sidi ancestor-saints are not divided into distinct 'tribes' as they are in Zanzibar, but are conceived to represent a single class in which female and male ancestors are linked by brother-sister ties. These are further distinguished in 'real' and 'ritual' brother-sister relationships, the former arising from biological descent, the latter from master-disciple relationships conceptualised in the Sufi idiom of *pir-murid* relationships (Basu 2000). The *pir-murid* relationship introduces a system of ranking and allows, in principle, for the inclusion of an unlimited number of ancestral/saintly personages within the category of spirit-saints. The kinship group is further internally differentiated according to age grades, gender and special dispositions conceptualised in the opposition of 'hot' and 'cold' temperaments. The highest rank is accorded to a group of 'real siblings' consisting of two brothers and one sister. However, while in Zanzibar classes of spirits embody links to distant localities, in Gujarat this aspect is attributed to individual ancestor-saints who symbolise connections to Africa. Thus, each one of these spirit-saints is named after a region in Africa. The eldest brother is popularly known in Gujarat as *Bava Gor*, but every Sidi is aware of his original name which is 'Sidi Mubarak Nobi' (Nubia). The younger brother is called *Bava Habash* (Abyssinia/Ethiopia) and the sister *Mai Mishra* (Misher in Egypt). And as with the different classes of Zanzibari spirits, Sidi ancestor-spirits are distinguished by the specific types of food each one prefers, by their own smells (incense and perfume) and colours. Unlike Zanzibari spirits, however, they are not represented through specific styles of dress. Finally, and most significantly, the musical instruments used in *goma*-performances are classified according to gender, identified with named ancestor-saints and considered to give them a voice through distinct styles of rhythms. Thus, male ancestor-spirit-saints, particularly Bava Gor and Bava Habash are embodied by the footed drum (*mugarman*), whereas the rattles used are called 'Mai Mishra' and embody female ancestor-spirit-saints.

Oral narratives of Sidi migration to Gujarat focus upon these three ancestors in whom history has become compressed. Serving as vehicles of memory, the idealised construction of the superior moral powers of these ancestral spirits/holy men and women buries that what is forgotten: the enslavement of Sidi in the past. However, different modes of ancestral travel reminiscent of different routes of African migrants are remembered. Thus, Sidi Mubarak Nobi is believed to have taken the route by land, whereas his brother and sister had crossed the sea in *dhows* at different times. They came to Gujarat on a specific mission which is set in the spirit realm: to liberate the land from sorcery and evil spirits led by an indigenous demoness, a leader of the underworld. Before Sidi Mubarak Nobi reached Gujarat, he became the disciple (*murid*) and ritual son of a Sufi master (Ahamad Kabir Rifa'i) in Bagdad from whom

he received his spiritual name (Bava Gor). Becoming a ritual son of a
Sufi master through initiation brings the adept closer to God and imparts
specific spiritual powers of intercession upon him. Thus, the ancestors
accomplished the defeat of the indigenous evil spirits not by a bloody
military battle but by overcoming the evil trickery of the demoness
through cleverness, knowledge of spirits and the support of God. This
struggle of the ancestors serves as a template for rites of expelling evil
spirits performed at Sidi shrines. A Sidi *dargah* is both a major site for the
performance of *goma/damal* in honour of the ancestors and a Sufi place
of worship situated between heaven and earth. Sidi shrines are
approached by heterogeneous groups of believers from different social
and religious backgrounds. Some may look primarily for a cure from a
possession illness, others, mostly Muslims, pray to the African saints and
seek their intercession because they are believed to be specially loved by
and thus closer to God. The narrative explains Sidi fakirs' inherited skills
of healing possession and the efficacy of their prayers on behalf of
supplicants. In healing, the ancestor-spirits call the spirits afflicting the
host in their 'drum-voices', expelling them through both the language of
drumming and Sidi mediums as their embodied counterparts. Inter-
cessionary prayers performed by Sidi complement the power of the
drums/ancestor-spirits. They are thought to be most effective in bringing
about the desired ends of a supplicant approaching Bava Gor and other
Sidi saints. Thus, a Sidi *dargah* presents a kaleidoscopic view of
cosmology which may otherwise be best described as a combination of
mutually exclusive angles: displaced patterns of African spirit possession
are fused with interpretations and practices of Sufi-Islam.

Thus, in Gujarat, Sidi *dargahs* have become unique places to
experience and communicate with the Islamic divine through the actions
of Sidi fakirs, situated as they are at the junction of spirit possession and
Sufi saint veneration. Practically, *goma* performances are infused with
Sufi forms of praying while, conversely, drumming is inculcated into acts
of inter-cessionary prayers (*du'a*). This infusion comes particularly into
the fore in two related contexts. The first is the annual saint's day
celebration (*urs*); this is the occasion for the congregation of large
numbers of Sidi of all ages and from all over the region in order to play

goma together. The second is supplication in the form of making vows. Giving a promise to a *pir* with the expectation of getting one's request granted constitutes one of the central modes of interaction between shrine clients and African saints. It requires the mediating actions of Sidi fakirs, namely the acts of praying and drumming. Both contexts are related in so far as Sidi fakirs regain their ritual powers needed for successful mediation in *goma* sessions that are specifically directed at the ancestor-spirit-saints during an *urs*.

As in East Africa, in Gujarat different types of *goma/dammal* are recognised. Here, traces of 'sacrificial *ngoma*' re-surface in 'saint's day *goma/damal*'; 'healing *ngoma*' has been transformed into 'inter-cessionary *goma/damal*' and 'competetive *ngoma*' is manifested in 'amusement *goma*' performed by professional and paid all-male dancing teams for cultural festivals and tourist entertainment patronised by the government. In each type of *goma/damal* one aspect of a multiplicity of meanings associated with drumming is particularly stressed: in saint's day *goma/damal* it is the communication between living descendants and dead ancestors through the language of the drums which leads to their ultimate unity through embodiment; in inter-cessionary *goma/damal*, drumming is used as a variation of praying and in amusement-*goma* it is the evocation of emotions of happiness and fun (*majha*) in the audience. Neither aspect is exclusive to the type of the performance; rather, the context determines which feature takes pre-eminence.

In the first two contexts, *goma/damal* inter-mingles with two forms of prayer, with 'remembrance of God', i.e. *jikar* (derived from *dhikr*) and *du'a'*, supplicatory prayers. Thus, in the context of vow making (*mannat*) inter-cessionary prayers are joined with intermediary drumming (*goma/damal*). The first step for a person making a vow is for them to 'show' their particular problem. Typical problems include barrenness, the search for a job, sickness of a relative and many of the other adversities arising from everyday life. A Sidi fakir (who may be a woman or a man) is asked to make the saints know about the problem by praying on behalf of the person to the saint most favoured by the supplicant. This is expressed in the request for 'doing my *du'a'*'. The second step towards making a vow is to promise a gift to the saints should the request be fulfilled. Whatever the promised gift might be (sugar molasses, money or new clothing for the tomb, for example), ritual gratitude is not complete without the assurance that a Sidi *goma* performance will be sponsored should the problem be rectified. In this case, *goma/damal* is performed by a relatively small group of children, women and men dancing together in a circle. Each man has slung around the waist a small double membrane drum (*dholak*) which they beat as they sing and move. Women and children use rattles or simply clap their hands. Those on whose behalf the *goma/damal* is performed watch the spectacle and throw coins into the circle along with others who happen to be present at the shrine for their own reasons.

A saint's day *goma/damal* performance contrasts with what I have just described because it is much more elaborate and involves a larger number of performers. Moreover, while non-Sidi clients of the shrine may attend the ritual, its main audience is the Sidi community as a whole. Such a performance bears a striking resemblance to patterns of song-drum-dance characteristic of *ngoma* as outlined by Janzen as well as to certain aspects of the rituals performed for Arab-Muslim spirits (*ruhani*) in Zanzibar described by Larsen. Thus, the series of rituals begin with prayers of referred to as *jikar* invoking God, the Prophet and finally the Sidi ancestor-spirit-saints.[13] A lead singer begins in the call-response style characteristic of African 'doing *ngoma*'. He sings two lines which are repeated by the chorus who responds with singing, drumming, the shaking of rattles and hand-clapping. Gradually, the drumming gathers speed and the singing accelerates until a climax is reached; after an abrupt ending it starts again, first slow, then faster and faster, ending abruptly, only to begin again. In the opening phase, while people sing *jikar* they remain seated. A second phase begins when the lead singer gets up and starts moving in a circle, drumming while singing. He is followed by other men carrying a drum and by women shaking rattles. While singing and drumming, the dancers encircle the shrine or the tomb until, finally,

---

13 The line *Allah hai* (Swahili 'God is living') sung in Zanzibar for *masheitani ya ruhani* (Larsen 1998: 134) is also sung in Sidi *jikar* in Gujarat.

they reach an open space where drummers form a circle, the arena for those who 'dance the ancestors' by embodying them. In contrast to the more formalised mimetic possession performances in Zanzibari *ngoma*, those performed by Sidi are improvisations and entirely unscripted. The possessed enact the particular characteristics of the ancestors, their hot or cool temperaments and their seriousness or playfulness. The movements of the ancestor-spirits, who cross spaces and times, are reflected in the movements of their 'sons' and 'daughters' in response to the drumming.

Conclusion

I have concentrated here on a buried strand of Islamic dissemination in the Indian Ocean: the migration of African spirit possession performances epitomised by the symbol of the drum. The overlapping landscapes of the slave-trade and African cults of affliction have been transposed to Gujarat, where Sidi shrines figure as memorial signs of the regions' connectedness to the Indian Ocean in the past. The combination of intermediary ritual practices, praying (*du'a'*) and drumming (*goma*), enabled historical actors from Africa to create multiple identities for themselves in the host society (Muslims, Sufi fakirs and African healers) which arose from symbolic practices of memory embodied in spirit possession performances. The empowering potential of African spirit possession to deal not only with adversity in terms of disease, but also with slavery, colonial repression and modern changes is confirmed by the agency of Sidis in Gujarat. The multi-dimensionality of *ngoma* allows for simultaneous acts of resistance, assimilation and communication of Sidis situating themselves actively in the host society of Gujarat. Here, remembered fragments of the past provided the means for creating a new spiritual world through performance. Moreover, the presumed antagonism inherent in the relationship between Islam and spirit possession has been transformed into a unified practice assimilated in the field of Sufism. Sufism in Gujarat, while under attack from Islamic reformers, provides a common frame of faith which allows for the articulation of social difference through a diverse range of ritual practices designed to express mystical truth. In this case, at least, African-derived forms of spirit possession represent one of the specific paths towards reaching the *unio mystica* towards which Sufi believers strive. In this way, to return to the question raised at the beginning of this chapter, African spirituality as embedded in *ngoma* cults of affliction has been reconstructed by Indian Ocean travelers far beyond the shores of Africa.

Bibliography

Alpers, E.A. 1975. *Ivory and Slaves in East Central Africa.* Berkeley: University of California Press.

—— 1997. 'The African Diaspora in the Northwestern Indian Ocean: Reconsideration of an Old Problem, New Directions for Research', *Comparative Studies of South Asia, Africa and the Middle East,* XVII.2.

—— 2002. 'Imagining the Indian Ocean World. Opening Address to the International Conference on Cultural Exchange and Transformation in the Indian Ocean World'. University of California, Los Angeles.

—— 2003. 'The African Diaspora in the Indian Ocean: A Comparative Perspective', in S. de S. Jayasurya and R. Pankhurst (eds), *The African Diaspora in the Indian Ocean.* Trenton: Africa World Press.

Assmann, A. 1999. *Erinnerungsräume. Formen und Wandlungen des kulturellen Gedächtnisses.* München: Beck.

Assmann, J. 1997. *Das kulturelle Gedächtnis. Schrift, Erinnerung und politische Identität in frühen Hochkulturen.* München: Beck.

Badalkhan, S. 2002. 'Coastal Makran as Corridor to the Indian Ocean World', *Eurasien Studies,* 1/2.

Basu, H. 1993. 'The Sidi and the Cult of Bava Gor in Gujarat', *Journal of the Indian Anthropological Society,* 28.

—— 1995. *Habshi-Sklaven, Sidi Fakire. Muslimische Heiligenverehrung im westlichen Indien.* Berlin: Das Arabische Buch.

—— 1998. 'Hierarchy and Emotion: Love, Joy, and Sorrow in a Cult of Black Saints in Gujarat, India', in P. Werbner and H. Basu (eds), *Embodying Charisma. Modernity, Locality and the Performance of Emotion in Sufi Cults.* London: Routledge.

—— 2000. 'Theatre of Memory: Performances of Ritual Kinship of the African Diaspora in Sind/Pakistan', in A. Rao and M. Boeck (eds), *Culture, Creation and Procreation in South Asia.* Oxford: Berghahn.

—— 2001. 'Africans in India – Past and Present', *Asienforum. International Quarterly for Asian Studies*, 32.3–4.

—— 2002. 'Afro-indische Besessenheitskulte im Vergleich (Sidi-Goma in Indien; Zar in Ostafrika; Candomblé in Brasilien)', *Zeitschrift für Ethnologie*, 127.1.

—— 2003. 'Slave, Soldier, Trader, Fakir: Fragments of African Histories in Gujarat', in S. de S. Jayasurya and R. Pankhurst (eds). *The African Diaspora in the Indian Ocean*. Trenton: Africa World Press.

Blokland, H. 2000. 'Kings, Spirits & Brides in Unyamwezi, Tanzania', in R. van Dijk, R. Reiss and M. Spierenburg (eds), *The Quest for Fruition Through Ngoma. Political Aspects of Healing in Southern Africa*. Cape Town: David Philip.

Braziel, J.E., and A. Mannur (eds) 2003. *Theorizing Diaspora. A Reader*. Oxford: Blackwell.

Camara, C. 2004. 'The Siddis of Uttara Kannada: History, Identity and Change Among African Descendants in Contemporary Karnataka', in A. Catlin-Jairazbhhoy and E. Alpers (eds), *Sidis and Scholars. Essays on African Indians*. Delhi: Rainbow Publishers.

Catlin-Jairazbhoy, A. 2004. 'A Sidi CD? Globalisation of Music and the Sacred', in A. Catlin-Jairazbhhoy and E. Alpers (eds), *Sidis and Scholars. Essays on African Indians*. Delhi: Rainbow Publishers.

Clifford, J. 1994. 'Diasporas', *Cultural Anthropology*, 9.3.

Cohen, R. 1997. *Global Diasporas. An Introduction*. London: UCL Press.

Connerton, P. 1989. *How Societies Remember*. Cambridge: Cambridge University Press.

Dijk, van R., R. Reiss and M. Spierenburg Dijk (eds) 2000. *The Quest for Fruition Through Ngoma. Political Aspects of Healing in Southern Africa*. Cape Town: David Philip.

Ewald, J. 2000. 'Crossers of the Sea: Slaves, Freedmen, and Other Migrants in the Northwestern Indian Ocean, c. 1750–1914', *The American Historical Review*, 105.1.

Fair, L. 2001. *Pastimes and Politics. Culture, Community, and Identity in Post-Abolition Urban Zanzibar, 1890–1945*. Oxford: James Currey.

Freeman-Grenville, G. S. P. 1971. 'The Sidi and Swahili', *Bulletin of the British Association of Orientalists*, 6.

Gilroy, P. 1993. *The Black Atlantic: Modernity and Double Consciousness.* Cambridge, MA.: Harvard University Press.

Halbwachs, M. 1985a. *Das Gedächtnis und seine sozialen Bedingungen.* Frankfurt/M: Suhrkamp.

―― 1985b. *Das kollektive Gedächtnis.* Frankfurt/M: Suhrkamp.

Hall, S. 1990. 'Cultural Identity and Diaspora', in J. Rutherford (ed.), *Identity: Community, Culture, Difference.* London: Lawrence & Wishart.

Harris, J. E. 1993 [1982]. *Global Dimensions of African Diaspora.* Washington: Howard University Press.

Jayasurya, S. de S and R. Pankhurst 2003. *The African Diaspora in the Indian Ocean.* Trenton: Africa World Press.

Janzen, J.M. 1992. *Ngoma. Discourses of Healing in Central and Southern Africa.* Berkeley: University of California Press.

Lambek, M. 1993. *Knowledge and Practice in Mayotte. Local Discourses of Islam, Sorcery and Spirit Possession.* Toronto: University of Toronto Press.

―― 2000. 'Localising Islamic Performances in Mayotte', in D. Parkin and S.C. Headley (eds), *Islamic Prayer Across the Indian Ocean. Inside and Outside the Mosque.* Richmond: Curzon.

Larsen, K. 1998. 'Spirit Possession as Historical Narrative: The Production of Identity and Locality in Zanzibar Town', in N. Lovell (ed.), *Locality and Belonging.* London: Routledge.

Lovejoy, P.E. 1997. 'The African Diaspora: Revisionist Interpretations of Ethnicity, Culture and Religion under Slavery', *Studies in the World History of Slavery, Abolition and Emancipation,* 2.1.

McPherson, K. 1993. *The Indian Ocean. A History of People and the Sea.* Delhi: Oxford University Press.

Meier, P. 2004. 'Performing African Identity: Sidi Communities in the Transnational Moment', in A. Catlin-Jairazbhhoy and E. Alpers (eds), *Sidis and Scholars. Essays on African Indians.* Delhi: Rainbow Publishers.

Minda, A. 2004. *An African Indian Community in Hyderabad. Siddi Identity, its Maintenance and Change.* Goettingen: Cuvillier Verlag.

Mirzai, B. 2002. 'Zar in the Context of the African Diaspora: An Overview', Paper presented to the International Conference on Cultural Exchange and Transformation in the Indian Ocean World. University of California, Los Angeles.

Monson, I. 2003. *The African Diaspora. A Musical Perspective.* New York: Routledge.

Obeng, P. 2004. 'African Indian Culture Articulation: Mediation and Negotiation in Uttara Kannada', in A. Catlin-Jairazbhhoy and E. Alpers (eds), *Sidis and Scholars. Essays on African Indians.* Delhi: Rainbow Publishers.

Pankhurst, R. 2003. 'The Ethopian Diaspora to India: The Role of Habshis and Sidis from Medieval Times to the End of the Eighteenth Century', in S. de S. Jayasurya and R. Pankhurst (eds), *The African Diaspora in the Indian Ocean.* Trenton, Asmara: Africa World Press.

Parkin, D. 2000a. 'Inside and Outside the Mosque: A Master Trope', in D. Parkin and S.C. Headley (eds), *Islamic Prayer Across the Indian Ocean. Inside and Outside the Mosque.* Richmond: Curzon.

—— 2000b. 'Invocation: *Salaa, Dua, Sahada,* and the Question of Self-Determination', in D. Parkin and S.C. Headley (eds), *Islamic Prayer Across the Indian Ocean. Inside and Outside the Mosque.* Richmond: Curzon.

Parkin, D. and S.C. Headley (eds), 2000. *Islamic Prayer Across the Indian Ocean. Inside and Outside the Mosque.* Richmond: Curzon.

Pearson, M.N. 1998. 'Indians in East Africa: The Early Modern Period', in R. Mukherjee and L. Subramaniam (eds), *Politics and Trade in the Indian Ocean World.* Delhi: Oxford University Press.

Pfleiderer, B. 1981. 'Mira Datar Dargah: The Psychiatry of a Muslim Shrine', in I. Ahamd (ed.), *Ritual and Religion among Muslims in India.* Delhi: Manohar.

Ranger, T.O. 1975. *Dance and Society in Eastern Africa: The Beni Ngoma.* London: Heinemann.

Risso, P. 1995. *Merchants and Faith: Muslim Commerce and Culture in the Indian Ocean.* Boulder: Westview Press.

Roberts, A. 2002. 'The Indian Ocean World and Area Studies. Opening Address to the International Conference on Cultural Exchange and Transformation in the Indian Ocean World'. University of California, Los Angeles.

Sheriff, A. 1987. *Slaves, Spices and Ivory in Zanzibar.* Oxford: James Currey.

Simpson, E. 2003. 'Migration and Islamic Reform in a Port Town of Western India', *Contributions to Indian Sociology,* (n.s.) 37.1&2.

Stoler, A.L. 1997. 'Histories of Racism and their Regimes of Truth', *Political Power and Social Theorie,* 11.

Toeloelyan, K. 1996. 'Rethinking Diaspora(s): Stateless Power in the Transnational Moment', *Diaspora*, 5.1.

Vertovec, S. 1997. 'Three Meanings of Diaspora, Exemplified among South Asian Religions', *Diaspora*, 6.3.

Werbner, P. 2000. 'Introduction: The Materiality of Diaspora - Between Aesthetic and 'Real' Politics', *Diaspora*, 9.1.

—— 2002. *Imagined Diasporas among Manchester Muslims.* Oxford: James Currey.

Whitten, N.E., and J.F. Szwed (eds) 1970. *Afro-American Anthropology. Contemporary Perspectives.* New York: The Free Press.

9

'I AM GULF': THE PRODUCTION OF COSMOPOLITANISM AMONG THE KOYAS OF KOZHIKODE, KERALA

Filippo Osella & Caroline Osella

A few weeks after our arrival in Kozhikode (known as Calicut during colonial times) we were introduced to Abdulhussein (Abdulbhai), an export agent who runs a family business together with his three younger brothers. He sat behind a desk in his sparsely furnished office on Beach Road. Abdulbhai is reading a Gujarati newspaper, while one of his younger brothers is talking on the phone in Hindi to a client from Bombay. The office is quiet and so is business: our conversation is only interrupted by the occasional friend who peeps into the office to greet Abdulbhai. He begins:

Business is dead, all the godowns (warehouses) along the beach are closed; all the other exporters have closed down. But at my father's time it was all different. During the trade season, there would be hundreds of boats anchored offshore, with barges full of goods going to and fro. There were boats from Bombay, from Gujarat, from Burma and Ceylon, but most of them belonged to Arabs. Down the road there were the British warehouses, and on the other end there is the Beach Hotel, only Britishers stayed there. The beach front was busy with carts and lorries and there were hundreds of Arab sailors walking up and down. The Arab boats arrived as soon as the monsoon was over, in October, and the last left the following May, before the rain started. Some of the boats were owned by Kozhikode businessmen, but the majority belonged to Arab traders. You could see the boat owners sitting on the verandas outside the offices of the exporters. They had telescopes and looked out for the boats: they could recognise boats by the size and shape of the sails. Some of these Arabs came to Kozhikode for the whole trading season, others had settled here. They married and had families, children. Arab sailors ate and slept in the godowns. They were away from home for a long time and they also took 'wives' here. So many Muslims here have an Arab father: everyone knows that! There were some really big traders to the Gulf here, very, very wealthy people. You can see their offices down the road. Some of these big traders were Arabs, two from Kuwait, one from Bahrain and another from Yemen. Even a black man from Sudan settled here. The last Arab boat came here in 1975. They found oil, made huge fortunes. What is the point of them coming here? Now it is Malayalis who go to the Gulf!

What Abdulbhai traces here is common knowledge and a shared Kozhikode-wide discourse. He tells a story evoking the continued connections between Kozhikode and the Gulf countries of West Asia, a circulation of people, goods and religious practices historically linking these two regions. The diverse experiences of the past – when commerce brought to Kozhikode traders from far and wide – and the present – when Kozhikode migrants travel to the Gulf to work and live alongside people from all over the world – are brought together in popular discourse to highlight the 'cosmopolitanism' of the city and its inhabitants. But for Koyas, a Kozhikode Muslim community, cosmopolitanism goes beyond a celebration of cultural sophistication.[1] Cosmopolitanism is a discourse through which a specific and exclusive local identity is objectified and valorised, at the same time assimilating and distinguishing Koyas from other communities in Kozhikode and beyond. The Koya residential area of Kozhikode – Thekkepuram, with its highly specific matrilineal *tharavadus* (joint households) – and the Gulf – connected historically to Kozhikode through trade and migration – become inseparable, braided reference points of Koya identity and claims for superior status. In turn, however, the experience of contemporary migration to and from the Gulf re-aligns historical notions

1 Fieldwork on which this chapter is based was conducted in Kozhikode, U.A.E., Oman and Kuwait from October 2002 to June 2004 with the support of the Economic and Social Research Council, UK (grant No. R000239766) and the Nuffield Foundation, UK (Social Science Small Grants Scheme). We have been affiliated to the Centre for Development Studies, Thiruvananthapuram, and the Madras Institute of Development Studies, Chennai. We are grateful for comments on earlier versions of this chapter to Geert de Neve, Jon Mitchell, William Clarence-Smith, the participants of the Gulf Migration Conference (Bellagio, June 2005) and the editors of this volume.

and practices of urban cosmopolitanism through which Koyas define their own and their city's identity.

What we find most useful in thinking about Kozhikode Koyas' discursive production of a sense of cosmopolitanism, and in understanding that actually it is not at all the product of a contradiction or a break or even an interaction between a 'global force' acting on a 'local place', is Anna Tsing's essay on 'The Global Situation' (2002; see also 2004). Tsing reminds us of the hubris of post-war modernisation theory, of its links to developmentalism, and asks us whether, in a rush to theorise globalisation, we are not in danger of repeating those same earlier mistakes. As she warns, 'Globalization draws our enthusiasm because it helps us imagine interconnection, travel, and sudden transformation. Yet it also draws us inside its rhetoric until we take its claims for true descriptions' (2002: 456). Tsing asks us instead to 'study folk understandings of the global, and the practices with which they are intertwined' (2002: 469). She also calls for more ethnography which demonstrates highly particularistic intersections of, and co-operations between, situated and specific 'projects', or 'historically specific collaborations' (2002: 472; see also Barendse 1998; Freitag 2003; Laffan 2002; Tarazi Fawaz et al. 2001). The study of 'concrete trajectories and engagements' (Tsing 2002: 475), set in an understanding of the importance of interests and identity offers us, she argues, an antidote both to grand theory inebriated by its own rhetoric, and to the nihilistic despair engendered by taking the global as always necessarily encompassing the grand scale of the planet in its entirety. Tsing is, after all, only reminding us of what anthropologists have always done best: to temper the reach of social theory with the gentle corrective of empirical material. This chapter is then an attempt to recount one such concrete set of highly specific and historically situated global engagements.

Kozhikode Town: Past and Present

With a population of roughly half a million people, Kozhikode is Kerala's third largest city and, although Muslims are not the majority, it is considered to be the Muslim capital of Kerala. Kozhikode Town, at the centre of Kozhikode district, sits right next to the Muslim-majority district of Malappuram, and there is plenty of coming and going between the two. Importantly, alongside local Muslims, Hindus and Christians in Kozhikode, there also live significant (economically and culturally, rather than numerically) immigrant trading communities, predominantly Gujarati Hindus, Jains and Bohri, but also Konkani Hindus and Muslims, who settled in the city towards the end of the nineteenth century.

Kozhikode was prosperous with maritime trade from the tenth to the fifteenth century, developing rapidly over the twelfth and thirteenth centuries as a commercial hub between West Asia, Southeast Asia and South Asia (Bouchon 1987, 1988; Das Gupta 1967; McPherson 1993). Akin to other Indian Ocean port cities of the time, Kozhikode had a noticeable population of visiting or resident 'foreign' merchants from the east (China, Java and Ceylon) and the west (Egypt, Yemen and Persia), as well as from Gujarat and Tamil Nadu. At the time of Ibn Battuta's visit in 1342 the chief merchant and harbour master was one Ibrahim from Bahrain, suggesting a strong Arab presence, confirmed by the existence of two mosques and a *qadi* (Muslim judge) of Arab origins (Shokoohy 2003). Almost a century later, the Chinese Muslim traveller Ma Huan reports that in Kozhikode 'many of the king's subjects are Muslims and there are twenty or thirty mosques in the kingdom', adding that the king employed two Muslim administrators (see Dale 1980: 27).

Vasco da Gama arrived in 1498 and began a long and bloody struggle to wrench away control of pepper trade from the 'Moors', merchants from Egypt and the Arabian peninsula. While it seems unlikely that the Portuguese presence completely disrupted existing trade networks in the Indian Ocean, its effect on Kozhikode was significant: for a period, the Portuguese monopolised pepper trade and, following continual harassment, Arab traders left the city (Barendse 1998; Bouchon 1987, 1988; Das Gupta 1967; cf. Subrahmanyam 1997). This is the period when Gujarati traders, encouraged by Portuguese policies, reinforced their presence in the city (Bouchon 1987: 167).

The second half of the seventeenth century saw the waning of Portuguese power, the rise of Dutch companies (Arasaratnam 1994; Das Gupta 1967) and, in the middle of the eighteenth century, the Mysorean conquest of Malabar. During this period, Kozhikode ceased to be a hub for trans-oceanic commerce; it remained, however, an export centre for local products and an entry point for goods from West Asia and North India. The eventual defeat of Tippu Sultan and the establishment of British rule in 1792 did not substantially change the position of the city: while Bombay developed as the main international export centre, trade from Kozhikode concentrated on the movement of goods to, and through, Bombay and Gujarat (Das Gupta 1967; Subramaniam 1996).[2]

Emerging as a major rice market in the region, Kozhikode also saw a resurgence of Arab trade from West Asia. From the nineteenth century until the middle of the 1980s, the colonial and post-colonial economy gave a major boost to local trade: the city became a world centre for timber export and, later, the centre for the commerce of copra. In the late 1970s, the timber trade declined and, following the Gulf oil boom, all resident Arabs left and Arab ships stopped coming to the city, leading to the eventual closure of all port facilities. As in the rest of Kerala, from the 1980s Kozhikode's economy became dependent upon the revenues and remittances of Gulf migration.

Koyas' Identities: Trade and Tharavadus
Kozhikode Koyas are a Muslim community closely connected to Thekkepuram (literally, 'south place'), a neighbourhood in the south-west of the city where the majority of the community either continues to live or has its roots. Thekkepuram is the oldest surviving part of the city, an area of (mostly crumbling) large joint households (*tharavadus*) and old mosques, delimited by the sites of the community's present and past economic activities: commodity bazaars to the north; retail bazaars to the east; coastal godowns to the west and river-side timber yards and wood mills to the south. Commerce in timber, copra and rice, together with trade with the Gulf countries are economic activities which have been, at different points in time, dominated by Koyas. Their successes allowed

---

2   Tipu Sultan (1750–1799) was the first son of Haider Ali. He ruled the Mysore Kingdom from 1782 to 1799. In 1783, following in his father's footsteps, he conquered the whole of Malabar.

the local middle classes to accumulate substantial capital from the mid-nineteenth century onwards.

Trade with the Arab peninsula occupies a special place in the historical imagination of Koyas, often well beyond its actual economic importance. Within living memory, Arab traders, some of whom had their own warehouses and either settled or spent a considerable part of the year in Kozhikode, are remembered to have brought goods from Basra, Kuwait and Oman and returned with spices, timber, coir and other locally produced consumer goods (cf. Onley 2004). But, as oral history recounts, the most lucrative side of twentieth century Kozhikode Gulf trade came from smuggling: during the two world wars it was tyres and petrol which went from Kozhikode to the Gulf; later it was gold, and later still it was migrants. From the 1950s onwards, until the 1990s liberalisation of import regulations, gold began to flow in the opposite direction, from the Gulf to Kozhikode.[3] Smuggling certainly brought enormous riches, not only to those directly involved in the trade, but to the whole of Thekkepuram, and it eventually replaced timber and spices as the major source of capital accumulation.

With the slow death of the timber and Arab trade, together with the incipient decline of commodity bazaars, migration to the Gulf has become the primary source of income. It is rare to find any household of Koyas without at least one member in UAE, Saudi Arabia, Bahrain, Kuwait or Oman. Migrants to the Gulf have been investing heavily in petty trade, whether on their final resettlement back in Kerala, or by financing the business activities of family members or friends. A few have set up successful trans-national or Gulf-based businesses.

Trade and commerce remain the preferred types of employment for Koyas, even when such activities rely on continuous financing from Gulf remittances. Defining themselves primarily as a business community, Koyas set themselves apart from the lower status Muslims who live along the coastal area of Thekkepuram, such as daily labourers in the bazaar,

---

3   Circulation of gold between the Gulf and South India has, of course, a long history, stretching well back to pre-colonial and early colonial times (see Barendse 1998; Prakash 2004).

fishermen and other non-Muslim Malayalis. But there are other Kozhikode communities with strong business orientations: traders of Gujarati origin and non-Koya Muslims. The Koyas distinguish themselves from the Gujaratis in terms of businesses practices (e.g. involvement in money-lending and inter-coastal trade) and orientation (stress upon economic planning and calculation), as well as lifestyle (saving, thriftiness). From non-Koya Muslims, differences are inscribed in status, kinship and residence, Koyas linking their own origins to historic relations with Arab traders (Fanselow 1996; cf. Mines 1973, 1975).

If trade is one pole the Koyas use to distinguish themselves from others, another is kinship. Unlike the majority of Muslims in Kerela, Koyas see themselves as a *marumakkatayam* (matrilineal) community whose exclusive status is maintained by generalised endogamy.[4] Ahmed Koya, a copra broker in his sixties, explained one evening as a group of friends sat *time passing* on a bench:

Koyas are the descendants of Arabs who came here to trade. They were very well received and respected by the Zamorin Rajah [erstwhile Hindu rulers of Kozhikode] who gave them land, allowing them to settle. At that time, Arab merchants and sailors had to stay here for a considerable time; they were away from home for many months and so they married local ladies [*mut'a* marriage]. These women were Nayars, they were *savarna* [caste] Hindus. The men were Muslims, so their children also became Muslims. The Rajah was so pleased with these Muslim traders that he even encouraged the parents to convert to Islam all children born on Fridays. Other local Nayars also converted, and that is why we are *marumakkatayam*, like Nayars.

This alleged Arab-cum-upper caste origin is used to draw distinctions between Koya and non-Koya Muslims. As Ahmedka continued to explain:

Muslims don't have castes like Hindus, but still we are not all the same. Here there are *onnum* number [number one] Muslims who are Koyas and live in

---

4 While Koyas define themselves as matrilineal, this is actually only partly the case. Unlike the truly matrilineal Kannur Muslims (the erstwhile royal family, the Ali Rajahs) and the northern coastal Muslim community, the Keyis (see Gough 1961: 415ff; cf. McGilvray 1989), Koyas are matrilineal only in so far as they recognise descent through female line; inheritance follows a combination of matrilineal traditions and *shari'a* law.

tharavadus [joint households]. They are *marumakkatayam*, of mixed Nayar and Arab origin and they are traders. Then there *randam number* [number two] who are also *marumakkattayam*, but live in small *tharavadus*; they are converted from lower castes like Tiyyas [casteless (*avarna*) Hindus related to Izhavas of Southern Kerala; [see Osella and Osella 2000], and worked as labourers or servants of *onnum numbers*. They are also Koyas, but different: *onnum numbers* don't marry with them. The last are *muunum number* [number three], the fishermen living along the beach. They are poor, illiterate and follow *makattayam* [patrilineal] system. Then there are Arabs from Yemen, like the *Thangals* [Hadhrami Sayyid families claiming descent from the Prophet; see Abdul Sathar 1999; Dale 1997; Freitag 2003; cf. Miller 1976: 255ff;], but they don't allow their women to marry others. They are the highest!

Kozhikode Koyas also distinguish themselves from Muslims from the interior of Malappuram district, the Mappilas, who are *makattayam* (patrilineal) and were largely agricultural, at least before they started to migrate to the Gulf (see Dale 1980; Miller 1976). While some intermarriage does occur, notably when urban Koyas trade their status for the rural wealth of Mappilas, a great distinction is drawn between the two communities and mutual antipathy often prevails. Status hierarchies are rationalised as substantial differences in *swabhavam* (essentialised nature, see Osella and Osella 2000: 231ff) between classes of people, expressed through notions of occupation (trade as opposed manual labour and fishing), class (wealthy traders as opposed to poorer labourers and fishermen), *culture* (educated *onnum numbers* as opposed to partially educated or illiterate *randam* and *muunu numbers*) and religious practice (reformist-inclined *onnum numbers* opposed to saint-worshipping *randam* and *muunu numbers*, see Bayly 1989: 71ff; Fanselow 1996; McGilvray 1998; cf. Mines 1973, 1975; Vatuk 1996).

These hierarchies of status are objectified in marriage and residence practices. Being a Koya belonging to one of the established and reputed matrilineages in Thekkepuram is a clear indication of long-standing prominence. But while *tharavadus* furnish Koyas with a measure of internal and external status, the cramped living conditions in houses which are often in disrepair and decay make *tharavadu* life unappealing for many. Amidst constant jokes that *tharavadus* are 'like hostels' and that the people living there might not even know how (or if) they are related to the people they live with, whoever has the financial resources, typically successful Gulf migrants, will build a new house and shift to a nuclear household. As a shortage of land and a high population density makes it practically impossible to build new houses in Thekkepuram, returnees from the Gulf have been following the established middle class in buying land from impoverished high-status Hindu landowners and relocating to high-prestige areas.

The history of Thekkepuram *tharavadus* expresses then the complex unfolding of Koyas' identity. On the one hand, *tharavadus* stand for claims to upper caste Hindu descent, and hence status. But stronger claims to *marumakkatayam* traditions puts Koyas in a difficult position vis-à-vis Islam, which of course prescribes patrilineal inheritance; and yet, Koyas claim superior status over patrilineal Muslims, such as fishermen and Mappilas. This tension, only partially resolved by the partial adoption of *shariʿa* inheritance, becomes even sharper following *Mujahid* (followers of post-1950s Kerala's Islamic reformist movements) campaigns for the adoption of 'true' Islamic practices where *marumakkatayam* has no part. Even strongly reformist Koyas embrace here the relativist discourse, otherwise dismissed as un-Islamic, justifying matrilineal orientations as a culturally specific adaptation of Islam, local custom (*adab*) which does not then breach the tenets of the Quran. *Tharavadus* also stand for Koya claims to Arab descent and early conversion to Islam via continuous trade with the Gulf; but they also testify to a strong involvement with the colonial economy, a period of history which has become muted in local historical narratives.

We Have Always Been Cosmopolitans
'We [Muslims] are different here in Kozhikode, we live next to each other' comments Ahmedka during another of the menfolk's evening meetings, 'we mingle with each other and do business together.' 'We have never been separated from Hindus,' chips in Basheer: 'We always had peaceful relations here. Look, in Kozhikode we dress like everyone else, you can't tell a Muslim from a Hindu or a Christian from what they wear. In North India, Muslims dress and speak differently, they stay

apart from others and therefore there are always troubles. But not here.'⁵ Ahmedka continues:

The first Arab trader who arrived here went to meet the Rajah. The Arab gave the Rajah a jar of pickle and asked him to keep it safe until the his return the following season. After one year he returned and the Rajah gave him the jar back. The trader opened it and took out a gold coin. It was a test: as the Rajah proved trustworthy, the Arabs began to trade in Kozhikode. The Zamorin Rajah was very fond of Arab traders and gave them honours and land. He encouraged local people to marry Arabs and convert to Islam. Koyas collected dues from the merchants on behalf of the Rajah and kept a portion to themselves.

Focusing on the benevolence and religious tolerance of local Hindu rulers, the pickle jar story underscores many themes commonly found in state-wide narratives.⁶ In a rhetoric shared by both left and centre political parties, communal harmony and tolerance are popularly represented as one of the distinguishing traits of Kerala. Communal harmony is represented as the clear expression of the spirit of tolerance which, together with a wider progressive orientation, defines the Malayali's unique identity. It is taken for granted that religious tolerance distinguishes Malayalis from other Indians who, on the face of recurrent episodes of communal violence, do not appear to be so inclined.⁷

In Hindutva (Hindu nationalist) discourse, on the other hand, the benevolence of Kozhikode's Hindu Rajahs, the Zamorins, takes an

---

5 This claim is made only, of course, for men. Although it is commonly made, it is not strictly true. All Malayali non-Muslim men, for example, even those with modest incomes wear gold neck chains, rings and identity bracelets. Only Muslims, for religious reasons, either totally eschew jewellery or limit themselves to rings made of silver set with semi-precious stones. While Hindu men generally prefer to wear a moustache, Muslim men will be, mostly, clean shaven. *Mujahid* men will invariably have a mark on their forehead as a result of prostrations during prayers (cf. Soares 2004).

6 The story of the pickle jar appears in different versions in the *Keralolpathi*, an eighteenth century collection of Kerala's popular legends (see Menon 1962).

7 In 2003, extreme communal violence did break out around the coastal fishing area of Marad. Most locals were keen to portray this as an isolated set of incidents, attributing it to the actions of ignorant and poor fishermen. Great efforts were made, especially among Muslim community leaders and social service organisations, to dampen things down and make peace. There was a strong will to limit the violence, stop it spreading and prevent re-occurrence (cf. Varshney 2002).

altogether different slant. It highlights that Hinduism, unlike Islam, is a broad-minded religion, capable of coexisting alongside different faiths and orientations (it must also be remembered here that Kerala has a substantial Christian population). The enlightened attitudes of the Zamorins are undermined by Muslims' zealous intolerance, represented here by the persecutions and alleged forced conversions taking place during the Mysorean invasions of Hyder Ali and Tippu Sultan, and later during the 1920s Mappila uprising. The rhetoric of Hindutva leads to negative comparison and a critique of contemporary practices: Muslims are accused of using their Gulf-acquired money aggressively, to push out other communities from business and residential areas.

Muslims like Ahmedka, however, characterise the Hindu rulers' piety differently, citing another popular story, which appears in the *Tohfut-ul-Mujahideen* (a sixteenth-century account of the Portuguese conquest of Malabar by Shayik Zaynu'd-din of Ponnani) and the *Keralolpathi*. This is the controversial story of the conversion of the last Cheraman Perumal (king of Chera dynasty) to Islam, a story taken as truthful by some historians (see Bahauddin 1992: 21–24; Ibrahim Kunju 1989: 14–20; cf. Logan 1989 [1887]: 192; Miller 1976: 46ff), but dismissed by others as fictional (see Menon 1962: 83, note 1). Based in the port town of Kodungaloor (erstwhile Cranganore), the Rajah converts to Islam, partitions his kingdom and decides to follow Arab Muslim traders back to their land. In Ahmedka's version of the story, the voyage takes place during the lifetime of the Prophet; eventually the Cheraman Perumal decides to return together with a party of Arabs led by one Malik Ibn Dinar, for some a Companion of the Prophet and for others a follower of the Sufi saint Hassa ul-Basri (see Ibrahim Kunju 1989: 20–21). In either case, the Rajah dies before setting sail. He leaves, however, a letter of introduction for his fellow travellers who, in time, reach Kodungaloor from where they propagate Islam peacefully and establish mosques right across Kerala.

Ahmedka concludes his story by stressing the wider cultural role of Arabs:

Arabs wore beautiful clothes, while people here had only a short *mundu* [cloth] across their waist and were bare-chested. It is the Arabs who brought clothes here. They were also very knowledgeable, in mathematics, astronomy and other things.

Ahmedka is making a case for Kozhikode's long-standing cosmopolitanism, understood not as a top-down or elite form of proto-globalisation (cf. Hannerz 1990), but as something more like Tsing's reading of circulation, as a highly specific and situated 'series of historically specific collaborations that create distinctive cultural forms of capitalism' (2002: 474). It is characterised in Koya narratives as a fruitful encounter between Arab and Malayali, set within a framework of a beneficent and peaceful expansion of Islam, bringing moral and economic well-being and engendering new identities and family forms even as it created new business. This period of overall prosperity is contrasted with the destructions and miseries brought by Portuguese conquest and the indignities and humiliations of British rule. Colonial decline is eventually redressed by independence – associated with the rise of the Muslim League to represent Muslim interests in post-independence Kerala – and, more crucially, by the 1970s beginning of Gulf migration.

Cosmopolitanism Revisited

Ahmedka's exemplary Koya-specific perspective is significant for its selective deployment of historical memories. In the neighbouring district of Malappuram, where Muslims are the majority, as amongst 'traditionalist' religious organisations, the colonial period evokes memories not just of resistance to the Portuguese, but, more importantly, to the British. The famous Mappila uprisings (see Dale 1980; Panikkar 1989) are presented as a powerful symbol of the heroic defiance by Muslims of foreign oppression and anti-Muslim rule, the culmination of a time-honoured tradition stretching back to the anti-Portuguese struggle (Kurup and Mathew 2000; Miller 1976: 68ff). But Koyas seldom mention the Mappila uprisings, a milestone in Malabar Muslim history. Now it must be stressed that public references to the rebellion are generally avoided because they might evoke unwelcome associations to the 'fanatical Muslims' of colonial and Hindu historiography (see

Hitchcock 1925; Nair 1923) from which the whole community seeks to distance itself at a time when Muslims in India and beyond are commonly associated to extremism and terrorist activities. But in Kozhikode, lack of reference to the rebellion is also indicative of the fact (nowadays rather unpalatable) that not only did Thekkepuram traders do relatively well under British colonialism, but also that many community leaders, members of the substantially anglophile middle class, sided with the British during the uprising.

The narratives of Koyas tend to focus instead on the post-rebellion period when Malabar's Muslims closed in upon themselves, distancing themselves from the processes of colonial-driven modernisation which were enthusiastically embraced all over Kerala by Christians and Hindus alike. Koyas then oppose Thekkepuram's self-ascribed cosmopolitanism and modern outlook to the conservative (read: backward) orientation of rural Malappuram Muslims. We were reminded many a time that in Malappuram Muslims refused to engage with modern education; instead, privileging Arabi-Malayalam over both English and written Malayalam, deemed respectively the languages of *shaitan* (the devil) and *kafirs* (non-believers). In Thekkepuram, however, the anglophile merchant middle-class had built two schools in the early twentieth century (Himayatul Islam High School, in 1908, and Madrasathul Muhammadiya Vocational High School, 1918) with the blessing of the colonial administration. Thekkepuram is proud of its educational achievements, perhaps modest compared to those of Kozhikode Hindus and Christians, but certainly significant in relation to Malappuram Muslims.

We have said that Koyas' sense of status and class distinction is translated in popular discourse as an opposition between Thekkepuram's 'modern cosmopolitan' orientation and the 'traditionalism' of rural Muslims; this opposition is also articulated at the level of religious practice. Regardless of specific religious affiliations or orientations, Koyas share Islamic reformist critiques of 'traditionalism' couched in terms of superstition, ignorance, blind following of 'traditional' religious leaders and overall cultural 'backwardness' (see Robinson 2004). The ideological influence of the *Mujahids* around Kozhikode is considerable. Reformism, focusing on religious learning and 'western' education, is generally associated both to a 'true' Islam' (to which Koyas claim direct descent via ancestry from or conversion by Arab traders) and to the modern outlook of the old and new local middle classes. Traditionalism has become associated, then, to ignorance, superstition and uncouthness; it is seen as characteristic of either rural (Mappila) or poor (*randam* and *munnum number*) Muslims, to the extent that even 'traditionalist' Koyas no longer participate openly in the annual festival of local shrines, so as not to be seen mingling with rustic rural and urban low status devotees. While 'traditionalist' practices are increasingly confined to the domestic realm, organisations devoted to the social and educational 'upliftment' of Muslims are thriving: from all-Kerala outfits such as the Muslim Educational Society and the Muslim Service Society, to local groups such as CIESCO (Citizens' Intellectual Educational Social and Cultural Organisation). Such organizations not only campaign for and support Muslim children's formal education but organise regular *camps* or seminars to 'enlighten' poor Muslims about the need for education, hygiene and, generally, a 'systematic life'.

Sympathies for reformism have also led to redefinition and critique of local orientations towards cosmopolitanism and modernity. 'The main activity here was gambling', remembered Aslam, a retired copra merchant.

In the evening men gathered in *clubs* above shops to play cards. Lots of money was lost! And there was also drinking. In the 1960s, strip-tease became popular. Now all this is finished: people realised it was bad. It is *haram*, forbidden for Muslims.

Abdul Gafoor, a timber merchant, continues:

Twenty years ago nobody went to mosques. There was not even need for a call for prayer! When someone died, people stayed outside the mosque, smoking ... When I was young [in the 1940s], if you were ill your mother would take you to a *Thangal* who would blow over a glass of water and give it to you to drink. What cure was that?

While these statements betray partisan support for *Mujahid* reformism, Gafoor and Aslam are giving voice to a general unease about the past. They present emerging colonial and post-colonial (secularising) modernism and enduring religious traditionalism as matching evils, leading respectively to moral corruption and reproduction of superstitious ignorance.

Critical appraisal of the past leads to a separation of progress from westernisation, hence explaining the erasure of colonial connections from the dominant narratives and the alternative associations of modernity and cosmopolitanism to the experience of the post-oil boom Gulf countries, to the modernising influence of pre-colonial Muslim Arab traders and to notions of pan-Islamic brotherhood. At the same time, Koyas are now re-evaluating their historical connections with Hadhrami settlers. *Thangal* families, arriving from the middle of the eighteenth century to the middle of the twentieth century, were formerly accorded religious and political leadership, but have now been substantially marginalised.

Have We Ever Been Cosmopolitan?

In Ahmedka's narrative, Koya cosmopolitanism, purged of its colonial and Hadhrami 'traditionalist' influences, is linked, via the history of Arab trade, to a sense of being part of the larger Muslim world. This sense is constantly re-kindled both during public religious functions where Arab scholars are invited, and through the recent experiences of Gulf migration. Koyas see themselves as more connected to the Arab world than to other Indian Muslims, such as the *randam* and *muunum numbers* with whom they interact on a daily basis, or to the Urdu speakers from the north of the country whom Koyas explicitly associate with illiteracy, ignorance, poverty, a past characterised by forced religious conversion and a present dominated by ethnic rivalries. All these lower-status Muslims are painted as part of the world of the contemporary national vernacular (cf. Pollock 2002), lacking the 'Arab connection'. Koyas indisputably feel themselves to be part of the *Dar al-Islam* (cf. Soares 2000; Werbner 2003). At the same time, the Koyas' sense of cosmopolitanism undoubtedly reflects the business ethic of a city whose past and present history is utterly intertwined with commerce (see Barendse 1998; cf. Das Gupta 2001; Fanselow 1996; Freitag 2003). But it is also true that although traders in Kozhikode's bazaars might belong to many different communities (though bazaars remain broadly Muslim dominated), in trade people seldom do business, in the sense of developing business ventures, across community boundaries.

While it is certainly true that some professional or trade associations, such as the Bar Council or the Chamber of Commerce, might have a wider-community support base, in practice many of these organisations may often be dominated by one group: an association of government employees may tend to be largely Hindu, an association of shopkeepers dominated by Muslims and so on. Likewise, although there are a few social organisations which have a mixed membership, such as the Rotary Club, the Round Table, the Lions Club or the (marvellously named and highly exclusive) Cosmopolitan Club, most people are more likely to be involved in their own community's organisations. And even if relationships in the workplace or schools might take place on a non-communal basis, cross-community friendships remain limited and circumscribed to public spaces: significantly, members of different communities rarely attend each other's life cycle ceremonies or celebrations, such as marriages or retirement parties. And, of course, they certainly do not marry each other (cf. Varshney 2002).

This is most surely the case among Koyas, whose main cultural and social referent remains Thekkepuram and its *tharavadus*. Married men retain strong relations with their natal *tharavadus*, where they continue to take their noon and evening meals. Even those who have started an independent household outside the neighbourhood take food two or three times a week in their mothers' or sisters' *tharavadu*. The sociality of Koya men revolves around Thekkepuram: every evening, after prayer, men get together in groups to exchange gossip, talk over daily political events or simply enjoy each other's company. Such groups of friends, who have often known each other since childhood, from school or are from the same or related *tharavadu*, meet every evening in the same place: a street corner, around a bench or outside someone's office. Some groups are more formal and may rent old shops to hold their daily meetings. In many groups, members take turns to organise a monthly communal meal or, during Ramadan, an *iftar* (fast-breaking) party. Thekkepuram friendships and groups are reproduced in the Gulf, where the more formalised associations will have 'branches' or 'chapters', meeting every weekend and organising fund-raising activities or 'family meets'.

If Gulf migration has led to an openness towards innovations coming from West Asia, it has also provided the basis for a withdrawal of Koyas into Muslim-dominated spaces. Inputs of Gulf money and the drive towards better education which, it is hoped, will rescue the community from dependence upon the declining bazaar and towards qualified Gulf jobs, have had significant impact upon the educational scene. In Kozhikode, local government schools generally recruit from particular residential areas; hence tend to be *de facto* segregated. In Kuttichira (Thekkepuram's central area) the government primary school is in a prevalently Muslim area and consequently the vast majority of students are Muslims from working class, non-*tharavadu* families. In the other local, but more prestigious, school (a government-aided school administered by a Muslim management committee) the student body remains predominantly Muslim, the curriculum is also designed around the all-Kerala syllabus, but the majority of the students come from low to middle class *tharavadu* Muslim families. While fifty and perhaps even twenty years ago the latter school was the preferred choice of local middle class Muslim students because the teaching of 'modern' subjects took place in an Islamic environment, nowadays, the wealthy prefer to send their children to one of the many expensive English-medium schools run by Christian management committees which offer a CBSE (Central Board of Secondary Education) syllabus. In sum, very few students complete their education in a 'mixed' or 'cosmopolitan' environment where they mingle with members of other communities. For many, education remains a segregated experience, with little or no contact with non-Muslims. And with the construction of more and more private educational institutions, at all levels, education is turning into an increasingly communalised affair (cf. Jeffery, Jeffery and Jeffrey 2004).

This move, which is common in various degrees to all castes and communities in Kerala, is apparent not only in education but also in a range of other services, such as hospitals. There is an often-expressed argument that such investment is necessary in order to encourage Muslims towards development; but the corollary of these shifts is at once an impoverishment of the state sector and an increasing tendency for community closure. Communal closure does not, however, affect Koyas in the same measure: professional and business elites strive to enter wider middle class lifestyle, moving, for example, to emerging 'cosmopolitan colonies'. But in embracing these new lifestyles and orientations, middle class Koyas do not have the same confidence as their Christian or Hindu counterparts. On the other hand, residence in Kozhikode has always been segregated community-wise. Historically, trading ports in the Indian Ocean had cosmopolitan populations living in conditions of extra-territoriality, cooperating with each other, but living separate from local population (see Pearson 1999: 13).

Koya womenfolk, meanwhile, also remain rooted strongly in the area, moving in even more tightly restricted (family based) circles. All women in this matrilineal-oriented community are strongly enmeshed in the lives of their female kin, sociality being the mainstay of Koya womenfolk's spare time. This is a daily matter in the case of *tharavadu* co-residents (and is certainly, of course, not always peaceful but often highly acrimonious) and less regular in the case of more distant relations. The lanes of Thekkepuram are always busy, and utterly thronged on Fridays and Sundays, with groups of women and their kids in auto-rickshaws, going to pay visits to relatives. Women from families who have moved out of the area frequently drop by the *tharavadu*, even if it means, as it often does, an hour-long bus trip. A shopping trip for new clothes for the kids or to exchange a gold chain is always turned into a social opportunity, sometimes extended by tea or food in the family room of a restaurant.

Koyas in Thekkepuram remain, then, a closely tied and to an extent closed community: exemplarily local. Even those families who have set up independent households in other areas tend to prefer areas already populated by Koyas, where Koya specific and Koya-exclusive forms of sociality can be reproduced and enjoyed. The degree to which such mixing takes place depends very much upon a number of highly-specific factors. In an area where there is a good mixed school, women whose children attend school together will be cordial and happily invite their children into each other's homes. But a strong Muslim presence is preferred: a woman who had recently shifted into a small new house outside Thekkepuram took Caroline into the backyard and pointed out all the neighbour's homes: 'Muslim, Muslim, Hindu, Muslim, Muslim; it's a nice area.' An architect in an interview affirmed that, 'the first priority when choosing a location for buying land is proximity of a mosque. It goes above a good school, nearby shops, anything else.' Given the requirement of five daily prayers and the increasing stress on public orthopraxy, this is, after all, reasonable, but its effect is to limit residence choices and favour closure.

Cosmopolitanism and the Gulf

We often heard the comment that 'Kozhikode used to be the Arabs' Gulf'; they came from a barren desert land to buy Indian commodities, and would be dazzled by Kozhikode's bazaar. From the 1970s, labour migration to the Gulf and post-liberalisation business opportunities have certainly increased traffic and intensified exchange while the direction of these flows has reversed, but all such connections are subsumed within a rhetoric that solely emphasises Kozhikode's long-standing relation with the Gulf.

We find strong connections between life in Kozhikode and life there. When we look at the life-cycle of a typical Muslim migrant family, we see a web of connections over time. Initially, men may go alone to the Gulf and reside with other Koyas. After marriage, a man might take his wife with him or may leave her in her own *tharavadu*, depending on finances and preference. A wife sometimes takes a visiting visa to spend a month or two with her husband; more often, women wait for menfolk to come home. Men's periods of leave and visits home range from one to six months and come at intervals of between one and five years. Women who go with their husbands to the Gulf in any case all come home and stay anything up to a year for the birth of a child. Professional men who can afford decent family housing and private schooling prefer to shift their families out with them; but even then, women often feel isolated and find a stream of good reasons, such as a family wedding, an ailing parent or a child's education, to make prolonged visits home. Even settled families have to send their children back home for college-level education; Gulf-raised teenagers often champ at the bit to finish their studies and get out of Kerala and back to what is for them home.

The constant traffic back and forth is not only made up of migrants going to work in the Gulf or visiting home; we have come across several Koya brides who have never lived in Thekkepuram before coming to get married. Khadeeja, 18, who had been brought up in Saudi Arabia, was happy to marry in Kerala and shift into her mother's *tharavadu*, where she had never lived; she found the stream of visitors, the rounds of dinners, shopping trips and weddings, and the throng of female company in the house exhilarating. Eventually, Khadeeja's husband may build his own house, at which time Khadeeja will move there; or perhaps the husband will, as is common, use his new Saudi Arabian connection to launch his own migrant career.

In the Gulf, in large apartment blocks (notably in Dubai, Sharjah and Kuwait) or small independent houses (in cities such as Ras al-Khaimah and Ajman), Koyas, where possible, will re-constitute groupings familiar to them from Kozhikode. If this is not possible, they will at least prefer as neighbours other Muslim migrants, such as other Muslims from Kerala, Pakistanis and so on.

Koyas' relationships with, and evaluation of, the Arab world gets considerably nuanced through the experience of actual close contact with Arabs. Inevitably, experiences are good and bad and lead them to reflect upon *Dar al-Islam* and ideals of Muslim brotherhood, upon the ways in which Malayali Muslims live and embody their religion, and upon Islam itself. Considerable ambivalence is of course what results. In Kuwait City, a city with strong historic trading links with Kozhikode, Filippo met up with a lively Koya community. Meeting every Thursday evening and Friday in each other's houses or on the coastal promenade, they describe themselves as a 'branch' of Thekkepuram. They are a mixed bunch: professionals, watchmen and drivers; those who have been there for more than twenty years, as well as the newly arrived (often re-locating from Saudi Arabia or Oman following the implementation of recent Arabisation policies); mature men and youngsters, the latter sometimes the sons of Kuwait's old hands. Filippo was taken for the usual visitor's tour of the city's sprawling shopping complexes and to meet Koya shop assistants of Kozhikode origin. Comments on the exorbitant prices were interspersed with criticisms of Kuwaiti shoppers. As Mohammed Ali, a mechanical engineer, expressed, 'Kuwaitis are very few and the government pays for everything. They get free electricity, free water, free housing, free education and free medical care. They have no expenses and so they have money to buy anything they want.' He added, 'Life is good here, I can't complain. But the Kuwaitis [...] well, they are difficult, they are too proud, like the Saudis. It is become worse since the liberation [from Iraq following the 1991 invasion].' Another friend chipped in: 'these Arabs really do suffer from a superiority complex over all of us and think they are the only proper Muslims.'

The following evening, Filippo's host decided to treat him to local food, taking him to one of the many open air restaurants outside the main *suq* (bazaar). They met up with Abdullah Koya, one of the oldest Koya residents in the city, who normally dresses in the 'Arab style' and speaks fluent Arabic. Sitting uncomfortably staring at the menus under the surprised gaze of Kuwaiti customers, no one knew what to order. Eventually, Abdullah called for the attention of an Egyptian waiter and ordered food for everyone. The food was eaten with great relish and, walking back to the cars, Abdullah confessed that in all the years in Kuwait none of them had dared enter an 'Arab restaurant' before. Later, they stopped outside an old mosque, one of the few remaining old buildings in Kuwait City, Abdullah called Filippo, 'Look there' he said, pointing to a plaque on the side of the mosque's entrance, 'it says that this mosque was built in the 1920s by Indian merchants. It must have been Koyas!' The group broke up, and Filippo got a lift home in Abdullah's car. Abdullah was a little annoyed with the others: 'They always complain about Kuwaitis, they say that they [Kuwaitis] are too proud. So what? Anyone with money and a luxury life will naturally be proud. When they go back to Kozhikode, they [the others in the group] are all proud!'

Now, Abdullah's sympathetic treatment of Kuwaitis is not incidental. His elder sister married a prominent Kozhikode-based Kuwaiti merchant who in the 1950s moved back with his Koya wife and children to Kuwait. After a few years, Abdullah joined them, learning Arabic and getting, through his sister's husband, a government job. Abdullah, extremely proud of his Kuwaiti family connections, was keen to take Filippo to his brother-in-law's *diwaniya*, a private weekly gathering of related men and their friends. When they arrived, the meeting had already started: sitting around a richly furnished room and served refreshments by Malayali servants, men talked to each other in small groups. Abdullah introduced Filippo in Arabic to the men who failed to show any particular interest in the two visitors. While Abdullah settled to watch television, Filippo explained the reason for his visit to a group of older men, retired traders who had spent their youth in Bombay. Overhearing the conversation, someone from the other side of the room asked loudly, 'What? Studying Keralites in India? Are there any of them left there? They are all here, you know. They come, bring all their family and want to be rich, always asking for something.' Abdullah, somewhat embarrassed, stood up, signalling Filippo that it was time to go.

Back in Kozhikode, Caroline met Shameela, whose impoverished family had married her, through a broker, to an Arab twenty-five years ago when she was a girl of sixteen. Now she returns to Thekkepuram annually to stay for four months in her natal *tharavadu*. Her children are grown up and have Omani passports, Arab names and habits and have never seen their mother's homeland. While her Arab husband is happy now to allow her visits home (he long back took another wife, with whom he lives), while the children were young, he never allowed them any connection with Kerala, and Shameela did not visit home for years. Shameela speaks Malayalam with a heavy Arabic accent, wears an Arabic-style housedress and *hijab* in the house, and puts henna on the soles of her feet like Arab women. We have no way of knowing how many women like her are moving between Kerala and the Gulf, but women like Shameela are strong forces in bringing the Gulf and its commodities, clothing styles, cultural practices and food items into the intimate spaces used by Kerala's women.

Kitchens' Cosmopolitan Particularism

The food practices of Koyas display strong tendencies towards cosmopolitanism and a willing adoption of new fashions and ideas.

Having previously worked among rural Hindus, who express widespread distrust of food items felt to be imported or not traditional, who avoid commensality because of purity anxieties, and who hold strong preferences for local (*nadan*) food, even to the extent of preferring to eat rice grown on their own land (Osella and Osella 1999), food is an arena in which we find the Koyas' openness to outside influences especially notable. Not only do Koyas accept new food influences, they seem actively to seek them out as part of their generalised interest in food, feasting and eating out.

Home-cooked trans-national dishes occasionally appear, such as the minced beef with macaroni served in some Gulf and Gulf-returned Koya homes as an exemplar of European or 'Araby' food, a notion of pasta transformed via Arab sensibilities into an index of Malayali sophistication. As Caroline compared recipes with Koya migrant women for pasta *al ragu* (original Italian version: pasta with minced beef), spaghetti Bolognese (UK version) or *macaroni* (Omani-style-Gulf-Malayali version), a non-migrant teenager marvelled. When 'tomato paste' was mentioned, she looked puzzled. Her mother in law, recently returned after fifteen years in Oman, smiled triumphantly and said: 'Tomato paste? Of course I know it: I am Gulf'.

Koya women like her are at the forefront of culinary innovation in Kozhikode. They want to learn to cook pasta, pizza, stuffed chicken, chocolate cake and so on. Cookery classes, demonstrations and competitions are a regular feature of life both in Thekkepuram and out in the Gulf. Caroline was astounded when she attended a cookery demonstration sponsored by Nestle and attended by lower middle-class Koya women, women whose husbands may be doing low-level labour in the Gulf, or running or working in small shops in the bazaar: all of the women used Maggi ready-made noodles regularly and most of them also knew and praised Maggi prawn powder as a useful kitchen ingredient. Among Hindu and Christian communities, this level of sophistication and enthusiasm for the new is seen only among the higher classes (cf. Caplan 1985).

Koya food itself is well-known outside the community and is highly specific. Reading descriptions of Arab food items (such as that of *harira or harissa*, the broth made from meat, grain and milk), we have recognised several Koya items and have begun to realise the extent of Arab and Muslim influence on the culinary traditions of Koyas. In some instances, food items are clearly simply imported and simply referred to by the original Arabic names, as in the drink *cava* (Yemeni *qahwa*) which is served after *biriyani* and at festive occasions, and claimed as typically Koya and Kozhikode by Koyas. In other instances, however, the connections are not so obvious, but we have experienced clear equivalences through travel and taste.

Food for Koyas is tightly linked to sociality and to hospitality. The party, more properly the *salkaram* (in Thekkepuram dialect the *takkaram*) is a greatly enjoyed aspect of Koya social life, part of the Koya value of *making jolly*. At a *salkaram* there will always be the ghee rice for which Koyas are famous or meat stew (*biriyani*) and sometimes both; then there will be *pathiri* (flat bread), both rice and wheat. Sometimes there is also fried rice and chapatti, the slightly exotic food of non-Koyas. As well as the necessary Koya food items, women also try to serve different dishes, surprise and novel, luxury or exotic foods. There will be a huge range of side dishes, at least seven; and two or more puddings; finally, two great platters, one of salad and one of cut fruit. The uncompromising non-vegetarianism of Koya food is mitigated by vast quantities of (imported) fruit. In the drive to try something new, we have recently seen the introduction of overseas-imported exotica such as lychees and kiwi fruit; and more local, but still costly and unfamiliar, items like strawberries. When unfamiliar items are offered, guests enjoy guessing what the ingredients are; there is a great sense of enjoyment and easy sociability at a *salkaram*.

The pleasure Koyas take in food exemplifies the complex braiding of influences at work in the community. While feasting and hospitality harks back to their days as hosts to Arab traders, nowadays it reinforces intra-community rather than inter-community bonds. Eating out and trying new dishes expresses simultaneously: a longstanding cosmopolitan and open orientation, also demonstrated by the vast difference in Koya dishes from the 'base' South Indian diet; an arena in which Koyas can claim distinction over less sophisticated 'others', via their awareness and demonstration of a range of 'exotic' food options; pan-Indian lower-middle-class aspirations towards global bourgeois 'lifestyle' options. Recent migration to the Gulf has intensified these processes, as visiting relatives bring items like custard powder, local supermarkets increasingly stock Gulf-imported items, *shawarma* and juice bars open up, and satellite television cookery programmes increase the culinary competence and range of those, like Koya women, sophisticated and open-minded enough to follow them.

Conclusions: Openings and Closures

While the cosmopolitanism of Koyas resonates with social theory, it does not easily fit characterisations found in recent debates (see Grillo n.d.; Vertovec and Cohen 2002). It entails an appreciation of cultural competence, of hybrid descent and of social tolerance, but also exclusion and closures, produced out of highly specific historical contingencies and practices, thus not simply an epiphenomenon of either modernity or globalisation. The cosmopolitanism of Koyas is just as much the product of the globalisation of labour (see Appadurai 1997; Clifford 1998; Hannerz 1990; or see Diouf 2002; Gidwani and Sivaramakrishnan 2003; Werbner 1999 for non-elite variants) as it is of long term connections across the Indian Ocean (see Al-Rasheed 2004; Barendse 1998; Chaudhuri 1990; Das Gupta 2001; Kearney 2003; Parkin and Headley 2000; Pearson 2005). But in both cases the experience of living, working or trading in heterogeneous social environments is highly nuanced and contradictory. While in the Gulf, interactions across community boundaries appear to be confined to the work place and where Koya migrants replicate familiar and exclusive forms of sociality, in Kozhikode the experience of colonial and early post-independence international trade, which, unlike earlier trade connections, remains vivid in people's memories, is simultaneously deeply embedded in the identity of Koyas and, for reasons which are both political and religious, publicly muted. And in any case the two experiences, of cosmopolitanism at home and abroad, produce relationships which are qualitatively different.

Arab merchants and sailors used to roam the streets of Kozhikode and were entertained in Koya houses as guests and friends, and sometimes as husbands; contemporary Gulf migrants might enter Arab houses only as servants or employees. While trans-nationalism and cosmopolitanism across the Indian Ocean are not solely twentieth century phenomena, regimes of labour circulation under contemporary global capitalism have radically transformed Koyas' everyday engagements with the wider world (cf. Al-Rasheed 2004). And yet, Koyas are neither 'trans-nationals' who simply reconstitute the *desh* in the *bidesh* or the home overseas (Gardner 1993) nor are they comfortably straddling 'multiple cultural worlds' (Gidwani and Sivaramakrishnan 2003: 361). Openings and innovations go alongside a progressive closing of the community onto itself, an enhanced localism which nevertheless impinges on an increased sense of being part of a wider *Dar al-Islam*.

Islamic reformism and recent experiences of Gulf migration have intensified existing Arab-identified and Muslim-identified strands of Koya identity. Through the embrace of an Islamic and Gulf-oriented modernity and way of life, Muslims re-nourish themselves at an imagined and sentimentalised heartland of Islam. This has the effect of intensifying processes of communalisation and community closure. The need for such a turn has been reinforced by political events: locally, the emergence of strong and successful Hindu and Christian communal and caste organisations which dominate the public sphere; nationally, the state of living 'post-Ayodhya' and under the rise of Hindutva; internationally, the Afghanistan and Iraq invasions and widespread post-9/11 Islamophobia giving a sense being a 'community under siege' which needs to stick together. We also note that Koyas, and Muslims in Kerala more generally, neither present themselves as cultural hybrids, which would expose them equally to Hindutva claims that Indian Muslims are 'really' Hindu and also to accusations of religious impropriety, nor do they want to overplay an exclusive Islamic identity, a stance which would make them foreign within the nation. It is of course the totalising discourses of nationalism which make it so difficult to talk in the same breath about the indigenous roots of Koyas, cosmopolitanism and Arab influences without a negative value being put on them.

Religion, especially following reformist influences, has acquired a dominant place in the daily life of Koyas, helping migrants deal with the hardships of migration and restoring community pride back in Thekkepuram in the face of economic decline. Islam is felt to shape cultural styles across places, and offers a stable framework which connects the different parts of one's life. All those we met rely heavily upon a benevolent God who will eventually help them get good opportunities for themselves and their families and make the right decisions in life. Religion (following the argument made by Waldinger and Fitzgerald 2003), does appear to bring about a sense of true trans-nationalism rather than mere internationalism. There is a certainly a feeling among Koyas that we know that there is something like a broader 'Muslim culture' (and equally a 'Christian culture'). They see Islamic modernity as a correct and good relationship to modernity; depending upon individual orientation, particular Gulf states are held to embody this perfection. At the same time, the rise of religious orthopraxy has been reinforced by the success of reformist discourses. Reformists have, for example, advised Muslims against taking part in any un-Islamic practices, such as celebrating Onam (Malayali new year; see Osella and Osella 2000) or Christmas with their non-Muslim neighbours; or taking part in public events with a 'Hindu flavour', such as lighting lamps onstage at inaugurations. Reformist critiques have accelerated recognition among Muslims that Kerala's secularist public sphere is in fact strongly marked as Hindu. Relationships between communities are being reformulated as 'unity in diversity', under the protection of a secular state which guarantees the rights of religious minorities.

The ways in which Koyas of Kozhikode render their home city and their own lives, histories and identities, is often through references to highly-specific places and to a braided culture which is at once particularistic and supra-local. Under discussion are not empirical locations but imaginary zones which exaggerate perceived negative and positive characteristics. In practice, of course, places are actually tightly linked, and resist clear lines being drawn between what is *nadan* (local) and what is *foren* (foreign). The inter-penetration and co-presence of the local and the foreign – in the case of Kozhikode and the Gulf, something which is extremely intense – also needs to be taken properly into account. As we have seen, the Gulf is hardly alien at all in Kerala. Apart from the ubiquity of households with migrant members, shops such as 'Gulf Bazaar', selling imported items, and pavement cafés such as 'Hot Buns' chicken *shawarma* bar are all part of the landscape. Muslim children begin to learn Arabic script as soon as they learn Malayalam or English, and all Muslims we meet in Kozhikode have some familiarity, sometimes a high competence, in Arabic language. Many television sets in Kerala receive not only local channels but also satellite channels such as Asianet Gulf, which is targeted at Gulf Malayalis and broadcasts daily news on Malayali life and social events in the Gulf. We feel that because of the intensity of the linkages, the frequency and ease of traffic back and forth, and the interpenetration of Gulf and Kerala, that the Gulf is actually part of Kerala, and not at all a separate *nadu*.

Turning to consider relationships between local and supra-local which then make up both cosmopolitanism and Kozhikode's own particular connection into global networks, we find that Koyas have both a strong local orientation, but that this is shot through with a sense of cosmopolitanism coming from both wider Islam and from the specific links to the Gulf. But we must not (following the argument made by Tsing 2002) think that 'local' and 'global' are pitted against each other, or that 'local' necessarily means vernacular, non-cosmopolitan. There is an extremely specific and exclusivist Koya identity, which is heavily dependent upon the right to claim roots in a particular bounded locality, Thekkepuram, and a set of cultural practices revolving around the *tharavadu* system, food, and sociality. But that highly specific and exclusive identity itself is recognised to be an outcome of wider links. It is prized as a historic product of cosmopolitanism itself: of descent from or meetings with Arabs; of a recent willingness to move into the mainstream of education; of a cultural sophistication which is open to innovation.

This sense of cosmopolitanism among Koyas is contrasted with those who lack these characteristics: the poor who cannot afford to go to the Gulf and who can claim no direct Arab descent or connection; the rural folk who lack access to Kozhikode's commercial and seafaring past with its rich commodities and contacts with Arabs; Muslims from North Indian who are stuck with a specific language marking them off from others and with an uneducated worldview which makes them prone to violence and prey to manipulation by communal-minded forces. Concluding, then, we take Koyas as embodying a highly particularistic cosmopolitan localism, in which the local extends to encompass the Gulf Arab world. This very specific and bounded Koya culture is made up of many strands from the sedimented past and contemporary experience: in all of this, encounters with Gulf Arabs are right at the heart of what it means to be a Koya.

Bibliography

Abdul Sathar, M.K.K. 1999. *History of Ba-Alawis in Kerala.* Unpublished PhD Thesis, University of Calicut.

Al-Rasheed, M. 2004. 'Introduction: Localizing the Transnational and Transnationalizing the Local', in Madawi Al-Rasheed (ed.), *Transnational connections and the Arab Gulf.* London: Routledge.

Appadurai, A. 1997. *Modernity at Large: Cultural Dimensions of Globalisation.* Delhi: Oxford University Press.

Arasaratnam, S. 1994. *Maritime India in the Seventeenth Century.* Delhi: Oxford University Press.

Bahauddin, K.M. 1992. *Kerala Muslims: The Long Struggle.* Trivandrum: Modern Book Centre.

Barendse, R.J. 1998. *The Arabian Seas: The Indian Ocean World of the Seventeenth Century.* Leiden: Research School CNWS.

Bayly, S. 1989. *Saints, Goddesses and Kings: Muslims and Christians in South Indian Society, 1700–1900.* Cambridge: Cambridge University Press.

Bouchon, G. 1987. 'Sixteen Century Malabar and the Indian Ocean', in A. Das Gupta and M.N. Pearson (eds), *India and the Indian Ocean 1500–1800.* Delhi: Oxford University Press.

——— 1988. *'Regents of the Sea': Cannanore's Response to Portuguese Expansion, 1507–1528.* Delhi: Oxford University Press.

Caplan, P. 1985. *Class and Gender in India: Women and their Organizations in a South Indian City.* London: Tavistock.

Chaudhuri, K.N. 1990. *Asia Before Europe: Economy and Civilisation of the Indian Ocean from the Rise of Islam to 1750.* Cambridge: Cambridge University Press.

Clifford, J. 1998. 'Mixed feelings', in Pheng Cheah and Bruce Robbins (eds), *Cosmopolitics: Thinking and Feeling Beyond the Nation.* Minneapolis: University of Minnesota Press.

Dale, S.F. 1980. *Islamic Society on the South Asian Frontier: The Mappilas of Malabar 1498–1922.* Oxford: Clarendon.

—— 1997. 'The Hadhrami Diaspora in South-Western India: The Role of the Sayyids of the Malabar Coast', in Ulrike Freitag and William G. Clarence-Smith (eds), *Hadhrami Traders, Scholars and Statesmen in the Indian Ocean, 1750s–1960s.* Leiden: Brill.

Das Gupta, A. 1967. *Malabar in Asian trade, 1740–1800.* Cambridge: Cambridge University Press.

—— 2001. 'India and the Indian Ocean, c.1500–1800: The Story', in U. Das Gupta (ed.), *The World of the Indian Ocean Merchant, 1500–1800: Collected Essays of Ashin Das Gupta.* Delhi: Oxford University Press.

Diouf, M. 2002. 'The Senegalese Murid Trade Diaspora and the Making of a Vernacular Cosmopolitanism', in C. Breckenridge et. al (eds), *Cosmopolitanism.* Durham: Duke University Press.

Fanselow, F. 1996. 'The Disinvention of Caste among Tamil Muslims', in C. Fuller (ed.), *Caste Today.* Delhi: Oxford University Press.

Freitag, U. 2003. *Indian Ocean Migrants and State Formation in Hadhramaut: Reforming the Homeland.* Leiden: Brill.

Gardner, K. 1993. 'Desh-bidesh: Sylethi Images of Home and Away', *Man* (ns), 28.1.

Gidwani, V. and K. Sivaramakrishnan. 2003. 'Circular Migration and Rural Cosmopolitanism in India', *Contributions to Indian Sociology* (ns), 37.1.

Gough, K. 1961. 'Mappilla: North Kerala', in D. Schneider and K. Gough (eds), *Matrilineal Kinship.* Berkeley: University of California Press.

Grillo, R. n.d. 'Betwixt and Between: Trajectories and Projects of Transmigration', Unpublished paper.

Hannerz, U. 1990. 'Cosmopolitans and Locals in World Culture', in M. Featherstone (ed.), *Global Culture.* London: Sage.

Hitchcock, R.H. 1925. *A History of the Malabar Rebellion, 1921.* Madras: Government Press.

Ibrahim Kunju, A.P. 1989. *Mappila Muslims of Kerala: Their History and Culture.* Trivandrum: Sandhya Publications.

Jeffery, P., R. Jeffery and C. Jeffrey. 2004. 'Islamization, Gentrification and Domestication: A Girls' 'Islamic Course' and Rural Muslims in Western Uttar Pradesh', *Modern Asian Studies*, 38.1.

Kearney, M. 2003. *The Indian Ocean in World History*. London: Routledge.

Kurup, K.K.N., and K.M. Mathew. 2000. *Native Resistance Against the Portuguese: The Saga of Kunjali Marakkars*. Calicut: University Press.

Laffan, M. 2002. *Islamic Nationhood and Colonial Indonesia: The Umma Below the Winds*. London: RoutledgeCurzon.

Logan, W. 1989 [1887]. *Malabar*. New Delhi: Asian Educational Services.

McGilvray, D. 1989. 'Households in Akkaraipattu: Dowry and Domestic Organization Among Matrilineal Tamils and Moors in Sri Lanka', in John N. Gray et. al (eds), *Society from the Inside Out: Anthropological Perspectives on the South Asian Household*. New Delhi: Sage.

———— 1998. 'Arabs, Moors and Muslims: Sri Lankan Muslim Ethnicity in Regional Perspective', *Contributions to Indian Sociology* (ns), 32.2.

McPherson, K. 1993. *The Indian Ocean: A History of People and the Sea*. Delhi: Oxford University Press.

Menon, S. 1962. *Kerala Districts Gazetteers: Kozhikode*. Trivandrum: Government Presses.

Miller, R. 1976. *Mappila Muslims of Kerala: A study in Islamic Trends*. Madras: Orient Longman.

Mines, M. 1973 'Muslim Social Stratification in India: The Basis for Variation', *Southwestern Journal of Anthropology*, 28.

———— 1975. 'Islamisation and Muslim Ethnicity in South India', *Man* (ns) 10.3.

Nair, G.C. 1921. *The Moplah Rebellion, 1921*. Calicut: Norman Printing Bureau.

Onley, J. 2004. 'Transnational Merchants in the Nineteenth-century Gulf: The Case of the Safar Family', in M. Al-Rasheed (ed.), *Transnational Connections and the Arab Gulf*. London: Routledge.

Osella, F., and C. Osella. 1999. 'From Transience to Immanence: Consumption, Life-cycle and Social Mobility in Kerala, South India', *Modern Asian Studies*, 33.4.

———— 2000. *Social Mobility in Kerala: Modernity and Identity in Conflict*. London: Pluto.

Panikkar, K.N. 1989. *Against Lord and State: Religion and Peasant Uprisings in Malabar, 1836–1921.* Delhi: Oxford University Press.

Parkin, D., and S. Headley (eds) 2000. *Islamic Prayer Across the Indian Ocean: Inside and Outside the Mosque.* RoutledgeCurzon.

Pearson, M.N. 1999. 'Introduction I: The Subject', in A. Das Gupta and M.N. Pearson (eds). *India and the Indian Ocean 1500–1800.* Delhi: Oxford University Press.

—— 2005. *The World of the Indian Ocean, 1500–1800: Studies in Economic, Social and Cultural History.* Aldershot: Ashgate.

Pollock, S. 2002. 'Cosmopolitan and Vernacular History', in C. Breckenridge et. al (eds), *Cosmopolitanism.* Durham: Duke University Press.

Prakash, O. 2004. *Bullion for Goods: European and Indian Merchants in the Indian Ocean Trade, 1500–1800.* Delhi: Manohar.

Robinson, F. 2004. 'Other-Worldly and This-Worldly Islam and the Islamic Revival', *Journal of the Royal Asiatic Society* 14.1.

Shokoohy, M. 2003. *Muslim Architecture of South India: The Sultanate of Malabar and the Traditions of Maritime Settlers on the Malabar and Coromandel Coasts.* London: Routledge.

Soares, B. 2000. 'Notes on the Anthropological Study of Islam and Muslim Societies in Africa', *Culture and Religion*, 1.2.

—— 2004. 'Islam and Public Piety in Mali', in D.F. Eickelman and A. Salvatore (eds), *Public Islam and the Common Good.* Leiden: Brill.

Subrahmanyam, S. 1997. *The Career and Legend of Vasco Da Gama.* Cambridge: Cambridge University Press.

Subramaniam, L. 1996. *Indigenous Capital and Imperial Expansion: Bombay, Surat and the West Coast.* Delhi: Oxford University Press.

Tarazi, F., C. Bayly and R. Ilbert (eds) 2001. *Modernity and Culture from the Mediterranean to the Indian Ocean, 1890–1920.* New York: Columbia University Press.

Tsing, A. 2002. 'Conclusion: The Global Situation', in J. X. Inda and R. Rosaldo (eds), *The Anthropology of Globalization.* Oxford: Blackwell.

—— 2004. *Friction: An Ethnography of Global Connection.* Princeton: Princeton University Press.

Varshney, A. 2002. *Ethnic Conflict and Civic Life: Hindus and Muslims in India.* New Haven: Yale University Press.

Vatuk, S. 1996. 'Identity and Difference or Equality and Inequality in South Asian Muslim Society', in Chris Fuller (ed.), *Caste Today*. Delhi: Oxford University Press.

Vertovec, S., and R. Cohen. 2002. 'Introduction: Conceiving cosmopolitanism', in Steven Vertovec and Robin Cohen (eds), *Conceiving Cosmopolitanism: Theory, Context and Practice*. Oxford: Oxford University Press.

Waldinger, R., and D. Fitzgerald. 2004. 'Transnationalism in Question', *American Journal of Sociology*, 109.5.

Werbner, P. 1999. 'Global Pathways: Working Class Cosmopolitanism and the Creation of Transnational Ethnic Worlds', *Social Anthropology*, 7.1.

—— 2003. Pilgrims of Love: The anthropology of a Global Sufi Cult. Bloomington: Indiana University Press.

AFTERWORD

Michael Pearson

Maybe, as the Introduction to this volume suggests, anthropology is struggling with history, but historians are too. Poor old history, under attack from all sides. Post-modern critics say we are too totalising, finding meta-narratives only by indulging in selective research which ignores the coded messages in our much prized 'documents' and other 'sources', and which privileges elite written sources at the expense of those revealing the real lives of real people. It is claimed that historians are still constrained by the archive, which elevates events, charters and treaties over and above the real complexities of social life. Meanwhile, the 'reading public' want us precisely to produce broad surveys which tell them how they got to where they are, and even what's going to happen next. Partisans of particular historical stories (and who is not?) complain of obvious bias and a very selective use of sources. The Taj Mahal is really a Hindu palace – or is it a Muslim tomb? Take your pick. Anthropologists and other 'social scientists' (these days a rather dated designation anyway) deride us as mere gap fillers, along the lines of Bernard Cohn's Lucy Lacuna. It is claimed that we think there are objective social, cultural and historical 'facts' which can be collected, thus 'filling a gap' (interesting to note though that Cohn thought anthropologists did this too). And where are the people in our histories? Why do we ignore legends, interviews and oral traditions? For us, the Holy Grail is a document that no one else has seen, untouched, hopefully musty and partially illegible, ours to do with what we want.

To be sure, much of this is caricature. Today, one seldom finds an historian who claims innocently to be merely 'telling a story'. We know that they are immediately making a subjective choice, for what story they tell is a matter of selection, and this selection is not value-free. Among other things, we historians today are aware that history is culturally and textually constructed and inseparable from the relations of power which produced it. Even when we use archives, they are approached in a critical

spirit. Nick Dirks (1994) wrote a 'biography of an archive'. Nor would
we today dare to write a study on say India derived entirely from an
imperial archive in London. On site inspection, an attempt at immersion
in the locale we are writing about, is considered to be essential, even if we
lack the training (routinely given to anthropologists) which would enrich
this modest fieldwork.

We are increasingly aware of the value of archaeology, especially in
areas like the Swahili coast where the written record before the arrival of
Europeans is spotty indeed. Over the last few decades, we welcomed the
New Archaeology which broadened the field very considerably, and
made it much less antiquarian. In particular, scholars often now try to
combine archaeology, anthropology and history, and indeed some throw
in other disciplines too. This is particularly to be seen when scholars use
archaeology and history together to write on medieval or early modern
historical periods (see Johnson 1995, for example).

Archaeology has not stood still, and nor have historians. We even try,
these days, to use oral traditions, difficult though they may be. We used
to try and correlate these with what 'texts' and 'documents' told us, and
this usually ended up disadvantaging, even discrediting, the oral source.
David Beach (1994) used them for the Zimbabwe plateau. In a
somewhat self-indulgent book, he provided a detailed discussion of
Shona oral traditions, and of his own personal use of, and battles with,
them. He stresses the difficulties. As one example, northern Shona oral
traditions tell how the Mutapa dynasty began late in the seventeenth
century, which is of course two centuries too late. In this volume,
Simpson believes that historians dismiss such sources as 'fanciful', but in
fact today we, like him, know that the point, one which anthropologists
have helped us understand, is that oral sources have been filtered through
generations of recipients and transmitters, with each adding, modifying
and deleting according to what is important or significant at a particular
time. Indeed, oral sources can be seen as subsumed by the present,
whenever that may be. As such they can tell us much about what
particular people thought, how they constructed their 'history', at
specific times.

What of big pictures? The public want us to do this, and some of us oblige. In the academy at least the totalising ambitions of world-system theorists are much debated, admired and denounced, but at least they have the temerity to try and explain how we got to where we are: as Bob Marley so correctly sang, 'If you know your history, you will know where you're coming from'. The greatest practitioner, Immanuel Wallerstein, even dares to predict the end of what he regards as the inherently vicious and malevolent system of capitalism. But maybe, like Marx, he has failed to acknowledge capitalism's apparently inexhaustible ability to bend, modify and reinvent itself. World History, as disseminated from Hawai'i in the *Journal of World History*, is less ambitious, and in general privileges, at the expense of 'theory', comparison and contrast in arenas not bounded by states. The editor, Jerry H. Bentley, is clear that world history does not have to include the whole world; rather, it is 'a historical perspective that transcends national frontiers' (1990). Scholars need 'a regional, continental, or global scale' to look at many important forces in history. The key is to get away from national, state-based histories. The Indian Ocean, to which we will turn presently, is one example of an area much loved by world historians.

In this volume, Caroline and Filippo Osella write that anthropology did best when it 'tempered the reach of social theory with the gentle corrective of empirical material.' This is what historians do too, but there is still a place for bold over-arching pictures. Future drudges can niggle about the details later. But maybe this is a bit dismissive, for any grand picture invites modification and needs fleshing out as more 'facts' are unearthed. Nevertheless, I unapologetically claim that we do need, now more than ever, 'a global explanation of the past which gives sense to the present and guidance to the paths of the future', or, in Marc Bloch's words, 'the only true history, which can advance only through mutual aid, is universal history' (see Olabarri 1995: 29). Bloch also wrote, again implicitly recommending meta-history, that 'the comparative method can elicit from the chaotic multiplicity of circumstances those contrasts which were generally effective' (quoted in O'Brien 2006: 5).[1] Similarly, a recent book very cogently argues, as an underlying theme, that human history 'has long-term and large-scale patterns, and that it is important, both intellectually and politically, to comprehend these patterns' (Sanderson 1995: 9). David Christian (2004) has gone much further for he writes of Big History. He deals with the globe from the origins of the universe to today.

The contributors to this volume manoeuvre rather uneasily when they consider historical 'truth'. Whether or not there is a truth which can be found and universally accepted is at the heart of our endeavours. Nor is this merely an academic question, for history flows over into public debate, and even into action. We know that our stories, our analyses, are constructed and partial, but we claim that there is a line, inchoate to be sure, between differing interpretations of an event, and outrageous distortion for a particular, usually political, end. In Australia, our Prime Minister and a handful of academic historians have complained of the Black Armband view of our history – we weren't really that awful, and even if we were a little bit you can't blame me for it for it is, after all, 'history'. The 'debate' has sometimes been reduced to the triviality of arguing over how many indigenous Australians were killed on particular occasions. Yet, fortunately, this has no discernible effect on political matters, though it may be that the Prime Minister's preferred version reinforces a 'triumphalist' version of our past, with himself as the implied capstone of Australian achievement. More alarming is the way some African governments push the line that the Swahili are foreign. This perception of history has contributed to giving the Swahili an invidious position today, reinforced by interpretations of events in the nineteenth and twentieth centuries. The role of the Swahili at this time has led today to popular suspicion of the community, and reinforced the notion of them as being foreign. Inadvertently, the Swahili contributed to their future problems. In the Omani period, status was closely linked to Arab origins, and many Swahili manufactured this in order to thrive. They

---

1 Drawing on a vast array of recent writing to do with the practice of history, O'Brien's essay is a vehement statement of the utility, even necessity, of meta-narrative history.

also played a large role, under the Sultanate, in the slave trade, for the first time venturing far inland to pursue this occupation.

Even more malevolent, crossing over the line, is the debate over the history of India which has now raged for decades. I can't avoid value judgements here. There have been gross distortions of the evidence by proponents of Hindutva, and an ignoring of more sober, and more accurate, accounts by most qualified historians. A very recent controversy over school textbooks in California was concerned with what young students should be told about the early history of India. On one side were Hindutva proponents, on the other secular supporters. The latter won, and proclaimed this to be a victory for 'reason and historical accuracy', while the 'ahistorical and sectarian' versions put forward by the former were rejected.[2] It appears then that there is out there a non-sectarian and unbiased version of India's ancient past, and this is what young Californians should be taught. The Babri Masjid incident in December 1992 is a more extreme example. Under the previous Hindutva-oriented national government school textbooks were rewritten to present (or more correctly represent) India's Muslims (some 14 percent of the total) as descended from pillaging iconoclastic barbarian invaders from the northwest who perpetrated atrocities on Hindu temples and people. Alternatively, their 'history' shows that India's Muslims are all just converted Hindus, and they should now be encouraged/persuaded/coerced to 'reconvert'. Here, bad history has caused communal tensions and contributed more-or-less directly to riots and pogroms.

In all this, I am assuming that there is also good, that is 'truthful', history, or at least that one version is more likely than some other. Here is a rotund Victorian claim that there is such a thing as 'unbiased' history. Lord Acton wrote (in a letter! What was he like when he wrote a polished book?):

---

2   Michael Witzel message dated February 27th, 2006, accessed at goa-research-net [<goa-research-net@yahoogroups.com>] Digest Number 103, on March 1st, 2006.

The inflexible integrity of the moral code is, to me, the secret of the authority, the dignity, the utility of history. If we may debase the currency for the sake of genius, or success, or rank, or reputation, we may debase it for the sake of a man's influence, of his religion, of his party, of the good cause which prospers by his credit and suffers by his disgrace. Then History ceases to be a science, an arbiter of controversy, a guide of the wanderer, the upholder of that moral standard which the powers of earth, and religion itself, tend constantly to depress. It serves where it ought to reign; and it serves the worst better than the purest (from Fears 1985: 383–84).

Powerful stuff to be sure. Some of the essays which precede this Afterword either implicitly or explicitly address this central question. Thus Kresse's unpacking of a series of sermons notes that they 'are also an appeal to his audience, to seek knowledge of history, and use it effectively for the present. Implicitly, they show that historical knowledge is crucial for dealing with the present [...]'. He goes on to say that what is important is 'a social consensus about the reality of past events perhaps more than the establishment of such truth itself' which must mean that somewhere out there we can discover a version which is at least closer than others to the 'truth'. Maybe some lucky Philias Fillagap will happen on new 'evidence' which will advance the matter. Perhaps we should listen to Arjun Appadurai, who is quoted by several of our authors. Possibly correctly, he says that historians give too much attention to relativism ('Before you read the history, first know the historian', and 'Each generation must write its own history'). He claims, in a way that should appeal to the contributors to this volume, that there is indeed somewhere out there a 'truth' which has been authorised by the society under review, though this may not be one that a western-trained historian would consider to be of value.

All this of course is skirting around the issue Acton raised so emphatically: what is 'truth' in historical writing? As I noted, several of the authors of the preceding essays, wrestle with precisely this matter as they unpack the 'stories' they are told. Do we finally squib an answer, and merely say that some versions of a particular event seem more credible, reliable, or true than others? This indeed is what western-trained historians typically seek to do, yet other 'truths' can have powerful results. Those who destroyed the Babri Masjid believed it had been built on a Ram temple. Archaeologists and historians say there is no evidence for this. Yet, surely, it would be a dereliction of duty to allow equal authority to both versions. In this case, there may be no Holy Grail of incontrovertible 'truth' (though I must admit that I think there is), yet the scholars' version is at least closer to a demonstrable 'fact' than is the Hindutva one. An extreme case, no doubt, and one with very clear consequences, yet even when we look at more benign, less politically charged, conflicts one can I hope avoid false relativism (every view and theory and explanation is of equal weight, just as the romantic plots of Mills and Boon books or the Australian soap opera 'Neighbours' are as worthy of analysis as Shakespeare's plays) and at least say that in my present state of knowledge, and admitting the influence of my own sociology of knowledge, this version is closer to the 'truth' than the other one. We may lack the Victorian certitude of Acton, but this does not preclude us from, with all hesitancy, saying what seems to be the most likely explanation, the story which has more, even if not total, credibility.

Some of the essays in this excellent collection seem to see history and anthropology as opposed, irreconcilable. I find this strange. The person whose work inspired this volume, Bernard Cohn, was convinced of the utility of each discipline drawing on the other; indeed, as I know from a long intellectual and personal friendship with him, he thought they were if anything symbiotic. Far from struggling with history, anthropologists should, he urged, embrace it, and vice versa. Cohn was not one to write books much, but it is extraordinary how many of his articles stimulated detailed research projects by others, often graduate students. One could produce a long list of well-known books which sprang from engagement with Cohn's insights, but the real point is that these were written by both historians and anthropologists. What they show above all else is the artificiality of these two terms, which falsely find two separate distinct epistemologies. In the best work they merge and feed on each other (see Kessinger 1974 for example). I can personally attest to this. One of Cohn's earliest articles, written with McKim Marriott, was concerned with the notion of networks and centres in Indian civilisation. I used this concept, I hope usefully, in the last chapter of my first book. It was still history, for it was about early-modern Gujarat, but the analysis was, I hope, enriched, indeed dictated, by Cohn's insight (see Pearson 1976a: Chapter 6). At one time, we planned an edition of the writings of Francis Buckler, an eccentric yet undeservedly neglected writer on Muslim India. Cohn dropped out of this project, but I (Pearson 1985a) proceeded and wrote a long introduction on symbols and legitimacy which owed nearly everything to Cohn. Later, in his own book, he showed, in a rather Saidian way, how knowledge and power intersected in writings on British India (Cohn 1996).

This book is not just about disciplines of course. It is also about the Indian Ocean, or at least the western, Arabian Sea, sector. The central question is whether indeed there is such a thing as an Indian Ocean which can be studied, analysed and used as a heuristic tool just like say a state or a village. The contributors differ agreeably on this matter: some say yes indeed there was/is an Indian Ocean World, others say 'human connectivity in the region tends to be rather modest and limited'. The editors vigorously contest the whole notion of cosmopolitanism ('a community of strangers'), which in turn questions whether there is something called the Indian Ocean which has enough unity/similarities to be subject to analysis. When I was asked to write a book on the Indian Ocean (Pearson 2003) I obviously had to wrestle with this very problem, though I fear readers of the book will notice that I rather squibbed it and provided no clarion-clear answer. Yet, apparently, publishers think there is such a thing as a history of an ocean, for my book was part of a series called 'Seas in History'. My book contained copious information on the movement over the past few millennia of goods around the ocean, the trickle or relay trade, the influence of monsoons on trade, and so on. Although this obviously contributed to the creation of an Indian Ocean world, I will on this occasion take this as a given, and instead concentrate on other matters.

Maybe, we maritime historians need to question our basic assumption, that it was the ocean that made the history. Maritime historians have long wrestled with the problem of how far inland their studies should extend. We often quote Braudel's notion of a thousand frontiers for the Mediterranean, depending on time and place and the matter under discussion. Yet all this of course privileges the ocean and people who travel over it. In this book, Becker provides a useful corrective in the way she shows that we need to look to the *bara* (mainland/hinterland) as much as to the *dhow* when we write on the process of Islamisation in East Africa.

There are also several other matters worth considering. One was raised by Gilroy's *Black Atlantic* (1993), and the consequent partial reorientation of Atlantic history. Gilroy finds an 'internation' on both shores of the Atlantic. This black nation is demarcated not by land areas, immobile land space, but by its ties to the Atlantic Ocean. It is distinctive, an alternative to the dominant land-based society, and shows 'race' emerging strongly in conjunction with slavery, moving across national boundaries and histories. The self-proclaimed writer of a 'peoples' history' of the Atlantic, Marcus Rediker (2004), wants history written from the bottom up (as many historians have tried to do for decades now). According to him, maritime history is a 'traditional and conservative field'. It remains 'provincial', and many maritime historians show 'narrow antiquarianism' and refuse to address 'big and important issues to which their subjects were central'. They remain 'trapped in the stories of nations even though they spent their lives traversing their borders'. He wants as a 'unit of analysis not this or that nation, but rather their connecting body of water, the Atlantic'. Then he goes on to a more extravagant claim, which as he notes 'is a little trickier':

Maritime history is not simply the story of landed society gone to sea. Which is to say: we need to learn to see the world's seas and oceans as real places, where a great deal of history has been made, and indeed is still being made. Many maritime historians continue to see the oceans as unreal places, as voids between the real spaces, which are inevitably lands or nations. So maritime history has exhibited – and continues to exhibit – what, for lack of a better term, I will call *terracentric* bias, a land-based set of assumptions about place'. (2004: 197–8, original italics).

It seems that he wants an aquatic history of people divorced from land influences; a problematic aim indeed. Ships after all are built on land of materials found on land. Sailors have families on land, are paid on land and often hope to make enough money at sea so that they can retire to the land. Even societies most often cited as being aquatic still find the land impacting on them. The much studied Madan or Marsh Arabs in the Tigris-Euphrates delta area certainly lived on the water, yet their way of life, their very 'aquaticness', has been undermined over the last few decades by the policies of landed governments. Specifically, the marshes dried up because up-stream governments took most of the water for irrigation.

Another tactic is to look at the people around the coasts, as indeed many of these essays do. Here it is a question of whether there is something which we can call a littoral society which shows certain commonalities around the shores of the ocean. These coastal communities will have more in common with each other than with their hinterlands. Their most important connections are with their maritime forelands. So Kilwa and the surrounding coast has, in terms of culture, religion, food, livelihood and so on more in common with Aden or Calicut than with the Mutapa 'state' to its west. The editors raise the important question of just what was travelling: people, or only goods? This, with other matters, contributes to their scepticism about cosmopolitanism. If it is only goods then the littoral society notion is seriously weakened. My early-modern data seems to contradict this; people did move. As just one example, which could be replicated endlessly, consider this eye-witness (and thus 'accurate'?) account of the port city of Surat, where in 1663 Manuel Godinho found:

> [...] white Mughals, Indian Muslims, all types of pagans, Christians of various nationalities and, in fact, people from all over the world who have either settled in Surat or have come to the port on business. In Surat we find Spaniards, Frenchmen, Germans, English, Dutch, Flemish, Dunkirkians, Italians, Hungarians, Poles, Swedes, Turks, Arabs, Persians, Tartars, Georgians, Scythians, Chinese, Malabaris, Bengalis, Sinhalese, Armenians and an endless variety of other strange barbarian people (Correia-Afonso 1990: 47–9).

Another matter which seems to hint at people travelling is provided by the bold claim of Eleana Losada Soler (2000: 204), who writes that once the Portuguese entered the Indian Ocean they found Arabic acting as a *koine* (*lingua franca*). This must imply that indeed people, as well as goods, travelled. On the other hand, some apparent similarities may be mere happenstance, not pointing to any influence from elsewhere. For example, on the central Swahili coast the sacrifice of one or more goats is an important part of the construction, and launching, of a new *dhow*. In far away south Sulawesi also a live goat is sacrificed just before the launch of a *prahu*.

Yet we can extrapolate a bit more here. The editors stress 'internal struggles within the respective Muslim communities' (something not unique to Islam anyway), yet in both Lamu and Sulawesi Koranic verses are quoted, and the local *madrasa* (Quran school) students are actively involved in the launch of a new boat. There is, I think, an Islamic bond all around the shores of the ocean, with important commonalities and similarities. Indeed, the work of Islamic rectifiers today and for many centuries in the past has increased the tendency towards a 'normative' or 'orthodox' version of Islam. David Parkin has written that 'the idea of prayer in the mosque connotes unambiguous Islamic piety, while that outside points towards the possibility of other kinds of worship' (2000: 1). My claim is that while the 'other kinds of worship' clearly show some regional variations, all are still 'coastal' variants of Islam, while obviously 'prayer in the mosque' has strong commonalities all over the Islamic Indian Ocean world, indeed the Islamic world *tout court*.

In short, non-economic connections and linkages around the ocean were usually provided by Muslims, as several contributors to this volume have shown in previous publications. And certainly they can change over time. As is well known, modern technology, especially the steam ship and the printing press, helped these networks to spread, encouraged conversion to Islam, and facilitated the work of both 'missionaries' and 'rectifiers', that is Muslim exemplars who aimed to reform and 'purify' an existing Muslim community. Green shows how these and other connections were facilitated by British technology, and this was not new. In the sixteenth century, a Jesuit wrote that *cacizes* [Muslim divines] travelled as 'lascars, which is the same as sailors', on Portuguese boats even, and sowed their evil seed wherever the boat called, even as far as China, Siam and Java (quoted in Pearson 1994: 80–1). And it was not only Muslim divines who travelled. Green provides fascinating data on the international, ocean-wide, aspect of book publishing, and in a related way the extent and significance of these travels is made clear when we look at languages. Jan Knappert has found that there are some 5,000 words of Arabic influence in Malay, and more than that in Swahili, and about 80% of these are the same, that is in Malay and Swahili, so that we have a 'corpus of travelling Arabic words' (1985: 125). Compelling perhaps, except that linguists would claim that just because the same word means the same thing in different languages, or that the same word has different meanings in different languages, does not necessarily point to any influence from one to the other.

In any case, I have rehearsed these matters of Indian Ocean unity, and littoral society, several times (1985b, for example), and at present will merely say that I do think this is a notion which is useful in itself, and also contributes to our attempt to define an Indian Ocean World. It is related to another concept now on the scholarly agenda, that is the notion of a 'water world.' Dian Murray, an expert on piracy, wrote of a 'water world', where boundaries were indistinct (1987: 6–17). Robert Antony recently modified Murray slightly, writing of a water world of 'shared social, economic, and cultural activities, and patterns that are not easily defined and delimited by ethnic and linguistic differences or by national boundaries.'[3] He and Murray are concerned with the South China coast, but their findings apply precisely to other coasts. And, all this of course, contributes to the drive for a world history which transcends artificial and recent political divisions. Equally relevant here is the concept of Eurasia, that is an area which nullifies the tyranny of continents and sees powerful connections between at least the eastern Mediterranean and the Arabian Sea.[4]

---

3   Antony's version was presented in a paper called 'Giang Binh: Pirate Haven and Black Market on the Sino-Vietnamese Frontier, 1780-1802,' for the workshop 'Ports, Pirates and Hinterlands in East and Southeast Asia: Historical and Contemporary Perspectives,' Shanghai, November 2005. I have his permission to quote from his excellent paper.

4   See Fawaz and Bayly (2002) for a very flawed attempt to use this notion.

Even though some other contributors to this book would disagree, I think that Gwyn Campbell is quite correct when he writes that 'Indian Ocean Africa constituted an integral and dynamic part of the Indian Ocean World and its Muslim commercial and religious network from the rise of Islam in the seventh century until the European Scramble for Africa in the late nineteenth century.' His use of a beginning and terminal point is interesting, for this avoids the ahistoricism which sometimes plagues Indian Ocean studies. We still at times get echoes of the unchanging East as authors draw data from widely separate times and places to discover unity and connections. Yet, in fact, I agree with Campbell's implicit assumption that things changed in the nineteenth century, though being one trained in Indian matters I would stress not the scramble for Africa but rather the British conquest of India, along with the steam ships and so on that I mentioned above. This is because one who is, like myself, influenced by political economy matters must give primacy to industrial capitalism as a uniquely important agent of change. I have frequently argued that basic qualitative change in the Indian Ocean came only from the late eighteenth century, and was caused by the arrival of an industrialising England. Let the anthropologists make what they like of this meta-statement! I would however differ with Campbell over a date for the beginning of the Indian Ocean World, for, at least in political economy terms, the base (trade and movement of people) was changed little by the arrival of Islam, even if the superstructure (religion) was different. And, in any case, several of the essays in this collection remind us to avoid reifying 'Islam' into something hard centred and united. There were, of course, various splits, controversies and disunities around the ocean, yet I stand by my comments above about a certain hard core of similarity, at least in the mosque, and this despite the explicit rejection of this notion in the Introduction to this book.

Al-Ghazzali said that the best of the sultans listen to the *'ulama'*, and the worst of the *'ulama'* speak to sultans. In the past, this aphorism could be applied equally to both historians and anthropologists, that is that only inferior historians flirt with such anthropological matters as oral traditions, village studies and the technique of participant observation.

And the reverse: 'over time' studies had little role in mainstream anthropology. More recently (and Cohn's influence is plain to see here), there seemed to be an acknowledgement by anthropologists that yes indeed historians can contribute some useful empirical information which they could, cuckoo like, use, thus saving them the drudgery of hard work in musty archives. Meanwhile, some historians injected a bit of ill-digested 'theory' into their work. A final cautionary tale: I did this myself. Many years ago I published a fairly pedestrian analysis of the decline of the Mughal empire, but in order to impress I threw in a sentence, which I described as 'stimulating,' from the behaviourist Robert F. Berkhofer Jr: 'Behavior is not a direct reaction to the stimuli, but a response made in accordance with ideational mediation' (Pearson 1976b: 230).[5] This actually had nothing to do with the decline of the empire, and contributed nothing to the discussion. In many ways we seem to have gone far beyond this.[6] Barney Cohn and his many disciples paved the way, and today no one is 'struggling' with history, except perhaps some historians. It is pleasant indeed to find the dichotomy ignored or transcended in these excellent chapters.

Bibliography

Beach, D.N. 1994. *A Zimbabwean Past*. Gweru: Mambo Press.

Bentley, J.H. 1990. 'A New Forum for Global History', *Journal of World History*, 1.

Christian, D. 2004. *Maps of Time: An Introduction to Big History*. Berkeley: University of California Press.

Cohn, B.S. 1996. *Colonialism and its Forms of Knowledge: The British in India*. Princeton: Princeton University Press.

Correia-Afonso, J. (ed.) 1990. *Intrepid Itinerant: Manuel Godinho and his Journey from India to Portugal in 1663*. Bombay: Oxford University Press.

---

5 The quotation is originally from Berkhofer 1971. *A Behavioral Approach to Historical Analysis.*New York: Free Press: 46.

6 For a recent extremely comprehensive survey of the literature see Saloni Mathur (2000). I also very much admire a recent book by a 'geographer' (who could as well be an 'historian'), Philip E. Steinberg (2001).

Dirks, N. 1994. 'Colonial Histories and Native Informants: Biography of an Archive', in C. Breckenridge and P. van der Veer (eds), *Orientalism and the Postcolonial Predicament: Perspectives on South Asia*. Philadelphia: University of Pennsylvania.

Fawaz, L.T. and C.A. Bayly (eds) 2002. *Modernity and Culture: From the Mediterranean to the Indian Ocean*. New York: Columbia University Press.

Fears, J.R. (ed.) 1985. *Selected Writings of Lord Acton*, Vol. 2. Indianapolis: Liberty Classics.

Gilroy, P. 1993. *The Black Atlantic: Modernity and Double Consciousness*, Cambridge, Mass: Harvard University Press.

Johnson, M. 1995. *An Archaeology of Capitalism*. Oxford: Blackwell Publishers.

Kessinger, T.G. 1974. *Vilyatpur, 1848–1968: Social and Economic Change in a North Indian Village*. Berkeley: University of California Press.

Knappert, J. 1985. 'East Africa and the Indian Ocean', in J. C. Stone (ed.), *Africa and the Sea: Proceedings of a Colloquium at the University of Aberdeen, March, 1984*. Aberdeen: African Studies Group.

Mathur, S. 2000. 'History and Anthropology in South Asia: Rethinking the Archive', *Annual Review of Anthropology*, 29.

Murray, D. 1987. *Pirates of the South China Coast*. Stanford: University Press.

O'Brien, P. 2006. 'Historiographical Traditions and Modern Imperatives for the Restoration of Global History', *Journal of Global History*, I.

Olabarri, I. 1995. '"New" New History: A Longue Durée Structure', *History and Theory*, 34.

Parkin, D. 2000. 'Inside and Outside the Mosque; A Master Trope', in D. Parkin and S.C. Headley (eds), *Islamic Prayer across the Indian Ocean: Inside and Outside the Mosque*. Richmond, Surrey: Curzon Press.

Pearson, M.N. 1976a. Merchants and Rules in Gujarat: The Response to the Portuguese in the Sixteenth Century. Berkeley: University of California Press.

___ 1976b. 'Shivaji and the Decline of the Mughal Empire', *Journal of Asian Studies*, 35.

—— (ed.) 1985a. Legitimacy and Symbols: The South Asian Writings of F.W. Buckler. Ann Arbor: University of Michigan.

—— 1985b. 'Littoral Society: The Case for the Coast', *The Great Circle*, 7.

—— 1994. *Pious Passengers: The Hajj in Earlier Times.* Delhi: Sterling Publishers.

—— 2003. *The Indian Ocean.* London: Routledge.

Rediker, M. 2004. 'Toward a Peoples' History of the Sea', in D. Killingray, M. Lincoln and N. Rigby (eds), *Maritime Empires: British Imperial Maritime Trade in the Nineteenth Century.* London: Boydell Press in association with the National Maritime Museum.

Sanderson, S.K. 1995. 'Preface' in S.K. Sanderson (ed.), *Civilizations and World Systems: Studying World-Historical Change.* Walnut Creek, CA: Altamira Press.

Soler, E.L. 2000. 'The Encounter of Languages: Reflections on the Language of the Other in *Roteiro da Primeira Viagem do Vasco da Gama*', in A. Disney and E. Booth (eds), *Vasco da Gama and the Linking of Europe and Asia.* New Delhi: Oxford University Press.

Steinberg, P.E. 2001. *The Social Construction of the Ocean.* Cambridge: Cambridge University Press.

INDEX